Middle Powers and International Organisations

Australia and the OECD

Aynsley Kellow

Professor, School of Social Sciences, University of Tasmania, Australia

Peter Carroll

Professor, Tasmanian School of Business and Economics, University of Tasmania and Crawford School of Public Policy, Australian National University, Australia

EE Edward Elgar
PUBLISHING

Cheltenham, UK • Northampton, MA, USA

Published by
Edward Elgar Publishing Limited
The Lypiatts
15 Lansdown Road
Cheltenham
Glos GL50 2JA
UK

Edward Elgar Publishing, Inc.
William Pratt House
9 Dewey Court
Northampton
Massachusetts 01060
USA

A catalogue record for this book
is available from the British Library

Library of Congress Control Number: 2017931740

This book is available electronically in the **Elgar**online
Social and Political Science subject collection
DOI 10.4337/9781788110648

MIX
Paper from
responsible sources
FSC® C013604

ISBN 978 1 78811 063 1 (cased)
ISBN 978 1 78811 064 8 (eBook)

Typeset by Columns Design XML Ltd, Reading
Printed and bound by CPI Group (UK) Ltd, Croydon, CR0 4YY

Contents

Preface

In 2011 we published a study of the Organisation for Economic Co-operation and Development (OECD) that focused on its adaptation over time to meet the changing situations and issues faced by its members. That project began as an attempt to understand the relationship between Australia and the OECD, and was funded under that title by the Australian Research Council. A number of articles on Australia and the OECD were produced, but that book sought to fill an obvious gap with a comprehensive account of the organisation itself.

We realised, however, that a full understanding of the OECD required a similarly full understanding of its members' activities in relation to the organisation. Moreover, there were no studies of which we were aware that provided a detailed analysis of those activities, other than in relation to specific issues; indeed, detailed studies of how nation states engage with international organisations are few and far between. There were few studies of a comparative nature, examining, for example, government motives for taking up membership, the strategies they adopted, or not, to guide their work at the OECD, or how government attitudes to the organisation changed over time. Finally, there were no detailed historical studies of Australian activities in relation to the OECD, an area of particular interest to us, given that our academic base was in Australia. In addition, we were aware that Australia's membership of the OECD was part of a long-established trend to the membership of international, intergovernmental organisations, one that had commenced with its membership of the League of Nations, the International Labour Organization and the Permanent Court of International Justice.

We had also become aware that, based on our archival work in the UK, USA and Australia, as well as that in Paris at the OECD archives, there was a wealth of material available on which to base a study of national activity relating to the organisation. Indeed, with rare exception, the archival records of almost every government department or agency that we investigated demonstrated a lengthy, if varying, involvement with one or more OECD committees. Hence, we decided to complete a book-length study of the history of Australia's involvement with the OECD, commencing with its slowly expanding involvement as a non-member observer at a number of committees in the early 1960s.

It was clear that such a work would require access not only to archival records but access to more current records so that we could trace the varying nature of Australia's involvement over time. We have based what follows on archival records and both the current records of agencies participating in the OECD and those held by National Archives. We have also drawn on the insights provided by participants, including four successive Australian Ambassadors until research was completed in late 2014, as well as numerous other officials.

Our understanding of the OECD was assisted by off-the-record semi-structured interviews (sometimes more than once) with numerous people, whom we would like to thank. These include successive Australian Permanent Representatives to the OECD: Ian Forsyth, Veronique Ingram, Christopher Langman, and Christopher Barrett, as well as some of those who occupied the position in earlier days, notably Philip Flood, Ralph Hillman and Ted Evans.

Interviewees also include Kathy Laurent, for many years office manager and Assistant to the Ambassador at the OECD Delegation and who facilitated many appointments with delegation members, OECD Secretariat members and ambassadors of other Members (and her successor Natallia Kuchynskaya). Kathy was not only an immense help to us over successive visits, but also an informative interview subject, providing much depth on how the organisation of the Delegation had changed over the years. Among the members of the Delegation, we would especially like to thank: Patrick Blake, James Bullock, Tim Crowe, Matthew Flavel, Joanne Fredericksen, Deborah Fulton, Angela McGrath, Lyndal Manson, Rodney Muir, Margaret Pearce, Roland Pittar, Peter Waddell-Wood, Steve Unwin and James Wiblin.

An Australian in the Secretariat, John West (OECD Public Affairs) was of great assistance in providing information and facilitating interviews. Among the many members of the OECD Secretariat, past and present, that were kind enough to talk with us, we wish to thank all of them for sharing their insights. In particular we wish to thank: Angel Gurría (OECD Secretary-General), Rolf Alter, Sergio Arzeni, Ken Ash, Nicola Bonucci, Carolyn Ervin, Anthony Gooch, Jan de Geus, Lorens Lorentsen, Grace Perez-Navarro, Anthony Rottier, Janet West, John Dryden, Mario Pezzini, Michael Osborne, Michael Ryan, Nobuo Tanaka, Odille Sallard, Carlo Padoan, Stefan Tangerman, William Hynes, Sylvan Giguere, Donald Johnston (former OECD Secretary-General), Kumiharu Shigehara, David Henderson, Ron Gass, Barry McGaw, John Martin, Richard Carey, Alan Moran and Jean-Pierre Cotis. We would like to offer particularly heart-felt thanks to Michael Wenke and the staff of the Australian National Archives, and Jan-Anno Schuur and his colleagues at the OECD Archives Office, notably Sandra Willmott, who provided immensely helpful assistance on every visit to Paris. We would also like to thank Mark Primmer, Nicole Primmer, Hanni Rosenbaum, and Vanessa Vallée of BIAC, Roland Schneider of TUAC and Ronnie Goldberg of the USCIB.

We were also informed by interviews with a large number of Ambassadors of OECD Members, initially for our more general book on the OECD published in 2011, but their views have also informed the current volume. We therefore wish to thank Ambassadors Laurence Argimon-Pistre (European Commission); Fernando Ballestero (Spain); Joan Boer (Netherlands); Bruno Cabras (Italy); Sarah Dennis (New Zealand); Shin-ichi Kitajima (Japan); Tae-shin Kwon (Korea); David Lyscom (United Kingdom); Constance Morella (United States); Harald Neple (Norway); Steffen Smidt (Denmark); and Stephanie Lee (Deputy Permanent Representative, New Zealand).

Among the very many current and former staff of Australian agencies that provided valuable information and insights we would like to thank Gerry Antioch, Howard Bamsey, Terry Grandy, Stuart Harris, Carmel McGregor, Mark Pierce, Rhonda Piggott, David Turvey, Susan Holmes, Paul Coghlan, Paul Bradstreet, Jane Halton, Michael Hardy, Lisa Kelly, Chris Legge, Helen Liddy, Ian McPhee, Bob Pegler, Mike Roberts, Terry Sheales, David Smith, David Grecian, Tom Dale, Brendan Berne, Blair Comley, Kevin Keefe, Jenny Boshier, Lynne Tacy, Ian Watt, Craig Burns, Greg Brunner, Michael Nugent, Jessie Borthwick, Grahame Cook, William Thorn, Simon Bryant, Keith Besgrove, Steven French, Dean Parham, Wendy Jarvie, John Ryan. Eric Ford, Ian Lambert, and Alan Fels.

Similarly, a number of USA and UK officials provided information and advice, notably Thomas Barnett, Kitty Smith, Graham Branton, Joe Grice, Jonathan May, Ken Warwick, Margaret Sutherland, Susan Hazen, Terry Hawes and William Ricket.

The research for this book was conducted under Special Access Arrangements under s56(2) of the Archives Act 1983, and access to more contemporary files still held by agencies under security clearance. (An exception was the Australian Taxation Office, from which we were unable to obtain consent.) In both cases, agencies have read and approved what we have written, but they by no means share all our views, but (especially with more contemporary material) we have necessarily agreed upon language that recognises in places the need for sensitivity to ongoing relationships. The views expressed, of course, are our own, rather than those of the Australian Government and its agencies, or of the OECD.

At all times, we have owed an immense debt to Dr David Lee, Director, Historical Publications and Research Unit, Department of Foreign Affairs and Trade for his assistance and his wise counsel, and Christine Schaeffer at the OECD desk at DFAT.

And finally, we thank our families for their support and understanding throughout what has proven to be more than a decade dominated by things OECD.

The research for this book was supported by a grant by the Australian Research Council (DP0559803) and the work on tax was supported by another (DP1095946) granted to Aynsley Kellow with Richard Eccleston, for which we are grateful.

1. Introduction

The Organisation for Economic Co-operation and Development (OECD) occupies a unique place in the global architecture of international economic governance. It was not part of the so-called Bretton Woods Institutions agreed to in 1944 to govern and rebuild the post-war global economy: the World Bank, the International Monetary Fund (IMF), and the International Trade Organization (ITO), the latter being stillborn after the US Senate refused to ratify the Treaty of Havana. Rather, the OECD had its origins in the Marshall Plan (the European Recovery Program, or ERP), an American initiative to help rebuild European economies after the end of the Second World War in the face of a growing Soviet threat. The OECD grew out of the Organisation for European Economic Co-operation (OEEC), established in 1948 to administer the Marshall Plan, and which helped build a cooperative spirit among European economies – though not those of Eastern Europe, which were gathered into the rival USSR sponsored (and controlled) Council for Mutual Economic Assistance (or Comecon).

The OEEC was seen as providing value, and was continued after the end of the Marshall Plan in 1951. Much of its work was centred on the European Payments Union, the Codes of Liberalisation and the European Productivity Agency. Further, a European Nuclear Energy Agency was established under its auspices in 1958. The OECD was formed from the OEEC through a desire to carry forward its work on a wider stage and a founding convention for the OECD was negotiated and concluded in Paris on 14 December 1960 among the OEEC members and the US and Canada.

This spirit of North Atlantic and European cooperation was limited and short-lived, as discussed in more depth in Chapter 2, as OEEC members split into the six that developed the Treaty of Rome and the European Economic Community in 1957, and the 'outer seven' that formed the European Free Trade Area in 1960. The OECD came into being on 30 September 1961, and its reach was extended beyond the North Atlantic with the early accession of Japan in 1964, followed later by others such as Finland (1969), Australia (1971) and New Zealand (1973).

The OECD today has 35 member countries, all with a commitment to the core goal of fostering sustainable economic growth and with a commitment to liberal democratic norms. As a result, and because the members are all advanced economies, there is considerable like-mindedness among the members, and considerable sharing of policy learning and policy transfer, which is achieved through such processes as subjecting the policies of members to the discipline of 'peer review' (which it inherited from the OEEC) and the collection and publication of usually, but by no means always, highly-regarded statistics that are collected on a consistent basis. Peer reviews began with members' economies, but then spread to other functional areas.

Not only do OECD work programmes influence members' own policy positions, but its work has influence in other arenas. For example, analytical work on trade in agriculture was influential in helping to achieve a degree of trade liberalisation during the Uruguay Round of the GATT. Similarly, a range of other OECD agreements have fostered trade liberalisation in many other ways, from ensuring that national policies to manage chemical and biotechnology risks do not constitute barriers to trade to laying down guidelines that facilitate the digital economy. The capacity of the OECD Secretariat means that forums such as the G7 and G20, which lack analytical capability of their own, often refer work to the OECD. It played this role on climate change in the late 1980s and early 1990s, for example, receiving references from the International Negotiating Committee developing the Framework Convention of Climate Change before the Convention entered into force and its own secretariat was established.

While the OECD has only a few members, relative to the number of states in the global system, it has achieved considerable influence by both expanding its membership and by its 'outreach' or 'enhanced engagement' activities with non-members. With the collapse of communism the OECD assisted countries in Central Europe to prepare for a transition to market economies. In 1990 it established the Centre for Co-operation with European Economies in Transition (succeeded by the Centre for Co-operation with Non-Members) and in 1991 it established the 'Partners in Transition' Programme to aid Czechoslovakia, Hungary and Poland, which soon became members, along with Slovakia. Mexico and South Korea also acceded in the 1990s, building its presence in the Asia-Pacific. Chile, Estonia, Slovenia and Israel became members in 2010. In May 2013, the OECD Council decided to launch accession discussions with Colombia and Latvia; in April 2015 Costa Rica and Lithuania were invited to open formal accession talks.

It has been able to extend its influence also by engaging with countries that are either not ready for, or not interested in, membership. The rapid emergence of the 'BRICSA' group (Brazil, Russia, India, China and South Africa) has seen all except Russia – plus Indonesia (largely through Australia's sponsorship) – come to be regarded as 'Key Partners' of the OECD and contribute to its work programmes. Russia was the first of these to be placed on a pathway to formal accession, but this process was suspended after its annexation of Crimea in 2014. The membership, plus the key partners, means that OECD work can involve 39 countries accounting for around 80 per cent of world trade and investment. Its deliberations can thus have considerable impact, while the relatively small number of parties involved can potentially assist in raising the quality of outputs by lessening the need for lowest common denominator decisions.

The OECD, through its Development Assistance Committee and Development Centre, also plays an important role in benchmarking and assessing aid programmes and policies of donor countries, but does not itself play a role in programme delivery here or in other functional areas.

THE OECD IN AUSTRALIAN EYES

The merits of the OECD are not immediately obvious, and it comes in for some criticism, especially from those who do not agree with the broad direction of the organisation, which – it is fair to say – has varied. The diffuse nature of the OECD, its brief and the absence of any major operational tasks make it difficult for the worth of the OECD to be appreciated. However, as Ron Gass (its Director of Social Affairs, Manpower and Education from 1972 to 1989) stated:

> The fact that the OECD does not have major operational responsibilities like the IMF, WTO and the World Bank – together with its cross-sector analytical capability and multi-policy committees machinery – gives it a comparative advantage when it comes to setting out the forward-looking policy options. (Gass, 2002: 10)

The OECD has, on occasion, had substantive operational roles, though usually for only a few years at a time. Working Party 3 of its Economic Policy Committee, for example, was once (before the age of floating exchange rates) the venue where the conditionality of IMF loans under the General Agreement to Borrow were partly, perhaps largely, determined. Rather, the major, though not only value of the OECD is widely regarded as its epistemic nature as a source of policy ideas that spread not just throughout its membership but beyond, through policy learning and policy transfer. The large part of the value of the OECD lies in the conduct of high quality economic analysis, not just on national economies, but also of problems and policies in other policy domains. It is often described as an international 'think tank' that enhances the quality of public policy among its members and beyond. Ron Gass sees the OECD's defining role as that of a 'policy pathfinder' for the policy responses to the economic and social challenges facing member countries. 'Policy innovation: that is the determining feature of its culture' (Gass, 2002: 10). Peter Nicholson in a review of the OECD noted that the Organisation plays a unique role by virtue of one or more of the following:

> (i) its intergovernmental character; (ii) the broad range of Member countries (as compared for example with the EC or the G7); (iii) the more focused capacity for policy analysis among a like-minded group (by contrast with UN agencies); (iv) the 'non-negotiating' context in which most OECD bodies meet; (v) the unique cross-national data sets and deep analytical capability of many OECD divisions; and (vi) the highly evolved OECD capacity to do benchmarking and peer reviews. (Nicholson, 2003: 9)

At various times the OECD has been seen as reflective of Keynesian economics, but at others as the embodiment of neo-liberalism, and more recently criticised for its promotion of sustainable development and 'Green Growth' rather than the economic growth that lay at the heart of its foundation. Economist Judith Sloan, for example, has opined in exaggerated fashion that the 'Sludge-producing OECD has outlived its welcome' (Sloan, 2012). She has also asked whether Australia should 'pull out of the OECD? This will allow the remaining OECD members to pay for idiotic reports, slapping each other on the back as their economies simultaneously go down the gurgler.' What must be understood, however, is that the OECD's changing economic directions have reflected the preferences of a majority of its members, including Australia, as the OECD is very much a 'member owned' organisation. Which is not to argue that Australia or any other member always support all of its activities, outputs and outcomes.

The OECD performs many functions, such as facilitating the benchmarking of the policies of members in its many functional areas, aided by its collection and publication of comparative statistics that allow international benchmarking. Sloan (quite appropriately) has questioned the quality of some of the comparative statistics, noting (for example) that those on Australian education expenditure were of dubious value because they failed to incorporate the fees paid by tertiary students. However,

Sloan herself, in subsequent opinion pieces, has cited OECD statistics in discussing taxation (Sloan, 2013), unemployment (Sloan, 2013a), and education, which demonstrate the value of at least some of its work for this Australian critic (Sloan, 2013b).

Australia has found value in its membership of the OECD. As a review of that membership put it, the OECD was:

> [T]he only international organisation of its type dealing with matters relevant to our national economic and social policies and concerns. The Organisation's role in developing its members' policies on relations with developing countries, including the North/South dialogue, makes it important for Australian foreign policy as well. (NAA, 1981)

The review made the important point that membership of the OECD was important for a relatively isolated middle power, not part of the major economic blocs. Membership was seen as remedying Australia's relative geographic isolation from the major economic, political, and strategic groupings.

> For the most part Australia is outside the major economic, political and strategic groupings which have such a profound impact on our interests. We are not a participant in the Economic Summits of 'the Seven', we are not a member of the Group of Ten Western Finance Ministers, and we are not a member of NATO, the E.C. and the Council of Europe. The OECD is the only developed country forum in which we interact with Japan, North America and Western Europe. (NAA, 1981)

Value was, and is, also seen as deriving from the personal contacts made by the participation of public servants in the numerous committees and subsidiary bodies, both in terms of the development of participating staff and the international networks established through meeting peers from other member governments in Paris. The assessment of the review was that Australia had 'on balance undoubtedly benefited substantially from membership'. Nevertheless, very few Australian officials have an appreciation of the work of the OECD as a whole, however, a point made by the Australian Ambassador to the OECD in a cable in January 2002:

> It is evident that the breadth and volume of the OECD's work means that no one in Canberra is in a position to be across the totality of this work and that, as a result, its overall value can be both under-rated and over-rated. (NAA, 1981)

While the Australian view of the OECD has been overall positive, at times it has seen some unwelcome developments. For example,

Ambassador Ian Forsyth warned in a cable briefing Canberra prior to the 2003 Ministerial Council Meeting:

> Some European and other ministers will probably stress social cohesion and sustainable development in their interventions – agendas that are, unfortunately, loaded with protectionist objectives and that are essentially anti-growth rather than pro-growth … . In our view much of this work is of dubious quality and value and we are resisting attempts to shift the focus of the OECD from sustainable economic growth, in which its real expertise and mission lies, to the European agendas on sustainable development and social cohesion. (DFAT, 2001)

Nor have ministers and the governments they constitute always had a high regard for the OECD, although indications of this are not always unambiguous. The two most recent Australian Ambassadors, for example, have been political appointments from outside the public service, whereas the position previously rotated between senior, career public servants in the Treasury and Department of Foreign Affairs and Trade (DFAT). However, such appointments could indicate a higher commitment by governments to economic diplomacy and that the OECD was seen as of greater value in this agenda, with the more limited diplomatic experience of the two counterbalanced by their more direct access to their ministers. Also, Australia has engaged very positively with the G20 Leaders' Summit, which it hosted in 2014, perhaps finding this a more productive forum than the OECD, though the G20 lacks a secretariat capable of undertaking the statistical and analytical tasks and, as with the G7/G8, often refers work to the OECD, as well as to some of the UN specialised agencies. Perhaps it would be more accurate to assert that it has found the OECD Council to be of more limited value, lacking the ability to drive major, international developments compared to the national leaders in the G20, while the remainder of the organisation, with its specialised committees and well qualified staff, retains its value.

Australia does see the recent enlargement of the OECD, especially the accession of smaller EU member states, as diluting its relative coverage of the global economy, as several Asian economies have grown more rapidly, and as having somewhat of a diminishing ability to reach high quality decisions (despite the introduction of provisions for a restricted degree of qualified majority voting). The OECD's traditional decision rule of 'mutual agreement', as discussed below, has allowed some flexibility, as Decisions are binding only on those voting for them, and members are able to abstain rather than cast a negative vote and veto proposals. This has made the OECD a useful forum for developing policy that might be built upon in wider multilateral forums such as the World

Trade Organization (WTO), and it has been the site for such development of ideas for many policies, from hazardous waste to trade. However, it may well lose a degree of its influence relative to the G20, which includes the rising economies in the Asia Pacific. This suggests, in turn, that the OECD may well find itself playing a diminished role, more limited to its 'think tank' role, supporting groups like the G20, but less often used as a venue where a limited number of like-minded members can develop important elements for the architecture of global governance.

THE AIMS, ORGANISATIONAL STRUCTURE AND DECISION PROCESSES OF THE OECD

The OECD is a complex and changing organisation. The objective of this section is to outline, in summary, its major aims, organisational structure and key decision processes for the reader with little or no prior knowledge of the organisation so that the material in the following chapters can avoid frequent repetition. A more detailed elaboration can be found in Carroll and Kellow, especially Chapter 3 (2011).

The aims of the OECD as set out in its Convention at Article 1 are to promote policies designed:

(a) to achieve the highest sustainable economic growth and employment and a rising standard of living in Member countries, while maintaining financial stability, and thus to contribute to the development of the world economy;
(b) to contribute to sound economic expansion in Member as well as non-member countries in the process of economic development; and
(c) to contribute to the expansion of world trade on a multilateral, non-discriminatory basis in accordance with international obligations.

Mindful of the very broad remit for policy development in current and new areas of policy they were endowing upon the organisation, its founders drew up a design for an organisational structure aimed at achieving a high degree of control by its members in three major ways: (1) by designating the Council as the ultimate decision making body from which all authority derives, comprised of the Secretary-General plus representatives of the member states (Article 7); (2) by requiring that the Secretary-General present an annual budget and accounts to Council for approval in accordance with a Council-approved set of Financial Regulations (Article 20), aiming to control the allocation and flow of resources needed for all activities; and (3) by the use of a complex committee system, organised in hierarchical fashion, its members drawn for the most part from representatives of the member states, not from OECD staff members. In other words, while the OECD was endowed with a capacity for change, it was to be closely controlled and guided change, in the interests of its members (Carroll and Kellow, 2011: Chapter 14).

The committees are a key means by which members exercise control and guidance over the OECD's work, but they are also important as:

- Channels of communication between the member governments and OECD staff, providing access to the current and evolving views, wishes and, at times, ideas of an enormously wide range of national departments and agencies. They provide authoritative and often critical feedback on existing work and act as an 'early warning system' that enables astute staff to identify possible future work requests and undertake appropriate changes in work programmes.
- Authoritative sources of more detailed leadership and direction for the OECD staff who for the most part undertake the approved work programmes.
- Relatively secure supportive locations within which negotiation, bargaining, compromise and agreement between members can take place. In addition, given the large number of committees involved within the one organisational structure they enable, usually at the levels of parent committee, the standing committees of the OECD Council and in Council itself, cross-committee negotiation, bargaining, compromise and agreement in which a concession in one committee or working party can be traded for support in another. In this sense the committees are stalls in a complex market place in which a variety of exchanges can take place, with the market place, the OECD, being owned by the stall holders.

The OECD Council and the Secretary-General

The Council is composed of all the OECD members and is the supreme decision making body. Its membership consists of either elected Ministers, one for each member, usually meeting only once per annum, or of Permanent Representatives, with the rank of ambassador, usually senior public servants from national foreign affairs or finance/treasury departments, meeting on a monthly or more frequent basis. The chair of the Council of Ministers is drawn annually from one of its members, while the chair of the Council of Permanent Representatives is the Secretary-General.

The Secretary-General is appointed by the Ministerial Council for a period of five years to assist it in all 'appropriate ways', and has the right to submit proposals to Council and to appoint required staff, though subject to the Council approval of organisational plans and staff regulations. Article 11 of the OECD's Convention makes it clear that the Secretariat is to be independent by specifying that its members:

> [S]hall neither seek nor receive instructions from any of the Members or from any Government or authority external to the Organisation.

It was to be independent of the individual member states and external authorities, but not, of course, independent from the members acting collectively in the shape of the OECD Council.

In essence, the Ministerial Council (MCM) meets once a year to discuss a carefully scripted set of key issues and to endorse a set of largely predetermined and agreed priorities for continuing and future OECD work. The MCM is important, not for the discussion that takes place at the meeting, but for its authoritative, ministerial endorsement of the organisation's strategic priorities and its current and changing work programmes. It is an endorsement that finds form in the final communiqué from the MCM and it is treated by the Secretariat and the Heads of Delegations (the Permanent Representatives) as the mandate for terminating, encouraging, prioritising and adding to the OECD's future work programme.

Ministers also meet on a less frequent basis in sectoral meetings of Committees at the ministerial level (Ministerials) that correspond to one of the major OECD committees. The Committee for Agriculture, for example, was one of the first sectoral Ministerials meeting four times in the 1962–68 period (OECD, 1988: 118). The OECD Ministerial Council has responsibility for approving and convening sectoral Ministerial meetings, reviewing agendas and accompanying documentation. It also takes note of any Declarations, Decisions and Recommendations developed at the sectoral Ministerials and, where agreed, is responsible for their adoption (OECD, 1988: 119). The role of sectoral Ministerials is broadly the same as that for the OECD MCM meetings, but without the latter's influence and legal status. Nevertheless, they give a degree of added weight to major recommendations from the relevant committee (for example, the Agriculture Committee and the Health Committee) that are submitted to the Secretary-General, then the Budget Committee and the OECD MCM for new or modified work programmes and, most importantly, necessary budgetary resources.

The Council of Permanent Representatives (CPR) has four major roles and is supported in its work by four standing committees, the Executive, Budget, External Relations and Evaluation committees. The committees act as filters for Council by dealing with and resolving most of the matters submitted to Council, leaving it free to focus on areas of major concern or disagreement. The first role is an essentially political role, comprising a continuing process whereby the CPR assesses the political implications of the issues placed before it by the Secretary-General for the countries they represent and, in so far as it is relevant and possible, their common interests in both regional and global contexts. This is especially so where Council is considering a proposal for any one of the three formal 'acts' of the organisation, a Decision, Recommendation, Resolution and, in addition, while not a formal act, a Declaration.

A Decision is rare as it is binding upon all members, except where otherwise specified and for members abstaining on the matter, so is subject to very close attention. A Recommendation is not binding but represents a policy commitment by governments, relying for its force upon peer group pressure and the adverse impact upon reputation that might follow if a country does not implement a Recommendation it has endorsed. A Resolution is a decision concerning the internal workings of the OECD. A Declaration is not a formal act as it is not specified in the Convention, nor does Council adopt or approve declarations, merely noting them by means of a resolution. They are developed in other committees or bodies of the OECD and aim to give the topic covered by the Declaration an added weight and 'solemnity' (OECD, 1988). In practice it is rare for Council to reject any proposal for an act or Declaration as proposals likely to be highly sensitive, contentious or divisive are filtered out informally or in earlier discussions in one of the standing or substantive committees, with all parties mindful of the requirement for consensus.

The second role is that of providing strategic direction for the OECD. While CPR meetings are not the venue for detailed strategic planning they do provide, or at least attempt to provide, a sense of strategic direction for the Secretariat and the major committees by identifying and agreeing strategic priorities to be taken into consideration in the development of the work plans and budgets prepared for its later approval. Interestingly, it was not until 2005 that Council finally developed a formal, systematic process for establishing a set of strategic, medium term objectives (the MTO) to indicate work priorities in the medium term (Bourgon, 2009).

The third and perhaps most important role is that of resource allocation, centred in the politics of the budgetary process. This is a difficult role for the CPR as the members of the OECD's major committees, responsible for developing budgetary proposals for their proposed work programmes, are themselves delegates from a wide range of departments in members' national governments. In agreeing and recommending their draft work programmes for Council they are acting on behalf of, and on the basis of instructions from, those departments. Hence, given this situation, while Council has the Convention-derived authority to make decisions regarding the budget and proposed work programmes, if it makes major changes to those proposed it risks the ire of those departments and the governments they serve. However, at the same time, they face constant pressure from the national governments to constrain or reduce the overall budget, a difficult and essentially political task involving frequent compromise and, for the most part, 'behind the scenes', or 'in the corridors', negotiations. As always, organisational continuity and change are essentially the results of complex political processes.

The OECD budget is funded on the basis of a system of required, formula based and also voluntary contributions from members and, occasionally, by external bodies. Part I of the budget is formula based, with funds being a proportion of each member's taxable income, although there are sometimes voluntary contributions for Part I activities. Part II concerns programmes funded for the most part by members' voluntary contributions. The formula is subject to three constraints: (1) no member's rate of contribution should exceed 25 per cent; (2) no member's rate of contribution should be less than 0.1 per cent of the total; and (3) no member's rate of contribution to any budget should increase by more than 10 per cent from one year to the next. In general, the larger the GNP the more each member contributes, up to the maximum of 25 per cent of the budget total, a maximum imposed following strong pressure from the USA and Japan.

In essence, the Part I funding system means that each member pays a different 'price', for the bulk of the 'products' of the OECD, regardless of how much they have 'consumed' of those products. Members with a smaller GNP are, in effect, heavily cross-subsidised by those with a larger GNP. The USA typically funds very nearly 25 per cent of the Part I budget and Japan 22–24 per cent, with Iceland and Luxemburg, in marked contrast, only 0.1 per cent. Hence, the politics of the OECD's budgetary process is complex and challenging, as the larger countries typically try to reduce their share of the total and move work programmes to the voluntarily funded, Part II of the budget. This is against a background of near-constant pressures from the major committees for budget increases to fund existing and proposed new programmes (usually strongly, if discretely supported by the OECD's directorates that stand to benefit from increased allocations). It is made even more challenging by the fact that Council decisions, as specified by Article 6 of the Convention, have to be made by mutual agreement, that is, by consensus. This does not require a unanimous vote by all members on all issues, only a unanimous vote by those actually voting, leaving others free to abstain.

Fourth, is the performance evaluation role, based on a slowly developed, integrated management cycle within which two major evaluative mechanisms are embedded, the Programme Implementation Report (PIR) and the in depth evaluations of committees. The PIR provides Council with annual reports on the extent to which the planned work outputs or results in the previous year's work programme and budget have been achieved. The in-depth evaluation of committees is designed to supplement the PIR with a mechanism that enables Council to judge whether the substantive committees are conducting processes, delivering outputs and achieving impacts that are in line with Members policy expectations and priorities and with the comparative advantage of the OECD; and that represent value-for-money to capitals.

The Role of the Delegations

All OECD members maintain a permanent delegation in Paris, though they vary greatly in size, with the members geographically most distant (such as Korea), tending to have larger numbers of staff than European members partly in order to reduce costs, partly in an attempt to ensure more effective coordination of their inputs to the myriad of committees. (The Australian delegation is modest, and New Zealand's even more so.) The latter task is achieved in a number of ways: (1) most permanent delegation staff represent their countries on a small number of committees and working parties, especially those of lesser importance; (2) they liaise closely with their relevant, national departments and agencies on all matters likely to be of interest; (3) they liaise closely with the Secretariat staff that undertake the relevant committee work programmes, gaining a detailed knowledge of the organisation; and (4) while the major, level one committees are nearly always attended by delegates sent directly from national capitals, they are usually accompanied at these meetings by one or more members of the permanent delegations.

The heads of delegations are the ambassadors that constitute the CPR, with overall responsibility for representing their countries' interests at the OECD and, in many cases, responsible for managing the permanent delegations. As well as sitting as members of Council they often have particular responsibilities as chairs, vice chairs or members of one of

Council's key standing and special purpose committees. In addition, they meet as members of one or more of the broad 'factional' groupings of members, notably the EU, Nordic, APEC (Asia-Pacific Economic Cooperation forum) and G7/8 groups, to identify, develop and pursue common interests across a wide range of issues, including key policy, structural, process and staffing issues. The groupings are by no means entirely cohesive, nor could they be given the range of national interests involved, though the EU grouping is the most cohesive, in the past meeting weekly in the attempt to ensure a common position for the European Commission representatives on Council and at the committees they also attend.

Committees and Directorates

The OECD's committees, at present some two hundred plus (the number varies over time), are its beating heart, for as an OECD working party put it:

> Through its committee structure the OECD's substantive policy agenda and outputs respond directly to the needs of, and are closely monitored by, senior policy officials from capitals in a way that may be unique among international organisations. It is these committees that produce the outputs of the OECD, the policy advice, guidelines, principles ('soft law') and best practices. The working methods of the committees are one of the institution's hallmarks, the source of its added value and the support it enjoys in capitals. (OECD, 2008a: 24)

The committees are the bodies to which Council delegates its powers and they are the key actors that play a major role in determining the complex and dynamic agenda of the OECD. Indeed, it is more accurate to speak of the agendas of the OECD, rather than one agenda, with each 'first level', major committee developing and pursuing its own agenda, subject to the agreement of Council. Indeed, in many respects the OECD committee system is analogous to a multi-sectoral, permanent, inter-governmental conference. The committees constitute a series of highly specialised smaller nodes, each with their own network of links extending within and outside of the ambit of the network governor, the OECD. In regard to other international organisations, for example, the OECD's committees are linked to at least 68, though only five or so have been granted a formal status, notably the World Health Organization (WHO), the World Bank, Asian Development Bank, Inter-American Development Bank and United Nations Conference on Trade and Development (UNCTAD) (Carroll and Kellow 2011: 194).

The thirty-nine first level committees are, in general, the most powerful of the committees, responsible to no other body but the OECD Council and they, in turn, commonly delegate increasingly specific responsibilities to various subcommittees and working groups. While the number of committees and subsidiary bodies, over two hundred, may seem large, they are responsible for a very wide range of work in almost all policy areas of interest to their members.

Committee Membership

The membership of the committees varies somewhat, depending on the aims and importance of the committee in question, but most are open to all OECD members and many include one or more non-members as observers, for example, the WHO, IMF and World Bank, or a non-member state, notably those from BRICSA. Council approval is required for all observers for a specified duration and for the renewal of their participation. The bulk of the membership of the committees consists of representatives from the member governments, drawn either from the permanent delegations that they maintain in Paris, or from domestic departments or agencies ('capital based delegates'). Representatives from the delegations have the advantage of being located close to the OECD in Paris for the period of their assignment and gain a greater familiarity with its operations and staff, with the potential to become somewhat more effective and influential in pursuing their national interests. However, at the same time, with the exception of those from member countries in close proximity to Paris, the staff of national delegations are somewhat removed from their departmental base and the latest national developments relevant to the areas of their responsibility, despite the intensive use of modern communications systems.

A number of national departments, notably Finance or Treasury departments, typically assign their most promising staff to their Paris delegation for one or two years in order to gain experience in discussions and negotiations at the international level. It is an experience also considered valuable for developing personal contacts with similar staff from other countries, part of the network of contacts typical of, and much used by, senior public servants. It is noticeable in discussions with both staff and delegates that committee attendance by, as the OECD puts it, capital based delegates, is usually valued more highly than attendance by members of national delegations, often on the basis of the assumption that the capital based delegates are more senior in rank and in influence.

In general the committees meet only once or twice per annum, for two or three days per session, so that while they might represent the beating heart of the OECD, it is a heart that beats rather slowly, if regularly. However, the total number of delegate days per annum for each committee and its subsidiary bodies can vary considerably, from 3,929 for the Development Assistance Committee (DAC) to only 35 for the Steel Committee (Nicholson, 2003: 35). While the OECD's budget is drawn up on programme lines, the resources allocated in support of work overseen by the committees varies substantially. In 2001–2, for example, the approximate resources allocated ranged from 8.2 million Euros for the Economic Development Review Committee (EDRC) to virtually nothing for the Tourism Committee. The largest seven committees and their subsidiaries are allocated over 50 per cent of the resources and the largest fifteen are allocated approximately 90 per cent. The reasons for the differences in resource allocation are caused largely by differences in the extent and type of work undertaken for the committees by the Secretariat. Those responsible for large-scale data gathering and analysis activities, especially when combined with major peer review activities, typically require and gain the largest share of resources, such as the EDRC, Economic Policy, Environment, Agriculture and Trade committees.

Committee Structure and Work Processes

The bulk of the committees have a largely common and simple structure consisting of a usually small bureau, the remaining members and a secretary, the latter drawn from the staff of the relevant OECD directorate. The bureau consists of an elected chair (as approved by Council, in the case of standing committees) and a number of vice chairs (appointed by the members of the committee) who, together, are responsible for setting the provisional agenda, guiding discussion and ensuring that the business of the committee is followed through in an appropriate fashion. They often meet separately before the full committee and, both before and after committee meetings, engage in email, phone or, less commonly, video conferences in order to reach agreement on the draft agenda and outstanding issues, and to monitor programme development and implementation.

The actual work of each committee can be divided into two broad phases: the between-meeting activities and the meeting. The former, in turn, falls into two broad types of activity: (1) those concerned with achieving the actions agreed in the last committee; and (2) those concerned with preparations for the next committee. As the bulk of the substantive work is undertaken by members of the OECD Secretariat, the follow-up actions of the committee for the most part involve the chair and vice chairs and, to a lesser extent, the other members of the bureau in providing advice in reply to questions raised by its support staff and commenting upon drafts or part drafts of forthcoming reports on work authorised by the Committee.

All members of the committee also report back to their respective national departments or agencies on the business of the committee meetings and later, related developments, reports usually also copied to the permanent delegations in Paris, whose members typically have responsibilities for overseeing as well as participating in the work of a number of committees. The second type of between meeting activities focus on drawing up the agenda for the next meeting, with the committee secretary (a member of the Secretariat) typically drawing up successive drafts on the basis of the views of the chair, following their sounding out of the interests of the bureau. While agendas vary their typical substantive content includes: progress reports on projects prepared by OECD staff; draft final project reports for consideration; initial proposals for new or modified projects; notes and related documentation from the Secretary-General on OECD-wide matters; occasional papers prepared by experts external to the Committee, sometimes for presentation at the next meeting. The bulk of the papers for the meetings are prepared by OECD staff.

The second phase often commences with a meeting of Committee members with their 'social partners', for example, representatives of Business and Industry Advisory Committee (BIAC) or the Trade Union Advisory Committee (TUAC), or other interest groups, focused on presentations or/and papers prepared by the representatives related to the business of the Committee meeting. Members' attendance at these 'pre-meeting meetings' varies and it is not uncommon for BIAC or TUAC to indicate their disappointment as to their value.

The meeting of the Committee is structured around the agenda items and, after approval of the agenda and minutes, typically commences with a presentation from a senior member of the relevant directorate, often the Director, reporting on recent and future events and issues of interest to the members. This is followed by the presentation of progress reports regarding ongoing projects and initial proposals for new projects, usually by staff from the Directorate, the discussion of which might spread over the bulk of two days. Less frequently, the chairs of subcommittees and working parties will make presentations and, where they do not, they often lead discussion of the tabled progress reports relevant to their subcommittee. The meetings are generally quite formal in style, a frequent criticism of members keen to see more open-ended discussion with a broader range of participation rather than the common, member by member presentation of formal briefs (as reported by most of those committee members interviewed).

The Peer Review Process

An important part of the work of many of the major committees is the system of peer review, which consists of an examination of one state's performance or practices in a particular policy area by other states. These provide both a means of subjecting the policies of member states to critical scrutiny – a 'quality assurance' check – and a means of identifying and sharing best practice among the membership (and beyond). The process places as much emphasis on the 'peer' as the 'review', because it reflects the fact that the OECD is an intergovernmental organisation. The involvement of peers (other members) in the conduct of the review means that it involves equals, rather than a superior body that will hand down judgement or prescribe punishment. This is central to their value, because a state is more willing to accept criticism, and other members to give it, if all parties know it does not commit them to a particular position or course of action. Peer reviews can help encourage dialogue that helps clarify positions in a non-adversarial setting.

Committee Decision Making

As noted above, decision making in the OECD is for the most part made on the basis of mutual agreement, that is, by consensus, as specified in the Convention, which makes no distinction between more important or less important decisions although, in practice, a number of committees and other OECD bodies have agreed, by consensus, to adopt a variety of qualified majority voting procedures for minor matters. Hence, in theory, any decision can be blocked by even one dissenting vote. However, in practice, the consensus principle only presents difficulties where there are major and persisting differences between committee members. This is because all members appreciate that unreasonable, frequent refusals to reach agreement by a member would lead to a similar response from other members, a perception that acts as an effective constraint.

As a result the typical decision making process in OECD committees involves up to three broad and often overlapping stages, stages which constitute the very core of OECD politics. The first is a pre-committee meeting period in which one or more members engage in a process of discussion with actors at the national level to determine what action or decision is desired. In this stage the OECD delegates provide information and advice to the relevant national department or agency about the likely acceptability of, and support for, the proposed activity, but the position to be adopted is usually determined in the relevant capital. The second stage, again in the pre-committee meeting period, often on an iterative basis, is one in which delegates (particularly permanent representatives) engage in consultation within the OECD aimed primarily at communicating the desired activity or decision and, on that basis, identify the views of other members on the issue in question, including the major groupings (EU, APEC, Nordic, G7/8) and influential members within the groupings, notably the USA, Japan, Germany, UK and France. In addition, the views of senior members of the Secretariat responsible are often sought (typically at heads of division level, grade A5 and above) and, to a more limited extent, the views of key interest groups such as BIAC and TUAC.

On relatively minor issues that fall clearly within the mandate of the committee in question the consultation is largely confined to the committee members, especially the members of the bureau. Larger, more complex issues require more extensive consultation, possibly including discussion in the regular meetings of Heads of Delegation and, for issues such as the accession of new members, bilateral or plurilateral discussions between foreign affairs departments outside of the OECD. While such consultations can and do take place at any time they are most frequent and intense where resource allocations are necessary, focused, unsurprisingly, in the biennial work programme and budget process (PWB).

The third stage can be described as the compromise and, for more complex decisions, programme design phase. In essence, the aim here is to shape the contents of a decision that will achieve the desired result by means of a negotiation and bargaining process. A degree of compromise is often necessary, both to ensure a significant majority of committee members support the design or solution and to ensure that those not supporting the decision will at least abstain on the issue. Those decisions dealt with in the budgetary process have to gain consensus both within the sponsoring committee and, of course, within Council's Budget Committee and, finally, Council. At this level attention focuses for the most part on new or substantially modified programme proposals, rather than continuing programmes. Those that align most closely with the agreed OECD priorities and that are accompanied by the promise of voluntary contributions from interested members are most likely to be successful. As might be expected, new proposals that require funding from what is called Part I of the budget, based on set, annual contributions from members, are the most fiercely contested for, in the context of limited or no growth budgets that have characterised the OECD since the mid-1990s, agreement to a new proposal means that one or more existing programmes will have to be reduced in scope, altogether cut, or increased efficiencies gained.

The OECD committees are supported by a range of bodies, notably the various directorates and their staff. It is the latter that undertake the detailed policy research, monitoring and surveillance work mandated by the various committees, with each directorate being responsible for supporting one or more committees. About 750 staff fall into one of three key types, economist, policy analyst and administrator, with the bulk at grades A2 or A3 and smaller numbers at grade A4 or A5 (Head of Division), with a varying, smaller number of statisticians. Grade A5 staff are expected to have considerable senior level experience in an international context, the ability to lead discussions in committees and working parties and very wide experience in a national and international policy context in a relevant field. Interestingly, they are also expected to have considerable political judgement. In addition, at any one time approximately another 500 staff are working on a short-term basis, with increasing numbers seconded from and paid by national administrations to work on specific projects. The remaining staff consists predominantly of translators, interpreters, secretaries and relatively junior administrative assistants.

There are currently fourteen directorates (twelve if the Executive and Public Affairs directorates are excluded, and they are variously and confusingly described as directorates, centres and departments), though the number has varied over time in line with the changing interests and emphases of the members.

The OECD also has a range of what it calls 'Special Bodies', created to meet particular demands at differing times over the life of the OECD and its predecessor, the OEEC, for example, the Africa Partnership Forum, Development Centre, Financial Action Task Force, International Energy Agency and the Nuclear Energy Agency.

OECD Staff, Their Role and Influence

A large part of the output of the OECD consists of a seemingly endless stream of data and reports on a very wide range of topics. The bulk of this output is produced by small teams of OECD Secretariat staff working under the direction of one or more of the committees of national delegates that, subject to the overall authority of the OECD Council, determine the direction and nature of each directorate's work. Moreover, as the organisation has little formal authority to impose its decisions on its members, its power relies primarily upon its ability to persuade its members of the accuracy and value of its data, its reports and the conclusions and recommendations they contain (Marcussen, 2001; Sharman, 2005: 6; Carroll and Kellow, 2011).

It is the quality, credibility and usefulness of that output that has earned the OECD Secretariat's generally high, if variable reputation. In turn, it is that high reputation that endows its current and future outputs of data and reports with a high degree of credibility and influence – it is expected of them. Similarly, that combination of reputation and quality endows the members of its Secretariat with a substantial degree of autonomy and influence provided, of course, that the quality of its work remains high and, most important, of value for its members.

The quality of the Secretariat's output is brought about by the interaction of at least three factors. The first is its institutional structure and associated processes, notably the role of its committees and its programme of work and budget processes that both provide the Secretariat with a varying degree of independence and, at the same time constrain that independence. The second are its discussions with a surprisingly large range of external stakeholders, notably national departments and agencies, other international organisations, but also public and private foundations and, increasingly, non-member countries in relation to the OECD's expanded, global relations programme (OECD, 2007). The third is the undoubted, if varying capacity of OECD staff.

As noted above and in contrast, for example, to the IMF or the World Bank, the representatives of the member states of the OECD are deeply engaged with the work of the OECD, largely by virtue of the central role they play as members of the two hundred plus OECD committees, subcommittees, working groups, roundtables and global fora. These bodies not only request work to be done by the members of the Secretariat, they contribute to, review and, less often, recommend the adoption of the conclusions of the data and reports they receive to the OECD's governing Council. Indeed, where OECD resources or expertise are limited, or both, the members, typically working with colleagues in their national administrations, sometimes undertake detailed research work to supplement that done on their behalf by their Secretariat support staff. In essence the committee structure represents a series of key veto points that constrain, to varying extents, the activities and influence of the Secretariat but, at the same time, contribute to its quality. This applies to proposals for specific projects, the development of projects once approval has been gained and, finally, the data and reports that result.

CHAPTER OUTLINES

Chapters 2 and 3 provide the historical context for understanding Australia's membership of the OECD. In particular, Chapter 2 shows that

Australia and its officials had had several decades of growing experience of working within the context of international, intergovernmental organisations, with day to day responsibility being allocated to those departments with relevant, domestic policy responsibilities, before joining the OECD. While substantial hopes had been placed in the UN and its specialised agencies much of that hope had not been realised with the development of the Cold War, leading to the growth of regional organisations. Australia was not a member of any of those established in the North Atlantic and Western European areas, such as NATO, the EEC and the OECD, so that Australian decision makers were relatively and, it was felt, increasingly isolated from important discussions held within their boundaries. This relative isolation was exacerbated by the increasingly obvious decline in the value of the Commonwealth, an Australian perception that British governments were not taking Australian interests sufficiently into consideration and, of course, the feeling of betrayal that accompanied the first British application for membership of the EEC. It was in this context that Australian officials began to consider and promote the value of OECD membership.

Chapter 3 argues that in contrast to the earlier decisions relating to membership of most of the UN special agencies such as the WHO, Food and Agriculture Organization (FAO), and United Nations Educational, Scientific and Cultural Organization (UNESCO) that concerning the OECD was very cautious, revealing substantial differences between key ministers and their departments that took a decade to resolve. Those supporting membership were officials contained, for the most part, in Treasury and the Department of External Affairs (DEA), searching for greater Australian access and influence in what was seen as an increasingly important organisation as regards international economic affairs, the coordination of foreign aid in the face of growing Soviet threat, and international trade. The opposition was centred around Deputy Prime Minister 'Black Jack' McEwen and his officials in the Department of Trade and Industry and, to a lesser extent, Prime Minister Menzies, concerned about the potential of OECD membership to result in increased pressure for the Australian stance of 'protection all round' as the basis for its economic development to be weakened or terminated.

Chapter 4 examines how the relationship with the OECD has been administered and the challenges of securing effective engagement by a middle power such as Australia in a remotely located international organisation. The work of the OECD in numerous committees and subsidiary bodies requires an extensive engagement of personnel and Australia's remoteness from Paris has placed demands for both travel and on the Delegation that are unusual when compared to many

Members. Communication has been particularly important, especially given the large volume of documents produced by the OECD, and (as the chapter shows) this has sometimes been problematic. Also considered are the financial arrangements for the cost of the engagement and some aspects of the arrangements for Ministerial Council Meetings.

Chapter 5 is the first of three chapters that focus on the roles played by DFAT in leading and organising Australian involvement at the OECD, its work in relation to export credit and foreign aid. It shows DFAT's role in relation to the OECD has been and continues to be, challenging and sometimes frustrating. This commenced before membership with a competition with Treasury and Trade for the position of lead agency for OECD matters. While the competition for lead agency status for the most part ended with the achievement of membership, organisational issues and challenges continued. Those associated with its work on export credit soon emerged and have continued to the present day, largely as a result of Australia's relatively minor position and influence as a middle power, able only occasionally to substantially influence the activities and policies of the major OECD actors.

Chapter 6 shows how Australian views regarding OECD work on trade and agriculture have varied over time. They changed from those dominated by considerable concern at the implications of membership for Australia's trade policy, soon allayed, to one of mixed, rather disappointed views regarding its early lack of influence and the mundane nature of much of the OECD's early work on trade in agriculture, the primary focus of the chapter. However, the late 1980s and early 1990s demonstrated more optimistic views, showing how a new and relatively small member of the OECD such as Australia could be more influential, if by no means always successful in its continuing drive to persuade members to move towards free trade in agricultural products. The reasons for optimism can be found in: (1) a more coherent strategy aimed at furthering Australia's trade interests, developed in 1986–87; and (2) the benefits of working in cooperation with like-minded members such as the USA, Canada, New Zealand and especially the members of the Cairns Group. However, again, following the initial success in establishing the WTO, disappointment came to the fore as little or no progress could be achieved at the OECD in relation to freeing up trade in agriculture.

Chapter 7 demonstrates how Australia's engagement with the Development Assistance Committee commenced at a relatively high level of intensity, conceived as an important first step to eventual full membership of the OECD, then slowly fell in both intensity and importance for most of the following decades. Participation in DAC became more selective and, for the most part, of a lower priority, though providing valuable learning experiences and, in particular, providing access to its aid statistics, reports and guidelines. The learning that took place was accompanied by, for the most part, the acceptance of the classifications, meanings and norms developed by the OECD and its members. The chapter asserts, however, that Australia did not simply accept what was developed by DAC, but also made important contributions, most recently in regard to policies and practices of value in dealing with fragile states. In addition, the DAC's regular reviews of Australia's aid policies and programmes enabled officials to learn from its peers at the DAC, as well as providing them with, at times, valuable information to support the case for greater aid allocations in annual budgets.

Chapter 8 is the first of two chapters that examine the role of the Treasury and agencies in its portfolio, the most extensive involvement of all government portfolios in OECD work. The full range of the portfolio's work cannot be covered in this study, so the chapter contains only a selection of its work, commencing with an examination of Treasury's role in promoting Australian membership of the OECD, before moving on to provide an outline of the varying extent and intensity of the Treasury Department's involvement with OECD committees. This is followed by a brief description of the involvement of the major agencies in the Treasury Portfolio, with the final section providing an in-depth examination of Treasury involvement with the EDRC, the reviews of which have often provided considerable challenges for the Department, largely as regards their political sensitivity when they are critical of current economic policy.

As discussed in Chapter 9, the second of the two chapters focusing on the Treasury portfolio, Australia had minimal initial engagement with the OECD's tax activities at the time of accession, but now plays a focused, though significant role in that work, both learning from shared experience and providing OECD members with its own valuable insights. While the OECD has proven a useful arena for developing tax policy for the Council of Europe and the United Nations, the intersection between arenas has given rise to some problems for Australia, particularly membership of the Commonwealth and its relations with small tax havens in the Pacific.

Turning to the environment, Chapter 10 describes how Australia initially was somewhat unenthusiastic about environmental matters in the OECD, despite perhaps an excess of enthusiasm on the part of Environment Minister, Moss Cass, at the first Ministerial Meeting. As with Education, the then limited Commonwealth role in environmental policy provided one factor explaining this, though as Commonwealth jurisdiction regarding the environment increased so did Australian engagement. Participation developed over time and provided opportunities in both the OECD and in 'pull aside' meetings with Members and non-members alike, and both on environmental policy issues and those environmental issues with important linkages to areas such as agricultural trade. A proposed Council Act on lead, for example, prompted an especially active role on both that specific issue and in developing broader principles for risk management.

Chapter 11 shows that Australia has played a prominent role in education at the OECD. It has been an eager participant and has committed substantial resources to this activity and it has made a greater contribution of staff to senior levels of the Secretariat than any other Directorate, with Australians having filled the roles of Deputy Director and Director. Australia was nevertheless initially a somewhat reluctant participant because of the limited role for the Commonwealth government in education in the Australian federation at the time of accession, but also because of a rather negative view conveyed by the United Kingdom and a reluctance to commit voluntary funds to the Centre for Educational Research and Innovation (CERI), the locus of early education activity.

Chapter 12 describes Australia's involvement in the health work of the OECD, an involvement that was only of minor interest for over twenty years but that increased sharply from 1997 to 1998. It was a rapidly increased and successful involvement, resulting in a programme of health work that brought it substantial influence. Moreover, it was an influence that persisted for over a decade and demonstrated that a middle power with a clear strategy, experienced officials and a willingness to provide significant funds to support its proposals could achieve an influential position in an international organisation. The change in strategy that spurred this development commenced under the first Howard government with a period of 'forum shopping', that resulted in the selection of the OECD, rather than the WHO, as the forum for an expansion of health work in which the Department of Health and Ageing was interested. The chapter then moves on to illustrate the difficulties faced in promoting increased health work at the OECD at a time of severe budgetary constraint and the desire of successive Australian ambassadors to the OECD to curtail the growth in the breadth and cost of its work.

Chapter 13 examines in further detail the organisation and management of Australia's engagement with the OECD, together with changing views as to its value. Australia has constantly considered the cost of engagement and the need to ensure the OECD delivers value for money, following on a tradition established by its representatives in the League of Nations. The coordination of the input of the largest number of participating Australian agencies found in any international organisation, and the performance of that role by DFAT is examined. It also examines how the value of OECD membership has come under increasing scrutiny as arenas such as the G20 have emerged, and the apparently political nature of the two most recent ambassadorial appointments. While DFAT and Treasury enthusiasm for the OECD shows some signs of decreasing, that of most other agencies has increased or at least been relatively stable.

Chapter 14, the concluding chapter, asserts that the experiences and views of Australian agencies in relation to the OECD have changed over time, although the dominant view has been that the organisation continues to provide an important means of influence on a wide range of international issues and, most importantly, an unrivalled means of enhancing policy learning and policy capacity.

BIBLIOGRAPHY

Bourgon, J. 2009. 'Reform and Modernization of the OECD', the Centre for International Governance Innovation, Working Paper No. 42, May, accessed on 19 January 2017 at www.cigionline.org/sites/default/files/wp_42-web.pdf.

Carroll, P. and Kellow, A. 2011. *The OECD A Study of Organisational Adaptation*, Cheltenham, UK and Northampton, MA, USA: Edward Elgar Publishing.

DEWR 2001. Cable 7 January 2002, Paris OECD to CBR, OECD: an overview and assessment from HOM, File ET01/11368 government relations – Committees 1358 – Organisation For Economic Co-operation and Development (OECD) – Cables and Reports.

DFAT 2001. Cable 29–30 April 2003, PAR to CBR MCM 11/4/03, File 01/050759 OECD EC 2001.

Gass, R. 2002. 'The OECD as a "Culture" as Seen by an "Old Timer"', *@mosphere, OECD*, 10 October, pp. 10–11.

Hawkins, D. and Jacoby, W. 2006. 'How Agents Matter', in D. Hawkins, D. Lake, D. Nielson and M. Tierney (eds), *Delegation and Agency in International Organizations*, Cambridge: Cambridge University Press, pp. 199–228.

Lintott, H. 1949. 'The Organization for European Economic Cooperation', *International Organization*, 3: 269–277.

Marcussen, M. 2001. 'The OECD in Search of a Role: Playing the Idea Game', Prepared for presentation at the European Consortium for Political Research (ECPR), 29th Joint Sessions of Workshops, Grenoble, France, 6–11 April.

NAA 1981. Organisation for Economic Co-operation and Development – Review of Australian Participation – June 1981. A6343 B1981/162.

Nicholson, P. 2003. 'Maximising the Impact of the OECD – Reorganising the Committee Structure and Related Matters', Report by Mr Peter Nicholson, SG(2003)1, 15 January 2003.
OECD 1988. 'Manual for the Guidance of Chairmen of the Subsidiary Bodies of the Organisation', June, Paris: OECD.
OECD 2007. 'The OECD's Global Relations Programme', Paris: OECD.
OECD 2008a. 'Rules of Procedure of the Organisation', Paris: OECD.
OECD 2008b. 'Participation of Non-Members', Paris: OECD.
Salzman, J. 2005. 'Decentralized Administrative Law in the Organization for Economic Cooperation and Development', *Law and Contemporary Problems*, 68: 189–224.
Sharman, J. 2005. 'OECD Reputation as OECD Effectiveness', Paper presented to the International Studies Association Meeting, Honolulu, Hawaii, 1–5 March.
Sloan, J. 2012. 'Sludge-producing OECD has Outlived its Welcome', *The Australian*, 6 October.
Sloan, J. 2013. 'Give and Take That Taps Touchy Topic of Taxation', *The Australian*, 30 March.
Sloan, J. 2013a. 'Surely you Weren't Wrong, Mr Swan?', *The Australian*, 13 September.
Sloan, J. 2013b. 'Chalk One Up for Free School', *The Australian*, 15 October.

2. Australia, international organisations and foreign policy

The aim of this chapter is to outline the development of Australia's involvement with international governmental organisations (IGOs) to the late 1950s in order to provide a more detailed, comparative context within which to examine its membership of the OECD. It indicates that Australian governments and public servants had had considerable experience in working within IGOs for several decades before gaining membership of the OECD, as well as having at least a basic understanding of the activities of its predecessor, the OEEC, especially in relation to its European Payments Union (EPU) and the Codes of Liberalisation, as well as a limited involvement as an observer at a number of the OEEC's Productivity and Applied Research Committee's subcommittees (NAA, 1953a, 1953b). While Australian views as to the value of IGOs were mixed, middle powers such as Australia typically have a preference, if variable in its intensity, for working through IGOs and promoting international legal norms (Ungerer, 2007: 539).

The chapter is divided into three major sections, followed by a conclusion. The first briefly examines the development of Australian foreign policy pre-1939, focused on the League of Nations, the International Labour Organization (ILO) and the British Empire. The second examines the varying position of Australian governments regarding the Commonwealth, the United Nations and its specialised agencies in the post-1945 period. The third section focuses on Australia's growing concern for European integration and its implications for Australian interests, with a focus on the OEEC, the OECD's predecessor.

AUSTRALIA AND INTERGOVERNMENTAL ORGANISATIONS BEFORE THE SECOND WORLD WAR

Much of the early, pre-1939 experience of Australian decision makers with external affairs was gained within three major IGOs, the League of Nations, the ILO and the British Empire as it commenced its slow metamorphosis into the Commonwealth of Nations. In these early years there was little or no mention of Australia as a middle power and the access to information and influence that membership of the three organisations might provide, but such membership was clearly seen as providing a degree of influence that might not otherwise have been attained.

The British Empire and the Commonwealth of Nations

In the years before 1914 and for most of the period up to 1939 successive Australian governments, labour and conservative, attempted to achieve their foreign policy goals primarily by influencing British policy. They accepted, for the most part, the convention of a single imperial foreign policy and the overall responsibility for its making and implementation by the British government, hopefully taking into account Australia's interests, especially in the Pacific. This is not to argue that Australian governments were keen to see a quasi-federal constitution for intra-imperial relations. This smacked too much of a continuing, subservient, colonial dependence. Indeed, one of Prime Minister Hughes' three major aims at the 1921 Imperial Conference was to prevent any such development (Edwards, 1983: 62). Rather, the aim was to ensure a full consultation by British governments with their Australian and other counterparts before the making of major decisions involving their interests, an aim pursued with varying degrees of success. It remained an aim of Australian governments until after 1945 (see, for example, Bruce's position in regard to the Balfour Declaration in Lee, 2010a: 65–8).

The dependence on Britain, if increasingly less colonial in nature, was accompanied by a high degree of reliance on the British for information related to external affairs, a reliance made the greater by repeated government decisions not to create any significant administrative support for external affairs (see, in particular, the meetings of the Commonwealth Economic Consultative Council and the Commonwealth Liaison Committee, as noted in NAA file series A3211). In turn, this inhibited the capacity of successive Australian governments to develop a fully autonomous foreign and defence policy, even had they so wished, an inhibition that caused, for example, later Liberal Party Minister R.G. Casey to express his concerns as to the wisdom of such dependence as early as 1931. He noted the progressive deterioration of the idea of Empire 'into a loose-jointed conglomeration of States called the British Commonwealth of Nations' (Edwards, 1983: 68).

Despite this slowly decreasing, dependent stance and limited capacity, as Lloyd notes, most of the British Dominions, including Australia, became, if slowly and at differing rates, international actors shortly after the First World War when they became founder members of the League of Nations, the ILO and the Permanent Court of International Justice (Lloyd, 2001: 10). They had, of course, attended international conferences and taken part in IGOs before, as well as engaging in a growing number of bilateral relations, but as members of the British Empire, a single diplomatic entity, without, at least formally, separate foreign policies (Beckingham and Kooyman, 1993: 1–9).

As well as the traditional reliance on Britain and the other Dominions for defence purposes, the 1930s saw the emerging Commonwealth of Nations developing a more pronounced economic dimension, hastened by the Depression (Singleton and Roberston, 2002: 244). In particular it saw the development of what became the sterling area and a more complex system of trading preferences. In summary, as nation after nation became increasingly protectionist and unemployment rose very sharply in the 1930s Britain and the Dominions, including Australia, turned inward for defensive purposes.

Australia and the League of Nations

Australia's membership of the League of Nations was on a largely part-time basis as it did not have permanent representation, with Hudson concluding that the League was 'a gentle introduction into world politics' (Hudson, 1980: 186). Successive Australian governments had rather ambivalent views as to the value of the League. Prime Minister 'Billy' Hughes, for example, was somewhat sympathetic with its aims but not prepared for a moment to cede any of Australia's newly won autonomy to an IGO and sceptical as to its potential for ensuring world peace (Twomey, 2000).

Prime Minister Stanley Bruce was more positive in his views on the League than was Hughes, but he also opposed any attempt to make the League a supranational body and was well aware of its inability to provide for collective security (Hudson, 1980: 4–5). He did not, however, oppose attempts to make the League more effective, arguing, for example, in favour of Germany's admission in 1925 (Lee, 2010a: 60). In later years, especially after he became Australian High Commissioner in London, an increasingly respected Bruce often represented Australia at the League's annual Assembly and, from 1933 to 1936 as a member of its Council. Initially rather unenthusiastic about the League and its prospects, his negative experience of economic protectionism in the 1930–33 period led him to increasingly argue for greater international economic cooperation within the context of the League. Hence, he began to play a more significant role in the League, though only in the years of its decline.

In summary, as Hudson notes, Australia was a ‘conscientious, responsible but distant member’ of the League, taking few substantial initiatives and largely opposing efforts to significantly change its role (Hudson, 1980: 6). It lacked the administrative capacity to undertake a consistently more active role and, for the most part, was content to follow the British lead in League affairs. The few more positive initiatives that it undertook sprang largely from the efforts of Bruce in the second half of the 1930s, focused on social and economic matters that were overshadowed by the League’s increasing failures to provide effective collective security for its members. While Bruce’s activities had little impact at the time, they helped provide at least a little of the basis for the development of the UN and its specialised agencies, perhaps owing more to Bruce’s personal status than the influence of Australian governments.

Australia and the ILO

While Australia became a founding member of the ILO, the conservative governments that were in office during its early years were by no means enthusiastic or strongly supportive, failing to attend the first Labour Conference in Washington in 1919, then again in 1922 and also deciding not to appoint a permanent representative in Geneva. Prime Minister Hughes regarded the ILO’s Constitution as ‘unworkable’, later seeing the organisation as largely irrelevant to Australia’s higher living standards and industrial conditions (Paterson, 2003: 43). Hughes’ successor as Prime Minister, Stanley Bruce, also lacked enthusiasm for the ILO, especially as in 1923 the USA, Germany and the USSR were not members, reducing its influence and coverage. He argued, as with Hughes, that the ILO’s conventions and recommendations were largely irrelevant, suggesting that Australians should be thankful that it could not interfere with the economic development of Australia, a country ‘“taken from the black man” because he could not develop it properly’, a view shared by the opposition Australian Labor Party (ALP) (Paterson, 2003: 49).

In this context it is perhaps not surprising that from 1919 to 1929 successive conservative governments developed the view that the power of the Australian Commonwealth to put into effect as domestic legislation most international treaties was limited by the constitutional division of powers between the Commonwealth and the states. This included ILO conventions, where their position was that the Commonwealth government would not ratify a convention, even if its contents were acceptable, unless the Constitution gave it express legislative power regarding the subject matter of the convention in question, given that the Constitution largely reserved labour matters to the states.

Article 19(9) of the ILO's Constitution permitted the government of any federal state to treat a convention as only a recommendation and Australian conservative governments acted in accordance with the article. Hence, in 1924 the Bruce government informed the ILO that it was the states of the Commonwealth that decided whether or not draft conventions should be ratified or applied, excluding those which clearly fell within the power of the Commonwealth. As a result up to 1931 Australia had ratified only one convention, Convention 9, in 1925. This was despite the fact that Sir Robert Garran, Secretary of the Attorney General's Department, advised that there were 'strong grounds' for believing that the Commonwealth government did have the authority to make laws enforcing international treaties that it had agreed, even where they customarily covered issues normally the responsibility of the state governments (Garran, 1921).

In contrast to the positions taken by the Hughes and Bruce governments, the Scullin ALP government of 1929–32 took a more positive view of the ILO, strongly supported by the union movement, with Scullin becoming the first Australian Prime Minister to visit the ILO's headquarters in Geneva. It ratified four conventions in just over two years, but was succeeded by the conservative governments of the 1930s, which returned for the most part to the positions of the Hughes and Bruce governments. Again, as with the League, Australia can be characterised as a conscientious, responsible but minor member of the ILO, although membership of it and the League were seen as an important recognition of Australia's growing independence.

The experience of operating in the Commonwealth, the League and the ILO meant that Australian decision makers were by no means unfamiliar with a multilateral, consultative and negotiating environment when faced with the new American drive to multilateralism, both during and after the Second World War. Nevertheless, the foreign policy capacity of Australian governments remained very limited, so that by the end of 1936 the Department of External Affairs (DEA) had a staff of only ten officers and four typists in Canberra and three officers and two typists in London. It grew slowly but steadily from this base, divided into a Political Section and the International Co-operation Section and was complemented by the international activities of Bruce as High Commissioner in London.

The records for this early period show a degree of ambivalence as to the value of IGOs, in so far as there was any sustained analysis of their value by leading government members or, for that matter, by the few public servants involved. The limited evidence in the records suggests that very little sustained, systematic analysis took place, Australia's foreign policy stance being characterised, for the most part, by a reluctance to surrender any aspect of Australia's new found autonomy to the League of Nations and the ILO. Two reasons stand out for this stance. The first was an understandable reluctance to surrender what it had only just gained, foreign policy autonomy, the second being the realisation that the new League could not provide the security that the British Empire might be able to provide, although this was a view that was increasingly qualified in the 1930s and 1940s. In essence, there was a largely instrumental use of all three IGOs and, while there were somewhat differing positions held by the conservative and ALP governments in relation to all of them, they were largely ones of emphasis, rather than principle.

POST-1945 IGOS AND FOREIGN POLICY

As noted, in the period to 1939 there was a distinct ambivalence as to the value of IGOs in the minds of Australian government decision makers. In the years from 1939 to the election of the first post-1945 Coalition government in 1949 this ambivalence at first declined substantially under ALP governments, with a considerable commitment to the new UN system, then re-emerged as the very limited capacity of the UN system and its associated set of specialised agencies to cope with the issues posed by the Cold War became apparent.

As regards economic and financial matters in the post-1945 period Australian decision makers focused on three major, interrelated areas. The first was Britain and the Commonwealth, particularly on issues involving, or likely to involve, the sterling area and the system of Commonwealth preferences, given that Britain was still Australia's major trading partner. The second was the USA, which was of increasing political and economic significance, especially given the general shortage of US dollars. The third, linked to the second, was the largely US-led attempt to develop a new, global system of rules for international economic relations, enshrined within, and managed by, what became known as the Bretton Woods institutions, the International Monetary Fund (IMF) and the World Bank. A third organisation was to join the latter two, the International Trade Organization (ITO), but opposition from the US Congress meant that it suffered a stillbirth, with only an incomplete set of trading rules remaining, in the shape of the General Agreement on Tariffs and Trade (GATT).

In two of these three areas IGOs were playing, or soon would come to play, an increasingly important role. The first was the Commonwealth, where the needs of financing the war effort had led to a more coordinated system of preferences and a more cohesive sterling area. The second was the emerging, global system of international economic relations, where the IMF, the World Bank and the GATT came to play an important role and, to a lesser extent, the other specialised agencies. Moreover, as Australian representatives were soon to discover, a number of issues involved more than one IGO, with Australian policies in relation to one having to be balanced against those of another. They were perhaps most obvious in relation to sterling, the Commonwealth, the OEEC's European Payments Union and the IMF, and Commonwealth preferences and the GATT.

Australia and the Commonwealth Post-1945

The Curtin, Chifley and post-war Menzies governments all saw an important, continuing defence, trade and financial involvement for Australia in the Commonwealth, as did Evatt during his lengthy period as Minister for External Affairs (Bongiorno, 2000: 42–3; Lee, 1990, 1995). The Australian goal was an 'equal partnership', in a Commonwealth that was an association of independent states, a position developed at length by Evatt (Ede, 2008: 14–29). However, there could be little doubt that the status and value of the Commonwealth was declining. As a result the Commonwealth came to have a more limited, but still important, value in Australian defence policy under the post-war Chifley governments, with a growing emphasis on attempts to gain a closer relationship with the US (Lee, 1992: 453–5). The Menzies' governments continued, more successfully, to develop a closer relationship with the US, especially after the Korean War, resulting in the ANZUS pact. They also accepted, at least initially, the British argument that a global war with the USSR was most likely to take place in Europe and the Middle East. Hence, it was agreed that Australian forces would be likely to fight in the Middle East, though a final decision as to the actual deployment of Australian forces would not be made until the time arose (Lee, 1992: 452).

In contrast to defence, the post-1945 value of the Commonwealth was greater in relation to trade and the sterling area, although the Curtin government was at first prepared to see a reduction in Commonwealth preferences, provided that it was accompanied by a compensating reduction in trade barriers by other countries, as proposed by the US in its push for a multilateral world. However, this could not be achieved in relation to agriculture and, combined with a US reluctance to place a priority on multilateral policies designed to maintain full employment and the importance of maintaining the value of Australian sterling balances held in London, it led the Chifley governments to re-emphasise the importance of the pre-war Ottawa Agreement, the sterling area and their potential for promoting economic growth. The change in policy was based, as Lee notes, in large part on fears of a post-war depression whose impact, it was hoped, could be ameliorated by continuing membership of the sterling area and Commonwealth preferences (Lee, 1990).

Interestingly, despite Menzies' personal attachment to the Commonwealth, his governments were increasingly critical of the sterling area and Commonwealth preferences for their often adverse impact on Australia's economic development, and gradually moved back to the Curtin government's earlier policy of working for the incorporation of the sterling area within the multilateral framework urged by the US, rather than within the European Payments Union of the OEEC, whose membership was restricted to European states, including the UK. Despite this move, which was unsuccessful, as the 1950s progressed the decreasing value and changing nature of the Commonwealth rapidly became clearer. It lost the cohesion provided by its earlier, smaller, more homogenous membership as well as its defence and economic significance, as brought firmly home to the Australian government with the development of the North Atlantic Treaty Organisation (NATO) and the OEEC, the Suez fiasco and the first British application for membership of the European Economic Community (EEC). In the UN its declining value was driven home with the loss in 1966 of the Commonwealth seat on an enlarged Security Council. As Lloyd notes, after Suez:

> [T]he Commonwealth connection counted for little. The meetings there were either appallingly dull or nastily argumentative, especially when Krishna Menon was on hand for India. (Lloyd, 2001: 22)

Australia, the UN and the Specialised Agencies

Despite the largely negative experience of the League of Nations the years immediately after 1945 saw the development of the United Nations and a number of specialised international agencies grouped loosely under its ambit, notably the IMF and the World Bank. In contrast to its earlier experience in relation to the League and the ILO, Australian representatives played a fuller role in these developments, commencing during the war years, with Australia taking up membership in all of the initial specialised agencies. It also undertook a far more systematic consideration of the potential value of the UN and its agencies, based largely on the work of the Department of Post-War Reconstruction (DPWR), under H.C. 'Nugget' Coombs, responsible to Ben Chifley as Treasurer, strongly supported by ALP governments and the foreign policy leadership of H.C. Evatt. Evatt, in particular, played a significant role in establishing the UN and had, initially, great hopes for the role that might be played by its Economic and Social Council (ECOSOC).

Nevertheless, an article written fifty years after the founding of the UN by Sir Arthur Tange, one of the DEA's first appointments to the Australian delegation to the fledgling United Nations and later to be its Secretary, noted that:

> New agencies to handle economic and social activities were set up separately from the UN and they evaded effective oversight by the ECOSOC. Significantly, the organisation which most firmly distanced itself from the body containing the full employment pledge was the International Monetary Fund where our first efforts had failed. Burton's hopes of a central UN powerhouse (backed in Australia by more authority housed in External Affairs) collapsed in New York and in Canberra. (Tange, 1996: 266)

It was not only in regard to ECOSOC that the hopes of Evatt and J.W. Burton, Secretary of the DEA, for effective international economic policy coordination were dashed, for, as Tange further noted, the relevant Commonwealth departments took little or no notice of ECOSOC's work and recommendations:

> I began to recognise these realities after sitting in sessions of the ECOSOC and, after returning to the Department in Canberra in the late forties, observing the lack of discernible impact of UN recommendations on the formulation of Australia's fiscal and trade policies in other departments which retained sole responsibility for them. (Tange, 1996: 266)

The change to a Coalition government under Menzies in Australia following the 1949 federal elections led to the appointment of Percy Spender as the minister for external affairs and a distinct downgrading of the importance of the United Nations and ECOSOC in government policy until the election of an ALP government in 1972, under the prime ministership of E.G. Whitlam (Beaumont et al., 2003).

AUSTRALIA AND EUROPEAN IGOS

Australian political and economic relations with the countries of mainland Europe, east or west, were very limited in the 1940s and early 1950s even though Europe's political significance in the context of the Cold War was clearly understood. Moreover, much of the political and economic intelligence available to Australian decision makers came 'second hand' as it were, via the offices of the British government and its much more extensive array of bilateral and multilateral contacts in Europe, including the OEEC, although the network of Australian embassies and consulates was growing.

The policy and negotiating positions of the major European countries soon became of considerable and direct interest as the discussions that led to the establishment of the Bretton Woods organisations took place, especially regarding the ITO and GATT. They were of interest as in many cases they were either opposed to, or lacked sympathy with, several of the proposals being pursued by Australian negotiators. In early discussions about the possibility of an ITO Australia repeatedly voiced its concerns regarding the lack of attention to agriculture, whereas, for example, Belgium, France, Norway and the Netherlands generally supported the US position, which was to exclude agriculture, with Britain being somewhat ambivalent but eventually supporting the US position (see, for example, Irwin et al., 2008: 96). Similarly, Australia in the context of discussions on trade opposed most European states in arguing strongly for protection for its infant industries and economic development, being keen to further promote its own industrial base (Irwin et al., 2008: 97–8). While it was supported by countries such as India, Australian representatives received little support from most European countries.

When GATT came into existence with its trade rules and associated tariff concessions in 1948, much to the Australian government's disappointment and increasing frustration those rules largely excluded trade in agriculture at a time when the bulk of Australian exports were in that area. As a result Australia's relations with most of the European and North American GATT members regarding trade were difficult and largely negative over the next two decades. In particular, Australia received little support for its repeated proposals for greater attention to the removal or reduction of barriers to trade in agriculture from either the bulk of European members (excepting the Nordic states) or, more significantly, from the USA (Snape, 1984).

In the late 1940s and 1950s Western European and North American governments increasingly developed a preference for regional organisations, a preference brought about by: (1) the failure to establish the ITO; (2) a rapidly growing disenchantment with the performance of the UN and most of its specialised agencies as the Cold War developed; and (3) considerable dissatisfaction with GATT's performance. This increasing preference for regional organisations also came to be shared by Australian decision makers. In the interdepartmental discussions leading up to the application for OECD membership in 1970, for example, the DEA's Mr L. Corkery was noted as stating that:

> It was unlikely there would be conflict between Australia's membership of UN specialised agencies and the OECD. Indeed, in the trade field, the OECD had become the main forum in which developed countries decided policy on UNCTAD matters. Much of the strength of the OECD lay in the fact that in some areas the specialised agencies of the UN were no longer the forums for serious business between developed countries and consequently the OECD had become the 'economic club' of the developed nations. (NAA, 1970)

One of the first major steps in this 'regionalisation' of post-1945 international economic relations came about with the Marshall Plan and the creation of the OEEC, the OECD's predecessor. It was a process of regionalisation from which Australia, as a state far removed from Europe, was excluded, having to rely initially for much of its information upon British government sources and regular briefings by British officials from the Commonwealth Relations Office to the Commonwealth Liaison Committee, based in London.

Australia and the OEEC

While never a member of the OEEC, Australian governments had a distinct interest in the organisation from the start. This focused first on an initial, unsuccessful proposal for a European Customs Union (ECU), and second, on the decision to locate the new European Payments Union (EPU) and a Code of Liberalisation of capital movements in the OEEC. It was an interest that sprang out of two sources. The first was out of a concern as to the possible impact of British membership of the OEEC on Australia's membership of the sterling area and its related trading interests in the system of Commonwealth preferences. The second was a concern for the positions that might be adopted by OEEC members in GATT trade negotiations.

While the Australian government recognised the value of increased European economic and defence integration in the face of a growing

Soviet threat and the potential for a larger European market for its primary produce, it was concerned that an ECU might lead to the dilution of the sterling area, the end of the system of Commonwealth preferences and increased competition for Australian exports. Prime Minister Chifley expressed his concerns to Clement Attlee in 1948, when stressing that:

> I cannot emphasise too much or too often the seriousness of taking decisions clearly involving us, or in expectation of our support, without the fullest prior consultation. One instance where we are completely uninformed is the matter of a Customs Union. We are being asked and will no doubt be questioned in parliament, as to our knowledge of this matter. We can only say that we have no knowledge as to how the union is to work. (Kunkel, 2004: 5)

However, Australian fears were soon allayed as the ECU talks were unsuccessful.

The EPU, signed in 1950, was an agreement under which the members of the OEEC settled their payments surpluses and deficits with one another on a multilateral basis (see Ransom, 2010; Flexner, 1957). The underlying aim of the EPU, especially as promoted by the USA, was to persuade its members to remove quantitative restrictions on intra-European trade by providing a more efficient, multilateral payments system that also provided credit for countries in deficit. This, in turn, from the Australian perspective, might lead to increased demand for Australian exports as well as providing growing markets for its exports, as European trade expanded.

After lengthy and difficult discussions, it was agreed that the sterling area would be incorporated in the EPU. The arrangement, as noted by Singleton and Robertson (2002: 151), was of concern for Australia as it might threaten the value of Australia's sterling holdings, which constituted about 90 per cent of its total reserves until the end of the 1940s, when it began to run down the proportion that was held in sterling (Schenk, 2010: 89). It also might divert British capital to OEEC markets rather than the Australian. The latter was of particular concern given successive Australian governments' focus on national economic development and the need for capital to that end, most of which came from Britain. However, as soon became apparent, the EPU did not threaten Australian interests as it was applied solely to current account transactions. Indeed, it may have provided an incentive for European members of the EPU to import Australian primary produce by enabling them to use for payment the sterling balances they accumulated in the EPU. It should not be thought that the Australian government was slavishly devoted to sterling, for, as early as 1949 it had started to gain US dollar loans from the World Bank to support its goal of industrialisation (Singleton and Robertson, 2002: 63).

The OEEC's Code of Liberalisation came into being shortly after the establishment of the EPU in 1950, as a scheme for the gradual removal of quantitative restrictions on intra-European trade that was to accompany the EPU. It was an agreement whose rapid development contrasted sharply with similar, painfully slow efforts to free up trade in agriculture in the GATT, where the stalled Torquay Round of negotiations was taking place. In combination with the EPU, the Code gained substantial success in assisting in the elimination of quantitative restrictions on trade, largely in regard to manufactured goods, though progress was uneven and, at times, difficult (see Kock, 1969; Brusse, 1997).

Australian views in relation to the Code of Liberalisation were mixed. On the one hand the possible achievement of a reduction in barriers to trade in line with the Code had some promise, although trade in agricultural products, the area of most interest to Australia, was excluded from the Code's coverage. On the other hand, there was the danger that OEEC members might more effectively organise their negotiating positions in GATT on the basis of earlier consultations within the OEEC, to the possible disadvantage of Australian interests, especially in relation to its continuing efforts to include trade in agriculture more firmly within GATT's ambit, which most OEEC members opposed. Equally as important was the fact that the Code's success in getting its members to reduce barriers to intra-European trade in manufactured products would, if extended successfully to the GATT, pose a significant problem for Australian efforts to continue to protect its developing industry with a range of trade barriers. At a meeting of GATT in January 1955, for example, Britain and the USA proposed that the Code be extended to GATT members. While the proposal was rejected, it was an example of exactly the kind of development that Australian negotiators in the Department of Trade feared (Lynch, 1997: 143–4). Moreover, if Britain was persuaded to open up its markets to imports from European members of the OEEC, which proved to be the case, this might endanger the preference given to Australian and other Commonwealth imports.

Thus, Australia had developed a considerable and mixed interest in European IGOs by the later 1940s, focused initially on the OEEC. It was an interest that was sustained and sharply increased at the end of the 1950s as it became apparent that the British government was likely to consider applying for membership of the EEC. Once that application was made and for the rest of the 1960s and early 1970s, Australian interest in the implications of British membership continued at a high level and was one of the factors in determining its successful bid for membership of the

OECD in 1971. Not only was the level of interest sharply increased, the growing complexity and competitive nature of the European integration process, focused on the EEC, then the European Free Trade Agreement (EFTA), posed an increasing management challenge for Australian decision makers.

Competitive European Integration and Australian Interests

While Australian interest in Western European economic integration was established by the end of the 1940s and early 1950s, monitoring, evaluating and advancing those interests became more difficult in the 1950s as the members of the OEEC split, increasingly acrimoniously, into two broad camps. The first consisted of those who favoured a greater degree of economic and political integration based on a body with a degree of supranational authority, in essence the future members of the EEC. The second consisted of those, particularly the British, who favoured the continuation of the OEEC, and who later became members of EFTA. The USA and Canada, associate members of the OEEC, looked on with concern at the growing split between its allies, as did Australia.

The split was evident from the early 1950s with, for example, major differences in relation to the European Coal and Steel Community (ECSC), whose treaty was ratified in April 1951. It had a mixed response from OEEC members and the British government was particularly opposed to the notion of a supranational authority, as earlier it had been in relation to the proposed powers of the OEEC, and it feared that any new authority would discriminate against OEEC non-members in regard to the supply and price of coal and steel (Laursen, 1997). Despite such concerns, the ECSC came into being and the years from 1952 to 1955 saw a series of disagreements and disputes between it and several non-ECSC members of the OEEC (Laursen, 1997). Similar disputes arose in relation to a proposed 'Schuman Plan' (the 'Green Pool' discussions), for agriculture that, while initially unsuccessful, formed part of the basis of the later Common Agricultural Policy (CAP) (Milward, 1994: 301–8). The split between the two camps became more obvious as the 1950s progressed and the original core function of the OEEC, the management of Marshall Aid programmes, was completed and the question of the future role of the OEEC came to the forefront of members' discussions.

France, Belgium, West Germany, Italy, Luxembourg and the Netherlands, broadly satisfied with the performance of the ECSC, were keen to see further progress in this direction and met at Messina in 1955 to consider prospects for a broader, common market. The fact that their meeting took place outside of the OEEC indicated that it was not seen as the likely venue for the type of development they envisaged, given British opposition. The British government was invited to attend the Messina talks but, in November 1955, announced its withdrawal. Moreover, it proposed that a looser Free Trade Area (FTA) be established within the context of the existing OEEC, where it was chair of the Council and hoped to better control the agenda. The ploy was immediately recognised for what it was by the Six, an attempt to 'sideline Messina and smother it', and the US expressed its concern (Griffiths, 1997: 236–7).

As might be expected, the OEEC discussions regarding the proposed FTA were difficult, increasingly bitter and, eventually, unsuccessful (Griffiths, 1997, Chapter XVIII). They did not de-rail the moves to create the EEC, with the Treaty of Rome being signed in 1957. Nevertheless the FTA talks continued on until 1958 when the French (with US support) indicated that they saw no point in their continuation (Griffiths, 1997: 239–40). In 1959 the seven non-EEC members involved in the FTA talks discussed a free trade area of their own, which became EFTA in 1960. The contrast between the 1948 and 1958 situations, still characterised by Cold War tensions, was now very marked: that between a largely unified OEEC, motivated by access to Marshall Plan funds; and the 1958 position of a bitterly divided OEEC, increasingly rivalled by the existence of the EEC and a possible EFTA.

It seemed that the OEEC was doomed. However, US and Canadian concern at the extent of divisions in Western Europe in the face of the continuing Soviet threat, especially given its new moves in less developed countries, led to a US proposal to continue the existence of the OEEC in a new format with modified functions. The proposal proved persuasive for the members of both the Six and the Seven and it was announced at a December 1959 summit meeting between Eisenhower, De Gaulle, Adenauer and Macmillan that a group of twenty countries, plus the Commission of the EEC, would be established to examine the OEEC's prospects (Griffiths, 1997: 244). The outcome of the meeting was the establishment of a 'Group of Four', eminent persons to examine the OEEC and make proposals for its reorganisation. Their proposals were accepted in principle and then elaborated in detail by a Preparatory Committee of senior officials to form a compromise agreement in which most OEEC acts were retained in a reorganised and renamed OEEC, the OECD, which commenced operations in 1961 (Griffiths, 1997: 249–50; Carroll and Kellow, 2011: 48–9).

Australia, the EEC and the FTA

As the process of European integration became more challenging during the 1950s the task for Australian decision makers necessarily became more complex and of more concern. In summary, they were faced with a situation in which the protection afforded to their trade and monetary interests in Western Europe by the leadership of British governments keen to retain the role of sterling as a major currency and the Commonwealth as a major trading block became increasingly less certain. Moreover, as noted by Ludlow, having relied for the most part upon British representatives to protect Australian trading and monetary interests within the OEEC, at a time of growing uncertainty the Australian government increasingly realised that it lacked well established ties with most of the states of Western Europe, especially those in the EEC, other than those gained within the context of the conflict-ridden GATT negotiations and the UN specialised agencies, notably the IMF and World Bank (Ludlow, 2001: 285).

In general, Australian governments had been sympathetic to European integration, at least of the 'milder' type favoured by successive British governments and embodied in the OEEC. Later, Percy Spender, for example, had been sympathetic to the British notion of a Free Trade Area within the OEEC context as early as 1956, so long as agriculture could be excluded, in order to avoid the potential loss of British markets for Australian primary produce and, on a more positive note, the possibility that British membership of the FTA would lead to a greater liberalisation of trade by Western European governments (Singleton and Robertson, 2002: 155). Such sympathy, however, was accompanied by increasing concerns regarding Australian trading interests, as noted by both the Department of Trade and the Department of Primary Industry. The departments pointed to the increased competition Australian firms might face if an FTA was created and to the possible establishment of FTA trade barriers. Nevertheless, the proposed FTA raised far fewer fears than did the prospect of the EEC, especially for Australian Deputy Prime Minister and Trade Minister 'Black Jack' McEwen and the senior staff of his department (Ward, 2001: 51–6).

Australian interest in, and support for, the FTA grew as its representatives became aware that the Six seemed likely to increase controls over agricultural trade in the EEC. John Stone, later Treasury Secretary, felt that a formal association with the FTA would give Australian representatives direct access to the rival decision making processes in Europe, access that would be essential if the FTA were to be established and the threat of the EEC contained. John Bunting, the new Secretary of the

Department of the Prime Minister went further, noting that Australia would get a greater benefit from membership of such a European grouping than it would in the Commonwealth. Such was the extent of interest that it was suggested that Australian representatives should participate directly in the FTA discussions, a proposal acceptable to the Netherlands, Germany and Denmark. However, the British government rejected the proposal on the grounds that it would tend to draw unwelcome attention to the British negotiating positions on trade in agriculture and tariff barriers (Singleton and Robertson, 2002: 160).

The British rejection of the proposal was part of a developing pattern of British resistance to the more direct and frequent involvement of Australia in such discussions. In 1959, for example, at the regular Commonwealth Liaison Committee meeting, the Australian and New Zealand representatives proposed that a 'collective' approach to the EEC be developed by Commonwealth members that, if successful, would enable greater access to the EEC market for their exports. A study group was established to see if a joint trade strategy could be agreed, but it was unsuccessful, lacking significant support from the British government, as well as the Canadians and most of the African and Asian members. Further, while the study group discussions were underway, much to the irritation of the Australian government, the formation of EFTA was announced, without consultation with Commonwealth governments (Singleton and Robertson, 2002: 163–4).

Such resistance to fuller Australian participation, or at least the lack of support by the British government, also tended to reinforce slowly growing concerns as to the extent to which it fully represented Australian or broader Commonwealth interests in multilateral settings. There was, for example, considerable Australian irritation when it was discovered that the British government had given an exchange guarantee to the Western European holders of sterling under the European Monetary Agreement (the successor to the EPU), but had neither informed, offered or given such a guarantee to Australia, with its much larger holdings of sterling. It was only after repeated representations by Australia that the British government decided to withdraw the guarantee, causing considerable resentment by the European recipients of the guarantee.

Hence, at the end of the 1950s, the Australian government was faced with an economically divided Europe in the shape of the EEC and EFTA, a failed attempt to create an FTA within the OEEC that now threatened the latter's very existence, and growing concerns as to the British position in relation to these developments and the role of the Commonwealth and the sterling area. In addition, it was clear that GATT was, from the Australian perspective, continuing to be an inadequate instrument for protecting and advancing Australian trading interests. McEwen, for example, had attempted to persuade both the USA and British governments to challenge the EEC, its Common External Tariff and developing Common Agricultural Policy in GATT, but had failed to gain any support (Ward, 2001: 55).

CONCLUSION

The end of the 1950s marked some forty years of Australian experience of working within IGOs. It had been a mixed experience in which, with the partial exception of the early post-1945 years, IGOs were regarded primarily as only one of a range of means of achieving or protecting national interests, especially economic. It was also a period in which the Australian capacity to support the activities of its representatives within the IGOs had grown substantially, especially from the mid-1940s. However, that growing capacity, while centred in the DEA, was also dispersed across a number of departments, each primarily responsible for the IGOs that related to its major policy concerns, making effective coordination an increasing challenge. The Treasury, for example, was responsible for the IMF and the World Bank, Education for UNESCO, Trade and Commerce for the GATT and the DEA for the UN.

The end of the 1940s was marked by a growing disillusionment by Australian ministers and officials with the UN and most of the specialised agencies, excluding for the most part the IMF and the World Bank. It was a disillusionment shared with the US, Britain and most of the countries of Western Europe. It was not, however, a disillusionment that reduced the role and importance of IGOs. Instead, it was one that, combined with a rapidly growing Soviet threat, led to an increasing use of even more, new, but regionally based IGOs such as NATO, the OEEC and the EEC. Australia was not a member of any one of these new bodies, so that Australian decision makers were relatively isolated from important discussions held within their boundaries. In essence, one of the key means by which a middle power such as Australia could exercise a degree of international influence – working within IGOs – was not available to it as regards developments in the North Atlantic and Western European area. This relative isolation was exacerbated by the increasingly obvious decline in the value of the Commonwealth, an Australian perception that British governments were not taking Australian interests sufficiently into consideration and, of course, the shock that accompanied news of the first British application for membership of the EEC. It was against this background that Australian interest in gaining membership of the OECD arose.

BIBLIOGRAPHY

Beaumont, J., Waters, C., Lowe, C. and Woodward, G. 2003. *Ministers, Mandarins and Diplomats – Australian Foreign Policy Making 1941–1969*, Carlton VIC: Melbourne University Press.

Beckingham, P. and Kooyman, M. (eds) 1993. 'Australia and Britain: The Evolving Relationship', P. Monash ANZ Centre for International Briefing, Melbourne, Victoria, pp. 1–9.

Bongiorno, F. 2000. 'Commonwealthmen and Republicans: Dr. H.V. Evatt, the Monarchy and India', *Australian Journal of Politics and History*, 46(1): 33–50.

Brusse, W. 1997. 'Liberalising Intra-European Trade', Chapter 9 in R. Griffiths (ed.), *Explorations in OEEC History*, Paris: OECD, pp. 123–138.

Carroll, P. and Kellow, A. 2011. *The OECD A Study of Organisational Adaptation*, Cheltenham, UK and Northampton, MA, USA: Edward Elgar Publishing.

Cook, J. 1925. 'Report from High Commissioner of Commonwealth, 1925', in the Joseph Cook Papers, NAA: CP611, M3582–7, p. 13.

Ede, E. 2008. 'Internationalist Vision for a Postwar World: H.V. Evatt, Politics & the Law', a thesis submitted in partial fulfilment of the requirements for the degree of BA (Hons) in History, University of Sydney.

Edwards, P. 1983. *Prime Ministers and Diplomats – The Making of Australian Foreign Policy 1901–1949*, Melbourne: Oxford University Press.

Flexner, K. 1957. 'The Creation of the European Payments Union: An Example in International Compromise', *Political Science Quarterly*, 72(2): 241–260.

Garran, R. 1921. 'Secretary to Attorney-General', June, NAA: A981 (981/4) INTI.

Griffiths, R. (ed.) 1997. *Explorations in OEEC History*, Paris: OECD.

Hudson, W.J. 1980. *Australia and the League of Nations*, Sydney: Sydney University Press.

Irwin, D., Mavroidis, P. and Sykes, A. 2008. *The Genesis of the GATT*, Cambridge: Cambridge Books Online, Cambridge University Press.

Kock, K. 1969. *International Trade Policy and the GATT, 1947–1967*, Stockholm: Almquist and Wiksell.

Kunkel, J. 2004. 'Perfidious Albion Revisited: Anglo-Australian Trade Relations and European Economic Integration', National Europe Centre Paper No. 88, Australian National University, Canberra.

Laursen, J. 1997. 'Integration at Cross-currents: the OEEC and the European Coal and Steel Community 1952–1956', in R. Griffiths (ed.), *Explorations in OEEC History*, Paris: OECD, pp. 149–158.

Lee, D. 1990. 'Protecting the Sterling Area: the Chifley Government's Response to Multilateralism 1945/9', *Australian Journal of Political Science*, 25(2): 178–195.

Lee, D. 1992. 'Australia, the British Commonwealth and the United States 1950–1953', *The Journal of Imperial and Commonwealth History*, 20(3): 445–469.

Lee, D. 1995. *Search for Security: The Political Economy of Australia's Post-war Foreign and Defence Policy*, St Leonards: Allen & Unwin in association with the Department of International Relations, RSPAS, ANU.

Lee, D. 2010a. *Stanley Melbourne Bruce – Australian Internationalist*, London: Continuum.

Lee, D. 2010b. 'Stanley Melbourne Bruce: The Forgotten Prime Minister', Paper presented at the National Archives of Australia, 11 April, accessed on 19 January 2017 at www.naa.gov.au/collection/publications/papers-and-podcasts/prominent-people/lee-transcript.aspx.

Lloyd, L. 1997. 'Britain and the Transformation from Empire to Commonwealth', *The Round Table: The Commonwealth Journal of International Affairs*, 86: 333–360.

Lloyd, L. 2001. '"Us and Them": The Changing Nature of Commonwealth Diplomacy, 1880–1973', *Commonwealth & Comparative Politics*, 39(3): 9–30.

Ludlow, N. 2001. 'Too Far Away, Too Rich and Too Stable: The EEC and Trade with Australia During the 1960s', *Australian Economic History Review*, 41(3): 267–286.

Lynch, F. 1997. *France and the International Economy: From Vichy to the Treaty of Rome*, New York and London: Routledge.

Milward, A. 1994. *The European Rescue of the Nation State*, London: Routledge.

NAA 1953a. 'OEEC Productivity and Applied Research', File A987 987/4, E777 Part 1.

NAA 1953b. See documents in File 1838 1838/1 791/4/2/3A.

NAA 1970. 'OECD Membership Interests, Record of Interdepartmental Meeting', 9 September 1970, File A1838-724-4-30 Part 6 'Accession'.

New York Times 1947. 'Evatt Urges UN Aid Economic Side: Holds Social Council is "All Harness No Horse" – Latin Commission Sought', 19 September.

Paterson, W. 2003. 'Desire for Social Justice: Equal Pay, the International Labour Organisation and Australian Government Policy, 1919–1975', unpublished PhD thesis, University of Newcastle, Australia.

Ransom, J. 2010. 'A Little Marshall Plan: Britain and the formation of the European Payments Union, 1948–50', *The International History Review*, 32(3): 437–454.

Schenk, C. 2010. *The Decline of Sterling*, New York: Cambridge University Press.

Singleton, J. and Robertson, P. 2002. *Economic Relations between Australia and Australasia 1945–1970*, London: Palgrave, St Martin's Press.

Snape, R. 1984. 'Australia's Relations with GATT', *The Economic Record*, 60(168): 16–27.

Tange, A. 1996. 'Plans for the World Economy: Hopes and Reality in Wartime Canberra. A Personal Memoir', *Australian Journal of International Affairs*, 50(3), 259–267.

Twomey, P. 2000. 'Versailles and the 1920s', Chapter 4 in Carl Bridge and Bernard Attard (eds), *Between Empire and Nation: Australia's External*

Relations from Federation to the Second World War, Melbourne: Australian Scholarly Publications.

Ungerer, C. 2007. 'The "Middle Power" Concept in Australian Foreign Policy', *Australian Journal of Politics and History*, 53(4): 538–551.

Ward, S. 2001. *Australia and the British Embrace the Demise of the Imperial Ideal,* Melbourne: Melbourne University Press.

3. A search for access and influence

The end of the 1950s marked some forty years of Australian experience of working within IGOs, an experience not always positive, as the growing disillusionment with the UN indicated. Nevertheless, the value of IGOs for a smaller power such as Australia was still well regarded, at least by professional diplomats. The Australian Permanent Representative to the UN in 1957, Ronald Walker, later to become Australia's first ambassador to the OECD, for example, in a despatch to his Minister R.G. Casey, noted that Australia's membership of the UN enabled regular contact with delegates from countries in which Australia had no independent representation. Also, he noted, given that the UN in New York was a major centre for American diplomatic activity, it provided an additional opportunity for contact and discussion. Casey had made much the same point in a 1954 radio broadcast, noting the value of informal contact with foreign ministers over lunch at the UN (Lowe, 1997: 174).

The disillusionment with the UN did not apply to all IGOs, although greater Australian attention began to be paid to regional, rather than global IGOs during the 1950s and into the 1960s, in common with the major Western powers (Padelford, 1954: 174). This trend had commenced in the later 1940s and continued in the following decades. In the North Atlantic area it included, for example, the OEEC (1948), NATO (1949), Council of Europe (1949), ECSC (1951), the EEC (1958) and the OECD (1961). Even within the UN context there was, at least in the 1940s, a greater, regional focus with the establishment of the Economic Commission for Europe (ECE, 1947). However, while the plethora of new organisations was of varying interest and concern for Australian foreign policy, it was a member of none in the North Atlantic area until it gained membership of the OECD in 1971.

Regional IGOs developed more slowly in the Asia-Pacific area and, in contrast to the North Atlantic situation, Australia became a founding member of most of them, including, for example, the South Pacific Commission (SPC 1947), Colombo Plan (1950), South East Asian Treaty Organisation (SEATO 1954), and the Asian Development Bank (ADB 1964). As with the ECE, there also developed a greater UN focus on regional bodies in the Asia-Pacific, with the establishment of the Economic Commission for Asia and the Far East (ECAFE, 1947, to become the United Nations Economic and Social Commission for Asia and the Pacific (ESCAP) in 1974). Despite initial reservations, Australia became a founding member of ECAFE, one of six non-Asian members with France, the Netherlands, USSR, the UK and the USA, and only four Asian members, China, India, the Philippines and Thailand, symbolising the recent or ongoing colonial status of several states in the area at this time.

The motivation for Australian membership of these new Asia-Pacific bodies was two-fold: (1) to enhance Australian security by entering into alliance with like-minded, anti-communist states (SEATO); and (2) to provide development assistance to countries in the regions (SPC, Colombo Plan and the ADB), although a significant part of the motive for such aid initially was to help promote political stability in the area, making it better able to resist what was seen as increasing communist encroachment. More slowly, a third motive also came into play: the desire to open up markets for Australian exports to the area, though this took place on a largely bilateral basis until the creation of APEC in 1989. As Ravenhill has noted, for the first thirty years after the end of the Second World War, security considerations dominated Australia's relations with Southeast Asia (Ravenhill, 1998: 274).

In summary, by the early 1960s Australia had had extensive experience of working as a member of both global and regional IGOs, an experience that had enabled it to expand its network of contacts with, arguably, a much wider range of states than it would have been able to afford on a bilateral basis. It was an experience that it valued, if to varying extents, for both security and economic reasons. However, Australia was not a member of any one of the new, North Atlantic and Western European organisations, so that Australian decision makers felt increasingly isolated from important discussions held within these organisations, discussions that increased in importance as Western states increasingly preferred to pursue several of their interests outside of the UN context. Moreover, this relative isolation was highlighted by the declining political and economic importance of the Commonwealth for Australia, an isolation brought into sharp relief by the first British application for membership of the EEC (Carroll, 2014).

It was in this context that discussion of the merits of membership of the OECD began in 1960, for it seemed to several of those in the DEA and Treasury that it would provide a means for overcoming, at least in part, Australia's 'diplomatic isolation'. However, this was by no means the only view and it was one met by a strong and successful, decade-long opposition to proposals for membership by Trade Minister and Deputy Prime Minister 'Black Jack' McEwen.

OECD MEMBERSHIP: UNCERTAINTY AND ARGUMENT, 1960–65

The 1960–65 period was one of uncertainty and increasing argument regarding the OECD in Australian government circles. In 1960–61, in particular, there was an understandable uncertainty over the status, possible future role and significance of the planned new organisation in relation to Australian interests, an uncertainty that, in turn, exacerbated differences of view as to what should be the nature of Australian relations with the new organisation. The uncertainty persisted, not surprisingly, until final decisions were reached as to the establishment of the OECD by its founding members. It led, for example, to a 1960 Cabinet decision to turn down a suggestion from the British government that Australia (and New Zealand) might wish to participate in the work of the recently established Development Assistance Group (DAG), later to become the OECD's Development Assistance Committee (DAC). It was felt that there would be little purpose in membership of DAG, at least at this stage of its development, with Australian aid being channelled through the Colombo Plan (British National Archives, 1964).

Two dominant views emerged in this uncertain situation. One was that Australia should consider an application for membership of the new OECD, supported increasingly strongly by the Treasury and more cautiously by the DEA. The second was that membership, at least for the foreseeable future, was not in Australia's best interests, especially as regards trade, a view supported primarily by the Department of Trade, its influential minister, Sir John McEwen and its two departmental secretaries in this period, Sir John Crawford (to 1960) followed by Sir Alan Westerman (to early 1971). In addition, Prime Minister Menzies seems not to have been initially enthusiastic about membership, based on departmental advice and the influential views of McEwen, who was also Deputy Prime Minister and the leader of the Country Party. The latter's influence was probably bolstered by the very narrow, two seat majority the Liberal–Country coalition gained at the December 1961 federal election.

It should be noted that, at least until the early 1970s and the advent of the Whitlam, ALP government in 1972, the proponents of the two different views did not question the overall setting of existing economic policy, domestic or international. It was a setting that was dominated by what Castles described as the politics of domestic defence, with the protection of domestic manufacturing industry by means of high tariff barriers as one of its central pillars (Castles, 1988: 91). Sometimes described as 'protection all round', it was a setting strongly advocated by the Country Party under McEwen and by most members of the Liberal Party, characterised by a complex pattern of assistance programmes and accompanying subsidies for the import-competing industry sector and for these areas of the rural sector focused on domestic markets. There were few in either the coalition parties or in the ALP that questioned this policy of protection until the later 1960s.

In this context the DEA and Treasury view of OECD membership was not in any sense designed to erode the 'protection all round' setting of Australian policy (though this might have been the increasing view of some Treasury officials), but aimed at securing additional access and influence over the policies of the major powers that might endanger this policy setting. The 'McEwenite' view was that the risks involved were too great to warrant membership, not, at least to begin with, because of fears for their potential to greatly threaten 'protection all round', but because membership of this 'rich mans' club', might endanger Australian attempts to gain the support of developing countries in the GATT in the push for greater access for agricultural products in OECD and Asian markets.

1960–61: Uncertainty

The British announcement of the decision to apply for membership of the EEC was made known to Prime Minister Menzies in a letter from British Prime Minister Harold Macmillan in April 1961 and came as a great shock to the Menzies government. As John Bunting, Secretary of the Prime Minister's Department noted:

> All our international arrangements have been entered into on the basis of a particular relationship with the United Kingdom – whether they are commercial or political. This arrangement will no longer exist. Our whole fabric of international ties and relationships will need re-thinking. (NAA, 1961a)

The announcement also stimulated a series of DEA departmental position papers, assessing the implications of the British decision for Australian interests (Ward, 2001: 73–98). They indicated a growing interest in the implications for Australian interests of not only the development of the EEC but of the OECD. Up to this time the bulk of Australian interest in both organisations and their predecessors had been in the Department of Trade.

The DEA pointed out that with British membership of the EEC the Commonwealth was likely to decline and eventually disappear. It implied, also, a need to consider the extent to which the British representation of Australian interests in organisations such as the new OECD, let alone within the EEC, could be relied upon, should its EEC application be successful. If it could not be relied upon, then other means for communicating and pursuing Australian interests needed to be found, including possible Australian membership of the OECD, as well as a more traditional expansion of diplomatic representation in the capitals of Western Europe. In May 1960, for example, staff in the Australian Embassy in Paris noted that a preliminary consideration of the first proposals for a reorganised OEEC indicated that it was not explicitly confined to European countries and that they had examined the potential for future Australian membership, should the government wish to do so at a later date. Their tentative conclusion, subject to further investigation, was that it would be possible (NAA, 1960d).

However, the very next day staff in the Australian High Commission in London reported, on the basis of discussions with senior British officials, that the question of membership had not been decided, with two schools of thought emerging. The first, the view of most Europeans, was that it should be restricted to Europeans, with the exception of the USA and Canada. The second, the very strong American view, was that membership should be left open for non-Europeans, with Japanese membership in mind, arguing, successfully, that the term 'European', should be dropped from proposed title for the new organisation (hence the final title 'Organisation for Economic Co-operation and Development', rather than the retention of the title 'Organisation for European Economic Co-operation'). A British official noted that there was no present intention to offer membership to a non-European country and the British were firmly of the view that it should be restricted to Europe and North America. He further noted that, once established, it would be 'entirely proper', for the new organisation to have 'relations' with non-European states (NAA, 1960e).

The Department of Trade's influential Secretary, Sir John Crawford, was well aware as to the implications for Australian trading interests of the creation of the proposed OECD. Trade officials in the London High Commission, for example, provided him with advice as to a range of alternative actions that could be taken regarding the organisation in May 1960. They noted that while it would not be 'practicable', to suggest to the major powers that the 'whole idea be dropped', that it might be worthwhile to try to persuade them that it should have no role regarding trade, or that its role in relation to trade should be 'watered down', for fear that it would form a block in the GATT with predetermined views, to Australia's disadvantage. It went on to suggest a range of possible alternative actions for Australia, ranging from that of full membership of the OECD, which, in contrast to the recent views of DEA officials, was seen as 'a theoretical possibility only and not worth serious consideration', to that of some kind of associate status in regard to some of its activities. It also suggested the possibility that a request for observer status in the new organisation be made, including a provision in its rules for consultation with non-members, at their request, when matters involving their interests were under consideration (NAA, 1960a). The officials in London indicated that they were inclined to favour the status of observer though noting that they appreciated it might lead to a further weakening of the GATT if other GATT Contracting Parties were also to be offered such an association.

In a cable to all relevant posts of 20 May 1960 the DEA, in addressing the question of the government's position in relation to an association with the new organisation, indicated that no decision as regards membership had been reached on the matter, should the possibility be offered. It also indicated, echoing Trade's views, that, while appreciating the value of the proposed organisation for discussion of 'European problems', its proposed power to take decisions binding on its members might well result in what had been feared, the development of a large and influential OECD group within the GATT committed to policies already agreed on at the OECD. In such a situation, the chances of influencing decisions in GATT on these policies, it was felt, would be nil.

The topic was raised again later in 1960, in a submission by McEwen to Cabinet regarding European economic integration and its implications for Australia. He noted that at some stage Australia would be asked about an association with the OECD but, in line with departmental advice, was of the view that such a stage had not yet been reached (NAA, 1960b). As noted above, thought already had been given as to the potential for OECD membership in the DEA and also in the Prime Minister's Department, as early as April 1960. Moreover, it was thought that also searched for reasons as to how Australia could become a member of 'the reorganised OEEC', without exciting similar claims for membership by other, non-European countries, for example, by New Zealand. Indeed, it was thought by some officials that if such a reason could be found then Australia might avoid the possibility of New Zealand becoming 'a nuisance hanging around our necks', anticipating one of the reasons later put forward by US officials for opposing Australian members of the DAC and, later, of the OECD (NAA, 1960c).

The possibility of membership had now received wide consideration, culminating in McEwen's July 1960 Cabinet submission. Cabinet agreed with McEwen's view that the time had not yet been reached for membership. It is clear from the records that the DEA and Treasury saw this decision as one which largely concerned the timing of an application for OECD membership, rather than a rejection of such a possibility. In a brief for the Australian representative to attend the Commonwealth Economic Consultative Council in May 1961 that focused on developments in European economic integration, for example, it was noted that Ministers had recognised in July 1960:

> [T]hat at some stage Australia would be faced with the question whether association should be sought with the OECD, but in the meantime Australian interests should be watched carefully and no opportunity lost to influence developments in such a way that the Australian point of view would be taken into consideration by the participants in the new organisation and that the effectiveness of GATT in the field of European trade and elsewhere should not be undermined. (NAA, 1961b)

The early proponents of Australian membership of the OECD thus faced not only the strength of McEwen's opposition to membership, but would also have been aware that, should Britain's first, 1961 application for EEC membership be successful, and later the EEC and EFTA merge, then the OECD, arguably, might have little purpose. The Australian Embassy in Brussels, for example, reported in June 1961 that M. Brunet, from the French EEC Mission, had noted in a conversation with the DEA's Alan Renouf, that 'he did not quite see what the OECD would do, if the Six and Seven question were solved' (NAA, 1961c).

A more positive view of the OECD's future was presented in a note from DEA representative C.G. Woodward of the Office of the Australian High Commission in London, to the Secretary of the DEA in 1962. He noted that in a talk with a Mr Scott of the British Foreign Office, he had been shown a copy of a planning paper that indicated that Britain should aim to build up the OECD to become an effective economic forum for cooperation in the widest sense between the USA and the European Communities and, importantly, that it 'associate' other developed countries such as Japan, Australia and New Zealand with its work, where appropriate (NAA, 1962a).

It was this continuing uncertainty as to the importance of the role that the new OECD might play, an uncertainty brought about, in turn, by continuing uncertainty as to the future of the EEC and EFTA, combined with McEwen's concerns regarding its impact on the trade regime that guided Cabinet's 1960 decision not to consider membership at that time.

1962–63: Continuing Differences and the First Small Step towards Membership

In the 1962–63 period there was a growing appreciation of what seemed to be the increasing importance of the OECD, accompanied by a greater knowledge and sophistication in the arguments put forward by those supporting membership, especially by Sir Roland Wilson, the influential Treasury Secretary. However, significant differences of view and related sensitivities persisted, sufficient for Cabinet to again reject the possibility of membership when it was considered, somewhat unexpectedly, in 1963.

The extent of the sensitivities can be seen in the contrasting DEA and Treasury reactions to a proposal from a US State Department official in Washington about the possibility of Australian membership of a Development Assistance Committee (DAC) ad hoc consultative group on Thailand which was being formed, with the aim of better coordinating donor aid to Thailand. He stressed that it was not aimed at getting Australia to increase its aid contributions, nor to get Australian membership of DAC, unless Australia was interested (NAA, 1962b). DEA's Minister Barwick approved attendance by his officials at the group's meeting, though on the strict understanding that it did not involve an increase in Australian aid to Thailand or Australian membership of the DAC (NAA, 1962b).

Barwick's action was not well received by the Treasurer, Harold Holt, whose reactions, when added to the views of McEwen, indicated the strength of opposition to either OECD or DAC membership within the Australian government at this time. Holt took umbrage at Barwick's action, stressing in a note to Barwick that in 1960 Cabinet had disapproved such moves because, mainly, of likely US pressure for Australia to increase its aid flows. Holt also noted that the US had promoted 'country confrontations' at DAC in order to put more pressure on countries to provide more aid and that Australia was likely to be similarly 'confronted', in the ad hoc group. Holt urged Barwick, then Prime Minister Menzies, that the US be told that Australia did not want to be associated with the Thai group. The matter went to Cabinet where it was agreed, however, that Australia should take up membership in the ad hoc working party, given that it did not involve any financial commitments (NAA, 1962c).

Barwick's successful Cabinet submission in support of his position also argued that the ad hoc group was only to coordinate aid to Thailand and that it would 'not report to the DAC or keep minutes; each member will report to his own Government'. He further noted that a lack of knowledge of such activities was hampering Australia's aid programme, that European countries were now showing more interest in aid to Asia than in 1960 and that it would be in Australian interests to encourage this, both politically and economically. Further, he argued that Australia should cooperate with the US in such matters, especially given military developments in Vietnam and Thailand, pointing out that Australia was involved in a similar group for Vietnam, though not one linked to DAC. Finally, as he pointed out, Australia was subject to pressures to increase aid from a variety of sources, such as the UN, and had successfully dealt with them, so that the US proposal was no real threat to Australian interests (NAA, 1962d).

The first half of 1963 saw two further Australian Cabinet decisions regarding the OECD. Both originated in an unexpected communication on 21 February 1963 from the British High Commissioner in Canberra. It took the form of a note to the Prime Minister's Department, circulated to the DEA, Trade and Treasury, advising that the Japanese government was very keen to gain full membership of the OECD and that if the Australian and New Zealand governments so wished, the British government would sponsor their applications for OECD membership. Menzies introduced the note at Cabinet on 27 February and indicated that he was somewhat dubious about such an application and in no hurry to consider it further.

A brief discussion followed in which Barwick indicated that he'd had preliminary discussions with the DEA but its advice was not yet finalised. At this point Secretary Bunting broke in to inform members that there had been a new message from the British requesting a reply that week. While Menzies indicated that a decision could not be made that quickly, Treasurer Holt suggested that it should not be dismissed without further study, but that it should be deferred for a year or so, when a later opportunity for membership might arise. McEwen indicated that he'd discussed the matter with the DTI's Secretary, Alan Westerman, but felt the answer was 'no'. Menzies brought the matter to a swift conclusion, indicating that there would be a report from officials and that 'a few of us', could consider the report when available (NAA, 1963a).

The DEA's initial advice to Minister Barwick was that the DEA should adopt a position in favour of membership in discussion with other departments, to which he agreed. The advice noted that:

> There would undoubtedly be political advantages in Australian membership. The OECD Council, Executive Committee and other committees comprise policy making members of European administrations. Australian membership could be a useful method of making the members more conscious of Australian interests and the contribution Australia has to make in international affairs. (NAA, 1963b)

This was much the same view as had been suggested by a Special Adviser to the OECD's Secretary-General Kristensen, Dr Saxe, on a visit to Australia in January 1963. In a conversation with senior public servants in Canberra he is reported as saying 'half-jokingly', that the only way to get European countries to listen to Australian economic health and security interests was to increase its aid programme and join in OECD deliberations, further noting that there had been some talk of Australia joining the OECD (NAA, 1963c).

Saxe's views received substantial support in late February and March 1963 from three influential sources, each of which stressed the value of Australian membership of the OECD in relation to opening up channels of communication to the EEC and European capitals. The first took the form of a lengthy telegram from Dr Robert Whitelaw, a senior Treasury official, who had been sent to the UK in order to gain a more detailed picture of the British reasons for suggesting Australian membership of the OECD. Whitelaw had managed to discuss the matter with Sir William Armstrong, head of the UK Treasury, who was reported as saying that there was no specific reason for British support other than having 'like-minded persons' in international gatherings and that 'Australian views might be welcome when UK was faced with firm Common Market or North American views' (NAA, 1963d). Given the recent British failure to gain admission to the EEC in January 1963, Australian support within the OECD clearly was seen as of some value by the British. Importantly, it also suggested the value of OECD membership as a channel for Australian access to and, possibly, some influence over, EEC members and the European Commission.

A similar view, possibly based on that presented by Whitelaw, was received the same day in a telegram from Sir Allen Brown, the Australian Deputy High Commissioner in London, previously an influential Secretary of the Prime Minister's Department from 1949 to 1959, who argued that:

> On the merits of the proposition I believe that we would be very foolish if we let slip this chance of becoming members of this body. It is a heaven-sent opportunity to get acquainted at first hand with European and American thinking in the economic field and in my opinion an opportunity that we cannot afford to reject. (NAA, 1963e)

Brown's telegram was followed the next day by a similar telegram from the DEA's influential Ambassador to France, Sir Ronald Walker, who stressed that Australia 'cannot afford not to take this opportunity as OECD is developing a major role in a number of areas'. He went on to point out that with the British government's failure to gain EEC membership the Australian government 'must be increasingly concerned over ways of establishing stronger influence and image throughout Europe' (NAA, 1963f).

The credibility and status of these views, combined with additional information on the OECD and its activities, was sufficient to spur a meeting in Treasury on 11 March between Sir Roland Wilson (Treasury Secretary), Dr Westerman (Trade Secretary), a Mr J. Nimmo (standing in for Bunting, Secretary of the Prime Minister's Department), and Sir Arthur Tange (DEA Secretary), to discuss whether Australia should re-open with ministers the possibility of Australia joining the OECD alongside Japan. Wilson was very keen to see Australia gaining membership of the OECD. Tange was a little more cautious, suggesting that some form of associate membership would be valuable (it appears that the DEA was not aware at this time that, at least formally, there was no such category of associate membership available). Westerman, however, in line with the position Trade had adopted since 1960, was not in favour of an application for membership, pointing out that Australia was in the process of seeking membership of the ECAFE region in the UN General Assembly and that a parallel application for OECD membership would raise suspicions as to Australian motives in South East Asian countries. He did, however, also state that if Australia was to go ahead with an application for OECD membership, then it was an opportune time to do so.

In the record of the discussion that took place at the meeting is further evidence of the growing perception of the value of the OECD. Wilson, for example, was reported to Prime Minister Menzies by Nimmo as stating that:

> [T]he OECD was a place where important decisions were made or trends developed among the countries representing the powerful economies of the world. Australia was becoming more isolated: we should aim to get back into a position where our voice counted. Europe would continue to be of great importance for investment, manpower, scientific knowledge and trade, whatever the results of our efforts in Asia. The organisation was consultative: there was no reason why we should be forced to accept policies with which we did not agree. (NAA, 1963g)

Tange was reported as putting forward similar, but more cautious views, stating that he:

> [T]hought it wise for Australia to try to obtain membership of an influential grouping now extending to cover all the industrialised countries of the

> Northern hemisphere: while, in some places, this would be regarded as joining a 'neo-colonialist' grouping, [he] did not think this should deter us. In the External Affairs view, a lonely Australia should be trying not merely to get into Asian associations but also using our diplomacy to make the greatest possible impact on the people whose opinions counted in the capitals of Europe. In this context association with the OECD would be a move in the right direction: whether membership or something short of that should be determined in light of Trade and Treasury views on the implications for them. (NAA, 1963g)

The view that Australia was now increasingly 'isolated' and 'lonely', not only in regard to Europe but North America, was one that was to be repeatedly made in the next few years.

Nimmo's advice to Menzies following the meeting was that a policy of 'go slow' was appropriate in line with the views expressed by Menzies at the earlier Cabinet meeting, noting that Secretary Bunting had informed him and that he, in turn, had informed the meeting that there was a lack of enthusiasm by ministers when they were informed of the British offer to sponsor an Australian application (NAA, 1963g). Nimmo also told the meeting that the US was keen to get Japan in for 'major political reasons', and, of more concern, that an aide memoire received by the PM's Department from the US Embassy in Canberra had indicated there were some doubts about US support for membership. He noted, in conclusion, that Sir Roland Wilson would approach Menzies separately on the matter.

Wilson's approach was unsuccessful, for the matter was considered on 17 March 1963, not by full Cabinet, but by a small, ad hoc Cabinet committee, consisting of Prime Minister Menzies, Treasurer Holt and Minister for Trade, McEwen (NAA, 1963h, 1963i). Barwick's absence from this meeting (he was attending an ECAFE conference in Manila), left Holt without support and the result was that the proposal to consider OECD membership at this time was rejected, although it was agreed, in line with the views expressed by Holt, that Treasury could reopen the issue at a later date if it wished.

As noted in the meeting, there were two main reasons for not proceeding with an application. The first, not unreasonably, was a feeling that there was simply not enough time to undertake an appropriate evaluation in the time available, constrained as it seemed to be to a similar timetable as that already agreed for the Japanese application. The second was that the US Administration had indicated that it would prefer it if Australia did not proceed with an application at that time as it might encourage applications from Argentina and Brazil and those, in turn, might prejudice or complicate its first priority, that of gaining membership for Japan (NAA, 1963h, 1963i).

Hence, by 1963, while differences persisted regarding the value and timing of OECD membership, it was not rejected outright, leaving the way open for future consideration, a consideration that soon developed.

1964–65: Continuing Differences and a Second Step towards Membership

In January 1964 the DEA initiated moves to gain Cabinet approval for OECD membership, with a request to Minister Barwick for authority to sound out other departments regarding possible membership of the OECD's DAC. This had the 'avowed intention' that it lead to full membership of the OECD. The authority was granted, as was later authority to prepare with Treasury a draft Cabinet submission recommending membership (NAA, 1965a). Matters moved slowly, however, especially with the change in the DEA's Minister from Garfield Barwick to Paul Hasluck in April 1964, and it was not until 7 September 1965, following a recommendation by the Vernon Committee for Australian membership of the OECD, that a formal submission from the DEA and Treasury was considered by Cabinet (NAA, 1965a). The detailed submission contained a much fuller rebuttal of the arguments of McEwen and his department and suggested five main advantages of membership (NAA, 1965a).

The first advantage was that membership would ensure that Australia's interests would be considered in the 'principal Western forum where international financial and economic matters of high importance to us are now discussed', interests of particular concern to Treasury. The claim was supported by reference to five issue areas: sterling, international capital, international liquidity, the European Monetary Agreement and the OECD's influential Economic Policy Committee. The reference to sterling, indicative of Treasury's continuing concerns in this area, focused on the recent, 'very active', discussions in the OECD's Economic Policy Committee and its Working Party 3 regarding the measures necessary to enable the UK to balance its external accounts and to restore confidence in sterling. Australia was at this time, after the UK, the single largest holder of sterling, so any agreement on the measures to be taken would likely also impact on the value of its holdings and, as the submission noted, 'It is obviously not good enough from our standpoint that we are not a party to such discussions' (NAA, 1965a: 9).

The reference to international capital lent greater weight to the claims regarding sterling, noting that the OECD was undertaking work on the freeing up of capital markets. This work was encouraged, allegedly, by the USA, which was keen for the Europeans to open up their markets for outside borrowers. Australia had been drawing attention to this situation in both the IMF and the IBRD and, if a member, the submission argued, it would also be able to do so within the OECD. If successful, it would open up those markets to Australian borrowers. In addition, in the context of the sterling crisis, the submission pointed out that the UK had restrained capital outflows to non-sterling markets, leading to criticisms of such discrimination by the USA and European governments. The latter, the submission noted, had also suggested that the UK restrain its capital outflows to the sterling area, a matter of considerable, potential concern for Australia, given its policy of support for Australian economic development and the international capital this required (NAA, 1965a: 9–10).

In regard to international liquidity, the submission noted the increasing tendency of Western powers to reach consensus positions on international liquidity and the monetary system outside of the IMF, in two main bodies, Working Party 3 of the OECD's Economic Policy Committee and the Group of Ten (G10). As the submission noted, the membership of Working Party 3, with the exception of Belgium, was identical with that of the Group of Ten. Both the G10 and Working Party 3 had been examining the existing structure of the international monetary system, culminating in the publication of a commissioned 'Report of the Study Group on the Creation of Reserve Assets', the Ossola Report. The Report included a proposal that the US dollar and sterling be 'displaced', as international reserve currencies by a new reserve unit 'set by a very limited group of Western countries'. As the submission noted, given Australia's dependence on sterling, it needed to do all that it could to ensure that its interests were not ignored in this situation, and OECD membership would assist in that regard. It was only in a later section that the submission noted that membership of the key Working Party 3 was in fact restricted and that it would be some time after it had gained membership of the OECD before Australia was likely to gain membership of the Working Party (NAA, 1965a: 12).

Membership of the OECD, the submission further argued, would also give access to the reports of the Board of Management of the European Monetary Agreement (EMA), which reported to the OECD Council on several matters involving sterling and long- and short-term guarantees provided by the British government to EMA holders of sterling. It noted, further, that it had been only in recent years that the Australian government had discovered that the British government had provided guarantees as to the future value of sterling to European holders under the terms of the EMA, but not to Australia, even though the latter had greater sterling holdings than the EEC and EFTA combined (NAA, 1965a: 11–12). It had taken 'repeated representations', to persuade the British to withdraw the guarantee. In addition, limited, short-term guarantees had been provided by the British to the USA and European governments for the financial support they had provided in the sterling crisis. Hence, membership of the OECD would provide both difficult to obtain information as to such activities and, importantly, an opportunity for Australia to have its views made known at the OECD's regular reviews of the EMA.

The fifth issue area was the value that would be gained by the potential of membership of the Economic Policy Committee's Working Party 3. While admitting that this would not be immediately available, the submission argued, rather optimistically, that because of Australia's role in the sterling area and the importance to Australia of many of the matters coming before the Working Party, Australia could expect to become a member in due course, and that the UK had indicated the Australian representative would probably be able to attend as an observer in the meantime (NAA, 1965a: 12).

The second major advantage claimed the submission, was the apparent value of membership of the DAC, described as 'one of the most effective activities of the OECD', membership of which would help 'make the Australian aid effort better known', and ensure the aid policies of the major Western powers were not 'formulated in ignorance' of Australian interests. No evidence was provided to support this assertion other than that the DAC members had been able to coordinate their activities at the 1964 UNCTAD meeting by virtue of the DAC 'machinery', a machinery that was also providing more general assistance to its members in the coordination and planning for the allocation of aid resources (NAA, 1965a: 12–14). In a somewhat contradictory fashion, the submission then went on to assert that there was no reason to expect that membership of the DAC 'would force us to alter the character or direction of our aid'. While the assertion was correct in that DAC members could not 'force' Australia to make such alterations, it failed to note the influence it might have in persuading the Australian government to modify policy and practice.

The third advantage simply grouped together the views of the Commonwealth Scientific and Industrial Research Organisation, the Atomic Energy Commission and the Department of Primary Industry, all of whom had indicated that membership would be of value in enabling participation in the OECD's activities (NAA, 1965a: 14). It is, in retrospect, difficult to understand why more was not made of these views in promoting the case for membership, given that powerful opposition was expected from Minister McEwen and his department. The space allocated to describing their views was only one short paragraph in total compared, for example, to over a page for DAC and three and a half pages for the international economic advantages.

The fourth claimed advantage, overlapping with the first and third, was the opportunity membership would provide for making the Atlantic powers, especially the USA and the Europeans, 'more conscious of Australia, its achievements, its potential and its needs', helping to turn Australia from an 'outsider', to an 'insider', in what was becoming an increasingly 'institutionalised' environment for the conduct of economic and political relationships (NAA, 1965a: 4–15).

The fifth and final advantage noted in the submission was the opportunity that membership of the OECD's Trade Committee would provide. Given McEwen's position, this was always going to be a contentious issue, as the submission noted, though it claimed that even if there were net disadvantages to membership of the Trade Committee 'it should not be allowed to stand in the way of achieving the other benefits to Australia which full membership of the OECD would bring' (NAA, 1965a: 17–18). In favour of membership was the fact that most of Australia's major trading partners were already members, so it was a forum in which Australian representatives could keep its trade problems constantly 'under the notice' of those trading partners and seek to influence their policies regarding Australia. Also, noted the submission, as trade consultations in the OECD were 'non-coercive', Australia had nothing to fear from membership. Further, it pointed out that the Vernon Committee of Economic Enquiry very recently had recommended the value of trade discussions in the OECD, arguing that this alone warranted Australian membership (NAA, 1965a: 16). Interestingly, Sir John Crawford, formerly Secretary of the Trade Department, was the vice chair of the Vernon Committee and perhaps its most active member. The government's rejection of all of its main recommendations was apparently one of his greatest disappointments (Miller, 2013). This included the recommendation for OECD membership which Crawford now supported. His position was that full membership would: provide information as to what Europe and North American were thinking; draw attention to and enable consultation on Australia's problems; and enable Australia to provide 'a friend at court', for developing countries (Arndt, 1965: 325).

The submission noted McEwen's argument that as Australia was a major exporter of primary produce and more heavily reliant upon it than the USA, Canada and Denmark, Trade Committee membership would place it 'too close', to the major OECD members on trade matters and that a closer relationship with developing countries in arguing for improved trade conditions for commodities would be more appropriate (NAA, 1965a: 17). However, in contrast, the submission argued that membership would provide Australia with the opportunity to comment on the trade policies of other members and that there was nothing to prevent it adopting whatever position it thought was appropriate for Australian interests in other arenas.

Other than those that might be posed by membership of the Trade Committee, the submission identified only two major, possible disadvantages of OECD membership. The first was that developing countries might perceive an application for membership as a declaration that Australia was aligning itself with the 'advanced' countries, making them reluctant, for example, to ally with Australia in regard to pushing for the freeing up of trade in commodities in the GATT. In contrast, the submission asserted, it might well result in an increase in Australia's standing in Asian eyes, given that Japan was already a member and, in practice, Australia was likely to gain greater support from the Western Group of OECD members in bodies such as the UN than it was from developing countries (NAA, 1965a: 18).

A second disadvantage, one brought up in Cabinet's 1963 decision not to consider membership, was that membership of the DAC might result in pressures to increase Australia's foreign aid effort. However, the submission indicated that the extent of Australia's foreign aid, especially the expanded subventions to PNG, made such pressure unlikely, with Australia in fifth position on the DAC's comparative scale of aid donors, outranking most current DAC members. Moreover, Australian aid was entirely in grant, as opposed to loan, form, in line with DAC recommendations. A third, possible disadvantage was the fact that OECD members were expected to consult with members before taking major economic and financial decisions likely to impact on other members, consultation that might result in pressures to modify the proposed action. However, the submission noted that this obligation worked both ways and was no different from that often found in other international organisations such as the IMF and the GATT (NAA, 1965a: 19).

In summary, the submission argued that there was no real alternative to full membership of the OECD if the listed advantages were to be gained, though it did admit that if an application was unsuccessful or if Cabinet chose not to accept its recommendation, then membership of the DAC 'would be worth seeking', noting that Japan had gained full membership after a period as a member of the DAC. In concluding it recommended that:

> [W]e should be prepared to consider an offer of membership in the Development Assistance Committee but should endeavour to obtain some assurances that this would be proposed as an introductory step towards full membership of the OECD. (NAA, 1965a: 25)

However, the recommendation for membership was rejected by Cabinet, for much the same general reasons as had been put forward in 1963, combined with McEwen's continuing, if slowly declining, influence in again arguing strongly against membership. As a sign of that decline, Cabinet on this occasion did not entirely accept his views, agreeing that Australia should seek membership, not of the OECD, but as recommended in the submission, of the DAC, overturning its 1960 decision, and that it would leave open 'for later consideration', the question of an application for full membership.

1965–71: Agreement and the Application for OECD Membership

A successful bid for membership of the DAC was made in 1965 following the Cabinet decision, with Australia taking up membership in 1966. In summary, the application for the most part went smoothly, with all DAC members other than the USA expressing support. The initial American position was that it opposed Australian membership of the DAC. It did agree, eventually, that it would not lobby against Australian membership, though it would make its position known, if asked. In response to Australian queries as to the reasons for its opposition, it was indicated that Australian membership would only encourage other, unwelcome requests for membership and that Australian cooperation in relation to UNCTAD, organised through the OECD at meeting to which Australian and New Zealand representatives had been invited, had not always been forthcoming. As an example it was noted that Australia had announced 'without forewarning', its intention to give preferences to developing countries, at a time when other OECD members of the Western Group (consisting largely of OECD members) were still considering their positions (NAA, 1965b). Finally, in the face of the fact that all other DAC members supported Australian membership, it was agreed on 18 November 1965 that the US would not veto the Australian application and Australia's formal application for membership was lodged on 26 November 1965. On 15 February 1966 the OECD Council formally approved the application.

DAC Membership, Learning and Differing Views: 1966–68

Australian views and activities in relation to the OECD in the 1966–68 period leading up to the decision in January 1969 to reopen the question of full membership, were characterised by two major trends. The first was the continuation of the division of opinion in Australian government regarding the merits of membership. The second was the valuable learning experience that membership of DAC brought about, an experience that was largely positive and used by the DEA to bolster support for membership in the OECD.

The continuation of division can be seen in the somewhat surprising attendance by McEwen at the OECD's annual Ministerial Council meeting (MCM) in 1967. In September Sir Ronald Walker, based at the Paris Embassy, contacted the DEA Secretary to suggest that a Minister might attend those sections of the MCM concerned with the DAC and related development matters. A handwritten note on the cablegram, obviously aware of Department of Trade and Industry views, indicated that a year ago the DEA would not have considered such a move as Trade and Industry would have opposed the suggestion, but that it was now 'a more open question', although it might still be inappropriate, given McEwen's concerns (NAA, 1967a). Another note on the same page, possibly the Secretary's, indicated agreement with the view but asked that the invitation be sent on to Trade and Industry for comment 'but without expressing our views'.

It might have come as something of a surprise, and certainly a concern, when McEwen, following a discussion with DEA Minister Paul Hasluck decided that he would attend the MCM and requested permission to attend from the new Prime Minister Harold Holt (Menzies had retired in January 1966). His lengthy letter of request noted his opposition to OECD membership, at least from the Trade perspective, but argued that as the MCM would be considering tariff preferences and food aid for developing countries, issues of major concern for Australian trading interests, he should attend, especially as he would be attending GATT talks at about the same time. McEwen was opposed to what he saw as the OECD's largely negative view regarding UNCTAD proposals to open up OECD markets to agricultural commodities from developing countries and to what he described as a 'grandiose scheme' for increasing food aid, 'the real purpose of which will be the disposal of the dairy products surpluses of Western Europe'(NAA, 1967b). Moreover, he asserted:

> I remind you that, if we had been full members of the OECD, we would, for example, have found it virtually impossible to have signed the Free Trade

> Area Agreement with New Zealand or introduced our preference scheme for less developed countries. (NAA, 1967b)

This assertion was incorrect and was probably seen as such by most officials involved, for the OECD had no formal authority to enforce its views on its members regarding any free trade agreements, nor preference schemes for less developed countries. Moreover, it had not at this time reached any agreed position on either issue because of disagreements among its members, further undermining McEwen's assertion. Nevertheless, whether or not he was aware of McEwen's exaggerated claims, Holt agreed that he could attend the MCM, where he delivered his views in his normal, forceful fashion.

The second trend, the learning experience that membership of DAC brought about, was visible in at least two respects: (1) in the increasingly accurate information about the OECD, including DAC, provided for departments in Canberra by Philip Flood, the Australian representative to the DAC and First Secretary at the Australian Embassy in Paris; and (2) the opportunity it provided for Flood to encourage more sympathetic views about, and understanding of, the OECD on the part of Australian officials. J.C.A. Roper, a member of the British Delegation to the OECD, for example, noted that he had been given lunch by Philip Flood and by a J. Richardson, the Australian Minister (Commercial), in Brussels, a senior official in McEwen's department. Flood had privately explained to Roper in advance of the lunch that he would welcome Roper's help in overcoming Richardson's doubts regarding the OECD.

McEwen, writing in 1967, was well aware of this potential for learning that membership of the DAC entailed, noting to the Prime Minister in support of his request for attendance at the 1967 MCM that:

> I have considerable misgivings that, as a result of attendance at normal OECD meetings, we would be so drawn into its discussions of trade policy matters as to lose our own freedom of manoeuvre and find inhibited our initiative in trade matters of vital importance to us. (NAA, 1967b)

Moreover, it was a realisation that might explain McEwen's very blunt response to Flood's attempts to persuade him of the merits of OECD membership during a meeting between the two in Paris in 1968. The Minister concluded the meeting with the statement that 'Australia will only join the OECD over my dead body' (Flood, 2011: 55).

While Flood was responsible for DAC affairs, as he later noted:

> Since my work with the DAC would not take up all my time, I would also have a brief to obtain information on the OECD as a whole and to report on OECD assessments of developments in the global economy. (Flood, 2011: 49)

Ambassador Walker apparently gave Flood a largely free hand as regards the DAC and to begin an assessment of the OECD as a whole and the benefits Australia might derive from membership. As Flood noted, Australia's interest in the OECD was increasing exponentially and he was soon 'working sixty to seventy hours a week' (Flood, 2011: 53). Flood did not always meet with success in encouraging support for Australian membership, as he noted in correspondence to a friend within the DEA in 1968 when bemoaning the difficulty he was having in encouraging visits to special, Paris-based DAC meetings by 'home-based', senior officials and experts:

> [T]his sort of special meeting is a test of our seriousness about the DAC. My impression is that virtually all members will send experts from capitals. *It is not unrelated to our ultimate prospects of OECD membership* (sic). (NAA, 1968a)

It was in 1968 that the reopening of the issue of OECD membership again developed. While the available records do not provide a full explanation as to why this was the case, discussion seems to have been sparked off by a communication from Flood to the DEA Secretary informing him of the formal invitation to take up membership that had recently been offered to Finland (NAA, 1968b). In the letter, Flood noted that after the OECD Council meeting at which the invitation to Finland had been agreed, the Canadian Permanent Representative, a Mr Short, had remarked to him that 'Australia will have to hurry up now', further stating that some Council members had said Finnish membership would be the last. Flood also noted that the previous week, as a result of dissatisfaction with the somewhat cursory nature of the application process for Finland, the Council's Executive Committee had decided to review and strengthen the requirements for membership. Short also suggested that 'special status' countries such as Australia should apply sooner rather than later. Flood's reply to the Canadian was that while two years of DAC membership had increased the interest of Australian officials in the OECD as a whole, the government's position remained the same. A copy of Flood's letter was also sent to the Senior Treasury representative in London.

A further letter from Flood to the Secretary in September 1968 provided additional details about the accession process for Finland, in the hope that they would be of use, as Flood put it, 'if Ministers should later decide to press for full membership for Australia' (NAA, 1968c). The letter also pointed out that the US Ambassador to the OECD, Trevise, had spoken out in favour of more thorough criteria for membership to be applied to future applicants. While unstated, there was a clear implication that it might be in Australia's best interests to consider reopening the question of membership sooner rather than later, for fear that stricter conditions might be applied. Discussions within the DEA took place in late 1968, leading to an informal meeting of officials from the DEA, Treasury, Prime Minister's Department and the Department of Trade and Industry on 10 January 1969 (NAA, 1969a).

Approval to Informally 'Sound Out' Views as to Australian Membership of the OECD

Cabinet's 1965 decision to leave open for further consideration the question of an application for full membership was finally acted on in January 1969, when it was decided at the 10 January meeting of officials that three 'on the spot' reports would be drawn up as regards the advantages and disadvantages of Australian membership. A decision would then be made as to whether or not to request Cabinet for authority to approach the OECD as to the likely terms and conditions of membership. Flood would report for the DEA, J.R. Short for Treasury and J. Richardson for the DTI (both Short and Richardson were based with the Australian High Commission in London). The three officials talked in confidence and at length with a variety of senior OECD officials, including the Secretary-General, Thorkil Kristensen, and a number of delegates, including the British, US and Canadian. The fact that not one, but three reports were prepared indicates the continuing differences and considerable degree of sensitivity regarding OECD membership that persisted. However, all three reports were positive in their recommendations, though that from Richardson of the DTI, as might be expected, given his Minister's views, was very cautious, culminating in the somewhat tortuous note that:

> [H]aving regard to the essentially consultative character of the Organization, I would think that the pressures would not be such that we could not successfully resist them in relation to the practices which we considered to be justifiable. (NAA, 1969a)

It took some time for the DTI to indicate its view following the receipt of the three reports and it was not until 7 July 1969 that its First Assistant Secretary J. Fogarty could inform the DEA that DTI could now agree to 'put under study the essential conditions which would have to be satisfied if Australia were to enter into negotiations for membership' (NAA, 1969c). He acknowledged that some of the concerns of the DTI had been allayed, but that others remained. In particular, Fogarty noted that this view was that of the Department, not of the Minister, McEwen, who had not been able to provide his reaction to its view because of a journey to Washington.

It was agreed that it was now appropriate to consult with other interested departments and a full interdepartmental committee meeting, as planned, was held on the 8 July, chaired by Sir James Plimsoll, Secretary of the DEA, with representatives from Attorney General's Department, National Development (including the Australian Atomic Energy Commission), External Territories, Shipping and Transport, Health, Education and Science, Labour and National Service, Primary Industry and the Commonwealth Scientific and Industrial Research Organisation (CSIRO). The aims were to inform the 'marginally interested Departments' of progress to date and to gain agreement to the establishment of a small group consisting of the DEA, Treasury, DTI and the Prime Minister's Department to draft a paper for Ministers that would indicate the advantages and disadvantages of membership and the major issues to be addressed and, probably, to request authority from Ministers to authorise detailed discussions in Paris, though not at this stage to ask them to decide for or against membership.

The views of the newly involved departments were brief and tentative though largely positive, with a limited number of common concerns emerging that were later developed at greater depth regarding: (1) the capacity of the OECD to bring pressure to bear for modifications to domestic policies; (2) fears regarding the rigour and intrusiveness of the OECD's 'confrontation', technique (now referred to as peer review); (3) the position of the state governments; and (4) the extent of the information provided by, and required by, the OECD from its members. The interdepartmental committee agreed to the aims, the later circulation of departmental views regarding membership and that a drafting group commence work (NAA, 1969d).

A first draft Cabinet submission was prepared largely by the DEA and circulated in July 1969. However, the planned meeting of the interdepartmental committee to consider the draft submission was delayed as: (1) the DTI felt that it needed to consult with McEwen before participating in the drafting group and, while he endorsed its views, he decided to submit a separate submission; (2) McEwen decided that the DTI would not be a co-signatory to the Cabinet submission; (3) the relevant Treasury officials were heavily involved in budget discussions; (4) the absence overseas for part of the period of both the Treasurer and Minister for External Affairs; and (5) as matters dragged on, the announcement of the

October 1969 federal elections and the accompanying convention that major new decisions not be taken in the run-up to the election (NAA, 1969d).

Hence, it was not until early 1970, following the federal elections that matters progressed, based on a shorter draft submission prepared by Treasury which became the basis of the final Cabinet submission. In summary, it recommended that Cabinet authorise: (1) that steps be taken to 'sound out' the likely reactions by existing OECD members to an Australian application; and (2) that, assuming the soundings were 'not unfavourable', an official approach to the OECD could be made to ascertain the terms and conditions on which Australia might be offered membership (NAA, 1970a, 1970b). As anticipated, McEwen submitted a separate submission and, in line with what DEA officials informally had been led to believe, while it indicated that that he would not support membership from the Trade point of view, it further noted that if the Treasury/DEA submission were supported by other Ministers, he would not oppose the recommendation, which proved to be the case (NAA, 1970b).

It is difficult to be certain as to the exact reasons for McEwen's somewhat grudging change of position, though a number stand out. First, with the retirement of Menzies in 1966 and his replacement as Prime Minister by Harold Holt, then by John Gorton, he was missing the support of a Prime Minister that had long supported him, for the most part, in Cabinet. Second, while still cautious and constrained, the views of senior officials in the DTI had changed from opposition to support for Australian membership. Third, McEwen's energy and enthusiasm were probably in decline as he had been in Parliament since 1934 and a Minister since 1949, so that the thought of a major Cabinet row might have been unattractive. He retired in 1971.

1970–71: Formally Sounding Out Views, the Approach to the OECD and the Accession Process

The process of sounding out the views of OECD members as to Australian membership took less than two months, in May and June of 1970. As expected, all members were in favour except one, as were the senior members of the OECD Secretariat, including the Secretary-General, with several being enthusiastic. The exception was the USA.

American opposition can be traced back to at least 1963 in the context of the unexpected British offer to sponsor Australian membership, an offer that Cabinet declined, in part because of US reservations regarding an Australian application, probably for fear it might complicate a

Japanese membership bid that the US had proposed and strongly supported (NAA, 1963g). Again, in 1965 there had been initial and quite strong US opposition to Australian membership of the DAC on the grounds that: (1) it would only encourage other, unwelcome requests for membership; (2) that Australian cooperation in relation to UNCTAD had not always been forthcoming, implying it might be a 'difficult' member of DAC, given its decision to introduce a system of preferences for imports from developing countries without waiting for discussions on the matter at the OECD to conclude (NAA, 1965d); and (3) that it might lead to a later bid for full membership.

Hence, it was expected that there would be US reservations to an application for full membership when the sounding out of views began in 1970. However, initial discussions on the fringes of the OECD's 1970 Ministerial Council Meeting indicated that the strength of the US reservations had lessened. These discussions (with Nathaniel Samuels, the Deputy Under Secretary of State in the State Department, Joseph Greenwald, the US Ambassador to the OECD and Benson Timmons, the American Deputy Secretary of the OECD), indicated three reservations. First, the US was concerned to ensure that the 'essential character of the membership', had to be preserved, a somewhat nebulous reservation that referred to the relatively high degree of homogeneity of OECD membership, a homogeneity that made the reaching of agreement somewhat easier than was the case in larger organisations such as the UN. The second was the desire, for political reasons, not to encourage applications from countries such as Israel and South Africa, applications it was felt might be encouraged if Australia were to commence the accession process. The third was the desire to keep out countries which had not reached 'a sufficient stage of economic maturity', such as Argentina, although it was recognised that several existing members, notably Turkey, Spain and Portugal might be regarded as similarly immature, but had been admitted for reasons associated with the politics of the Marshall Plan and the fact that they were European. All three reasons seemed to boil down to one, that the US was concerned that an Australian application would encourage applications from less desirable states (NAA, 1970c).

A further discussion took place in Washington on 12 June 1970 with Alexis Johnson, acting Under Secretary of State, Julius Katz from the State Department's European Bureau and Edwin Cronk from its Economic Affairs Bureau (NAA, 1970d). The meeting confirmed the earlier views that US opposition had largely evaporated. Katz did indicate that the US did not want to be seen to be influencing Europeans to admit a non-European member, but Johnson, his superior, stated that as Japan was now a member of the OECD it could no longer be described as a European or North Atlantic organisation, but an association of developed states. The meeting concluded shortly thereafter with Johnson authorising the Australian Ambassador to inform Canberra that the US would support Australian membership. Again, the fact that all other OECD members, plus the Secretariat supported Australian membership, combined with the fact that, as with Japan, Australia had been a well-regarded member of the DAC for nearly five years before commencing the accession process, overcame American reservations.

With American support assured, formal discussions as to the terms and conditions for Australian membership commenced in July 1970, as authorised by the OECD Council (NAA, 1970e) and concluded with its decision to invite the Australian government to accept membership on 24 May 1971. The offer was accepted by the Australian government on the 25 May. Provision for accession to the OECD was made in its founding Convention at Article 16:

> The Council may decide to invite any Government prepared to assume the obligations of membership to accede to this Convention. Such decisions shall be unanimous, provided that for any particular case the Council may unanimously decide to permit abstention, in which case, notwithstanding the provisions of Article 6, the decision shall be applicable to all the Members. Accession shall take effect upon the deposit of an instrument of accession with the depository Government. (OECD, 2013)

There is no other specification in the Convention as to the accession process apart from Article 16, nor were there any detailed, formal criteria that its members had agreed should be applied in determining accession that were then available to guide the Australian government, although there had been some discussion as to the value of setting formal criteria in the OECD's Executive Committee in 1968, as noted above.

Rather, the accession process was designed and led by the Secretariat, involving at this time three broad phases. The first involved the selection and distribution of relevant documentation by the Secretariat and its assessment and clarification by Australian agencies, including the identification of any issues as regards, in particular, Council decisions and recommendations, notably those contained in the OECD's two Codes of Liberalisation (collectively known as the 'Acts' of the organisation). Where issues were identified discussion first took place at the national level between the department raising the issue and, as necessary, one or more of Treasury, DEA and DTI representatives (see, for example, NAA, 1970g, concerning issues brought up by the Department of External Territories regarding Papua New Guinea, which posed a range of issues not faced by most other departments). If they could not be resolved at this level, requests for advice were sent to the Australian representatives in Paris, with most issues being resolved without significant negotiation. A relatively small number of more serious issues, especially those concerning aspects of the two Codes, were negotiated at greater length, as in the shipping example discussed below.

The second stage was the negotiation and drawing up of a declaration or statement that would contain: the acceptance of the OECD Convention, its two Codes of Liberalisation and its Acts; and agreed reservations and remarks. In effect, this represented the terms and conditions of membership as agreed by the applicant and the Secretariat and, as regards reservations regarding the two Codes, by the OECD's Committee for Invisible Transactions. The agreed terms and conditions were then submitted to Council for its approval, which, in turn, issued an invitation for membership. The Australian representatives for these negotiations consisted of a small group of senior officials drawn from the DEA, Treasury and the DTI and took place at the OECD, for the most part, in late 1970 and early 1971, focused on the remaining unresolved areas identified by departments and likely to require reservations or remarks in the final declaration. The third stage was a largely formal one of depositing the instrument of accession with the French government, the depository under the Convention.

In practice and as expected, the first phase of the accession process proceeded smoothly and rapidly, with a focus on the examination and discussion of the applicability of the OECD's Code of Liberalisation of Capital Movements and the Code of Liberalisation of Current Invisible Operations (largely the responsibility of the Treasury and, in parts, the DTI and the Department of Shipping and Transport) (NAA, 1970h). In large part this smooth and rapid progress came about because the bulk of relevant Australian legislation, regulation and policy was already compatible with that contained in the OECD's decisions and recommendations. In addition, under the terms of the OECD's Convention there was considerable scope for existing members and acceding states to enter abstentions from, and reservations to, specific decisions and recommendations, with the acceptance of recommendations being on a voluntary basis. Indeed, all existing members had entered one or more abstentions or reservations, typically to one or more items listed in the two Codes, so that there was ample precedent for Australia to enter reservations in the final agreement, as acknowledged and expected by OECD negotiators (NAA, 1970h).

Hence, the visit by the small team of Australian officials to Paris for negotiations took only ten days (NAA, 1970i). In a letter to L.S. Corkery in the DEA commenting on a progress report presented by the Secretary-General to the OECD Heads of Delegation, C.R.S. Rodgers the First Secretary in the Australian Embassy in Paris noted that there had been no questions raised by the Heads at the meeting and that Timmons, the Deputy Secretary-General, had stated that the talks had taken place in an 'excellent atmosphere' (NAA, 1970j). The return to Australia of the officials marked the beginning of the second phase of the accession process, the drawing up of a statement by the Australian government of its position in relation to the OECD Acts.

Only one area caused protracted difficulties. As noted by the Secretariat following an examination of the relevant documents during the first phase of the discussions, it felt that there were two issues of concern in relation to shipping and the Invisibles Code. The first concerned the Closed Conference System employed by shipping lines servicing Australian trade, in relation to Annex A, Item C/1 and Note 1 of the Invisibles Code. The Conference System was an association of shipping operators aimed at controlling competition between its members by setting freight rates, rebates to shippers and restricting access to the Conference. However, later legal opinion to the Secretariat was that this was not, as at first thought, inconsistent with Annex A, Item C/1 and Note 1 of the Invisibles Code, as the Australian government did not participate in fixing the terms of the Conference agreements, a participation that would have been inconsistent with the Code (NAA, 1970k).

However, the OECD asserted that this was not the case for the second, related item, concerning the Overseas Cargo Shipping provisions (Part XA) of the Australian Trade Practices Act 1965–66. In the OECD's legal opinion, Part XA could be viewed as granting to the Australian authorities the power to discriminate in favour of Australian flag carriers, contrary to the provisions of Item C/1 and Note 1 of the Invisibles Code. Deputy Secretary Timmons first outlined the issue to Australian officials on an informal basis, requesting their views on the OECD's legal opinion and the relationship between the Australian legislation and the Invisibles Code. He also suggested that if, as had been indicated by Australian officials in the earlier discussions, the Trade Practices Act had not been applied in any way contrary to the letter or spirit of the Code, then a declaration to that effect, combined with a declaration that it would not be so applied in the future, would strengthen the Australian case (NAA, 1970k).

Australian legal opinion, based on that provided by the Attorney General's Department, was that the OECD's legal advice was incorrect and, therefore, that there was no need to make the declaration proposed by Timmons, nor a reservation to the Code (NAA, 1970l). It was also noted that both the USA and France practised extensive flag discrimination. However, the new Minister for the DTI, Doug Anthony, after a prolonged delay, decided that the matter was of such importance that he wished for further guidance from Cabinet before Australian officials in Paris had further discussions with the Secretariat.

Both the Department of Foreign Affairs (DFA – formerly the DEA) and Treasury were concerned that such a submission and request for Cabinet guidance would be misleading if it were considered in isolation from the overall picture of successful negotiations on other aspects of membership, and were of the view that, in addition, a more balanced viewpoint should be presented to Cabinet (NAA, 1971a). It was agreed that such a 'balancing', submission should be made, even though it and the Anthony submission would further delay the accession process (NAA, 1971b). News of the delay and allegations that the accession process was being subverted by 'McEwenite' views had already been leaked to the press, which also alleged that the OECD was 'awestruck by McEwenistic isolationism' (NAA, 1971c).

However, the tone of Minister Anthony's Cabinet submission was relatively mild, simply describing the nature of the issue and recommending: (1) that the OECD's tentative legal opinion be challenged on the grounds that there was no conflict with the Code and, hence, that no reservation should be made; and (2) that if this failed other options be explored. The 'balancing' submission was made by the new Treasurer, William 'Billy' Snedden in 1971, in the form of a progress report to Cabinet. It noted that as far as the Current Invisibles Code was concerned 'Australia is able to accept the Code, virtually without reservations', and that the shipping issue was the only serious problem, with, discounting shipping, only three reservations having to be made (NAA, 1971d). It recommended that Cabinet note the report and endorse, subject to a satisfactory solution to the shipping issue, an attached list of proposed reservations to the Codes.

Cabinet endorsed both submissions, leaving it up to the Attorney General to come up with an appropriate form of words for the OECD, keen to leave legal argument aside and achieve membership (NAA, 1971d). It is possible that Cabinet was encouraged in its desire to see membership achieved rapidly by news of a letter from the US Secretary of State William Rogers, to new Prime Minister William McMahon. The letter indicated that the USA was keen to see Australia join the OECD and that Rogers would like to welcome Australian membership at the Ministerial Council Meeting on 7–8 June, which he would chair. As the DFA's First Assistant Secretary W.J. Cumes noted to his new Minister, Leslie Bury (who had succeeded McMahon as Minister on 22 March

1971), the message from Rogers 'offers us a chance to give a new impetus to our discussions on membership', noting that Anthony's Cabinet submission on the shipping issue had been circulated that week. Cumes also suggested that Bury write to Prime Minister McMahon urging that we press on with 'all possible speed', to achieve full membership by June, a suggestion rapidly adopted (NAA, 1971e, 1971g).

'All possible speed', was achieved, with the OECD Secretariat accepting the Attorney General's advice regarding the shipping issue and submitting it to the Invisibles Committee, which, in turn, accepted that there was no inconsistency with the Code (NAA, 1971f). A final submission was made to Cabinet with a full statement of the obligations of membership and relevant reservations, recommending that Australia seek full membership and that following the invitation from the Council of the OECD an instrument of accession should be lodged with the French government. The recommendation was accepted (NAA, 1971h).

CONCLUSION

In contrast to the decisions relating to membership of the UN special agencies such as the FAO, and UNESCO, those involving the OECD were very cautious, revealing substantial differences between key ministers and their departments that were only resolved after a decade of discussion. Those supporting membership were officials contained, for the most part, in Treasury and the DEA, searching for greater Australian access and influence in what was seen as an increasingly important organisation as regards international economic affairs. The opposition was centred around Black Jack McEwen and his officials in the DTI and, to a lesser extent, Prime Minister Menzies, strongly opposed to membership of an organisation that seemed to have the potential to exercise significant influence in opposition to the Australian stance of 'protection all round' for its economic development.

An important part of the motive for Australian membership of the OECD was the increased access it would give to Western European decision makers, including those in the EEC. It was a motive given increased weight by the shock of the first British applications for membership of the EEC. Australian interest in the EEC and the OECD was not new, but the most recent manifestation of interests in powerful international organisations that went back to earlier efforts at European integration in the later 1940s and 1950s. However, the British applications for membership of the EEC added weight to those arguing for Australian membership of the OECD for a wider range of other purposes.

Australian membership of the OECD also demonstrates that while there was a growing emphasis in Australian external and economic policy towards the Asian region it was not at the expense of a dilution of effort as regards Europe. Rather, it was accompanied by an extension of Australian activities in Western Europe, such as membership of the OECD, activities designed to provide greater access to decision makers and to reduce the earlier dependence on British representation of Australian interests.

BIBLIOGRAPHY

Arndt, H. 1965. 'Australia – Developed, Developing, or Midway?', *Economic Record*, 41(95): 318–340.

British National Archives 1964. 'Australian and New Zealand Relationship with OECD. Summary of Correspondence, 1960–64', the Annex to 'The Future of the OECD Relationship with Australia and New Zealand', a Note by the Commonwealth Relations Office for the Cabinet External Economic Relations Committee, dated 30 September 1964. File DO162/82 273341.

British National Archives 1969. A note dated 7 February from J.C.A. Roper to R.G. Britten, of the Trade Policy Department, Foreign and Commonwealth Office, File MTD 28/345/1.

Carroll, P. 2014. 'Gaining Greater Access to Western European Decision-Makers: A Motive for Australian Membership of the OECD', *Australian Journal of Politics and History*, 60(2): 229–240.

Castles, F. 1988. *Australian Public Policy and Economic Vulnerability: A Comparative and Historical Perspective*, Sydney: Allen & Unwin.

Flood, P. 2011. *Dancing with Warriors: A Diplomatic Memoir*, Melbourne: Australian Scholarly Publishing.

Lowe, D. 1997. 'Australia at the UN in the 1950s: The Paradox of Empire', *Australian Journal of International Affairs*, 51(2): 171–181.

Miller, J. 2013. 'Crawford, Sir John Grenfell (Jack) (1910–1984)', Australian Dictionary of Biography, National Centre of Biography, Australian National University, accessed 13 February 2013 at http://adb.anu.edu.au/biography/crawford-sir-john-grenfell-jack-1391/text22223.

NAA 1960a. 'Organisation for Economic Co-operation and Development', Outward Cablegram, 12 May 1960, For Crawford from Trade, File A987/4.

NAA 1960b. Cabinet Decision 615, 4 February 1960, File A3092.

NAA 1960c. 'Consultation with New Zealand', a note dated 22 April 1960 regarding a phone call from Dr Salter in the PM's Department for Dr Cumes in the DEA, File A1838 724/4/3 Part 1.

NAA 1960d. Unsigned Cablegram from the Paris Embassy to the DEA, requesting further advice regarding membership, 3 May 1960, File A987-4 E1395-1961- Part B.

NAA 1960e. Unsigned Cablegram from the Australian High Commission in London to the DEA, 4 May 1960, File A987-4 E1395-1961- Part B.

NAA 1961a. A note from Secretary John Bunting to Prime Minister Menzies, 7 July 1961, File A4940/1, C3368 Pt 2.
NAA 1961b. 'European Economic Integration', May 1961, File A1838-724-4-3 Part 3, contained in 'Australian Brief – Commonwealth Economic Consultative Council', Item 2(c).
NAA 1961c. 'Memorandum EEC/59/61', 8 June 1961, from Australian Embassy Brussels to DEA, File A987/4 'Organisation for Economic Co-operation and Development'.
NAA 1962a. 'European Economic Integration', 3 December 1962, a note from C.G. Woodard, Office of Australian High Commission, London to Secretary, DEA. File A1838-724-4-3 Part 3.
NAA 1962b. 'OECD-DAC Development Assistance Committee (including Ad Hoc Committee)', 7 May 1962, copy of a cablegram from DEA to Australian Embassy in Paris, Prime Minister's Department, File A1029, File No. 62/992.
NAA 1962c. 'OECD-DAC Development Assistance Committee (including Ad Hoc Committee)', 17 May 1962, copy of a letter from Holt to Barwick, Prime Minister's Department File, File A1029, No. 62/992.
NAA 1962d. 'OECD-DAC – Ad Hoc Group on Aid to Thailand', 10 December 1962, DEA submission to Cabinet, File A1029, No 62/992.
NAA 1963a. 'Possible Australian Membership of the Organisation for Economic Co-operation and Development', Cabinet Minute, Decision No. 676(HOC), 12 March 1963, and a Draft Cabinet Submission 'Organisation for Economic Co-operation and Development Suggested Application by Australia for Membership', undated, File A4940-C3754.
NAA 1963b. 'European Economic Relations Integration', note from D.L. Harry of the DEA's Economic Relations Branch to Minister Paul Hasluck, 26 February, File A1838-724-4-3 Part 3.
NAA 1963c. 'European Economic Integration', record of a conversation with Dr Saxe, 8 January 1963, File A1838-724-4-3 Part 3.
NAA 1963d. 'European Economic Integration', cablegram from Dr Whitelaw to Treasury, 1 March 1963, File A1838-724-4-3 Part 3.
NAA 1963e. 'European Economic Integration', cablegram from Sir Allen Brown to Treasury, 1 March 1963, File A1838-724-4-3 Part 3.
NAA 1963f. 'European Economic Integration', cablegram from Sir Ronald Walker to DEA, 2 March 1963, File A1838-724-4-3 Part 3.
NAA 1963g. 'Possible Australian Membership of the OECD', 11 March 1963, a note from Mr J.F. Nimmo in the Prime Minister's Department to Prime Minister Menzies. File A4940-C3754.
NAA 1963h. 'Organisation for Economic Co-operation and Development – Suggested application by Australia for membership', March 1963, A4940-C3754.
NAA 1963i. 'Australian Relationships with the Organisation for Economic Co-operation and Development', Cabinet Submission No 1037, Copy No 73, File A1838 724/5 Part 4.
NAA 1965a. 'OECD and DAC – Australian Relations With'. The file contains a copy of Cabinet Submission No 1194, 1965, which rejected the proposal for

possible membership of the OECD, but agreed to an application for membership of the DAC and left open for later consideration the question of an application for full membership. A1838, File No 724/5 Part 4.
NAA 1965b. 'Development Assistance Committee', a Cablegram from the Australian Embassy in Washington to Canberra, dated 23 October 1965, reporting on discussions with US officials regarding Australian's application for membership of the DAC. File A1838-724-5 Part 4 'Membership to DAC'.
NAA 1965c. 'Australian Relations with OECD', a note for the Minister, 6 September 1965, NAA A1838, File No 724/5 Part 4.
NAA 1965d. 'OECD – DAC (including ad hoc committee)', Cablegrams to the DEA, dated 6 October 1965 and 23 October 1965, NAA File No. A1209.
NAA 1965e. 'Report to the Minister for External Affairs by the Interdepartmental Committee to Review Australian External Aid', 25 March 1965, A4311, File No. 147/2.
NAA 1967a. A copy of a cablegram from Walker to the Secretary dated 21 September 1967, in NAA A724-4-26 Annex Part 1.
NAA 1967b. A letter of request from McEwen to the Prime Minister, in NAA A724-4-26 Annex Part 1.
NAA 1968a. A letter to a friend in the DEA, NAA in A724-4-26 Annex Part 1.
NAA 1968b. A letter from Flood to the DEA Secretary dated 23 July 1968, NAA A1838, File 724/4/16.
NAA 1968c. A letter from Flood to the DEA Secretary dated 2 September 1968, NAA A1838, File 724/4/16.
NAA 1969a. 'OECD and Australia', a note from K.C.O. Shann for the Secretary of the DEA, Sir James Plimsoll, dated 4 July 1969, in NAA A1838 724-5-16.
NAA 1969b. 'Australia and OECD', record of a conversation with J. Fogarty of DTI, 7 July 1969, with K.C.O. Shann and L. Corkery of the DEA present, NAA A1838-724-4-30 Part 2.
NAA 1969c. 'Australia and the OECD', letter to the Secretary Department of the Treasury from L. Corkery in the DEA, dated 14 July 1969, NAA A1838-724-4-30 Part 2.
NAA 1969d. 'Organisation for Economic Co-operation and Development (OECD)', an information note for the Minister, dated 10 September 1969, from K.C.O. Shann in the DEA, NAA A1838 – 724-4-30 Part 3.
NAA 1970a. 'Possible Australian membership of the Organisation for Economic Co-operation and Development (OECD)', copy of a draft Cabinet submission, dated 13 March 1970, signed by William McMahon, the new Minister for the DEA, A1838 NAA, A1838 – 724-4-30 Part 3.
NAA 1970b. Copy No 35 of Cabinet Minute 'Decision No 305', dated 30 April 1970, referring to Submission No 174 (the DEA and Treasury joint submission) and Submission No 176 (the McEwen submission), NAA A1838 – 724-4-30 Part 4.
NAA 1970c. 'Australian Membership of OECD', a Report on Discussions at Ministerial Meeting, Paris, 20–22 May 1970, by J.W.C. Cumes, dated 2 June 1970, in NAA A1838 724-4-30 Part 5 – Accession.
NAA 1970d. 'OECD', a cablegram from the Washington Embassy to the DEA in NAA A1838 724-4-30 Part 5 – Accession.

NAA 1970e. 'OECD', a cablegram from the Paris Embassy to the DEA, dated 7 July 1970, noting that the OECD Deputy Secretary Timmons had phoned to indicate that the Council had authorised the Secretary-General to examine the terms and conditions of an invitation for membership to Australia, NAA A1838 724-4-30 Part 5 – Accession.

NAA 1970f. 'OECD: Examination of the Obligations of Possible Australian Membership', a memo from L.S. Corkery in the DEA to participating departments, dated 21 August 1970. Attached to the memo was a list of the policy areas that were to be the responsibility of each department, NAA A1838 724-4-30 Part 5 – Accession.

NAA 1970g. 'OECD: Examination of the Obligations of Possible Australian Membership', dated 18 September 1970, a letter from the Secretary of the Department of External Territories to the Secretary of the DEA, advice on the letter from A.M. Campbell to L.S. Corkery in the DEA, dated 22 September 1970 and a cablegram from DEA to the Australian Embassy in Paris dated 25 September 1970 asking for advice on the issues, all in NAA A1838 724-4-30 Part 6 – Accession.

NAA 1970h. 'OECD', a cablegram from the Paris Embassy to the DEA dated 16 October 1970, summarising progress to date, following a meeting with Timmons, the OECD's Deputy Secretary-General and senior advisors, NAA A1838 724-4-30 Part 6 – Accession.

NAA 1970i. 'Statement to the Heads of Delegations Meeting on 20th October 1970, Regarding the Discussions Held to Date with the Australian Authorities', in NAA A1838 724-4-30 Part 6 – Accession.

NAA 1970j. A letter from Rodgers to Corkery in the DEA dated 21 October 1970, in NAA A1838 724-4-30 Part 6 – Accession.

NAA 1970k. As contained in the annex to a letter from Deputy Secretary-General Timmons to the Australian Ambassador, Alan Renouf, regarding the issue, dated 24 November 1970, NAA A1838 724-4-30 Part 7 – Accession.

NAA 1970l. A note prepared by L. Corkery for Sir K. Bailey, dated 15 December 1970, in NAA A1838 724-4-30 Part 7 – Accession.

NAA 1971a. 'Organisation for Economic Co-operation and Development', a note for the Minister from J.W.C. Cumes in the DFA, dated 19 March 1971 in NAA A1838 724-4-30 Part 8 – Accession.

NAA 1971b. 'OECD', a confidential note from J.W.C. Cumes to Ambassador Renouf in Paris, dated 17 March 1971 in NAA A1838 724-4-30 Part 8 – Accession.

NAA 1971c. 'Australia the Quibbler', a front page article by Maximillian Walsh in the *Australian Financial Review*, 15 January 1971.

NAA 1971d. 'Possible Australian Membership of OECD – The Codes of Liberalisation of Current Invisible Operations and Capital Movements', Cabinet Submission No 54, Copy No 59, dated 16 April 1971, in NAA A1838 724-4-30 Part 9 – Accession.

NAA 1971e. 'OECD: Australian Membership Letter to Prime Minister from United States Secretary of State', a note from J.W.C. Cumes to the Minister dated 2 April 1971, in NAA A1838 724-4-30 Part 10 – Accession.

NAA 1971f. 'OECD', a Report summarising an interdepartmental meeting of 30 April 1971 regarding the final stages of the accession process, in NAA A1838 724-4-30 Part 8 – Accession.

NAA 1971g. Copy of a letter from Minister Bury to Prime Minister McMahon, undated, in NAA A1838 724-4-30 Part 12 – Accession.

NAA 1971h. 'Cabinet Minute Canberra 4th May 1971 Decision No. 145' regarding Submission No. 80, 'Australian Membership of O.E.C.D.', in NAA A1838 724-4-30 Part 11 – Accession.

OECD 2013. 'Convention on the Organisation for Economic Co-operation and Development', Paris: OECD, accessed on 26 February 2013 at www.oecd.org/general/conventionontheorganisationforeconomicco-operationanddevelopment.htm.

Padelford, N. 1954. 'Regional Organization and the United Nations', *International Organization*, 8(2): 203–216.

Ravenhill, J. 1998. 'Adjusting to the ASEAN Way: Thirty Years of Australia's Relations with ASEAN', *The Pacific Review*, 11(2): 267–289.

Ward, S. 2001. *Australia and the British Embrace: The Demise of an Imperial Ideal*, Melbourne: Melbourne University Press.

4. Organising the relationship with the OECD

This chapter examines in some detail how the relationship with the OECD has been administered. The work of the OECD in numerous committees and subsidiary bodies requires an extensive engagement of personnel, and Australia's remoteness from Paris has placed demands for both travel and on the Delegation that are unusual when compared with most OECD members. Communication has been particularly important, especially given the large volume of documents produced by the OECD, and this has sometimes been problematic. Also considered are the financial arrangements for the cost of the engagement and some aspects of the arrangements for Ministerial Council Meetings. In summary, the chapter shows in some detail the challenges faced in securing effective engagement by a middle power such as Australia in a remotely located international organisation.

ORGANISING AUSTRALIA'S ENGAGEMENT

In September 1971 an interdepartmental meeting took place regarding the organisational arrangements for Australian representation at the OECD, attended by a range of senior staff and chaired by Dr Cumes of the DFA. He noted that Cabinet Decision 145 of the 4 May 1971 had provided for a delegation of eight persons, including the ambassador. Treasury and Trade would each have two members, as would the DFA. The Delegation would operate as a whole to represent 'the totality' of government interests, stressing that:

> To a far greater extent than in any other Embassy or Mission, there would be an interaction of inter-departmental interests in the OECD Delegation and this necessitated a) provision for clear direction and guidance of the Delegation by the Ambassador and b) coordinating machinery in Canberra to be carried out by Foreign Affairs within a broad framework of consultation with interested departments. (NAA, 1971)

The attendance list indicates the number and range of agencies with interests relevant to the OECD: Attorney-General; Census and Statistics; CSIRO; Education and Science; Environment, Aborigines and the Arts; External Territories; Foreign Affairs (five in attendance, including Ambassador Sir Ron Walker, Mr Philip Flood and Dr Cumes (chair)); Health; Immigration; Labour and National Service; National Development; Primary Industry; Public Service Board; Shipping and Transport; Trade and Industry (four in attendance); and Treasury (three in attendance) (NAA, 1971).

Ambassador Walker indicated resource and distance constraints would inevitably limit the scope of Australian participation and Delegation staff would have to cover areas outside departmental interests. He anticipated a monthly Savingram would review developments. Dr Cumes stressed clear lines of communication were vital, and recognised the different nature of the OECD and the challenges that posed:

> The objective would be to ensure that there were clear lines of communication between Paris and Canberra and that the Delegation performed a unified role of representing the Commonwealth Government. Departments had not had experience of a comparable flow of reports and documents from any other international organisation, OECD presented unique problems, and it might therefore become necessary to look again at procedure in six months' time in the light of experience. (NAA, 1971)

Cumes indicated that direct correspondence between departments and the Secretariat was prohibited, with correspondence with the Delegation to go through the DFA, except for those departments with representatives on the Delegation, although the DFA would have to be consulted on, and receive a copy of, any such instructions. Walker informed the meeting that departments could call on staff from other Delegations, but the Delegation in Paris and the DFA would have to receive copies of reports of meetings attended. He advised there was list of OECD meetings three months in advance, leaving time for consideration by the Overseas Visits Committee that had to approve international travel at that time.

There was interest at the 1971 IDC in placing high quality Australian staff in the Secretariat, but there was caution expressed that Australia had no wish to fill its 'quota' too rapidly with 'positions of a minor importance from a policy view point'. There was no Australian holding a senior position of Deputy Director or above and only 15 Australian staff in the Secretariat (1 A5, 1 A4, 8 A3, 2 A2, 1 Consultant, 1 trainee). Some Mediterranean countries had attempted to raise as a general issue the proportions of nationalities in the Secretariat. Australia thought the merit principle was more important. The special provision whereby France held one Deputy Secretary-General position as host, and the US the other as the major contributor was noted, although for the most part the 'carve-up' of Secretariat positions on the basis of nationality, prevalent in several other international institutions was largely avoided. Nevertheless, it was noted that the OECD was still a very European/United States oriented organisation, and while the prime responsibility for increasing awareness of Australia's interests lay with the Delegation and visiting delegates, it was felt that a few Australians in more senior positions would be useful.

A review of Australia's OECD engagement in 1974 reflected on a 'very active' year, with the annual review of the Australian economy and aid performance plus ad hoc reviews of manpower, science, trade and industry policies. Reviews of education and fisheries were being prepared for 1975. 'Apart from delays in the manpower review and a disagreement over references to energy policy in the independent examiners' report on Australian science policy, they proceeded without serious problems' (NAA, 1974).

A more negative Australian attitude towards some aspects of the organisation's work emerged on matters where Australia's national interests diverged from those of some other members. While the Australian position was appreciated and accepted if substantiated and argued consistently, and areas of difficulty flagged in advance to avoid misunderstandings during preparatory discussions, in some instances, such as the 'reluctant acceptance of the trade pledge', Australia gave the impression of 'attaching little weight to the general interest in cooperative action aimed at maintaining conditions favourable to world trade' (NAA, 1974). It was suggested that in other areas where vital Australian interests were not affected, some strategic acceptance might be used: 'In such areas there would seem to be little real cost associated with an attitude more accommodating to the views of the great majority of members' (NAA, 1974).

It was also suggested Australia could improve on its reluctance to exchange information and experience. Australia was, in effect, learning to adapt to the mores of the OECD in order to maximise its influence on matters more important to it:

> It is suggested that these considerations warrant continuing attention in Canberra on an interdepartmental basis, so that a better perception will exist of the totality of the Australian stance in OECD. A reputation for a generally negative, even obstructive, attitude, can lead to Australia not being consulted and not exercising the influence it might do on the nature of the activities undertaken. (NAA, 1974)

The Delegation in 1974 was far from self-contained. Assistance was provided from the London and Geneva posts, for example, and non-OECD activities (totalling at least 18 weeks of effort) also occupied Delegation members, who were making contributions to other agencies, including FAO, GATT, UNCTAD, and UNESCO. For some months the Deputy Head of Delegation initially was also accredited to France and expected to divide time equally between the OECD and bilateral matters. Five members of the Delegation were replaced during the year and in one case (Science Counsellor) the replacement arrived four months after the departure of the predecessor. A sixth (Education Counsellor), the only one to serve a normal three-year posting, had returned in July and was yet to be replaced some months later.

There were issues also with support staff. Secretary-typists were being recruited from the UK, but there was rapid turnover, and given the difficulties in recruiting 'suitable locally-engaged English language secretaries', it was recommended consideration be given to recruiting Australian-based (hereinafter A-based) staff.

The documentary demands of the OECD were large, with numerous reports, including various revisions and final versions, emanating from committees and their subsidiary bodies, in addition to notes by the Secretariat. The cost (including freight) appeared substantial, while there were concerns that the Diplomatic Bag – even by air – took six days plus the time for distribution within Australia (barring strikes). Nevertheless, the Delegation 'joined in the general effort to reduce the despatch of cables'. It was clearly concerned to manage costs and expressed the view that priority should be given to a reduction in the numbers of officers sometimes accompanying senior visitors, rather than in the number of separate visits by A-based participants in deliberative bodies. This quest for parsimony even extended to entertainment allowances:

> [S]ome officers regard their present allowances as being in excess of the requirement for activities appropriate to a Delegation to the OECD, in particular in relation to the level of representation allowances of, and the degree of reciprocal entertainment by, other Delegations. The Secretariat is, of course, not expected to reciprocate. (NAA, 1974)

The composition of the Delegation was by no means immediately settled after accession, nor for several of the following years. The Garland Committee on Overseas Representation recommended in 1977, for example, that the Department of Education position on the Australian delegation to the OECD be abolished (Australia, 1977: 8). The Committee considered Australia should be represented at Education Committee meetings either by Education officers sent direct from Australia or by DFA officers at the post (Australia, 1977: 49). On the basis of this Report, and the report of an IDC, Cabinet then decided (Decision No. 3873 (Ad Hoc)) that one position should cover all of Science, Environment, Education and Manpower. The Delegation at that time contained the representatives from Treasury, Foreign Affairs, Trade, and two officers covering Science/Environment and Education/Manpower and Social Affairs.

The decision was not well received, not least by the Ambassador, Mr F.P. Donovan, who cabled Canberra, stating that 'amalgamation has serious consequences for this Delegation in its task of representing Australia in an effective manner at the OECD'. He added it was 'not possible for one officer to provide an adequate standard of service to the four departments' (DSEWPC, 1976). The view in Paris was supported by R.B. Landsdown (Secretary, Department of Environment, Housing and Community Development) in a letter to Mr K.C.O. Shann (previously of the DFA, now the Chairman of the Public Service Board) on 26 September 1977 stating that 'This Department was not represented on the IDC nor were its views sought. We had no opportunity to comment on the IDC report nor on the draft Cabinet Submission.' The Ambassador further wrote to the Secretary, DFA on 5 December 1977 arguing that 'in a more fundamental sense the Delegation operates as an integrated team whose continued effective functioning overall would be prejudiced by the non-functioning of any of its parts'.

Eventually, in September 1980, subject to the views of Departmental Heads, the Public Service Board agreed conditionally to an additional position, subject to interdepartmental negotiation. Before any final agreement could be reached, however, the Fraser Government instituted a Review of Commonwealth Functions (by a committee known colloquially as the 'Razor Gang') in early 1981 (Australia, 1981). The Public Service Board also conducted a review of Australia's participation in international organisations, which included an examination of overseas posts including the OECD Delegation, and consideration of reinstating the Counsellor position lapsed.

Conditional approval for an additional Counsellor for Labour, Education and Social Affairs was to wait until November 1985 (NAA, 1982), but the interdepartmental rivalry over positions in the Delegation continued. The Secretary of the Department of Industry, Technology and Commerce made a bid for a counsellor position in the Delegation in 1987, having first made an approach to the Secretary of Foreign Affairs, Stuart Harris, in October 1985 while the latter was preparing a review of Australia's overseas representation. Writing to Ambassador McGoldrick on 10 February 1987, he argued that his Department now had the 'dominant interests in the affairs of the Science, Technology and Industry Directorate and that were the Government's interests in that Directorate to be brought together they would fully employ one member of the Delegation' (NAA, 1982b).

This attempt was met with a gentle rebuff by the Ambassador, no doubt having been sensitised to the matter by the Department of Housing, Aboriginal Affairs and Environment, which had found 'common cause' with the Department of Science in interdepartmental discussions in resisting the creation of a new DITAC-staffed post in the Paris mission. It was expected they would probably prevail in the short term, but (correctly) anticipated that the issue would surface again in a few months' time (NAA, 1982a).

By the 1980s, in addition to the Delegation, about 50 A-based officers participated in OECD meetings each year. Despite this, it was noted that Australia attended relatively fewer OECD meetings than any other member country of comparable size, and it was therefore considered to be essential that it make the very most of any opportunities to inject an Australian viewpoint and benefit from the meetings it did attend. To this end, it was recommended that consideration be given to increasing A-based visits (NAA, 1982a).

The patterns and problems of participation varied from committee to committee. For example, with the Committee on Fiscal Affairs, Australian representation (for which 65 half days were proposed for 1980) was mainly by the Permanent Delegation, because the distance from Australia, combined with the shortness of meetings generally mitigated against representation from Australia. Briefings were usually provided from Canberra and from the Australian representative at the Committee itself, and, for important sessions, from the Counsellor (Taxation) in London. Sometimes an Australian official was unable to attend less important meetings because of other commitments (NAA, 1982a).

With Energy, Australia only joined the OECD's International Energy Agency (IEA) in 1979, nearly five years after its establishment, and had a number of concerns in relation to the late release of Secretariat papers, a frequent complaint in many areas, and one that was exacerbated by the factor of distance. This allowed little time for coordination of Australian policies and made prior consultation with other IEA members 'difficult and sometimes impossible'. This had been improved by the introduction of a facsimile system, but only with the introduction of OLIS and email was Australia's disadvantage largely overcome (see below).

Guidance for Engagement

From the beginning of 1999 guidelines prepared by the Delegation were provided to departments for officers participating in OECD meetings (DEWR, 1998). Similar documents were previously provided on delegates' arrival in Paris, but some subsidiary bodies met elsewhere, and it was decided they should be used for all OECD meetings, wherever located. It was stressed that it was important that the guidelines were observed to ensure there was a consistent Australian approach at all meetings. The Ambassador also asked that departments inform the Delegation, through their designated departmental representative, when Australian-based officers attended OECD meetings to ensure they were briefed appropriately on relevant matters and on overall issues such the OECD Budget, on which Australia was seeking restraint, loosening somewhat DFAT's earlier, more detailed, coordinating role.

On matters such as the OECD's reform, restructuring and budget cuts the *Guidance* stated that 'a number of "systemic" questions need to be resolved if its future health and relevance are to be assured'. It briefed delegates on membership, reform of structure and working methods, and also (probably reflecting Treasury and DFAT views) set out Australia's problems with Secretary-General Johnston:

> In recent years, Johnston has argued that OECD's role is to help its members to strike a 'balance' between 'economic growth, social cohesion and good governance': this 'triangular paradigm', which posits (inappropriate) trade-offs between growth and social/political outcomes, has been criticised by Australia and others. Australia's consistent position has been that the OECD's mission is set out in its founding Convention, which emphasises the Organisation's core economic, structural and trade policy-development roles. (DEWR, 1998)

Another sensitive issue for Australia was 'Johnston's keenness to open the OECD to more non-governmental organisations, something to which Australia and others have adopted a cautious approach' (DEWR, 1998). Australian officials sought and received input from NGOs in Canberra and brought their views to Paris incorporated into positions on the issues. At the OECD, however, the NGOs making input were overwhelmingly European and North American in origin. The participation of environment NGOs, for example, was coordinated by the European Environment Agency. The OECD sought greater engagement with civil society primarily after the failed Multilateral Agreement on Investment (MAI) negotiation, where the Internet-based NGO campaign effectively provided cover, if unintended, for France's opposition, and there was therefore concern about any European bias in activism.

The *Guidance* set out Australia's interests and objectives including a number of key objectives for the strategic management of the Organisation – particularly budget and reform issues, membership, and relations with non-member countries, suggesting that Australian officials might wish to draw, as appropriate, on guidance provided in the document in discussions in committees and subsidiary bodies. On the Budget and Prioritisation the *Guidance for Delegates* emphasised: Australian support for 'value for money'; codification of committee priorities; fully costing new work and (ideally) ensuring it was funded by offsetting savings elsewhere in the work programme; and addressing inefficiencies in committee procedures, including through the development of an 'evaluation culture'. It noted that support for this position could be expected from the United States, United Kingdom, Canada, New Zealand, Sweden and, in recent years, Japan, Mexico and Korea.

On Decision Making, it noted support for adoption (for a trial period) of a qualified 'double majority' voting mechanism along the lines proposed by the Canadian Ambassador (in one version, 80 per cent of membership representing 80 per cent of budgetary contributions). The *Guidance* suggested officials support any moves by chairs to adopt more flexible processes. It emphasised the need for and search for 'Horizontal Policy Coherence', across the relevant range of OECD activities and directorates, in part to reduce the 'silo' mentality of directorates (DEWR, 1998).

On Voluntary Contributions, it noted that Australia, the US and UK in particular had questioned whether 'these funds are distorting the OECD's efforts by financing low priority work'. It asked that Delegates:

> [d]iscourage the Secretariat from soliciting voluntary contributions for low priority or marginal work. Because donors are not charged for all costs associated with their grants, this source of funds can 'crowd out' other committee priorities/activities. (DEWR, 1998)

This did not prevent Australia from employing voluntary contributions itself, for example to support its growing work on health (see Chapter 12 this volume).

On OECD Council Acts the *Guidance* asked delegates to flag clearly any proposals for Council Acts, Recommendations or Guidelines in their reporting to ensure whole-of-government responses (which sometimes required consultations with states and territories). For relations with non-member economies (including observerships of committees and subsidiary bodies), the *Guidance* stated:

> The OECD has been slow to re-orient its outreach efforts towards the emerging economies of Asia and Latin America, mainly due to resistance by some European members who see OECD outreach as an adjunct to bilateral aid efforts or a precursor to OECD membership (e.g. Nordic attitude to Baltic outreach). Observership of OECD committees is seen in a similar light. Australia has been the foremost advocate of strict application of the technical criteria for granting observership – *major player* in the relevant field and evidence of *mutual benefit*. (DEWR, 1998)

The document also asked delegates to ensure good links with the Permanent Delegation by maintaining open lines of communication, and by providing advance notice of forthcoming visits and reporting (preferably by cable) on the outcomes of meetings in a timely manner.

A June 2001 revision to the *Guidance* added a section on 'Australians in the OECD Secretariat' (DEWR, 1998). It noted there were at this time 60 Australians in the Secretariat, which at 4.23 per cent of total staff in 1999 was well above its *pro rata* level, with whom the Delegation maintained regular contact, as did Australia-based staff. There were, however, no Australians in the top three levels of the organisation. It stated that Australia supported quality applicants, but that appointments were the prerogative of the Secretary-General. It also stated that delegates were encouraged to have contact with Australians in the Secretariat, 'within the constraints on the OECD staff in relation to their responsibilities to the OECD'. The revision to the *Guidance* also drew the attention of agencies to the pool of casual consultants maintained by the Delegation, whose engagement could be especially useful for those departments and agencies without representation in the Delegation, an option 'shown to be very cost effective relative to (always) sending an officer from Australia'.

A footnote on Australian participation in a cable from the Head of Mission (HOM) in January 2002 provided a snapshot of Australian engagement with the OECD at that time. Australia provided 1.8 per cent of the Part I budget, which was the 11th largest of all members. In terms of voluntary contributions, Australia was 16th largest in making Part II contributions, with voluntary contributions by eleven Commonwealth departments and two state or territory governments, having grown by 93 per cent between 1994–95 and 1999–2000 (DEWR, 2001b). Ironically, this was a period in which the Australian delegation was pushing hard for the accelerating use of voluntary contributions to be reduced or constrained.

The Australian Mission at this time consisted of three A-based staff from DFAT, one each from the Department of Agriculture, Fisheries, and Forestry, AUSAID, Department of Education, Science and Training

(DEST)/Department of Employment and Workplace Relations (DEWR), Department of Family and Community Services, Department of Industry, Technology and Resources (DITR), and Treasury. Health was sometimes represented by a Geneva-based officer, and a pool of qualified spouses was also drawn upon to represent agencies' interests. Australia had more Minister-Counsellors (SES Officers) than any other delegation, largely to compensate for the difficulty and cost of providing Australia-based representation at OECD meetings. The Permanent Delegation also occasionally covered work of interest to the Department of Environment and Heritage, Attorney-General's, the Department of Finance and Administration, and Prime Minister and Cabinet. Over 230 officials from Australia, for example, visited Paris to attend OECD meetings in 2001.

Ambassadors, Continuity and Coordination

Australia-based staff are generally posted to the Delegation for three years. Most in interview expressed an awareness of the limitations of this rather short period, considering their effectiveness to be limited for the first several months while familiarising themselves with their roles and the OECD, and then a little unsettled in the final months of the posting. The orientation period is exacerbated by a prohibition of any overlap in post with their predecessor, so the hand-over is rather discontinuous. Most reported that they were at peak effectiveness for somewhat less than the three years. There are advantages in both cost and continuity in employing locally-engaged staff, often Australians working in Paris or accompanying their partners, and their number has slowly increased over time.

Participation in meetings is necessarily strategic, with limited time available given the sheer number of meetings that might possibly be attended, in addition to reading and researching the vast amount of printed material emanating from various work programmes and the additional time required for liaison with Canberra, and occasionally with other Australian missions. Then there is the considerable impact in assisting Australian visitors; visits by Ministers can be particularly demanding, though they rarely amount to more than three or four per annum. The Delegation must support Ministers attending the various committee meetings at Ministerial Level. During Ambassador Forsyth's term, for example, twelve Ministers came through in three years.

The Delegation is relatively large when compared with that of most other members, but this is of necessity, because of the difficulty in achieving participation in Committees and subsidiary bodies by staff flying in from Australia, which is easier for full committee meetings, but is often not cost-effective for shorter meetings of subsidiary bodies.

Smaller European members make do with delegations that are more modest in both size and accommodation. Norway, for example, rents modest offices in the OECD's Franqueville Building, and the Netherlands in relatively small quarters nearby. But they, like all European members, can fly in delegates from national capitals quite rapidly, or even after a short train ride of a few hours. Most delegations tend to be proportionate to distance from Paris, although New Zealand's is much more modest than Australia's, at the cost of lower engagement and concomitantly less influence, somewhat offset by working closely with the Australian Delegation on many issues.

Members of the Delegation are required to be flexible, and sometimes to attend meetings at short notice. And their activities have not always been limited to representing Australia, sometimes bringing an Antipodean sense of practicality to the rather internecine politics of Europe, such as the time a member of the Delegation provided French–English translation, because translation was demanded by the French representative in a working group (in accordance with the OECD commitment to bilingualism — and French insistence on the use of their language). The French representative could speak and understand English, but French linguistic pride resulted in the somewhat farcical situation where the Australian member provided a rather poor translation so that French honour was satisfied and the meeting could proceed.

The role of the Ambassador is important. Coordination of participating departments is addressed to a very limited extent by an Interdepartmental Committee on OECD Issues in Canberra which typically meets only once per annum, but DFAT has formal responsibility for coordination, although much is devolved to the Permanent Representative and the Delegation. One Minister-Counsellor remarked that there was, within the Delegation, much more of a whole-of-government approach than in Australia, simply because co-location meant there were closer personal links than in Canberra.

The Agenda for a meeting of the Interdepartmental Committee on OECD Issues held at DFAT on 20 April 2007, for example, had as an attachment a copy of a letter to Veronique Ingram as she began her appointment as Ambassador to the OECD, from Alexander Downer, Minister of Foreign Affairs, and Mark Vaile, Minister for Trade (DEWR, 2006), setting out the main priorities the government wished her to pursue during her assignment. The letter indicates not just the priorities for the government in the OECD, but also some details of the way in which the participation was managed, including, for example, an integration for logistics purposes between the OECD Delegation and the bilateral mission to France, with whom it was co-located: it noted that

'You … will need to cooperate closely with the Australian Embassy for support services.'

The brief for the Ambassador gave a clear statement of what the government wanted from OECD membership at that time (DEWR, 2006):

> Your principal objective will be to ensure that the OECD continues to deliver timely and high quality analysis and policy advice, consistent with Australian priorities and interests. The OECD's great value to Australia is its capacity for leading edge comparative analysis and policy evaluation of the major economic and trade issues facing the Government.

The ministers noted Ingram would be familiar from her career in Treasury with issues of trade liberalisation, structural economic reform, and macroeconomic policy but emphasised the importance of the OECD's involvement in issues such as agriculture, science and technology, health and ageing, education, environment and development assistance, and that she should ensure these matters were given appropriate attention. They also emphasised the 'need to encourage a whole of government approach to the work of the delegation and to official representation from Australia at OECD meetings'. Also stressed were the need to help ensure efficient resource use by the Secretariat, and, as with other international organisations, 'we expect budget discipline and prioritisation in the OECD's work; greater effectiveness in its decision-making processes; attention to the Asia-Pacific region; and a realistic approach to the admission of new members' (DEWR, 2006). A key policy objective was that of attempting to ensure the OECD work programme remained focused on supporting the successful completion of the WTO's Doha Round of negotiations.

Each Ambassador brings their own work style to the position, including how they familiarise themselves with the role. Ambassador Christopher Langman, for example, read approximately the previous 12 months of Ambassador Ingram's cables before taking up his new position. Being from DFAT, he knew that DFAT had limited capacity to receive and make sense of extensive cables, so he reported more extensively only on an as needed basis, particularly during the 2008 financial crisis, and sought instructions only when he thought he needed to.

A rather unusual appointment as Ambassador and Permanent Representative was made in 2011, when it was Treasury's 'turn' for the appointment, but an appointment was made from outside either Treasury or DFAT. The Gillard government, through Foreign Minister Kevin Rudd, appointed Christopher Barrett who took up his post on 1 August 2011.

Barrett was not a Treasury officer, but rather had served as Chief of Staff to Treasurer Wayne Swan from 2007 to 2010, and as a senior adviser to then Opposition Leader Kim Beazley from 1996 to 2002, his only prior public service having been at the state level, in the Victorian Department of Premier and Cabinet from 2003 to 2007. In January 2015, following the end of his posting, he was appointed as Executive Director, Finance and Economics, at the European Climate Foundation, meaning that he did not bring his OECD expertise and experience back into Treasury. He was succeeded by Brian Pontifex, former Chief of Staff to Western Australia Liberal Premier Colin Barnett, who had had experience working at the OECD. These appointments could be seen as an indication of the downgrading of the importance of the OECD in the eyes of both ALP and Coalition governments – but equally could be a sign that Australia is following the US example of making political appointments to more ambassadorial posts and ministers wish for ambassadors who are trusted and close to them. Career officers are not always the best advocates for the OECD, and Barrett, for example, was Chair of Executive Committee, exemplifying a higher level of engagement. These appointments can be seen as reflecting an elevation of the 'economic diplomacy' agenda by governments.

MINISTERIAL PARTICIPATION

When incoming Ambassador Fred Argy presented his credentials to Secretary-General van Lennep in September 1983, van Lennep expressed a wish that more Australians would come to work for the OECD, but he also expressed disappointment that only one Australian Minister had attended the last MCM, whereas other members were represented by both their Foreign Ministers and Ministers of Finance, and at times even their Trade Ministers. He also regretted Australia's poor attendance at the Executive Committee in Special Session, which, he said, 'provided a unique opportunity for senior Australian officials to tick-tack with the counterparts in other countries' (NAA, 1982).

Nevertheless, Australia persisted with its low valuation of the ECSS, with a 2004 Policy Planning Paper stating:

> We have made judgments about the relative value, and opportunity cost, of greater engagement in the OECD. For the past three years, for instance, we have not sent A-based representation to a single ECSS. That decision was the right one. (DFAT, 2004)

It has also persisted with the practice (apparent in van Lennep's statement) of sending only one minister to the MCM, typically, alternating for many years between the Treasurer and the Trade Minister, although Foreign Minister Bill Hayden attended the MCM in 1987, after Treasurer Paul Keating had attended in both 1985 and 1986. In recent years, it has been the Trade Minister who attends.

Representation at the MCM has not usually been controversial, but there was some jockeying for a position at the MCM held on 14–16 May 2001 (DFAT, 2001). Trade Minister Mark Vaile was to attend the MCM, and Energy Minister Nick Minchin asked Vaile to represent him at the IEA Ministerial which was to precede the MCM. Senator Robert Hill, the Environment Minister, was also to attend a Meeting of the Environment Committee at Ministerial Level just prior to the MCM and sought also to attend the MCM, at which climate change was to be discussed. Hill wanted to be the lead speaker on climate change, but this had to be cleared by DFAT and ultimately (after the Department of Prime Minster and Cabinet insisted the practice of one minister only be adhered to), only Vaile was approved for attendance at the MCM, probably in part because Hill was more supportive of action on climate change than either Minchin or Vaile, and the DFAT position was that it was hopeful that climate change could be 'contained at lunch' rather than spending five hours on 'sustainable development'. Vaile's travel was approved, at a cost of $50,000, and Hill was denied approval for travel on 27 April, but persisted (unsuccessfully) with his request to travel (as late as 30 April).

While Australian policy on ministerial participation has been relatively constant for 30 years, such engagement by other OECD members has declined to match that of Australia, which has been somewhat sceptical of some of the moves to reinvigorate the MCM, especially by taking on briefs from the G7/G8. It was noted in 2003 that attendance by Finance Ministers had been somewhat weak in recent years, and the MCM was consistently failing to attract finance or economic ministers from G7 members (except Japan). Attendance by trade ministers had been strong and the MCM seemed to have cemented its place in the annual round of trade ministers meetings. Secretary-General Johnston was keen that links with G7/G8 might be strengthened by holding the MCM immediately after the G7/G8 summit to take up some G8 mandates (OECD, 2003). Australia was less enthusiastic at the prospect of the Organisation pursuing the agenda of the G8, and had a difficulty with the proposed date as it would clash with the introduction of its Budget (DFAT, 2001a). For example, Australia was concerned to ensure that the OECD's work on food safety, referred from the G8 after an impasse there between the

US and the EU, was consistent with the OECD's comparative advantage and complemented the work of the FAO and WHO.

Johnston played an advocacy role for OECD on food safety issues provoking some Australian concern over the tendency to have the OECD undertake G8 commissions. On the one hand, this presented a chance to influence G8 positions, but was seen as carrying with it a danger of a loss of control to G8 on issues like food safety (DFAT, 2001b). Australia was supportive of reappointing Johnston for a second term, despite him being slower to reform the OECD than it would prefer, perhaps with an eye on European membership, and his enthusiasm for the food safety agenda was seemingly the reason why Agriculture, Fisheries and Forestry Australia (AFFA) was the only Australian agency to express opposition to his reappointment in late 2000. Australian thinking, captured in a Briefing Note dated 12 January 2001, was sceptical of the MCM taking on such mandates which might lead to a growing number of regulatory or voluntary instruments (DFAT, 2001c).

Just as the ambassadorship rotates between Treasury and DFAT, Australian attendance at Ministerial Council Meetings once alternated between the Trade Minister and the Treasurer, though the former now attends because the MCM often clashes with the bringing down of the Budget. This arrangement for Ambassadorial appointments is unusual among OECD members, as most are represented by Foreign Affairs Ministries or Departments of State, not Treasuries.

It is worth noting that Australia has taken its turn in chairing the MCM in 1977, 1993 and 2001, for example. Chairing the MCM provides some, if limited opportunity to play a slightly greater role in influencing the shape of the agenda and future work programme draft communiqué. Various Secretaries-General have visited Australia. Secretary-General Jean-Claude Paye made a visit to Australia in 1985 and Donald Johnston visited in 1978 and in 2002, and Angel Gurría twice in 2014, for the G20 Finance Ministers summit and the G20 Leaders' Summit.

COMMUNICATIONS

The OECD produces large numbers of documents, making rapid communications between the Delegation and Canberra important. Prior to the introduction of the OECD On-Line Information System (OLIS), documents were routinely duplicated in Paris and sent by air by diplomatic bag. Documents specifically requested or thought to be required urgently were faxed to departments and agencies in Australia at an annual cost in excess of $200,000. The introduction of the OLIS in 1991, perhaps the first such system for any international organisation, assisted Australia's engagement by making documents available electronically and immediately. (The OECD was also developing a system called COMNET to allow on-line conferencing.)

When OLIS was introduced, DFAT agreed to supply OLIS to departments via a system called Keylink on a cost recovery basis, with the marginal cost of 0.92c/line being increased to 1.2c/line to cover fixed costs. It seemed some agencies baulked at the cost, and some clients were receiving documents through channels other than Keylink. It was likely that some departments may have been creating and taking part in a 'back door' network (Treasury, 1985).

Australia quickly became the highest user of OLIS by 1994, but it took some time to bed down. When participating departments were asked if arrangements were working satisfactorily, they reported the system was not meeting expectations, but only four rated it as unsatisfactory (DFAT, 1995). To support its use, an Australian-based OLIS support consultancy was established in 1994 at DFAT's initiative. In terms of total bytes used on OLIS between 1 January 1994 and 30 August 1994 the relative shares were: DFAT 17.5 per cent; DPIE 15.4 per cent; DIST 12 per cent; DEST 6.8 per cent; Treasury 6.4 per cent; Department of Prime Minister and Cabinet (PM&C) 4 per cent; and the Delegation 7.3 per cent (DEWR, 2006).

By 1996 there were a large number of faxes being used, email was making inroads, and by September OLIS I was being replaced by OLIS II. A Government Electronic Mail Users Group (GEMUG) operated from 1992 to deal with the introduction of email and the issues that arose therefrom, and an OLIS II Users Group was established in DFAT. OLIS II had 1800 active users, with 60 new applications being received each month. Two OECD information technology staff visited Australia in June 1997 to conduct an OLIS workshop for 51 OLIS users, representing 30 government agencies at a cost of $250 per agency. There remained problems of communication beyond DFAT to other agencies involved, however. For example, DEST was seeking a new system to be able to receive low classification cables from DFAT, as it had to download OLIS documents, print and then circulate them in a purely manual system (DEWR, 2006).

Difficulties persisted. In the DEST files, handwritten notes on the Agenda for a meeting of the Inter-Departmental Committee on OECD in 2007 (DEWR, 2006) show concerns over the need for OLIS training, and a desire for access to the Secure Australian Telecommunications and Information Network (SATIN), to assist in the distribution of cables. Even at the time of writing, the more secure SATIN High is not available on the desks of officers in key agencies such as Treasury, meaning they have to access it in a separate secure communications room, so communication is not as smooth as in DFAT, where SATIN is essentially on every desk.

Changes were required by the use of the new means of communication. For example, previously DFAT cables were received as hard copy in the International Unit in DEST and distributed by photocopying, hand labelling and delivery by hand or the internal mail (DEWR, 1993). A cable from the Delegation to Canberra captured some irony in the context of the changing nature of communications:

> Our OLIS e-mail to the Secretariat, despatched some days ago, apparently disappeared into an electronic Bermuda Triangle somewhere between the 15th and 16th Arrondissements. However, following up by telephone, we were assured by Daniel that there would be no problem in providing us with the information you requested on the Australian break-down for access to documents on the 'ultra secure' list and details re access rights for universities. (DEWR, 2006)

It was not clear how access to documents on the 'ultra-secure' list would function. Apparently, those members not participating in the relevant group would not have access to those documents, and the working party in question was not listed because its documents were not put on OLIS in the first place. (Australia was interested in universal access rights that the US and some other OECD countries enjoyed.) The transition gave rise to some problems. For example, a Ministerial Communique in February 1996 was on OLIS I, but not immediately on the upgraded OLIS II, so the document had to be faxed. One officer concerned over the late appearance of the document on OLIS II sent a hand-written fax to the OLIS Help Desk: 'As I am at present unfamiliar with the e-mail system, I would be grateful for either a faxed reply or a faxed *and* e-mailed reply' (DEWR, 1996).

The Delegation sent fortnightly cables on 'Mission Commitments' listing the names of the person covering meetings, and flagged forthcoming publications in cables. While facsimile brought the rapid transmission for longer documents not previously possible with cables and the diplomatic bag, it brought new risks, because it allowed more direct communication than cables between agencies, rather than going through DFAT and being routinely copied to all interested missions. Faxes were also not automatically backed up and archived, making both whole-of-government consideration and coordination by DFAT more difficult.

This problem was addressed by a Minute from the Ambassador (Ed Visbord) to all Delegation staff in April 1989 specifying cables were to be used rather than faxes, especially because they were both quick and backed up. The range of available communication methods included cables, telememos, faxes, memos, minutes and letters, this last 'A fast disappearing species.' Visbord wrote that:

> [T]his Delegation represents the Australian Government in dealings with the OECD and it is appropriate that communications from the Delegation should normally flow through a universal channel where all interested departments in Canberra can participate in the benefits of our activities … I should add that I expect to receive copies of all official communications from or to this Delegation whatever form they take. As far as I am concerned, that is an absolute rule. (DSEWPC, 1989)

The mid-1990s were a period of some flux in communications, and there were problems aplenty as the facsimile was rapidly supplanted by emails. The transition was not always smooth, as some communications between the Delegation and DEETYA reveal. A fax from Annette Fraser in Canberra to Danielle Hoyling-Richard (Delegation) on 5 November 1996, for example, read: 'I have sent a couple of e-mail messages that do not look as if they have been read. Did you receive the attached one last week and did you respond? I have not received a reply' (DEWR, 1996a). The reply came back on 5 November: 'We continue to have problems sending e-mails to you. They keep bouncing back' (DEWR, 1996b). Three days later the Delegation emailed that 'we received a message from Mr Ruby's office advising us that the IT system in DEETYA [Canberra] is having problems in sending and receiving messages from overseas (not only Paris)' (DEWR, 1996c).

It must have seemed at times that facsimile, email and OLIS were combining in a perfect storm of 'dysfunctionality', exemplified by an email from Canberra to the Delegation the on 12 November on the subject 'OLIS strikes again':

> I have been persisting and getting some docs off OLIS. One doc came to us last week … off the fax containing only 38 pages (we were none the wiser and sent it out as was). Today through the bag the same doc arrived but this time containing 154 pages and missing page 63. I downloaded page 63 later on and forwarded new amount of pages to the area concerned, with apologies.
>
> I do hope OLIS gets better soon. (DEWR, 1996e)

Paris was apologetic, also hoping for improvement in OLIS. But even the sending of email attachments was problematic: 'Thank you for trying to send us the latest DEETYA organisation charts. Unfortunately, they are in MIME format which we are unable to decipher this end' (DEWR, 1996f).

A similar problem arose when the Delegation made an urgent request for copies of the Explanatory Memo and Second Reading Speech for the *Workplace Relations Bill 1996*, following a request from the Secretariat:

> Annette has printed off the Internet the Explanatory Memorandum, the second and third readings, the most frequently asked questions and answers, the Bill itself and other bits and pieces. All together, the pile of paper is approximately 15–16cm thick. We will be sending them by a diplomatic bag because even though you may have access to the Internet, you may not be able to download them, as Annette tells me, you need an Acrobat reader. (DEWR. 1996g)

Canberra then faxed copies of the departmental website on the Act. On 7 December it was reported that there was a problem with the fax line the previous day and the Delegation received no faxes from Australia. Even the diplomatic bag was not immune from problems, with the Delegation emailing Canberra on 11 December that while they had received envelopes 3 and 4 in the previous day's bag, 'One diplomatic bag is still missing so I guess the other two envelopes must be in that one' (DEWR, 1996h). Envelope 2 arrived by 14 December and it was hoped the outstanding Envelope 1 would be in the following week's OECD diplomatic bag.

Internal communication and coordination, even when the technology was functional, were problematic. DEETYA, for example, received cables addressed to Executive Officers within the relevant Division(s) who customarily replied to the Counsellor's cables directly, either by a facsimile or by email. In most cases, its International Division was not informed of replies sent to the Assistant Secretary nor of their content, which created confusion and, in some instances, duplication. In addition, individual officers and the Counsellor had been exchanging facsimile and email messages about various portfolio activities without notifying International Division, which became aware of these exchanges only if the Counsellor asked for urgent follow-up and no response had been received. International Division was unable to resolve the issue immediately if, for example, the action officer was away on leave (DEWR, 1996i).

Often the late arrival of key documents would hinder preparation of an Australian position paper to guide participants at OECD committee meetings. The following fax from Treasury in 1989 is not atypical:

> We have not received a copy of the above note by the Secretariat on 'Revision of the 1977 Model Convention'. As the note is listed for discussion at the next WP1 meeting, we would appreciate your sending us a copy of the note as soon as possible, so that any necessary briefing can be prepared. (NAA, 1985)

The coordination task within participating agencies was also a challenge, particularly Treasury, with its very extensive involvement in a wide range of committees (NAA, 1985a).

Eventually, email and cable systems and protocols were developed that ensured communication was direct and timely and appropriate divisions of agencies were copied in according to subject matter. Introduction of a secure communications system, SATIN, in 2000 provided a better basis for communication. SATIN has 145 points of access with 6000 users globally, and is used by over 40 agencies. It supports transmission and exchange of data from unclassified to top secret, for national security arrangements, general diplomatic business, international aspects of major government projects, and consular, passport and visa functions. It has low and high security networks – the 'Satin Low' business network and the 'Satin High' diplomatic communications network – and a 'Satin Voice' telephony network and a video conferencing network.

But the presence of SATIN does not guarantee perfect communication. For example, Treasury, at the time of writing, did not have Satin High on the desk of each officer, as does DFAT, and officers were required to go to a secure area to use it, requiring proactivity on the part of Treasury officers that cannot be taken for granted. In addition, one ambassador suggested that, excluding DFAT, officers participating in the OECD were not always diligent in writing cables summarising meetings they attended because they were not trained to do so habitually.

At the time of writing, communication systems are much improved, with both emails and cables being copied to those likely to need to know, although delivery does not ensure that communications are read. And from about 2003, the style of cables reflected the fact that Telex and its requirement for writing in capitals only (like the telegram) was long gone, and some cables began to appear in capitals and lower case, rather than in the capitals to which diplomats had no doubt become accustomed.

FINANCE

While the DFAT generally met travel costs of attendees immediately after accession (NAA, 1973), departments now meet their own costs of attendance and any Voluntary Contributions, while DFAT meets the Part I contributions plus the cost of the IEA and Nuclear Energy Agency (NEA) – over $7m in 2005 (DSEWPC, 2005). DFAT plays a coordinating role, however, in making sure participating agencies meet their Part II contributions when due, reminding them if they are overdue (as has sometimes happened).

In 1996 the US, United Kingdom and Australia pushed successfully for an outcomes-based budget system consistent with domestic reforms they had undertaken, and cuts of 10 per cent to the budget over three years. This placed the OECD ahead of most international organisations, except perhaps the World Bank, in planning for such cuts. The impact of these cuts was defused, however, because nothing was done to restrict members who wished to make voluntary contributions and the mutual agreement rule meant it proved difficult to kill off some programmes, as they required only one supporter on Council to live on long after most had considered them to be either without value or of low priority. This has not meant that Australia has not used voluntary contributions: it was, for example, one of the top two contributors to the Health Project in the early 2000s.

As the costs of overheads were often poorly provided for in those programmes funded by VCs, they were in effect subsidised from the Part I budget. Also, as Part II funds could be carried forward to future years, this gave the Secretariat the opportunity to shift costs to Part I functions and find Part II funds to continue activities that many on Council wished to terminate. This initially partly diminished the effect of the planned budget cuts, especially when combined with the effective veto of a single member and the ability of one or a few members to establish or continue a Part II activity, subject to approval by Council.

The level of financial commitment entailed in Australia's participation in the OECD, and the commitment of specific agencies to activities funded through Part II of the Budget were set out in a cable in May 2002 (DEWR, 2001). Australia's share of the 2015 OECD budget of €363 million was 3.28 per cent, or €11,906,400.

Administrative rearrangements in Canberra, of course, have required adjustments in the Paris Delegation, including adjustments to budgetary arrangements. For example, when the Department of Employment, Workplace Relations and Small Business was established in November 2001 by removing those functions from DEETYA to form DETYA, the budgetary allocation for the shared Counsellor – Education and Employment (a sum of $192,519) had subsequently to be transferred back to DETYA which was bearing the responsibility for the position (DEWR, 2001a).

Table 4.1 Australia's Budget Payments to OECD – 2002

OECD Budget	Australian Agency	OECD Programme	Euros
Part I			
	DFAT	General Expenditure	2,460,000
		Capital Expenditure	32,650
		Site Project	479,084
		Pension Fiscal Adjustment Scheme	29,394
		Annex Budget: Pension Scheme	197,298
		Pension Reserve Fund	510,469
Part II			
	DFAT	Control of Chemicals	29,786
		IEA	346,078
		NEA	164,795
	Attorney-General	FATF on Money Laundering	22,882
	DEST	CERI	53,012
		Global Science Forum	8,988
	DAFF	Codes and Systems/SEEDS	5,903
	DOTRS	Road Research	15,349
	DITR	Steel Committee	11,920
		Cooperative Action Program on Local Economic and Employment Development (LEED)	30,088
	DHA	Health Project (estimated)	300,000
	Total Euros		4,697,696

CONCLUSION

Australia's participation in the OECD has been made difficult by both distance and the complex nature of the organisation. It has been mindful of the cost of engagement and the need to remain focused and, in addition, to try to keep the OECD focused so that the cost effectiveness of participation has been maximised. The challenges provided by the OECD have included the initial need to manage and resolve the initial competition for lead department status, resolved by a compromise among

Foreign Affairs, Trade and Treasury (and consolidated further by the creation of DFAT in 1987). In addition, an ongoing challenge has been the need to coordinate the involvement of a larger number of participating agencies than is to be found in Australia's engagement with any other international organisation of which it is a member.

BIBLIOGRAPHY

Australia 1977. Parliament of the Commonwealth of Australia, House of Representatives Standing Committee on Expenditure, *Australia's Overseas Representation* (Garland Report) Report May 1977, Parliamentary Paper No. 100/1977.

Australia 1981. Ministerial Statement, *Review of Commonwealth Functions*, Canberra: AGPS.

DEWR 1984. Letter, Ian Castles, Sec Department of Finance, to Dr N. Fisher, Acting Secretary, Department of Education, 6 November 1985, Government Relations – Committees 1358 – IRB – Organisation for Economic Co-operation and Development (OECD) Review of Need For Counsellor Education and Social A, File C1984/56425.

DEWR 1993. Email to Dennis Bowler, Manager, OA Implementation Team, from Alison Russell French, Director, International Unit, DEST, 8 December 1993. Email Requirements, Government Relations – Committees 1358 – EPSD – PCS – Industrial Policy in Organisation for Economic Co-operation and Development (OECD) Countries – Annual Review 1992, File C1993/06657.

DEWR 1996. Cable 13 Auhust 1996 Paris to CBR OLIS II: Access Rights for Australian Users, File NO96/18936 OECD (OECD) Liaison with Australian Delegation – 1996.

DEWR 1996a. Fax Don Gray to OLIS Help Desk 21 November 1996, File NO96/18936 OECD (OECD) Liaison with Australian Delegation – 1996.

DEWR 1996b. Fax Annette Fraser DEETYA to Danielle Hoyling-Richard (Delegation) 5 November 1996, File NO96/18936 OECD (OECD) Liaison with Australian Delegation – 1996.

DEWR 1996c. Fax Shelagh Whittleston, Delegation, to Annette Fraser DEETYA 5 November 1996, File NO96/18936 OECD (OECD) Liaison with Australian Delegation – 1996.

DEWR 1996d. Danielle Hoyling-Richard to Annette Fraser email 8 November 1996, File NO96/18936 OECD (OECD) Liaison with Australian Delegation – 1996.

DEWR 1996e. Annette Fraser to Danielle Hoyling-Richard cc. Shelagh Whittleston, 12 November 1996, File NO96/18936 OECD (OECD) Liaison with Australian Delegation – 1996.

DEWR 1996f. Email, Danielle Hoyling-Richard to Annette Fraser, 26 November 1996, File NO96/18936 OECD (OECD) Liaison with Australian Delegation – 1996.

DEWR 1996g. Fax Gordana Burtmanis DEETYA to Danielle Hoyling-Richard, 4 December 1996, New Industrial Relations Legislation, File NO96/18936 OECD (OECD) Liaison with Australian Delegation – 1996.
DEWR 1996h. Email Danielle Hoyling-Richard to Gordana Burtmanis, 11 December 1996, ET01/19305 OECD (OECD) – Interaction.
DEWR 1996i. Minute Gordana Burtmanis FAS International Division 22 September 1997, Coordination of replies to Correspondence between the Department and Ms Shealgh Whittleston, Counsellor, Paris, File NO96/18936 OECD (OECD) Liaison with Australian Delegation – 1996.
DEWR 1998. 'Australian Delegation to the OECD. Background Information and Guidance For Australian-Based Officials Attending OECD Meetings', January 1999, File NO98/12816 Research and National Reporting (RNR) Section Involvement in Organisation for Economic Co-operation and Development (OECD) Indicators of Education Systems (INES) Network A – 1998.
DEWR 1999. 'Australian Delegation to the OECD. Background Information and Guidance For Australian-Based Officials Attending OECD Meetings. June 2001', File ET99/08976 OECD – Administration and Forthcoming Projects – 1999–2000.
DEWR 2001. Cable from Paris OECD to Canberra Call up from OECD for Australia annual contributions for 2002, 22 May 2002, File ET01/11368 Government Relations – Committees 1358 – Organisation for Economic Co-operation and Development (OECD) – Cables and Reports.
DEWR 2001a. Issues Relating Cost Sharing Between DETYA and DEWRSB for the Joint Paris Counsellor – Education and Employment, File ET01/16251 International Policy Branch.
DEWR 2001b. Cable, HOM, PARIS OECD, to CBR. OECD: An Overview and Assessment 7 January 2002, File ET01/11368 Government Relations – Committees 1358 – Organisation for Economic Co-operation and Development (OECD) – Cables and Reports.
DEWR 2006. ES06/04773 DEST Involvement in OECD Education – Non Specific Correspondence – 2006/2007.
DFAT 1995. OECD: Review of Australia's Interests, Discussion Paper: Membership, April 1995.
DFAT 2001. File 01/050418 Trade Policy – Conferences – OECD Ministerial Council Meeting (MCM) – PEU 01/03/01 to 30/04/01.
DFAT 2001a. File 01/050759 OECD EC 2001–02.
DFAT 2001b. File 01/050075 Secretariat – Secretary-General – Vacancies 30/11/2000 to 30/10/2002.
DFAT 2001c. File 02/020132 OECD Agriculture Committee 29/11/01–22/01/03.
DFAT 2004. 'Policy Planning Paper. Australia and the OECD: DFAT's Perspectives'.
DSEWPC 1976. Cable Paris OECD to Canberra 14 September 1978, File 76/1285 OECD ENV Committee 17th Session March 1976.
DSEWPC 1989. Minute to All Staff 17 April 1989 From Ed Visbord, Ambassador: On communications modalities (prepared by Mr R.J. McInnes, Dep Perm Rep), Organisation for Economic Co-operation and Development (OECD) – Environment Committee – 49th Session 12–14 December 1989, File 89/01022.

DSEWPC 1991. Environmental Planning Branch – Organisation for Economic Co-operation and Development (OECD) – Electronic Document Transfer – OLIS, File 91/08015.

DSEWPC 2005. Terry Grandy DFAT to DEH re OECD Budget Payments for 'Control of Chemicals Program', Email 7 November 2005, File 2005/06281 International Relations – Committees – Meeting Papers – Organisation for Economic Co-operation and Development (OECD) – Environment Policy Committee (EPOC) – 7 to 9 November 2005.

NAA 1971. 'OECD: Summary Record of Inter-Departmental Meeting held on 1 September, 1971', File A3753/14 71/282 Pt 1, Department of the Environment Aborigines and the Arts. OECD – Environment.

NAA 1973. Letter CRS Rodgers for the Sec DFAT to Sec D of Env and Cons 11 May 1973, File A3753/14 1972/246 PART 2, Department of Environment, Housing and Community Development, OECD – Environment Committee.

NAA 1974. 'Delegation to OECD: Annual Review for 1974. Australian Delegation to the Organisation for Economic Co-operation and Development. 1974 Review', File A3753/14 1972/246 PART 2, Department of Environment, Housing and Community Development, OECD – Environment Committee.

NAA 1982. Cable PAR to CBR 9 September 1983, File NAA A5343/18 82/309 Part 2, National & International Relations Section – OECD – Australian Representation.

NAA 1982a. 'Minute for the Acting Secretary by D.F. Gascoine FAS', 15 January 1987, File A5343/18 1982/309 Part 3, National and International Relations Section DHAE – OECD – Australian Representation.

NAA 1982b. Letter, Dr D.T. Charles, Secretary, Department of Industry, Technology and Commerce to HE Mr A.K. McGoldrick, AM 10 February 1987, File A5343/18 1982/309 Part 3, National and International Relations Section DHAE – OECD – Australian Representation.

NAA 1985. Treasury. J.P. Anderson, AS I&IT Branch, 7 February 1989 to A. Oster, Counsellor. Faxed: WP1 of the Committee on Fiscal Affairs: DAFFE/CFA/WP1/893, File A1985/219, IIT/INT: Organisation for Economic Co-operation and Development (OECD) – Committee On Fiscal Affairs (CFA) – Working Party No. 2 – Double Taxation.

NAA 1985a. Minute Paper. W. Stock Acting AS, Personal Taxation Branch to M.F. Shadwick, AS, International Economy Branch 13 December 1989. Distribution of oecd Documentation/Publications, File A85/201 Part 16, IIT/INT: Organisation for Economic Co-operation and Development (OECD) – Committee on Fiscal Affairs – Working Party Number 8 – Tax Avoidance and Evasion.

OECD 2003. Organisation of OECD Ministerial Meetings (note by S-G) 12 June 2003, CD C(2003)137.

Treasury 1985. Letter Jane Drake-Brockman, Ass Sec, Econ Orgs Br To GEMUG representatives, email, 15 April 1992, File A85/201 Part 16, IIT/INT: Organisation for Economic Co-operation and Development (OECD).

5. The Department of Foreign Affairs and Trade and the OECD

As with its predecessor the DEA, the Department of Foreign Affairs (DFA, now DFAT) had a major role in persuading the government to apply for membership of the OECD and, in addition, gained responsibility for Australian involvement in the DAC from 1966. On gaining OECD membership in 1971 the DFA's role focused largely on: (1) the continuation of its responsibility for DAC; (2) the establishment and operation of the coordinating machinery necessary for the involvement in the OECD of a growing number of Australian departments and agencies, several of which had only limited experience in international activities. In July 1987 the DFA's role in relation to the OECD grew significantly, with the merger of the DFA and the Department of Trade to form the Department of Foreign Affairs and Trade, bringing with it Trade's significant involvement with the OECD's trade work. It increased further in 1998 with the decision to move the Export Finance and Insurance Corporation (EFIC) to the DFAT portfolio. As the World Trade Organization (WTO) grew in significance in the later 1990s DFAT's involvement in the trade-related activities of the OECD has tended to be more variable, while that in the WTO has grown.

Hence, DFAT's role in relation to the OECD is an extensive one and is treated at some length in this chapter, as well as in Chapter 6, which focuses on its work in relation to trade in agriculture and in Chapter 7 in relation to the Development Assistance Committee (DAC). The aim of this chapter is two-fold: (1) to describe the competition for lead agency status in the years leading up to accession in 1971; and (2) provide an examination of its work related to export credit, including EFIC's role. At the time of writing day-to-day operating responsibility for the OECD is administered by the Trade Finance and OECD Section in DFAT's Trade and Economic Policy Division.

Most of the non-departmental agencies in the DFAT portfolio have relatively little direct involvement with the OECD, although several make regular use of its publications. The two exceptions are the EFIC and AusAID. The latter was absorbed back into the department in 2014, and is the subject of a detailed examination in Chapter 7. EFIC has a significant though varying degree of involvement in the trade-related, export credit work of the OECD and it is the focus of a section in this chapter. Its officials are often directly represented in the Export Credits Group (ECG) of the OECD, along with a representative from the Delegation and EFIC's work is guided by several OECD recommendations, notably the:

- OECD Arrangement on Officially Supported Export Credits;
- OECD Recommendation of the Council on Common Approaches for Officially Supported Export Credits and Environmental and Social Due Diligence;
- OECD Council Recommendation on Bribery and Officially Supported Export Credits;
- OECD Principles and Guidelines to Promote Sustainable Lending Practices in the Provision of Official Export Credits to Low-Income Countries; and
- OECD Guidelines for Multinational Enterprises.

THE COMPETITION FOR LEAD AGENCY STATUS

The concept of lead department is one of a range of instruments that are used in the effort to achieve effective coordination in government when two or more departments are involved. The gaining of lead department status bestows authority and responsibility upon the department in question, at least as regards the activities specified in their formal allocation to the department. It also bestows status upon a department, assigning it a 'higher' position in the informal hierarchy of department authority and prestige. Hence, it is not surprising that where it is likely that a department will be designated as the lead there is a degree of competition between likely candidates. The greater the authority and responsibility likely to be bestowed, the more intense that competition is likely to be, at least for departments keen to maintain or increase their status and authority. This is particularly the case where there have been previous disagreements as to which department should be allocated lead department status in relation to similar activities, as the gaining of that status can be seen as either reinforcing an existing status or, conversely, threatening that status where it is allocated to a competing department. In regard to the question of lead department for the OECD, the context at the end of the 1960s was one in which the DEA had been previously unsuccessful in gaining lead department status for several major international organisations, notably the UN's specialised agencies and, more recently, the Asian Development Bank.

Indeed, the DEA 'was not highly ranked in the informal Canberra public service pecking order until the 1970s' (Harris, 1999: 25). It had been established in 1935 and, while growing rapidly in the following years, its responsibilities in relation to the rapid post-1945 growth in the number of major international organisations had not grown, with the notable exception of the UN. In the 1940s, for example, responsibility for the new UN specialised agencies had been allocated to departments other than the DEA, being allocated to the department with existing, domestic and international responsibilities for the policy area in question. Responsibility, for example, for the IMF and the World Bank went to Treasury, for the WHO to the Department of Health, and for UNESCO, initially, to the Prime Minister's Department and to the Department of Education on a shared basis. The responsibility for the GATT, although not a UN specialised agency, went to the Department of Trade and Industry (DTI).

Hence, past precedents suggested that lead department status as regards the OECD was likely to be awarded to Treasury, given the OECD's primary focus on economic matters. Similarly, but to a lesser extent, given the OECD's work on trade, there was a possibility that the status would be awarded to the DTI, although its decade-long opposition to OECD membership made this only a slim chance. The DEA was also in the running, having been a major proponent of OECD membership with Treasury, and the fact that the bulk of pre-membership relations with the OECD had been conducted through its offices, notably the embassy in Paris.

However, Treasury had had over twenty years of experience as lead department in relation to the IMF and the World Bank and, from 1966, for the Asian Development Bank. Moreover, along with the DEA, it had been the major proponent of OECD membership since the early 1960s, submitting a series of joint Cabinet submissions with the DFA to that end. In addition, in his last year as Treasurer, 1969, as the final consideration of OECD membership commenced, William McMahon strongly asserted that the OECD was a Treasury matter and that the DEA should collaborate with Treasury as regards Australia's relations with the organisation, not vice versa (NAA, 1969a). Somewhat ironically, McMahon became the DEA's Minister in November 1969, shortly after asserting Treasury's major interest in the OECD, but, unsurprisingly, seems not to have continued his support for Treasury as lead agency in his new position.

It might have been that the rapid turnover of ministers that followed in the next two years somewhat impeded Treasury's chances of gaining lead department status. Leslie Bury, for example, was Treasurer from November 1969 to March 1971. When McMahon became Prime Minister in March 1971, he retained Bury as Treasurer, but only for twelve days, before moving him on to what was now the DFA, then sacking him altogether some four months later, in August. Bury was succeeded as Treasurer by 'Billy' Snedden, who also became Deputy Liberal Leader, but by then responsibility for the OECD had been allocated to the DFA.

What McMahon might not have been aware of in 1969 was that the then Treasury Secretary, Sir Roland Wilson, who retired in 1966, had in 1963 agreed that the Australian Ambassador in Paris, Sir Ronald Walker, a senior and very experienced DEA official, could head the delegation to the OECD should Australia gain membership, provided he was supported by 'top level men' from Treasury. He did, however, reserve the right to query whether Walker's successor in Paris would be fitted for the task of leadership (NAA, 1963a). Wilson was responding to an assertion by Sir Arthur Tange, DEA Secretary, that he would certainly regard the activities of an Australian delegation to the OECD as being part of the responsibilities of the Minister for External Affairs (NAA, 1963a). At this stage the DEA view, as expressed by Tange during the same meeting, was that there would be some advantage to a close association with the OECD, as either a full or an associate member. This was a more cautious view than that expressed by Wilson, who had called the meeting and was reported as being very keen to join and saying that Australia's chances of membership would be very much weakened if it did not join at the same time as Japan. He was reported as being 'keen for speedy action' and intending to approach the Prime Minister about it shortly after the meeting (NAA, 1963a).

While Wilson did not directly contest Tange's assertion that the OECD delegation should be the responsibility of the Minister for the DEA, his pointed claim that Walker should be supported by 'top level men' from Treasury and that he reserved the right to query the capacity of his successor as Ambassador, indicated that he was less than enthusiastic about Tange's claim. Moreover, it was Wilson and his Minister, Harold Holt, who seem to have taken the lead in developing in 1963 a draft Cabinet submission proposing OECD membership. Although the submission was unsuccessful it was agreed, in line with the views of Wilson and Holt, that Treasury could reopen the issue at a later date if it wished, with no mention of the DEA in that regard (NAA, 1963b). As Garfield Barwick the DEA Minister was overseas at the time the meeting took place there seems to have been no objection to Treasury's leadership on the matter expressed, at least publicly or for the record, at this time.

In January 1964 it was the DEA not Treasury that again initiated moves to gain Cabinet approval for OECD membership, with a request by officials to Minister Barwick for authority to sound out other departments regarding possible membership of the OECD's DAC. This had the 'avowed intention' that it lead to full membership of the OECD. The authority was granted, as was later authority to prepare with Treasury a draft Cabinet submission recommending full membership of the OECD (NAA, 1965a). The development of the joint submission proceeded very slowly. In June 1965 a DEA official reported that a Treasury official had informed him that the Treasurer would be submitting the recently completed Vernon Committee Report for Cabinet consideration towards the end of July and that Treasury was considering recommending to the Treasurer that the question of Australian relations with the OECD be pursued in this context, implying Treasury's frustration with the slow pace at which a revised proposal was being prepared. The Treasury official further stated, it was reported, that the Treasurer had earlier indicated that he would prefer to join with the DEA Minister in taking the question to Cabinet but that if he had not agreed by, say, mid-July, then Treasury might 'advise the Treasurer to pursue the OECD question in the context of the Report of the Committee on the Economic Enquiry' (the Vernon Committee, NAA, 1965b). In public service terms, this was a warning that further delays by the DEA were not likely to be tolerated.

The recommendation for OECD membership was again rejected by Cabinet, for much the same general reasons as had been put forward in 1963. It did agree, however, that Australia should seek membership, not of the OECD, but of the DAC and that it would leave open 'for later consideration', the question of an application for full membership without, on this occasion, noting that Treasury would be the department entrusted with that task. The DEA would be the lead department for DAC, in line with its general responsibility for Australian aid programmes. In this context the DEA was now on the front foot as regards the achievement of lead department status, with the much respected Sir Ronald Walker being appointed as Australia's Permanent Representative to DAC (in addition to his continuing duties as Ambassador to France). It meant that it was the DEA and its senior officials that provided the main conduit for Australia's relations with the OECD in the years leading up to full membership in 1971, a considerable advantage in any competition for lead agency.

There is little explicit reference in DFAT or Treasury records regarding lead department status after the 1965 Cabinet submission and the successful application for membership of the DAC until 1969, and the first and final application for full membership of the OECD. The staff from both departments as well as their ministers seem to have worked cooperatively during the DAC application process. Treasurer Holt, for example, was happy to lobby relevant ministers and officials in both the UK and the USA during a visit later in 1965, as part of moves to ascertain the extent of support for Australia's application, and both departments seem to have taken care to gain the approval of the other as regards their activities relating to the application (NAA, 1965c). As time progressed, however, there is some evidence that sensitivities regarding lead department roles and status were not far from the surface. In 1967, for example, Keith Shann in the DEA wrote to Frank Pryor in Treasury, asking for the latter's views on which of the two departments had principal executive authority for meeting the government's obligations regarding the DAC, noting that a difficulty had arisen in this regard and that Shann understood the responsibility to be the DEA's (NAA, 1967).

In 1969 as the process of gaining approval by Cabinet for the 'sounding out' of OECD members as to their views on an Australian application commenced, officials in the DEA seem to have been working on the clear assumption that they would have lead department responsibility for the OECD. In August that year, for example, in the context of a possible new building for the Australian Embassy in Paris, it was noted as regards possible staffing requirements in relation to the OECD that it was too early to be certain, but that early thinking was that space would be needed for a separate mission to the OECD, with an ambassador from DEA, plus two fairly senior staff from each of Treasury and the DTI (NAA, 1969b). However, the question of responsibilities soon came to the fore, focused on new proposals from Minister McEwen, should Australia gain OECD membership.

McEwen's proposals were contained in a submission to Cabinet that accompanied the joint submission from the DEA and Treasury. He noted that it was essential for any Australian application for membership to be subject to a number of conditions, including:

- Control by the DTI over matters under consideration in OECD of concern to it;
- Complete access by the DTI to economic matters under OECD consideration; and
- Full participation by the DTI in any membership negotiation (NAA, 1970a).

While the proposals were not a claim for lead department status, they could be interpreted as at least a demand for a share of that status, in two ways: first, in their unqualified claim for 'control', over all OECD matters of 'concern to it'. It was, however, a largely unnecessary claim, for the specialised nature of much of its work meant that, in practice, it would be officials from DTI who would have to undertake trade related activities in the OECD, as was largely the case in the GATT. It was also unnecessary as there had been no claim by the DEA for responsibility for such work. What the DEA did come to claim, in line with established practice, was responsibility for ensuring that trade related work was, as necessary, coordinated with the work of other departments at the OECD where that work had cross-departmental and cross-policy implications. Again, in practice, for relatively minor matters in this area coordination normally would be achieved informally between the two or more departments involved. It would be only on occasion, for more serious matters, that the DEA, in the shape of the Ambassador or his delegate, would take a more substantive role. Where agreement could not be reached at this level, then it would be referred back to Canberra to be dealt with at a more senior level. Hence, McEwen's claim, mindful of what was normal practice and assuming that McEwen and his officials were aware that this was the case, was likely to have been a claim for at least a share of lead department status.

The second way was McEwen's claim for 'complete access' to economic matters which, given that the bulk of the OECD's work was economic in nature, was, in effect, if not intended, a claim for unrestricted access to nearly all of its work, presumably including its documentation, reports and meetings. Again, this claim was largely unnecessary for, in practice, a lead department would provide such access to the interested and responsible departments as a matter of routine, usually on the basis of prearranged criteria, at least as regards areas relevant to a department's responsibilities. It could be argued that a lead department might choose to unduly limit such access, but to imply in advance, as this claim did, that this might be the case was rather insulting to the DEA. Moreover, if it did occur on any regular and significant basis it would not be long before the resulting disagreements were referred to higher levels, including ultimately Cabinet, and the offending lead department and minister taken to task. Hence, again, this second claim, mindful of what was normal practice and assuming that McEwen and his officials were aware that this was the case, could be construed as a claim for at least a share of lead department status.

If McEwen's claims were accepted, they would: (1) reduce the scope of the responsibilities and, importantly, the accountability of whichever department was granted lead department status; (2) lead to the potential for time consuming and costly interdepartmental arguments as to what was meant by 'control', 'matters of concern', 'economic matters', and 'complete access'; and (3) perhaps encourage other departments, particularly Treasury, to make similar claims, leading to a progressive diminution of the DEA's responsibilities and accountability. In such a situation the result might be an uncoordinated and less effective Australian presence at the OECD, shared between three departments. The DEA's Deputy Secretary Keith Shann drew attention to such possibilities in a Minute to his Minister that contained briefing notes for the Joint DEA–Treasury Cabinet submission regarding OECD membership. He highlighted the difficulty of defining what is relevant and what control actually means, going on to note that 'The Department of External Affairs would have to exercise some central direction over the totality of Australia's relations with OECD', and that questions of jurisdiction should be best left to a later, more definitive Cabinet submission (NAA, 1970b). However, McEwen's submission was endorsed by Cabinet at this stage, possibly in return for his final, if rather grudging acceptance of what was increasingly likely to be an Australian application for membership.

Given Cabinet's apparent acceptance of McEwen's submission and the claims it included, and Treasurer McMahon's 1969 assertions that the OECD was a Treasury matter, it is not surprising that Treasury officials continued to 'push', if rather more gently than had Minister McEwen, for lead department status. It took the form, primarily, of a search for information as to which ministers were responsible for the OECD among its existing member states. Treasury official J.R. Short, for example, in response to a request from Robert Whitelaw, the first head of Treasury's Overseas Economic Relations Division, noted that it varied, being the Foreign Affairs Minister in Austria, Denmark, Japan, Luxembourg, Netherlands and the USA. In France, Germany, Italy, Portugal, Switzerland, Turkey and Yugoslavia it was the Finance Minister, and in Belgium, Canada, Greece, Iceland, Ireland, Norway, Sweden and the UK it was the Trade Minister (NAA, 1970c). The fact that neither the USA nor the UK allocated lead department status to their respective Treasuries must have been disappointing, though it did not prevent officials from conducting further enquiries as the probability of Australia membership grew in 1970.

Treasury's J.C. Humphreys (later Ambassador to the OECD), wrote to Gordon Low, the Minister (Financial) in the Australian Embassy in Washington, asking how the Americans handled the administration of the

OECD 'at the Washington end', and whether responsibility rested with one Minister. He explained to Low that:

> You will realise of course that our interest in all of this stems from our consideration of the role that we in Treasury should have in OECD matters in the event that the Australian membership bid is successful. As you would no doubt anticipate, External Affairs in particular do not share any views we might have that it is appropriate for the Treasurer to be designated as the Minister primarily responsible for OECD matters. Any ammunition you can provide to support such a view would be welcome. (NAA, 1970d)

A copy of the letter was also sent to Treasury official Terry Larkin in Tokyo asking as to the Japanese arrangements (NAA, 1970d).

Gordon Low, following discussions in Washington, replied to Humphrey's letter with a similar, but more detailed reply to that which had been provided by Short earlier in the year. In summary, it was that responsibility for overall management regarding the OECD was vested in the State Department and had been since the establishment of the organisation. The basic argument, as provided by the State Department, was that as the OECD was an international institution and as it had responsibility for international affairs, then it was responsible for the OECD. However, Low also noted that the State Department normally selected an ambassador for the OECD with a good economics background and that, on the basis of a long-standing agreement with the State Department, the Deputy Head of Mission was a Treasury officer with the rank of Minister (NAA, 1970d, 1970e).

However, it was apparent by at least late 1970 that Treasury was unlikely to be designated as the lead department. After all the DEA could and did argue, successfully, that given the wide range of departments that might become involved with the OECD and its many committee-based activities, it was important that their input was effectively coordinated on a whole of government basis, not degenerate into a series of separate, perhaps conflicting series of representations, as could be implied by McEwen's claims. Perhaps most importantly, the coordination of a range of departmental interests via a Permanent Delegation was a mechanism for which the DEA was well equipped and in which it had had considerable experience, in the shape of its larger overseas missions, notably the UN.

Thus, Treasury's attention switched to that of ensuring that even if it did not gain lead department status, it would play a substantive role, given that 'It is agreed that the Minister for Foreign Affairs should have administrative responsibility for OECD ...' (NAA, 1971a). The failure to define what exactly was meant by 'administrative responsibility', meant that continuing differences of interpretation were likely to arise between what was now the DFA and Treasury, although the former was probably reassured by the lack of mention of McEwen's demands for control, access and participation in the final Cabinet decision agreeing to membership.

R.J. Randall, Treasury Secretary, in a minute to the Treasurer regarding the need to send a delegation to the OECD's Invisibles Committee as part of the application process, noted that:

> We've received a couple of indications from Foreign Affairs this morning that they would like one of their senior officials – or even the Ambassador in Paris – to lead the delegation. This, we believe, would be totally inappropriate. (NAA, 1971b)

He argued, largely correctly, that the DFA had little expertise regarding the area and the matters involved were predominantly Treasury matters, concluding:

> If Treasury is to play a significant role in OECD I believe it is important that we resist this first takeover bid from Foreign Affairs, and that we insist a Treasury officer lead the delegation to the Invisibles Committee. I would suggest Whitelaw for the job. He has been in charge of Treasury interests in the negotiations for the past nine months or so, and is fully conversant with the background and details of the whole exercise. Do you agree? (NAA, 1971b)

Also in April, Robert Whitelaw drew the Treasurer's attention to the aim of ensuring a substantial role for Treasury. He noted in regard to a forthcoming Cabinet submission, that:

> I should say that this will be the last opportunity Ministers will have to look at the OECD issue before taking a final decision. It is also the last opportunity the Treasurer and the Treasury will have to lay claim to a significant role in OECD affairs if Australia joins. We have not attempted to set these issues out in the draft. That, we consider, and we presume that you would agree, is a matter best taken up in Cabinet in a direct way at Ministerial level. (NAA, 1971c)

Further, in noting that the DFA's Minister would have administrative responsibility for the OECD, he went on to note rather bluntly, that 'this, very broadly, is where his responsibility should end'. He also suggested that the Minister for Trade should have responsibility for trade policy matters and Treasury for economic policy issues. Hence, he felt, if questions on such issues were raised in the House then the Treasurer, not the Minister for Foreign Affairs, should deal with them. Similarly, if Australia's position in relation to such matters needed to be advised to

OECD, then the Treasurer, not the Minister for Foreign Affairs, should be responsible for the provision of that advice. 'In other words, Ministerial responsibility should be preserved right along the line' and:

> It follows from this that you must be adequately represented in the permanent delegation in Paris. Indeed, since this is an institution for economic co-operation, you could well lay claim to some primacy in representation. How this would be worked out in practice would be a matter for Ministerial agreement. But it should not be the prerogative of the Minister for Foreign Affairs to make such decisions. (NAA, 1971c)

As with McEwen's earlier claims, Whitelaw's assertions were largely unnecessary. There had been no attempt, at least as revealed in archival records and secondary publications, that the DFA wished to take over substantive policy and operational responsibilities that were assigned to Treasury.

What was eventually worked out became apparent in a press release from the Prime Minister. Secretary Randall in a Minute paper to the Treasurer noted that the draft press release included the sentence:

> The Minister for Foreign Affairs will have the administrative responsibility for OECD but, it will of course be part of the Administrative Arrangements that other Ministers and Departments will have a principal interest in activities of direct concern to them. (NAA, 1971d)

Randall went on to point out that this arrangement was not too far from what 'we wanted and recommended to you to strive for', before gaining his Minister's approval for suggesting to the Prime Minister's Office that the sentence in question be slightly modified to read:

> The Minister for Foreign Affairs will have the general administrative responsibility for OECD but other Ministers and Departments will of course have the principal interest and responsibility for activities of direct concern to them. (NAA, 1971d)

The proposal reduced DFA's role somewhat to that of a 'general administrative responsibility', with its implication that this did not necessarily cover all administrative responsibilities and made it clear that other departments would have 'the', not just 'a' principal interest in relevant activities, as well as the 'responsibility for activities of direct concern to them'. A handwritten, rather laconic note on the Minute signed by the Treasurer indicated 'yes, if can be achieved'. It was achieved, for the modified proposal is contained in the final Prime Ministerial Press Release No 57/1971 (NAA, 1971d).

Just what was 'the general administrative responsibility' of the DFA remained to be worked out in practice and it was a practice that was planned to have one unusual feature, the rotation of the position of ambassador between DFAT and Treasury. The origins of the idea go back at least to 1971, when Treasury's Whitelaw was reported as being adamant, in a conversation with a DFA official, that while Treasury did not wish to take over responsibility for the administration or funding of the OECD, it should be given a turn at the ambassadorship. It was also noted that Whitelaw, who had had responsibility for coordinating Treasury's involvement in the accession process 'had a strong personal interest', regarding the role of ambassador (NAA, 1971e).

If accepted, Whitelaw's view would mean that the DFA would retain responsibility for administration, as delegated to the Ambassador on an operational basis, but that the Ambassador might be from Treasury or Trade. This would be an unusual arrangement. Whitelaw was not alone in his views, for acting First Assistant Secretary J.R. Short, in a minute to the Treasurer, advised that:

> [W]e do not believe that, because of the nature of the work of the Organisation, that there is any justification for the Head of the Mission position always to be filled by a member of the Department of Foreign Affairs. Treasury and, to a lesser extent the Department of Trade and Industry, both have a more direct interest in the main work of OECD than has the Department of Foreign Affairs.

He went on to note that the position of Ambassador could be filled by an officer of any one of the three principal departments, with:

> [T]he choice at the time of each appointment depending on the circumstances prevailing at the time. The Department of Trade and Industry, and we believe their Minister, share this view. (NAA, 1971f)

It was a view that prevailed, although after the amalgamation of Foreign Affairs and Trade in 1987 the position of Ambassador alternated between only DFAT and Treasury.

In September 1971 an interdepartmental meeting took place regarding the new arrangements, attended by a range of senior staff and chaired by Dr Cumes of the DFA. He noted that Cabinet Decision 145 of 4 May 1971 had provided for a delegation of eight persons, including the ambassador. Treasury and Trade would each have two members, as would the DFA. The Delegation would operate as a whole to represent 'the totality' of government interests, stressing that:

> To a far greater extent than in any other Embassy or Mission, there would be an interaction of inter-departmental interests in the OECD Delegation and this necessitated a) provision for clear direction and guidance of the Delegation by the Ambassador and b) coordinating machinery in Canberra to be carried out by Foreign Affairs within a broad framework of consultation with interested departments. (NAA, 1971g)

This was a view made clear by William McMahon, now Prime Minister, in a letter to 'Billy' Snedden, the Treasurer, in responding to a letter from the latter about the lead department issue and the role of Treasury. McMahon indicated that he had no difficulties with Treasury suggesting persons for the position of Ambassador to the OECD, as long as it came up through 'normal channels', notably the DFA. Moreover, he stressed that Australia's participation at the OECD should not evolve into a series of separate representations, but must remain a coordinated, harmonious and united representation of the Australian government, with the responsibility for achieving this going to the DFA (New Zealand Archives, 1981). This, of course, was a very different position from that he voiced when Treasurer, as noted above.

INTERNATIONAL TRADE AND THE ROLE OF EXPORT CREDIT

Chapter 6 will provide a detailed examination of Australian activities at the OECD in relation to trade, specifically trade in agriculture. An introduction to some of the sensitive issues involved in that area is also provided in this section by focusing on the issue of export credit. Export credit refers broadly to the lending, guarantee or insurance provided to support exporters. Much such credit is provided by private suppliers through the market in the form of loans, guarantees, credit insurance, letters of credit or political risk finance. However, the bulk of such credit is provided by governments, particularly those of the richer, more developed states, in the form of officially supported export credit for exporters competing for overseas sales, usually via a public agency or, indirectly, via a state-supported private sector agency. While exact figures are not available, it is estimated that the total finance provided or underwritten is approximately US$430 billion per annum.

As the terms offered for export credit are an important factor in determining which country's exporting firms are selected for purchases by overseas clients, export credit that is subsidised by governments provides an exporting firm with a competitive advantage. Hence, it is not surprising that in response to the provision of such subsidies there has been a marked growth in state-owned or supported credit agencies competing for business. It has been a growth accompanied by criticism that such credit distorts international and domestic markets (see, for example, Baldwin, 1970; de Meza, 1989). In contrast, governments providing such subsidies argue that they are a valuable policy instrument for helping to overcome market failures and to promote a variety of social, environmental and developmental aims (see, for example, Morrissey, 1993; Johnson, 1994). As early as 1956, for example, the Australian government had established the Export Payments Insurance Corporation to support Australian exporters and, in 1971, it approved a proposal for a 'buyer's credit facility', to authorise the Corporation to guarantee repayment of loans by lending institutions to overseas buyers of Australian capital goods, excluding services, leading to an amendment to the Corporation's statute. Further, in 1985 the terms of *The Australian Trade Commission Act, 1985*, enabled the government to underwrite export credit risks in the national interest, covering all areas of risk, as well as export credit.

As competition between state credit agencies and the cost of providing credit for the rapid, post-1945 increase in large-scale manufactured exports grew, the cost of subsidising agencies also grew, stimulating calls to manage the increasingly costly competition coming from a variety of national and international agencies. In addition, given the cost of purchasing large-scale manufactured products, deferred payment plans grew in importance for buyers, particularly those from developing countries unable to make purchases without some form of extended credit. However, private sector lenders were not keen to provide such credit, given the higher risk, especially political risk, involved. In turn, this led to greater pressure on governments to provide more and riskier credit.

The Berne Union, an association of state and private export credit agencies, proved unable to deal with the increased and costly competition between its members and non-members, so governments increasingly focused their attention on the OECD to help manage the situation. The OEEC had adopted recommendations against 'artificial aid', as it was then described, to exporters in 1955. In the early 1960s OECD members, in aggregate, accounted for approximately two-thirds of world trade and were by far and away the major suppliers, or lenders, of subsidised export credit, with relatively few of their members purchasing such credit, enabling less acrimonious discussion than within the organisation than in most other international organisations. Hence, in 1963 the OECD's Trade Committee established the Group on Export Credits and

Credit Guarantees (ECG), initially a rather secretive body, to attempt to manage competition by agreeing a set of guidelines for export credit and to assess national policies.

Discussions moved very slowly, at first focusing on procedures for the exchange of information and it was not until 1978 that 'The Arrangement on Guidelines for Officially Supported Export Credits' was put in place, spurred on by the first oil shock. The Arrangement was not a formal OECD legal instrument as it was not agreed by the OECD Council, but a voluntary, 'gentlemen's agreement', or 'soft law'. It applied only to official export credit with repayment terms of two years or more and also provided a set of rules as to how official support could be given. It excluded military equipment and, much to the disappointment of the Australian government, which had been a member since 1976, also agricultural products, with separate agreements ('disciplines'), applying to ships, nuclear power plants, civil aircraft, renewable energy and water projects. Negotiations to extend the agreement to agriculture were put in place following the establishment of the WTO, but failed to make significant progress, again much to the disappointment of successive Australian governments.

A separate committee was set up to administer the new system, somewhat clumsily known as 'The Participants to the Arrangement on Guidelines for Officially Supported Export Credits', commonly known as the Participants. It is not a formal OECD body, though it meets at the organisation and is serviced by the Secretariat. The original members were Australia, Canada, the EEC, Finland, Greece, Japan, New Zealand, Norway, Portugal, Switzerland and the United States. The ECG and the Participants are formally independent of each other, so that members can participate in either or both bodies, and are only obliged to support the export credit agreements of the group(s) in which it participates.

The Arrangement has been slowly expanded and tightened so that there now exists a set of voluntary agreements among Participants, as noted above. It is, arguably, an international cartel of credit suppliers serving primarily the collective interests of supplier states by: (1) attempting to control the predatory use of export finance to shift rents from one supplier to another; and (2) attempting to control the unintentional transfer of wealth from supplier states to buyer states (Evans, 2005). Others, including the Participants, would argue that the Arrangement is a necessary tool for managing unrestrained competition benefiting all players in the market for credit.

Australia and Export Credit

Australian involvement with official export credit began with the Export Payments Insurance Corporation in 1956. It was succeeded by EFIC in 1974 to widen the range of finance and insurance that could be provided, enabling it to compete more effectively with other state export agencies. Initially part of the Industry Portfolio, EFIC was transferred to the DFAT Portfolio in 1998, where it has worked closely with trade officials in the Department and with officials in the Department of Agriculture, Fisheries and Forestry and in Treasury. In addition to its normal work, if EFIC finds that export credit insurance, loans or credit have been granted on non-commercial terms by another state's export credit agency, it can appeal to the Minister for what is known as National Interest Cover. If this is approved, the Australian government assumes 100 per cent of the risk for amounts covered by EFIC for the organisation in question. EFIC manages what is called its National Interest Account operations by means of a service level agreement with DFAT and it is reimbursed for any losses on that account, remitting profits to the Australian government, with a fee for its administration (Productivity Commission, 2012: 5).

As well as the OECD-related agreements, EFIC is also guided by the WTO Agreement on Subsidies and Countervailing Measures. While the GATT, then WTO had had agreements prohibiting or limiting export credit and credit guarantees for several decades, they were largely ignored by its members and, in effect, when the Arrangement was developed within the OECD the GATT/WTO lost a great deal of authority in this area (Evans, 2005: 142–3; Coppens and Friedbacher, 2014). The WTO's present agreement (2015) allows an exception for export credit agencies that comply with the interest rate guidelines set under the OECD Arrangement, which are adjusted each month and are intended to be in line with commercial rates. Several export credit agencies, in effect, circumvent WTO rules by using the OECD Arrangement. Governments, for example, can provide export credit support for aircraft manufacturers if they comply with the OECD Arrangement, even though such support might otherwise fall into the WTO's definition of a prohibited export subsidy (Riley, 2014).

Managing Australian interests in this complex area requires, as a minimum, an active role by officials in the WTO and in the OECD, as well as an expert knowledge of technical developments, resulting in the need for close cooperation between EFIC, DFAT and often Treasury officials. It also requires expertise in regard to the implications of subsidised credit for Australia's foreign aid, requiring liaison with AusAID. The OECD's DAC, for example, in the context of a review of

Australian aid, felt that AusAID should be advising EFIC on the developmental impact of its operations, though Australian officials felt this should not be the case (DIST, 1999).

As a small, now relatively open economy Australia cannot compete effectively in export credits with the much larger credit programmes of the EU and the USA, which have the greatest impact on agricultural commodity exports, especially wheat exports. Hence, it was argued, and continues to be argued by successive Australian governments in a variety of international organisations, notably the GATT/WTO and the OECD, that the export credit offered for agricultural commodities was particularly damaging for the Australian economy, especially when accompanied by the agricultural subsidy programmes of the EU and the USA (Truss, 2007). In 1981, for example, Australia, supported by New Zealand, proposed, unsuccessfully, that rules be developed to regulate official credits supporting agriculture commodity exports and that they should be subject to a separate sector agreement in the Arrangement. This was followed in 1983 by an Australian paper tabled at the OECD that indicated its growing concern over the growth of export credit subsidies, noting that:

> [c]ircumstances are being created that will lead to widespread and disruptive competition on credit levels in the agricultural sector. (Evans, 2005: 208)

Canada and Australia also suggested that the major, non-OECD agricultural exporters be involved (Argentina, Brazil and South Africa), a suggestion that was not accepted.

The Australian and New Zealand proposals were opposed by the United States, although it did indicate that it would be happy to begin negotiations on all agricultural subsidies (a much larger problem), including export credit subsidies, but it would not agree to separate out for separate negotiations subsidies for export credit for agriculture. The US also decided not to support a separate European Community proposal to negotiate on export credit for agriculture, a position it maintained for over two decades (Evans, 2005: 205–7). The scale of the export credit issue was illustrated by an OECD publication in 1983 which showed that the amount of short-term official credits (repayment periods up to 180 days) had reached US$6.1 billion, although this underestimated the total amount as only twelve countries had provided information and it excluded longer term credits (OECD, 1983).

While discussions continued in the years leading up to the creation of the WTO, agreement could not be reached on a set of rules to govern subsidised export credit for agriculture at this time, though agreement to terminate the bulk of subsidies was finally reached in 2015, an agreement strongly supported by Australia (WTO, 2015). However, it was agreed that the signatories to the new WTO Agreement on Agriculture would work towards disciplines on the provision of export credit, export credit guarantees or insurance programmes and the OECD's ECG set up a working group chaired by Japan to draft a set of rules. Despite repeated urging from both the OECD's Ministerial Council and from the G8, little progress was made in drafting any rules, leading to continuing tension between the USA, EU, Australia and the other major agricultural commodities exporters. In 2000, for example, the Minister for Trade, Mark Vaile and Minister for Agriculture, Fisheries and Forestry, Warren Truss sent a letter to the Secretary of the USA's Department of Agriculture, Dan Glickman, expressing their concern regarding a recent US announcement of additional food aid and the continuing provision of export credit for wheat on non-commercial terms. It noted also that the Australian Wheat Board had written to his Department expressing its concern that US non-commercial export sales of wheat to Pakistan were eroding their competitive position and that Australia provided no special credit arrangements for wheat sales. The letter stressed that an agreed set of international disciplines were needed and that OECD negotiations should be brought to a successful conclusion (DFAT, 2000a).

The letter from Vaile and Truss had little impact, although later in 2000 at an informal meeting of Geneva-based Australian officials with US representatives the latter noted that one of the four major issues it had with export subsidies included state-owned or supported enterprises such as the Australian Wheat Board, with statutory monopoly powers that gave them the ability to attract rents and use them to provide non-commercial export credits. The US, Australian officials were informed, was developing a proposal regarding such entities that would be passed on to Australia and Canada for comment (DFAT, 2000b). The Australian officials reiterated the official Australian position that export credits were only provided by EFIC and that the Australian Wheat Board did not provide credit and that the latter was now a private company, but US negotiators continued to press the issue of what they saw as the unfair, competitive advantages of state trading enterprises in the export credit discussions. The Australian government also had indicated in 1997 that its position was that the WTO was the appropriate venue for negotiations regarding state trading enterprises in regard to export credit, not the OECD, where it was likely to gain support for its position from the many developing countries that possessed an often wide range of state enterprises (DAFF, 1997).

The members of the Cairns Group led by Australia were kept briefed on the discussions and their implications, especially those taking place at the OECD. It was emphasised that the draft disciplines being considered would not preclude the Cairns Group from pursing its goal of eliminating subsidised export credits in possible WTO negotiations. The latter negotiations, if they did take place at this time, were regarded by Australia and other Cairns Group members as likely to be very difficult for, if the OECD disciplines were brought to the WTO for negotiation, they risked being diluted given the presence of countries in that organisation (largely developing countries), that were the recipients of subsidised export credits and who would not wish them to be eliminated or substantially reduced (DFAT, 2000c).

A number of efforts were made to revive export credit negotiations regarding agricultural products following an OECD study indicating that the amount of export credits provided by fifteen OECD members had increased by US$2.4 billion between 1995 and 1998 (OECD, 2000). As a result, in 2000 the OECD Council indicated its disappointment with the failure of the Participants to reach an agreement as mandated in the Uruguay Round and urged that negotiations be resumed and completed by the end of 2000 at the latest. The lack of progress may have been a factor in what was perceived as EFIC's growing lack of interest in at least the technical side of OECD credit discussions and negotiations (DFAT, 2010).

While Australia continued at various times to continue to press for the introduction of disciplines for agricultural credit, in general officials seem to have felt that Australian interests had been 'well served', by the OECD Arrangement, with the general level of subsidisation in export finance having been substantially reduced, with the glaring exception of agricultural products (DFAT, 2003). However, even though Australia was and remains a major actor in international wheat sales, it lacks the extent of influence of the USA and the EU (where the Commission acts on behalf of EU members). Nor, in the case of the WTO, can it draw upon the support of the bulk of less developed countries, other than the few that are major agricultural exporters and are members of the Cairns Group, as most see benefits in the reduced prices brought about by subsidised credit rather than the longer term economic inefficiencies that it creates. At best, it can continue to raise issues and, importantly, provide or ask for more accurate information about trends related to the issues, helping to achieve more informed debate and very slow progress in moves to reduce subsidised credit. Janet West, head of the OECD's unit responsible for export credit from 1993 to 2009 and previously Director of the UK's Export Credits Guarantee Department, was reported as stating that Australia, as early as 1995, had played an important role in maintaining pressure on the US regarding export credits (DAFF, 1995).

CONCLUSION

DFAT's role in relation to the OECD has been and continues to be a challenging and often frustrating one as regards its position as the lead agency for OECD matters, and in relation to its more outwardly focused work on trade and export credit. The chapter also illustrates the continuing challenge faced by DFAT in coordinating the work of other agencies in its Portfolio, notably EFIC, with those of its own officials in the Department, both in Canberra and in Paris, and with officials from other departments, notably Treasury, but also with those in DAFF as regards trade in agriculture. Its coordinating work in this regard is analogous to the role of the Department of the Prime Minister and Cabinet, especially when its role in relation to foreign aid is considered, as explored in detail in Chapter 6.

While the early frustrations associated with the competition for lead agency status have long since ended, those associated with export credit for agriculture are continuing. In large part this latter frustration is a result of Australia's relatively minor position and influence as a middle power, able only infrequently to influence the activities and policies of the major OECD actors, the USA, the European Commission and Japan. This is particularly the case where those actors are unwilling to engage in substantial reform that might benefit Australian interests.

BIBLIOGRAPHY

Baldwin, R. 1970. *Nontariff Distortions of International Trade*, Washington, DC: The Brookings Institution.

Carroll, P. and Kellow, A. 2011. *The OECD A Study of Organisational Adaptation*, Cheltenham, UK and Northampton, MA, USA: Edward Elgar Publishing.

Coppens, D. and Friedbacher, T. 2014. 'A tale of two rules: The intersection between WTO and OECD disciplines on export credit support', Chapter 4 in *The Future of Foreign Trade Support – Setting Global Standards for Export Credit and Political Risk Insurance*, a Global Policy eBook, accessed 15 January 2015 at www.globalpolicyjournal.com/blog/26/11/2014/tale-two-rules-intersection-between-wto-and-oecd-disciplines-export-credit-support.

de Meza, D. 1989. 'Not Even Strategic Trade Theory Justifies Export Subsidies', *Oxford Economic Papers*, 41(4): 720–736.

DAFF 1995. A response from Craig Burns, Director, Multilateral Trade Strategy Section, Corporate Policy Division, dated 1995, to a request for comments from David Stafford, Director, Export Credit Policy, DIST, dated 31 August 1995, regarding the OECD's TD/CONSENSUS(95)33 'Discussion Document on an Outline Sector Understanding for Agricultural Products – With Options', for discussion at the second meeting of the WGP on Agriculture, 19–20 September 1995. Burns noted that at a meeting with Janet West, 'She suggested that a united front would help maintain pressure on the US', indicating also that she felt Australia had played an important role in maintaining pressure on the US, DAFF File No 95-009289 'Export Credits OECD GATT Disciplines'.

DAFF 1997. A letter dated 10 April 1997 from John Anderson, Minister for the Department of Primary Industry and Energy to John Moore, Minister for DIST, agreeing to the latter's proposition in a letter of 17 February 1997, that Australia should try to restrict the use of export credits for agriculture as much as possible and that while negotiations may become deadlocked, Australia should remain firm that the WTO, not the OECD, is the forum for discussion of state trading enterprises, File No 96-004898 'OECD: Export Credits for Agricultural Products'.

DFAT 2000a. Copy of a letter dated 13 March 2000 to Secretary Glickman from Ministers Vaile and Truss, DFAT File No 00/035783 Trade Policy-Committees-OECD Group on Export Credits and Credit Guarantees OEF Aspects – OEU.

DFAT 2000b. A note from the Australian Delegation in Geneva to DFAT Canberra dated 24 March 2000, reporting on a meeting in the margins of the WTO Committee on Agriculture of 22 March with US representatives Fritz (USDA) and Tvardek (Treasury), who were visiting Geneva specifically to discuss the US position with a number of participants in the OECD negotiations on agricultural export credits, DFAT File No 00/035783 Trade Policy-Committees-OECD Group on Export Credits and Credit Guarantees OEF Aspects – OEU.

DFAT 2000c. A note from the Australian Delegation in Geneva to DFAT Canberra dated 20 September 2000, regarding meetings officials had had with Cairns Group delegations in Geneva on 19 September, DFAT File No 00/035784 Trade Policy-Committees-OECD Executive Committee and Executive Committee In Special Session (ECSS)-OEU.

DFAT 2003. A note from the OECD Delegation to DFAT, dated 14 August 2003, regarding export credit discussions and various scenarios as to their future, DFAT File No 2003/110029 International Relations-Conferences-OECD-Trade Directorate-W/Party On Export Credit And Credit Guarantees-EFIC-Paris Club-OEU.

DFAT 2010. A note dated 5 February 2010 from James Wiblin of DFAT to Nick Williams and Joanne Frederiksen regarding briefing notes for the ECG of 3–4 February, DFAT File No 10/3856 Political-Economic-International Organisations-OECD- Advice on Arrangements on officially supported export credits, Meetings, 2010.

DIST 1999. A note from P. Keating to I. Anderson with an urgent request for information regarding the DAC Peer Review of Australian aid. Robin Davis of

AusAID advised that DAC would not let go of the idea that AusAID should advise EFIC and Keating indicated that it would be helpful if DFAT/EFIC would provide arguments to counter the suggestion. DIST File No C98/03545 'OECD: Development Assistance Committee: Export Credit Policy Group', Part 04: 1998.

Evans, P. 2005. 'International Regulation of Official Trade Finance: Competition and Collusion in Export Credits and Foreign Aid', a thesis submitted to the Department of Political Science on 23 May 2005 in partial fulfilment of the requirement for the Degree of Doctor of Philosophy in Political Science at the Massachusetts Institute of Technology, accessed on 20 January 2017 at http://dspace.mit.edu/handle/1721.1/33684.

Harris, S. 1999. 'Australia: Change and Adaptation in the Department of Foreign Affairs and Trade', Chapter 2 in B. Hocking (ed.), *Foreign Ministries – Change and Adaptation*, Basingstoke: Macmillan, 23–39.

Johnson, J. 1994. 'Financing the Arms Trade', *Annals of the American Academy of Political and Social Science*, 535: 110–121.

Morrissey, O. 1993. 'The Mixing of Aid and Trade Policies', *The World Economy*, 16(1): 69–84.

NAA 1963a. A Minute from J.F. Nimmo to the Prime Minister, 11 March 1963, reporting on a meeting he had attended on behalf of Secretary John Bunting with Sir Roland Wilson (Treasury), Dr Alan Westerman (Trade), Sir Arthur Tange (DEA), regarding the proposal that Australia join the OECD, NAA File No A4940-c3754.

NAA 1963b. 'Australian Relationships with the Organisation for Economic Co-operation and Development', NAA File No A1838 724/5 Part 4, Cabinet Submission No 1037, Copy No 73.

NAA 1965a 'OECD and DAC – Australian Relations With'. The file contains a copy of Cabinet Submission No 1194, 1965, which rejected the proposal for possible membership of the OECD, but agreed to an application for membership of the DAC and left open for later consideration the question of an application for full membership, NAA A1838, File No 724/5 Part 4.

NAA 1965b. A Minute from G.N. Upton to Mr Moodie, 25 June, 'OECD – Committee on Economic Enquiry', and copied to the Secretary for information, NAA A1838 724 5 Part 3 'Membership to OECD'.

NAA 1965c. A Minute from Alan Renouf, First Assistant Secretary in the DEA to the Minister, 15 September 1965, outlining the proposed steps to be taken in applying for DAC membership, NAA Folder A1838 724 5 Part 4 'Membership to DAC'.

NAA 1967. Letter from K.C.O. Shann to F.C. Pryor in Treasury, dated 18 May 1967, NAA File No 724/5/3 Part 2 'DAC – 1966 – 1967 Review of Australian Aid'.

NAA 1969a. 'Treasury Minute Paper', 23 September 1969 from the Secretary for the Treasurer, which summarised Treasury's activities in relation to the OECD and Australian membership. It concluded by asking McMahon whether Treasury should collaborate with the DEA in presenting a Cabinet submission, given the large extent of Treasury interests in the work of the OECD. A handwritten note attached to the minute, signed by McMahon, noted that 'Surely this is basically a Treasury matter. They should collaborate with us.' A further handwritten note on the minute indicates that the Secretary, Sir Frederick Wheeler 'had confirmed to him that it is the Treasury which has the *major* interest in OECD', NAA File No 69 2095 Part 4 'Reconsideration of Possible Australian Membership of OECD'.

NAA 1969b. Minute dated 4 August 1969, from R Miles Connolly to a Mr Marshall in DEA, NAA File No 1838 724 4 30 Part 3 Accession.

NAA 1970a. 'Possible Australian Membership of the Organisation for Economic Co-operation and Development (OECD)', a submission to Cabinet by McEwen, NAA A1838 724 4 30 Part 5 Accession.

NAA 1970b. Minute for the Minister from K.C.O. Shann, NAA File No 1838 724 4 30 Part 3 Accession.

NAA 1970c. A letter, dated 22 January 1970, from J.R. Short, based in the Australian High Commission, London, to R. Whitelaw, in NAA File No 69 2095 Part 4 'Reconsideration of Possible Australian Membership of OECD'.

NAA 1970d. A letter, dated 25 June 1970, from J.C. Humphreys in Canberra, to Gordon Low in Washington, NAA File No 69 2095 Part 6 'Reconsideration of Possible Australian Membership of OECD'.

NAA 1970e. A letter, dated 12 October 1970, from J.C. Humphreys to the Assistant Secretary, International Relations Branch, reporting on a meeting the former had had with Dallas Jones, the Counsellor for Economic Affairs in the US Mission to the OECD, NAA File No 69 2095 Part 8 'Reconsideration of Possible Australian Membership of OECD'.

NAA 1971a. A Treasury Minute 'Australian Membership of OECD', to the Minister from Robert Whitelaw dated 30 April 1971, NAA File No 69 2095 Part 11 'Reconsideration of Possible Australian Membership of OECD'.

NAA 1971b. A Treasury Minute for the Treasurer from R.J. Randall, the Secretary, dated 27 April 1971, NAA File No 69 2095 Part 11 'Reconsideration of Possible Australian Membership of OECD'.

NAA 1971c. A Treasury Minute for the Treasurer from R.J. Randall, the Secretary, dated 25 May 1971, NAA File No 69 2095 Part 12 'Reconsideration of Possible Australian Membership of OECD'.

NAA 1971d. Prime Minister's Press Release No 57/1971, NAA File No 69 2095 Part 12 'Reconsideration of Possible Australian Membership of OECD'.

NAA 1971e. A note to Phillip Flood in DFA from C.R.S. Rodgers in the Paris Embassy, NAA 1838 File No 724/5/48 Part No 3 'DAC Untying of Aid'.

NAA 1971f. A note dated 3 May 1971 from J.R. Short Acting First Assistant Sec to the Treasurer, 'Comments on Cabinet Submission No 80: Australian membership of the OECD', NAA File No 69 2095 Part 11 Reconsideration of Possible Australian Membership of OECD.

NAA 1971g. 'OECD Summary Record of an Interdepartmental Meeting held on 1st September 1971', chaired by Dr Cumes, NAA Series 1838 File 724/4/40 PART 1 OECD – Visit of Secretary-General to Australia – 1971.

New Zealand Archives, 1981. R17724827 Part 1, 'Miscellaneous International organisations – OECD – NZ Membership [01/1971–11/1981]', being a copy of a letter from P.M. McMahon to Treasurer Snedden, dated 1 November 1972.

OECD 1983. 'Summary of Replies to the Questionnaire on Export Credits for Agricultural Commodities', Trade Directorate, TD/Consensus/83.31, 10 June 1983, Paris: OECD.
OECD 2000. 'An Analysis of Officially Supported Export Credits in Agriculture', Paris: OECD.
Productivity Commission 2012. 'Australia's Export Credit Arrangements', Report No. 58, Final Inquiry Report, Canberra.
Riley, B. 2014. 'Foreign Export Credit Subsidies: Kill Them, Don't Copy Them', The Heritage Foundation, 12 September 2014, accessed on 14 January 2015, at www.heritage.org/research/reports/2014/09/foreign-export-credit-subsidies-kill-them-dont-copy-them.
Truss, W. 2007. 'Truss welcomes new Cairns Group Proposals on Food Aid and Export Credits', Media Release, 28 May 2007, accessed on 20 January 2017 at www.trademinister.gov.au/releases/2007/wtt045_07.html.
WTO 2015. 'Export Competition', Ministerial Decision of 19 December 2015, WT/MIN(15) /45 WT/L/980.

6. Trade and agriculture: developing an effective strategy

This chapter focuses on a range of Australian activities in relation to the OECD's work on trade and agriculture in the period from 1971 to the establishment of the World Trade Organization. It examines: (1) the impact of Australia's policy of 'protection all round', on proposals to gain membership of the OECD; (2) the manner in which the concerns of 'Black Jack' McEwen and senior officials in his department were allayed in the accession negotiations and in the OECD review of Australia's trade policy during its early years of membership; (3) the difficulties and disappointments caused by the High Level Group on Trade and the Trade Pledge as the 1970s progressed; and (4) the more positive experiences of the work of the OECD in relation to the Uruguay Round. It shows that as a new and relatively small member Australia was more effective in its continuing drive in helping to persuade members to move towards free trade in agricultural products when it did so on the basis of a coherent strategy and working in cooperation with like-minded members such as the USA, Canada, New Zealand and the members of the Cairns Group. Most recently, following a long period of failure to reach substantive agreements in the Doha Round of WTO negotiations, Australia has been a very active OECD and WTO member in helping achieve the WTO's 2015 Agreement on Trade Facilitation and its agreement to abolish agricultural export subsidies.

'PROTECTION ALL ROUND', AND OECD MEMBERSHIP

It should be noted that initially two departments had an interest in the OECD's work on trade and agriculture, the Department of Primary Industry (DPI) and the Department of Trade and Industry (DTI), but the latter was responsible for trade in agriculture. The DPI, in summary, and unlike the DTI, was more positive about the prospects of OECD membership. It had a wide range of interests in the OECD regarding its technical functions and its wider economic and development aid functions, and it had applied for membership of the OECD's seed certification scheme before Australia had commenced discussions regarding OECD membership, following consultation with the state governments (NAA, 1969c). In particular, the DPI stressed that OECD membership, which it supported, would enable it to participate in the development of the OECD's food regulations and related standards at an early stage, rather than having to try and argue for amendments after standards had been promulgated. Meeting these standards was an important step in gaining access to important European markets for Australian agricultural produce, particularly as the relevant EEC standards were based on those of the OECD. In addition, OECD standards were also an important influence on negotiations in the Codex Alimentarius.

However, in contrast, and as indicated in chapter 3 regarding Australia's accession to the OECD, the DTI was responsible for much of the early and successful opposition to proposals for OECD membership in the period 1960–69, led by Minister 'Black Jack' McEwen, and supported by two successive and influential heads of the department, Sir John Crawford and Sir Alan Westerman. Crawford, at least in later years, was critical of the continuing use of high tariffs to protect inefficient industries, a core feature of the established 'protection all round' policy stance, and a strong supporter of the Industry Assistance Commission that replaced the more protectionist Tariff Board (see, for example, Capling, 2001: 75; Banks and Carmichael, 2007). In contrast, his successor, Westerman has been described as an 'ardent protectionist' (Capling, 2001: 75).

McEwen was an ardent supporter of protectionist policies in support of manufacturing industry, accompanied by various support measures for agriculture to offset its higher production costs that protectionism entailed. He was supported strongly by Prime Minister Menzies, the bulk of the manufacturing sector, a range of rural interests, as well as trade unions and many of the Opposition members of the ALP, though not its leader, Gough Whitlam. In summary, there was little effective opposition to protectionism at the beginning of the 1960s, apart from the Commonwealth Treasury (Bell, 1993).

Largely as a result, and in contrast to the bulk of OEEC/OECD members, Australia did not participate in the multilateral tariff reductions negotiated in the GATT in the 1950s and 1960s, and by 1970 it had the highest manufacturing tariffs of the industrialised countries (Anderson and Garnaut, 1987). It justified this stance, in part, by the very limited attention paid to trade in agriculture at the GATT, with high levels of subsidies to agricultural exports being common, increasingly so in the

EEC under the Common Agricultural Policy (CAP), but also in the USA. Membership of the OECD was seen by McEwen and many of his senior officials as a threat to the 'protection all round' stance that had dominated Australian policy since the early years of the twentieth century and the structure of political interests in which it was embedded. It was seen as a forum for organising the trade interests of its members and their presentation in the GATT, largely to Australia's disadvantage.

ALLAYING THE CONCERNS

The Australian government's position on trade policy, at the request of the OECD Secretariat, was described in detail in a lengthy note to the Secretariat in April 1971 prepared by the DTI during the accession negotiations (NAA, 1971j). The report made the DTI's concerns regarding membership clear, though noting that Australia was an active supporter of multilateral trading principles. However, it stressed that the DTI had never been satisfied that the General Agreement on Tariffs and Trade (GATT), had made the major impact on trade in primary products hoped for by the proponents of the International Trade Organization. As an example, the paper noted that the stringent provisions of GATT Article XVI in relation to export subsidies for manufactured products contrasted with the relatively weak provisions regarding export subsidies for primary produce. Hence, given the high proportion of Australia's export income derived from primary produce, the 'imbalance' between manufacturing and primary produce export subsidies had been an important factor in Australia's decision not to subscribe to GATT's strong provisions regarding export subsidies on manufactures.

A number of developments helped largely allay the DTI's concerns regarding the OECD's work on trade. The first was the experience of the exploratory 1969 discussions with the OECD, combined with the following, 1970–71 accession negotiations. The second was the generally positive experience of the first OECD review of Australia's trade policies in 1973–74.

The 1969 Discussions and Accession Process

The DTI was closely involved in the preliminary accession discussions that were held in 1969 with senior OECD officials as well as a number of members. Mr Jack Richardson (of the DTI, then on attachment as a Minister (Commercial) to the Australian Embassy in Brussels) and the DEA's Philip Flood first met with Dr Simantov, Head of the Agriculture

Directorate, then Erhard Poincilit, the Director of Trade, and also with Phillip Trezise, the US Ambassador to the OECD from 1965 to 1969 (NAA, 1969a). The DTI's concerns regarding the 'intrusive' nature of the OECD's 'confrontations', or peer reviews, were allayed by Simantov, who explained that 'confrontations' on agriculture were being held but had been reduced from an annual to a five yearly basis, with the last having been held in 1966. It is likely that the bulk of European members and the European Commission had driven this development, at least in part to avoid critical questioning of the CAP and their domestic agricultural policies by their USA and Canadian peers. While Richardson might have been disappointed that he and his colleagues would not have an annual opportunity to press for a reduction in protectionism regarding agriculture and a greater market orientation in such confrontations, it meant also that the still strongly protectionist Australian trade policies would themselves also face only a five yearly examination.

Simantov also indicated that it was in the Joint Working Party on Trade and Agriculture that most discussion regarding agricultural exports took place, including discussion about the possibility of members providing advance notice to the Working Party of forthcoming policy changes in the area, an issue that had been of concern to the DTI as potentially limiting its discretion and capacity in trade negotiations in the GATT, and on a bilateral basis (NAA, 1969b). However, again Simantov was able to reassure Richardson and Flood by further noting that no agreement had been reached on the question of advance notice of proposed changes in members' policies and that the 1964–65 resolutions of the OECD Ministerial Council, while supporting such consultation, were not compulsory. They might also have been pleased to note that, as Simantov indicated, a recent meeting of OECD Ministers of Agriculture had reviewed the issue of the alarming 'increasing imbalance between production and demand', in agriculture and its adverse impact on income and prices and, most worryingly and as a result, the rapidly growing agricultural surpluses caused by the CAP. The Ministers had agreed that discussions on how to deal with the issue should take place in the OECD, supported by analytical work from the Secretariat, with Simantov indicating that Australia and New Zealand might be invited to participate. Such work was intended to complement that of the GATT, with discussions at the OECD being helped by its smaller size, the lack of formal written statements and the fact that they took place in the more general context of economic policy. Most importantly for Australia, membership of the organisation would enable its representatives to take part in any discussions regarding CAP and any solutions that might be developed. As it happened, this work did not commence until the end of the 1970s, as noted below.

USA Ambassador Philip Trezise, as with Simantov, also felt that the OECD was a valuable forum for consultation before issues moved into GATT, suggesting that if the latter reached an agreement it was because it had been first tackled in the OECD. Trezise also indicated that if another GATT Round was to take place he would not be surprised if the preparatory work was done in the OECD. Indeed, he noted that there was a proposal that a small group of OECD members do 'careful' work on agricultural trade problems in parallel with the work being undertaken in GATT (NAA, 1969a). While these views might have been of concern for the DTI as regards their influence in GATT negotiations, OECD membership, again, might increase its earlier knowledge of negotiating positions being developed in that organisation, as well as providing at least an opportunity to influence developments. It is a moot point as to whether or not OECD members would have been forthcoming with detailed information in the organisation about the details of their likely positions at any forthcoming trade negotiations, although they might have been expected to discuss at least the general principles that might underlie future trade relations.

At the meeting with Erhart Poincilit, the OECD's Director for Trade, Thierry Monnier, the head of the OECD's Division of External Relations was also present, reflecting the sensitivity of trade work, although the views of the two men were, again, largely reassuring. They were at pains to explain that there were no annual confrontations on trade policy, though there were occasional, ad hoc confrontations on specific trade issues. The bulk of current work was on the question of trade preferences for developing countries and, in particular, discussions at UNCTAD, the latter of which Australian officials were familiar with, given their earlier participation as observers in the OECD's work in this area. Richardson, mindful of the growing use of export credits and guarantees to subsidise agricultural exports, would have been especially interested in Poincilit's explanation that the work of the Group on export credits and export credit guarantees had 'run into considerable difficulties', as some members used these instruments for development aid purposes and others for trade competition.

As noted in the chapter on accession, the remaining concerns regarding trade following the 1969 discussions were further allayed in the formal accession negotiations, with the only concern being initial difficulties regarding the Overseas Cargo Shipping provisions (Part XA) of the Australian Trade Practices Act. A report from the DTI's F.P. Donovan, while cautious, noted that the DTI might not be able to retain complete flexibility in trade and related policies, but that the entry procedure would 'not necessarily', require any change in policies (NAA, 1970a). Sir Kenneth Bailey, appointed as a special advisor on international law to the Australian government, commented in detail on a draft statement of the formal obligations that Australia would sign regarding the OECD and noted in regard to trade that it would not be bound by any decisions of the Trade Committee other than by agreement (NAA, 1970b). Finally, the DTI indicated that it was happy with the conditions of accession and a major, domestic obstacle to OECD membership was removed (NAA, 1970c). It had been, for the most part, a relatively simple if extended process of learning.

The First Examination of Australia's Trade Policies at the OECD

Australian concerns regarding the OECD's trade work and its implications were further allayed by the experience of the first OECD examination of Australian trade policies. The Australian Delegation was informed in March 1972 that it was the practice of the OECD Trade Committee to examine the trade policies of new members, as had earlier been the case with Japan. While DFA officials in Canberra wondered whether such an examination was warranted given, they felt, that Australia did not apply such restrictive conditions as Japan, they did not oppose it in principle, but asked that it take place in 1973, following what were likely to be changes to trade policy with the recent election of the first ALP Whitlam government (NAA, 1972d). It was indicated that the examination was not a 'confrontation', such as took place in the EDRC reviews, but more of 'an informal round-table exchange of views and giving of information' (NAA, 1972e).

However, the changes introduced by the Whitlam government in 1972 proved greater than expected, including a number of proposed major changes to trade policy, and it was agreed that the examination be postponed until 1974, after the changes had been completed. The examination finally took place in the Working Party of the Trade Committee in May 1974 'in an atmosphere of cordiality', doubtless helped by the unilateral, 25 per cent across the board cut in Australian tariffs introduced by the Whitlam government in July 1973, and its clear policy of reducing, if cautiously, the level of protection for Australian industry (which, nevertheless, still remained high by OECD standards). The decision to cut tariffs had been based, in part, on advice from a taskforce chaired by Tariff Board chair 'Alf' Rattigan and the evidence provided by the use of the 'effective rate of protection' measure developed by Australian economist Max Corden, utilised by the Vernon

Committee, and further developed by the new Industry Assistance Commission (IAC). It was also a measure further developed by the OECD in the 1980s (Leigh, 2002; Corden, 1971; OECD, 2008: 25, 172).

The examination was regarded as of considerable importance by the Australian government, its concerns being illustrated by the unusually large size of the Australian contingent that attended. Sixteen Australian officials were present in Paris (though not necessarily all at the same time), with nine from Overseas Trade, and one each from Minerals and Energy, Customs and Excise, Primary Industry, Treasury, Secondary Industry, Northern Development and, unusually, Prime Minister and Cabinet. The size of the contingent might also have driven home to other delegates the importance Australia attached to its trade policy, as well as providing most of them with their first detailed description of Australia's trade situation and policies and the challenges it faced. It was also an important opportunity to clarify Australian policy positions in the context of the Tokyo Round of GATT trade negotiations that had commenced in September 1973.

Most questions at the examination, as anticipated, were addressed to: tariff policy; export controls and government purchasing; Australia's bilateral, preferential trade agreements with New Zealand, Canada and the UK; the trade implications of the UK's entry to the EEC; its increasing trade with Asia, notably Japan; and the role and authority of the new Industries Assistance Commission, the Temporary Assistance Authority and the criteria for industry protection (NAA, 1974a, 1974b). The Australian records of the meeting indicate that, as reported, discussions were largely cordial and focused on a fact-finding exercise as regards the several major changes introduced or planned by the Whitlam government. It is likely that delegates' attention was probably somewhat diverted by the adverse impacts of the first oil crisis, a crisis that had led in April 1974 to the OECD's 'Trade Pledge' (see below), in which context Australian trade policy was of limited importance (NAA, 1974a, 1974b).

Hence, by 1974, most, if not all of the remaining fears regarding the outcomes of OECD membership that had been repeatedly voiced by the DTI during the 1960s had been allayed.

TRADE ISSUES IN THE EARLY YEARS OF OECD MEMBERSHIP

If the discussions in the 1969–71 period, followed by the 1974 examination of Australia's trade policy, had allayed DTI concerns regarding the

OECD's trade work, other aspects of membership were less positive. In particular, these early years did not provide Australian officials, at least initially, with the degree of access to, and influence in, high level discussions that the proponents of OECD membership had hoped would be achieved. There was, in particular: (1) a disappointing lack of progress on issues of interest to Australia in the work of the Agriculture and Trade committees; (2) a failure to gain membership of the High Level Group on Trade (HLG), which, if achieved, might have provided Australia with somewhat greater influence on trade and agriculture issues; and (3) difficulties associated with the 1974 Trade Pledge. All of which made it clear that the politics of trade issues at the OECD could be both challenging and disappointing.

A Disappointing Lack of Progress: The 1970s

Much of the experience of working on trade issues in the early years after membership seem to have been something of an anticlimax and were often disappointing. At an interdepartmental committee meeting in Canberra in December 1972 to consider Australia's current and future participation at the OECD, for example, it was indicated by J.T. Fogarty, First Assistant Secretary of what was now the Department of Overseas Trade, that his division had had to spend much time and effort in persuading other divisions in the department of the value of active participation at the OECD. As regards the Trade Committee, he felt that the reluctance of the 'Europeans' to let the Committee take any initiatives was 'killing' the Committee with, as suspected, the EEC members acting as a bloc so that its work was unlikely to have any positive impact from the Australian perspective on the 1973 (Tokyo Round) GATT negotiations, with the GATT and UNCTAD remaining the most important forums (NAA, 1972c). Fogarty's views are not surprising as Australian officials often persistently expounded views in direct contrast to those of many members of the Trade Committee and its subsidiary bodies, especially those that were members of the EEC, for example, views critical of the CAP and the lack of progress regarding the contentious issue of export credit. Indeed, the trade aspect of agriculture was given comparatively little attention by the OECD throughout the 1970s and European Commission representatives at the OECD were often reluctant to discuss the impact of the CAP on trade in agriculture (Blair, 1993: 115–19; NAA, 1973).

The High Level Group on Trade

Australia acceded to the OECD in 1971, at a time when the organisation started to become a more active and important member in the global trade regime. In summary, the US Administration had been disappointed at the outcome of GATT's Kennedy Round trade negotiations, particularly as regards agricultural trade and the opposition of the EEC to its liberalisation. What resulted can be seen as part of the 'Nixon Shock', package of measures, in the shape of a push for a major new trade initiative at the OECD, rather than the GATT. The Nixon Shock, announced on 15 August 1971 by President Nixon, surprised world leaders by suddenly ending the ability of foreign central banks to convert their US dollar holdings into gold and imposing a 10 per cent surcharge on imported, manufactured goods. The policies were aimed at preventing a run on US gold reserves and to stop the deterioration in the US balance of payments by getting other countries (notably West Germany and Japan), to revalue their currencies, as well as heading off mounting protectionist pressures in Congress (Irwin, 2012). The policies, if successful, would, in turn, increase the price of imports to US markets and reduce the prices of US exports, over time helping to reduce adverse movements in its balance of payments. It marked the end of the Bretton Woods system of fixed exchange rates.

Australian officials had received an early indication of likely US thinking on trade at an interdepartmental meeting in Canberra in March 1971, where they had been addressed by J.A. Greenwald, the US Ambassador to the OECD (NAA, 1971c). He indicated that a new US initiative on trade would soon commence. The US initiative was taken up, in turn, by the OECD's new Secretary-General, Emile van Lennep, with the agreement of the US, in the form of the appointment of a new, ad hoc body of experts, the High Level Group on Trade (HLG), chaired by Belgian Jean Rey, a former EEC Commissioner (which could not have been a reassuring appointment from the perspective of Australian officials). It was to report on trade and related issues from a long term perspective, as part of a broader initiative aimed at strengthening cooperation on economic matters at the OECD.

Van Lennep saw the OECD's new role in trade as that of defining the key problems faced and working out possible, broad lines of action to remedy them which would then be handed to the GATT for detailed negotiation and implementation. Of particular interest to Australia was his view that, while it would be premature for a major negotiation on agricultural trade to immediately commence, given the opposition of EEC members regarding proposed changes to the CAP, early discussions on matters of common concern would be useful, as there had been little progress in the OECD's Agriculture Committee. While trade in agriculture had not been an issue included in the original US initiative, it was one of considerable concern to Australia. Alan Renouf, Australian Ambassador to France, met with van Lennep and indicated Australia's interest in gaining membership of the proposed HLG, suggesting that a person such as Sir John Crawford could meet the criteria for membership by relevant experts (NAA, 1971b). Canberra confirmed Australia's interest and saw merit in van Lennep's proposal, though noting its concern that it should not be seen as a rebuff to GATT work, where Sweden and Australia recently had proposed, unsuccessfully, a GATT study group on trade in agriculture. Canberra instructions to the Paris Delegation were not to press for membership of the HLG, given that Australia had only just gained OECD membership, but to indicate its interest in the topic, leaving a final decision until later (NAA, 1971d).

As OECD members lobbied for membership of the HLG in the latter months of 1971, delaying the commencement of its work, the Australian position changed, instructing its recently established Delegation to inform van Lennep that if the size of the HLG went beyond ten members then Australia would propose a candidate. There was concern that an expanded membership would include a disproportionate number of members of the EEC and applicants for EEC membership, to Australia's disadvantage, given the EEC's protectionist position on agricultural trade (NAA, 1971e). However, it soon became clear that membership would be ten or higher, with Australia excluded. Australia could have made its disappointment clear by opposing the establishment of the HLG in the OECD Council, but this might have eroded the goodwill that van Lennep had shown Australian representatives.

Also, Australian Trade Minister Doug Anthony felt that Australia would have to climb down eventually from a stance of opposition to the HLG proposal, so the Australian Delegation was instructed not to oppose the creation of the HLG and its larger membership, but to press van Lennep to arrange for a 'consultative role' for Australia that would enable officials to keep in touch with discussions in the HLG (NAA, 1971f). Van Lennep was not able to achieve a consultation role to the satisfaction of Canberra and, while not formally opposing the HLG in Council, Australia did make a reservation that noted its concerns as to its membership, a reservation it later withdrew, having made its point regarding exclusion from HLG membership. Minister Anthony also agreed that steps should be taken to ensure that the HLG did not develop into a permanent OECD group, a proposal to which the OECD Council later agreed (NAA, 1971g, 1971h).

As it happened, Delegation staff were frequently briefed on the content and progress of the HLG discussions by Canadian officials, with Canada being a member of the HLG. They indicated, for example, that William Eberle (the US member of the HLG and President Nixon's newly appointed Special Trade Representative) had asserted that the US would not agree to any further liberalisation of trade in industrial products unless there was some satisfactory progress in liberalising trade in agricultural products, a stance very much in line with Australian views (at this time the US was still persisting with the 10 per cent surcharge on imports by President Nixon). Canadian officials also strongly supported a proposal from Australia that it make a formal submission to the group as regards the importance of freeing up agricultural trade for countries such as New Zealand, Australia and Canada, so as to help focus the work of the HLG on the issue and, at least to some extent, balance the views of EEC members of the Group (NAA, 1971i).

The HLG membership issue was important in that, while it clearly indicated the limited influence of Australian officials in regard to major trade issues, they were able to make the Australian position clear and were also able to work with other, sympathetic OECD members, especially Canada, work that provided them with a clear picture of the views being expressed. However, as with their efforts in the GATT for most of its existence, the fact that agricultural trade was now also being discussed in the OECD did not bring with it any immediate increase in Australian access or influence.

The 1974 OECD Trade Pledge

If the first review of Australian trade policy at the OECD could be characterised as 'cordial', the same could not be said for the experience of Australian officials at a ten-hour long meeting of the Working Party of the Trade Committee in March 1975. The first oil crisis following the October 1973 Middle East war had seriously disrupted many countries' balance of payments and economies. The very sharp rise in oil prices resulted in rising trade deficits, especially for oil importing countries. As a result the spectre of a rapid rise in protectionist trade measures by members loomed large, with detrimental results for world trade. In order to help reduce if not prevent this development the OECD members agreed to work towards a joint declaration, the 'Trade Pledge', in April 1974. The Pledge was adopted unanimously in May 1974, with members agreeing to a co-operative approach to the difficulties caused by the oil crisis and, in particular, to consult regarding proposed measures and to avoid any unilateral actions to protect their balance of payments for one year.

Australia's trade position leading up to the Trade Pledge had been increasingly difficult, even before the first oil crisis. The UK's entry to the EEC in 1973 was beginning to have a major, adverse impact on Australian exports to UK markets at the same time as: (1) the EEC's massively subsidised sugar exports were cutting sharply into Australia's hard won Asian markets; (2) Canada and the US had cut their imports of Australian beef; and (3) in 1974 Japan had placed an embargo on the import of beef which led to a 60 per cent fall in Australia's total beef exports (Capling, 2001: 89). Also, inflation in Australia was running at 17 per cent, among the highest of the OECD members. In addition, Australian producers were still coming to terms with the major changes in policy introduced by the Whitlam government, as explained to the OECD Trade Committee in the review of Australia's trade policies. The impact of the first oil crisis severely exacerbated this already challenging situation.

While Australia became a signatory to the Pledge, Australian officials were not happy about its lack of precise detail, though appreciating its political and symbolic importance in signalling the commitment of OECD members to dealing with the economic dislocation caused by the oil crisis. Moreover, Australia's interpretation was that the Pledge did not apply to trade measures related to specific products covered by the GATT Article XIX, as noted in the Pledge. It was also indicated at the time of the agreement on the Pledge that Australia did not regard it as applying to its export controls on minerals, which had been in force for some time (NAA, 1975a). Indeed, Australia retained a 'reserve', regarding the Pledge until only a few days before the Ministerial Council meeting that agreed to the Pledge (NAA, 1975b). In the successful proposal that the Pledge be renewed in 1975, Frank Crean, Minister for Overseas Development, argued to Cabinet that it would harm Australia's international credibility if it did not renew its commitment because it would call into question Australia's widely stated position that its recent imposition of import restrictions on a variety of products was only temporary and not a reversal of its general policy of a more open and outward approach to international trade (NAA, 1975a).

Interestingly, Minister Crean's letter to Prime Minister Whitlam did not mention the considerable irritation that Australia's 1974–75 imposition of import restrictions on textiles and cars had caused to the US Administration, the Japanese government and OECD Secretary-General van Lennep. In January 1975, for example, the State Department noted its serious concern about the implications of the Australian textile import restrictions, allegedly introduced to counter rapidly rising unemployment, for fear it might spark off a series of 'beggar my neighbour', responses from other members. It had raised its concerns with the Australian Ambassador in Washington on 2 January and planned to raise the issue in Canberra (State Department, 1975a). In February van Lennep discussed the matter with the US Delegation, arguing that the recent imposition of import quotas on cars by Australia was a further and first major violation of the Pledge. He was aware of the Australian argument that the quotas were a sectoral action outside of the scope of the Pledge, made under the authority of GATT Article XIX, but considered that it was just a 'technical cover', and argued the actions should not be allowed to proceed without a strong OECD response, asking if other major countries would support his invoking the Pledge in the OECD Council so as to head off similar moves by other members (State Department, 1975b).

While sympathetic to van Lennep's proposal, US officials decided that it would be inadvisable to drag Australia though the Trade Pledge 'Court' of the OECD Council at a time when the US was keen to see the Pledge renewed, a move that might be harmed by a lengthy argument over the details of the issue. Australian officials, it was felt, would stress that the quotas fell within the GATT Article XIX 'escape' clause of the Pledge and, perhaps, point to the OECD's failure to deal with the recently imposed Japanese and US restrictions on meat imports. In addition, there were signs that the UK and New Zealand governments had reservations about renewing the Pledge. Also, on a distinctly pragmatic basis, from the US perspective it might itself be obliged to take similar 'escape clause' actions in the future. Hence, it was decided to first raise the matter on a bilateral basis with the Australian government and then in the 20 February 1975 meeting of the OECD Executive Committee in Special Session, to ask it for an assurance that the quotas and other restrictions were only of a temporary nature (State Department, 1975b).

On 13 March US Embassy officials in Canberra called on Lionel Bowen, the Special Minister of State and acting Minister for Overseas Trade, to express their concern at the Australian government's import restrictions. In an extended discussion Bowen assured the officials that the measures were emergency steps to meet unprecedented surges in imports and an unemployment crisis until the IAC could examine the situation and make recommendations for any longer term action. He also indicated that the US concern would be brought to the attention of the Prime Minister, indicating that it would be helpful in encouraging Cabinet to continue to carefully weigh up the international impact of such measures.

While Bowen's assurances were well received, the OECD Trade Committee's Working Party decided to examine the Australian case in detail at a meeting on 24–25 March (the British introduction of a system of 'inflation insurance', in effect an export subsidy, was examined at the same meeting). The meeting was far from cordial, lasting a gruelling ten hours, during which Mr B.F. Meere (Assistant Secretary, Department of Overseas Trade), repeated the official position put by Minister Bowen and was subject to a wide range of penetrating questions and critical views from members of the Working Party. The Canadian member, for example, representing a country usually sympathetic to the Australian cause as regards trade, was reported as stating that the trade restrictions in question might be only the tip of the Australia protection 'iceberg', while the Swedish member stated baldly that the measures were not in accord with the spirit of the Trade Pledge.

In conclusion, the Working Party took no formal position on the consistency of Australia's actions with the Trade Pledge but agreed that such actions should not serve as a justification for any similar actions other governments might contemplate. It was further agreed to keep a watching brief on the Australian situation and leave the matter open for further 'consultations', if warranted (State Department, 1975d). The incident could hardly have improved the likelihood of repeated Australian proposals for action to liberalise agriculture at the OECD and the GATT. While the US wanted to have agricultural products negotiated on the same basis as all other products during the Tokyo Round that had commenced in 1973, the EEC would not agree and the Australian government again decided not to participate in negotiations on industrial products during the Round as negotiations on agricultural commodities were not included in the negotiations on the same terms.

AUSTRALIA, THE URUGUAY ROUND AND THE OECD

In contrast to the difficulties associated with the High Level Group on Trade and the Trade Pledge, the end of the 1970s and, in particular, the1980s saw a more strategic and somewhat more successful approach by Australia to the trade-related activity of the OECD, focused on its use and value in relation to the preparations for the Uruguay Round of trade negotiations and, to a lesser extent, in the actual Round negotiations. This was in marked contrast to the somewhat reactive posture it had adopted in the early years of membership, where, in reference to the 1974 annual review of the OECD post by the DFA, the OECD Ambassador, R.J. Cameron noted that:

> All too often departments seem to want to merely react to other countries' attitudes and not to have a clear idea of the outcome they wish to see emerge. (NAA, 1975b)

The 1970s were a period of substantial change in agricultural policy in Australia, moving away from the ad hoc decision making undertaken in close cooperation with producer groups and overseen by Country Party ministers, to more systematic, more market oriented policies and programmes aimed at assisting structural change under the Whitlam, ALP governments (Throsby, 1972). This rather inward-looking focus, combined with the lack of substantial developments at the OECD, meant that Australian participation in the trade work of the organisation was relatively passive for much of the latter half of the 1970s, other than its constant and unsuccessful urgings for a reduction in protection for agriculture, including trade in agriculture, usually in support of the USA and Canada positions. Instead, as Capling notes, in the second half of the 1970s Prime Minister Malcolm Fraser engaged in an unsuccessful process of 'executive diplomacy', involving very critical attacks on the CAP. The government also undertook the negotiation of a series of bilateral agreements with the Quad countries (Canada, the USA, Japan and the EEC) that provided, however, only a minor improvement in access for Australia's agricultural products (Capling, 2001: 90–91).

It was not until 1979 that the OECD's Ministerial Council agreed to the commencement of the organisation's first comprehensive study of the problems of agricultural trade, stimulated by: (1) the increasing realisation of the rapidly growing costs to EEC members of the CAP, especially with further EEC enlargement looming; (2) similar, rapidly increasing annual budget costs for farm programmes for the USA; (3) continuing pressure for reforms in a pro-market direction by the USA, Canada and Australia; (4) developing recession or 'stagflation' with an accompanying slump in global commodity prices; (5) perhaps most of all, the damaging impact of the second oil price shock of 1979. The annual budget cost, for example, of EEC outlays on farm programmes doubled between 1975 and 1986, and the annual budget cost of US farm programmes increased five-fold, to US$26 billion, with a similar situation developing in Japan (Paarlberg, 1997). This study of the problems of agricultural trade initiated in 1979 was part of a wider, 'concerted action program', by the OECD that had commenced in 1978 (OECD, 1979).

However, at the end of the 1970s there were no independent measures of the actual extent of agricultural subsidies, measures essential if there was to be effective discussion and negotiation of their actual impact and reduction. It was in this context, as part of the study of agricultural trade requested by the 1979 Ministerial Council that the concepts of producer subsidy equivalents (PSEs) and consumer subsidy equivalents (CSEs) were initially applied and calculated at the OECD for Australia, Austria, Canada, the EEC, Japan, New Zealand and the United States for the period 1979 to 1981 (OECD, 2008: 26). The concepts derived from the work of Australian Max Corden and had been further developed by Tim Josling in work for the FAO (Corden, 1971; Josling, 1973, 1975). A PSE, whether it was an import tariff, export subsidy, or one of a range of possible payments per tonne to farmers, is the payment per unit of output that a government has to pay producers to generate the same impact on production as the policy measure in question. It captures explicitly all domestic agricultural policy measures that directly or indirectly affect trade, thus including all domestic policies causing trade distortions, not only those of explicit trade barriers.

While later modified and improved, the concept came to be used by or built upon by a number of states, for example, by the USA and Canada for the US–Canada Free Trade Agreement and in the European Commission's Aggregate Measure of Support (AMS). The PSEs and CSEs, most importantly, provided a basis for the OECD's Trade Mandate Study, as formally proposed by New Zealand Prime Minister Robert Muldoon, with the strong support of the USA and Australia at the 1979 Ministerial Council. As noted by New Zealand officials, their:

> [M]ain concern had been to stop agricultural officials from Community capitals who come to meetings from having an undue influence on the direction of the work and the content of the final text. This is an uphill battle. (New Zealand Archives, 1981)

The study brought together the Trade, Agriculture and Economic Directorates. It examined the consequences of reductions in the protection of the agricultural sector in member countries, work carried out by the Directorate for Food, Agriculture and Fisheries (OECD, 1987a, 1987b; Blair, 1993: 131; Lattimore and McKeown, 1995: 7). The model developed in this process then became the initial foundation for the annual monitoring of agricultural policy changes by members to determine the extent of protection existing and whether or not agreed reforms were being implemented.

With the convincing evidence of the very large costs of agricultural protection provided by the PSEs and CSEs showing that, for the most part, it was domestic agricultural policies that were responsible for the situation (notably the CAP), at the 1982 OECD Ministerial Council it was agreed that: (1) agricultural trade should be more fully integrated within an open and multilateral trading system; and (2) that the desirable adjustments in domestic policies could best take place if such moves were coordinated within a concerted multilateral approach aimed at achieving a gradual reduction in protection and a liberalisation of trade. The Secretariat was instructed to examine the various ways in which the aim of integration could be achieved and to draw up a detailed proposal for the implementation of the Mandate.

What should or should not be included in the implementation plan excited vigorous and at times contentious discussion in the Trade and the Agriculture Committees, as well as their Joint Working Party (DAFF, 1982). The outcomes of the discussion were felt to be generally satisfactory by Australian officials as the implementation plan was largely endorsed and they were able to gain the incorporation of some new elements in the plan, with the support of New Zealand, Canada and the USA (known informally at this time as the Pacific Economic Group, or PEG), including recognition that the work should be as quantitative as possible and that it should look at economy-wide effects of agricultural policies and measures (DAFF, 1982).

The first major results of the Mandate Study were released by the OECD in 1987, in its publication 'National Policies and Agricultural Trade', which provided a detailed analysis of the agricultural policies of individual OECD countries based largely on the PSE and related indicators (OECD, 1987a, 1987b). The study recognised the linkages between domestic and trade policies and concluded that in order to improve the trading environment actions were necessary on both trade barriers and domestic policies. While the study was only released in 1987 its findings regarding the sheer extent of subsidies relating to trade in agriculture and their origin in domestic policies had been a matter of intense discussion within the OECD for over a year and were an important factor in the gradual reduction of the EEC's resistance to OECD work on agricultural trade and to the inclusion of agriculture in the Uruguay Round (Kenyon and Lee, 2006: 56–7; Blair, 1993: 131).

Australian support was critical to the success of these studies, which were also strongly encouraged by the Trade and Finance Ministries of most OECD members and, while it was not made explicit, the studies were part of a strategy to increase awareness of the need for agricultural reform that was carefully stage managed by the Secretariat and key member countries, notably the USA, Australia, Canada and New Zealand to avoid them being undermined by European and Japanese opposition. Similar, detailed studies of the adverse impact of agricultural subsidies and protection also began to appear in a wide range of journals. In Australia, for example, the Australian Bureau of Agricultural and

Resource Economics (ABARE) published a series of monographs that outlined the agricultural policies of Japan, the EEC and the CAP, and DFAT commissioned the Industries Assistance Commission to conduct an analysis of the economic effects of alternative trade liberalisation scenarios, based on the OECD's WALRAS model (ABARE, 1985a, 1985b, 1988; Industry Commission, 1991).

In 1986 the Uruguay Round commenced and ALP Trade Minister Dawkins proposed that the Australian government's main priority should be to work towards more effective GATT provisions on controlling export subsidies for agriculture. Cabinet agreed and also established a small group of officials from relevant departments to examine its possible strategies for the Round (Kenyon and Lee, 2006: 56). The group concentrated on two strategies: (1) focusing efforts on gaining agreements to measures that would reduce the aggregate level of support for agriculture, based on the work developed in the OECD; and (2) negotiating the strengthening of GATT rules. The group also favoured the USA's position of aiming for a general prohibition on direct subsidies that would be introduced over a ten-year period. In addition, with the attention of the USA primarily focused on getting trade in services on to the Uruguay Round's agenda, and mindful of Australia's relative weakness in such negotiations, Trade Minister Dawkins and the new Department of Foreign Affairs and Trade (DFAT), focused on organising a group of similarly minded countries to push for agricultural reform (Kenyon and Lee, 2006). The assumption was that acting as a group the members would have greater influence in the Round, and the Cairns Group was established in 1986.

While the Uruguay Round negotiations in Geneva were the major focus of trade policy in the 1986–94 period, there was a frequent interaction between the OECD and the major actors involved in the negotiations as the actors drew upon the technical analysis of trade undertaken in the OECD. At the 1987 Ministerial Council, for example, Australia strongly supported the Council's endorsement of the Joint Report of the Trade and Agriculture Committees, 'National Policies and Agricultural Trade', which pointed out the costs and adverse impacts of agricultural protection and subsidies. The Council also endorsed a set of principles for their reform, 'the 1987 Principles', a proposal that an implementation plan would be developed, and that the progress of members in implementing the Principles would be assessed in an annual Monitoring and Outlook report, based on the PSE and CSE measures (OECD, 1987c). The implementation of the Principles proved a lengthy and difficult task, with only Australia, the USA and New Zealand taking significant steps to implement the Principles domestically (DAFF, 1993).

The May 1987 Ottawa meeting of the Cairns Group unanimously endorsed the OECD Principles and the three Group members who were also members of the OECD (Australia, Canada and New Zealand) sometimes took a coordinated approach to issues at OECD meetings, also feeding into the meetings Cairns Group ideas and views, often in cooperation with the USA. However, it proved difficult for the Group to exercise much in the way of influence at the OECD during the Uruguay Round with all of the latter's members being very sensitive to activities that might jeopardise their positions in the GATT negotiations (DAFF, 1993).

CONCLUSION

Australian views regarding OECD work on trade and agriculture varied over time. They changed from one of considerable concern at the implications of membership for Australia's trade policy, to one of mixed feelings where concerns were allayed by the cordial reception of its initial trade policy stance, but were accompanied by a growing disappointment at its early lack of influence and the mundane nature of much of the OECD's early work on trade in agriculture. Then, as the 1980s progressed, views became more positive as, working in often close cooperation with the USA, Canada, New Zealand and members of the Secretariat, their persistent lobbying for a detailed examination of the often adverse impact of members' domestic agricultural policies on trade met with increasing success. In turn, the information provided by a growing range of OECD studies, especially those using the PSE and CSE measures, provided a 'common language' for more informed and productive, if still difficult and sensitive discussions, ones that helped, in turn, the progress of negotiations in the Uruguay Round and the establishment of the WTO.

The period examined also showed how a new and relatively small member of the OECD such as Australia could be more influential in its continuing drive to persuade members to move towards free trade in agricultural products when it did so: (1) on the basis of a coherent strategy, finally developed in 1986–87; (2) when working in cooperation with like-minded members such as the USA, Canada, New Zealand and the members of the Cairns Group; and (3) when OECD work demonstrated the adverse costs of members' existing policies, providing objective evidence to support those arguing for change.

BIBLIOGRAPHY

ABARE 1985a. 'Agricultural Policies in the European Community', Policy Monograph No. 2, AGPS, Canberra.

ABARE 1985b. 'Intersectoral Effects of the CAP: Growth, Trade and Unemployment', Stoeckel, A, Occasional Paper No. 95, AGPS, Canberra.

ABARE 1988. 'Japanese Agricultural Policies', Policy Monograph No. 3, ABARE, AGPS, Canberra.

Anderson, K. and Garnaut, R. 1987. *Australian Protectionism: Extent, Causes and Effects*, Boston, London and Sydney: Allen and Unwin.

Banks, G. and Carmichael, B. 2007. 'Domestic Transparency in Australia's Economic and Trade Reforms: The Role of 'the Commission', accessed on 25 January 2015 at www.oecd.org/australia/39217022.pdf.

Bell, S. 1993. *Australian Manufacturing and the State: The Politics of Industry Policy in the Post-war Era*, Cambridge: Cambridge University Press.

Blair, D. 1993. *Trade Negotiations in the OECD*, London and New York: Kegan Paul International.

Capling, A. 2001. *Australia and the Global Trade System from Havana to Seattle*, Cambridge: Cambridge University Press.

Corden, M. 1971. *The Theory of Protection*, London: Oxford University Press.

DAFF 1982. A note dated 25 February 1983 to the Department of Agriculture, Fisheries and Food (DAFF), from the Paris Delegation regarding the Joint Working Party meeting of 21–23 February 1983, DAFF File No 435-5-375 Part 12DPI 'OECD Joint Working Party of Agriculture and Trade Committees', as held in DAFF Secondary Storage, Canberra.

DAFF 1993. 'OECD Committee for Agriculture Meeting Paris 13–16 April 1993', a 24-page briefing note for the meeting contained in an 8 April 1993 fax from Noel Benyon to Joanna Hewitt, DAFF File No 94-000240 'OECD Committee for Agriculture', held in DAFF Secondary Storage.

Industry Commission 1991. *SALTER A General Equilibrium Model of the World Economy Volume 2 Gains from Global Trade Liberalisation: An Illustrative Application of SALTER*, Canberra: Industry Commission.

Irwin, D. 2012. 'THE NIXON SHOCK AFTER FORTY YEARS: THE IMPORT SURCHARGE REVISITED', National Bureau of Economic Research, Working Paper 17749, accessed on 20 January 2017 from www.nber.org/papers/w17749.

Josling, T. 1973. 'Agricultural Protection: Domestic Policy and International Trade', c/73/LIM/9, FAO.

Josling, T. 1975. 'Agricultural Protection and Stabilisation Policies: a Framework of Measurement in the Context of Agricultural Adjustment', c/75/LIM/2, FAO.

Kenyon, D. and Lee, D. 2006. *The Struggle for Trade Liberalisation in Agriculture: Australia and the Cairns Group in the Uruguay Round*, Canberra: Commonwealth of Australia.

Lattimore, R. and McKeown, P. 1995. 'New Zealand's International Trade Performance Pre and Post Deregulation: 1970–1985 and 1985–1993', Research Report No. 231, Agribusiness and Economics Research Unit, Lincoln University, Canterbury, New Zealand.

Leigh, A. 2002. 'Trade Liberalisation and the Australian Labor Party', *Australian Journal of Politics and History*, 48(4): 487–508.

NAA 1960a. 'Proposed re-organisation of O.E.E.C.', an Outward Cablegram from the DEA to posts in Washington, Paris, Ottawa, Geneva and London, dated 20 May 1960, asking that officials make it known to all bodies with which they were accredited that Australia was concerned that the proposed OECD Convention appears to embrace functions in trade and economic policy 'that are not confined to purely European matters'. We fear that a large and influential body of OECD members would come to the GATT 'already committed to policy lines already agreed in Paris to which we were not a party and to which we might be opposed. Our chances of influencing decisions in GATT on these policies would be nil.' NAA Series 1838 File No 724/4/2 Part 1 Committee on Trade.

NAA 1960b. 'European Economic Conference Points for Discussion', 20 January 1960. This file also contains a number of urgent requests for information, NAA Series 1838 File No 724/4/2 Part 1 Committee on Trade.

NAA 1969a. 'OECD Question of Australian Membership'. Discussions with Simantov, Trezise and Poincilit, 10–11 March 1969, summarised in three separate reports, NAA Series 1838, File 'Examination of Australian Membership of OECD (1969)'.

NAA 1969b. 'OECD and Australia', dated 4 July 1969, a memo for the DEA Secretary from K.C.O. Shann, in which the Department of Trade and Industry's position regarding the OECD in 1965 is described, NAA Series 1838, File 'Examination of Australian Membership of OECD (1969)'.

NAA 1969c. 'OECD – Consideration of Australian Membership', a letter from the Secretary of the DPI, Walter Ives, to K.C.O. Shann in the DEA that outlined the views of the DPI regarding the OECD, NAA Series 1838, File 'Examination of Australian Membership of OECD (1969)'.

NAA 1970a. 'OECD – Question of Australian Membership Exploratory Discussions Paris 6–16 October, 1970', a Report by F.P. Donovan, later to be Ambassador to the OECD, from the Australian High Commission, London, NAA Series 1838 724-4-30 Part 6 Accession.

NAA 1970b. 'OECD', a memo dated 11 November 1970 from Mr Kenneth Bailey to Mr L. Corkery in the DFA regarding the legal implications of aspects of OECD membership. NAA Series 1838 724-4-30 Part 7 Accession.

NAA 1970c. 'OECD Examination of the Obligations of Possible Australian Membership', a letter from the DTI's First Assistant Secretary J.T. Fogarty to the Secretary of the DFA regarding the draft list. NAA Series 1838 724-4-30 Part 7 Accession.

NAA 1971a. 'OECD Summary Record of an Interdepartmental Meeting held on 1st September 1971', NAA Series 1838 File 724/4/40 PART 1 OECD – Visit of Secretary-General to Australia – 1971.

NAA 1971b. 'OECD Ministerial Council – Trade Item', Inward Cablegram from Alan Renouf to the Minister DFA dated 18 May 1971.

NAA 1971c. 'OECD', a summary of an interdepartmental meeting of 31 March 1971, addressed by Ambassador Greenwald, NAA Folder 724/4/44 PART 2.

NAA 1971d. An outward cablegram to the Australian Embassy in Paris providing instructions in regard to the proposed HLG, dated 20 May 1971, NAA Folder 724/4/44 PART 2.
NAA 1971e. An outward cablegram to the Australian Delegation to the OECD providing instructions regarding HLG membership, dated 7 October 1971, NAA Folder 724/4/44 PART 2.
NAA 1971f. An outward cablegram to the Australian Delegation to the OECD providing instructions regarding HLG membership, dated 11 October 1971, NAA Folder 724/4/44 PART 2.
NAA 1971g. An outward cablegram dated 24 November 1971 from Canberra for Ambassador Walker, noting the matter had been discussed and agreed with Minister Doug Anthony, NAA Folder 724/4/44 PART 2.
NAA 1971h. Inward cablegram dated 7 December 1971 from Ambassador Walker to Canberra, NAA Folder 724/4/44 PART 2.
NAA 1971i. Inward cablegram dated 14 December 1971 from the OECD Delegation to Canberra, NAA Folder 724/4/44 PART 2.
NAA 1971j. 'Notes on Australian Trade and Related Matters', dated January 1971, by the DTI, NAA Folder A1838-724-4-30 Part 11 Accession.
NAA 1972a. A handwritten letter dated 25 October 1972 from M.J. Dan in the OECD Delegation to FAS Jim Cumes, in DFA, NAA Folder A1838-724-4-2-5 Part 1 Australian Relations with OECD.
NAA 1972b. A Memorandum dated 1 November 1972 from FAS International Organisations, J.W.C. Cumes to the Deputy Secretary regarding the annual review of the post, NAA Folder A1838-724-4-2-5 Part 1 Australian Relations with OECD.
NAA 1972c. 'OECD', the record of a meeting at DFA on 19 December 1972 to review Australian participation at the OECD, NAA Folder 1838-724-4-2-5 Part 1 Australian Relations with OECD.
NAA 1972d. An outward cablegram from Canberra to the OECD Delegation dated 24 March 1972, NAA Folder A1838 724/4/10/2 PART 1.
NAA 1972e. An inward cablegram from the OECD Delegation to Canberra dated 24 March 1972, NAA Folder A1838 724/4/10/2 PART 1.
NAA 1973. 'OECD – Review of Agricultural Policies', dated 6 July 1973, from the DPI's Deputy Secretary, R.S. Swift, to the Secretary of the Department of Foreign Affairs. NAA Folder A1838 1 – 724-4-12-6 Part 2.
NAA 1974a. A detailed, inward cablegram from the OECD Delegation to Canberra dated 23 May 1974, NAA Folder A1838 724/4/10/2 PART 1.
NAA 1974b. 'OECD – Examination of Australia's Trade Policy', a letter and attachment dated 25 March 1974 from J.T. Fogarty, First Assistant Secretary, the International Trade Organizations Division of the Department of Overseas Trade to the Secretary of the DFA, NAA Folder A1838 724/4/10/2 PART 1.
NAA 1975a. 'OECD Trade Declaration', Briefing notes for the Treasurer dated 19 May 1975 in response to a proposal from the Minister for Overseas Trade, J.F. 'Jim', Cairns to Prime Minister Whitlam that the Australia agree to the renewal of the Pledge on the original terms and conditions, NAA Folder A571-110 – 1975 – 1224 Part 1.
NAA 1975b. 'OECD Annual Review for 1974', NAA Folder 1838 724-4-2-5 Part 2.

New Zealand Archives 1981. 'The OECD and New Zealand Membership – An Assessment', R17724827, Part 1, 'Miscellaneous International Organisations – OECD [Organisation for Economic Co-operation and Development] – NZ Membership [01/1971–11/1981].

OECD 1979. 'Meeting of the Council at Ministerial Level in June 1979 Communiqué', accessed 10 March 2015 at http://www.g8.utoronto.ca/oecd/oecd79.htm.

OECD 1987a. 'OECD National Policies and Agricultural Trade', OECD, Paris (Synthesis Report).

OECD 1987b. 'National Policies and Agricultural Trade – Country Studies: Australia; Canada; European Economic Community; Japan; New Zealand; United States', Paris: OECD.

OECD 1987c. 'Communique – Meeting of the Council at Ministerial Level in May 1987', Paris: OECD.

OECD 2008. 'OECD's Producer Support Estimate and Related Indicators of Agricultural Support: Concepts, Calculations, Interpretation and Use (The PSE Manual)', Paris: OECD.

Paarlberg, R. 1997. 'Agricultural Policy Reform and the Uruguay Round: Synergistic Linkage in a Two-Level Game?' *International Organization*, 51(3): 413–44.

State Department 1975a. Electronic Telegram, 1975STATE001803_b, 4 January 1975.

State Department 1975b. Electronic Telegram, 1975OECDP03454_b, 7 February 1975.

State Department 1975c. Electronic Telegram, 1975CANBER01592_b, 13 March, 1975.

State Department 1975d. Electronic Telegram, 1975OECDP07946_b, 28 March 1975.

Throsby, C. 1972. 'Background to Agricultural Policy', in C.D. Throsby (ed.), *Agricultural Policy: Selected Readings*, Ringwood: Penguin Books, pp. 23–32.

7. The Development Assistance Committee: a slowly declining priority

Australia became a member of the OECD's Development Assistance Committee (DAC) in 1966, some five years before it became a member of the OECD in 1971. The aims of this chapter are to: (1) briefly outline Australia's growing involvement in foreign aid from 1945 to 1965, providing the background against which interest in the DAC developed; (2) examine Australia's participation in the DAC in the years to 1971, with a focus on DAC's peer reviews and their publication, the volume of aid and tied aid; (3) investigate the continuing issue of aid volumes and their political sensitivity; (4) assess the increase in the use of tied aid, export credits and mixed credits in the 1970s and1980s; and (5) examine the relatively low priority attached to DAC work in the 1990s and early 2000s.

CONTEXT: AUSTRALIA AND DEVELOPMENT ASSISTANCE 1945 TO 1965

In the years after 1945 Australia's developing aid policy came to have a three-fold focus. The first was on the UN system, the second was on Papua New Guinea (PNG) and the third was bilateral aid, focused primarily through the Colombo Plan. Overall, Australian aid when entering the DAC in 1966 was almost entirely in grant form, rather than loans, with an emphasis on technical assistance using Australian experts and with a strong emphasis on scholarships for study and training in Australia. While aid to PNG was not technically tied, Australian aid to other countries in the 1950s and 1960s was tied to varying extents, requiring recipients to procure equipment and supplies from Australian sources, though Australian policies in this regard were viewed as relatively liberal by the DAC (OECD, 1969: 42). The impact of the notionally untied aid to PNG was to substantially reduce Australia's overall level of tied aid compared to most other DAC donors. However, as PNG aid was largely planned and administered by Australian officials in Australia and PNG (before independence), with the bulk of the aid used to purchase Australian goods and services it was, in effect, tied aid.

Philip Flood, later to become DFAT's secretary and head of AusAID from 1993 to 1994, was also Australia's first representative on DAC, from 1966 to 1969. He noted in his memoirs that on taking up the latter position, 'Australia's aid administration was a very rudimentary structure', though it made enormous progress in the years that followed (Flood, 2011: 225; Wilkinson 1976: 215). An interdepartmental review of external aid in 1964–65 shortly before membership of DAC, was the first overall review of Australian aid policy in over fifteen years and, while generally supportive of the current thrust of aid policy, was critical of the lack of coordination in its administration (NAA, 1965; Wilkinson, 1976). The committee had recommended membership of the OECD's DAC. A young Philip Flood had been one of the review committee's secretaries and was primarily responsible for drawing up the committee's final report (Wilkinson, 1976: 243).

THE DAC AND AUSTRALIAN MEMBERSHIP: THE EARLY YEARS

The Development Assistance Group (DAG), DAC's predecessor, sprang out of the Eisenhower Administration's interest in promoting and coordinating greater aid to the developing world by Western European states, an interest stimulated by: (1) the potential threat posed by growing Soviet interests in the developing countries; and (2) related to the first, the aim of getting the larger OEEC members to increase their flow of aid (Dillon, 1960). The group consisted of Belgium, Canada, France, Germany, Italy, Portugal, the UK, USA and the EEC's Commission. The Japanese government was immediately invited to join and the Netherlands joined in July 1960.

Australian diplomats had been aware of these developments from at least December 1959 and discussion took place as to whether or not Australia should express an interest in membership of the DAG. However, despite promised support from both Canada and the UK should Australia request membership, Cabinet decided in February 1960 not to pursue DAG membership, nor membership of the OECD as a whole as: (1) it was felt Australia was a net importer of capital and not able to make significant amounts available for aid purposes; (2) Australian aid was provided largely through the Colombo Plan, which had its own consultative machinery, so membership of the OECD's DAC was not necessary; and (3) fears that DAG or OECD membership would bring US pressure for an increase in Australian aid (NAA, 1960a, 1960b). In addition, there was the general opposition to membership of the OECD by influential Deputy Prime Minister, John McEwen, as described in earlier chapters. Further, there was a concern that too close an Australian association with the DAG might not go down well with some of the East Asian and South East Asian countries (excluding Japan), then increasingly being targeted as potential markets for Australian exports by the DTI.

Despite continuing ministerial disagreements regarding the value of membership of DAG/DAC and the OECD, the DEA decided to propose such membership to Cabinet in September 1965. The 1964–65 review had noted that if membership of the OECD was not acceptable, then membership of DAC, following Japan's example, would enable Australia: (1) to make the Australian aid effort better known; (2) ensure that the aid policies of the major Western powers were not formulated in ignorance of Australia's interests; (3) to bring home to an important group of countries the extent of Australian responsibilities in PNG; (4) draw European attention to the aid needs and development prospects of Asia; and (5) to coordinate its aid effort with Europeans and other aid donors. Also, there was no doubt that DAC membership was seen as a first step towards later, full OECD membership as it would provide a better understanding of the OECD and, hopefully, increase support for Australian membership. While Cabinet decided not to proceed with an attempt to gain OECD membership at this time, it did agree that an application for membership of the DAC could proceed, despite the lack of support from the US Administration (NAA, 1965a).

The period leading up to full OECD membership in 1971 saw the cautious establishment of Australia as a new DAC member, only the second, after Japan, from the Southern Hemisphere. Phillip Flood was appointed as Australia's first representative. His task was two-fold: (1) representing Australia's interests in the DAC; and (2) providing more detailed information regarding the OECD to Canberra, increasingly with a view to supporting moves towards full membership. He was supported by the appointment of K.C.O. 'Mick' Shann to head up the DEA division that included external aid (but not PNG), in April 1966. Shann was keen to upgrade the status and performance of the DEA's aid policy and programmes following the 1964–65 review, including its new links with DAC, and he attended its annual High Level Meeting (HLM) each year. In addition, James Ingram was appointed to a re-graded position of Assistant Secretary and made responsible for the formulation and implementation of aid policy in DEA. Ingram later became Director-General of the Australian Development Assistance Bureau from 1975 to 1982, when he was also the Australian representative on the DAC (Wilkinson, 1976: 237, 241; Flood, 2011: 5).

Despite this additional support the work of Australian officials at the DAC and its working parties was made difficult by the fact that documents from the Secretariat were often circulated less than a week before a meeting so that, at times, they had to operate without a briefing from Canberra for DAC meetings, a situation also often faced in the early years of Australia's full OECD membership (NAA, 1966a). A Treasury representative from the Australian High Commission in London attended several DAC meetings, including the first review of Australian aid and there was initial concern as to which department had responsibility for DAC (NAA, 1966b). However, attendance by Treasury officials at DAC meetings dropped off sharply in later years (NAA, 1968a).

As he later described it, Flood saw his role in these early years as being to ensure that Australia's aid policy was well understood, to seek to persuade member countries to take a stronger interest in Southeast Asia, and, more generally, to work to temper the influence of the European members of the OECD whose focus was on matters primarily of concern to Europe (Flood, 2011: 53). In addition, he had no doubt that as regards DAC a primary aim was to learn from its officials and members, noting:

> Even more importantly, I was charged with seeking knowledge and information that would enable Australia to strengthen the quality of its aid policy and bring added efficiency to the administration of its aid program. (Flood, 2011: 52–3)

Similarly, in praising the quality of the members of DAC, he noted that:

> Working alongside these and other talented professional colleagues brought home to me the weak nature of Australia's aid administration. Although some gains had been made following the conduct of the aid review of 1964–65, responsibility for running Australia's aid program remained divided among four departments: External Affairs, External Territories (responsible for aid to Papua New Guinea), Treasury and Education. Compared with the aid administration of many other countries, ours was not professional: it was not well coordinated; it placed little emphasis on innovation, research or evaluation; and it did not offer staff an effective career structure. (Flood, 2011: 52–3)

DAC Peer Reviews of Australian Aid

The DAC's assessment of members' aid policy and administration in its peer review process was a major focus of Australian interest at the DAC in these early years, the first Australian policy area to be subject to peer review by an OECD body before the EDRC reviews commenced after full membership in 1971. It was, in effect, a key, sometimes rather painful learning experience, primarily for the country being examined, but also for the examining members.

As the volume of Australian aid was increasing in this period the tenor of the early reviews was largely positive. The first took place in 1966 only two months after membership of DAC had been taken up, with a set of guidance notes provided for the Australian delegation, as well as the key questions to be asked by the examiners. The review's report was very positive in its findings, though largely exploratory in nature, with existing DAC members having little knowledge of the details of Australian aid and its development. As described by Laurence McIntyre, acting DEA Secretary in a note to his Minister, the examination by the Committee was lively and stimulating 'and at all times friendly and helpful', fully justifying, he felt, the government's decision to join the DAC. In particular, he noted that its advice could not fail to be helpful in formulating recommendations to the Minister in the aid field and in the development of aid policy. The latter, McIntyre suggested, in a less than subtle observation, had suffered in the past 'from an acute shortage of staff in the department'. However, he also warned that future reviews would be more probing (NAA, 1966c).

As McIntyre foretold, the second, 1967 review, while still somewhat exploratory in nature, was also in parts critical, focusing on three areas. The first was what the examiners felt was the relatively low level of Australian aid provided on a multilateral basis through bodies such as the World Bank, compared to most DAC members. The second was the unusually large proportion of aid to PNG, which constituted some 60 per cent of Australian aid at this time. Linked to this issue was the relatively small amount of Australian aid being provided to other Asian countries, although that provided in the context of the Colombo Plan received positive attention and the volume of aid to Indonesia was beginning to rise rapidly (Wilkinson, 1976: 231–2). These were issues that were to persist for several decades in the context of the reviews.

Deputy Secretary Shann was not at all happy with the second review, noting that it seems 'to be all the time looking for something to harp about', perhaps indicating that not all learning experiences, or the potential for them, were welcomed, though his was not an untypical response from those whose work was being evaluated by others and, at times, found wanting. Shann's views also indicated the political sensitivity that the reviews, or elements of them, could evoke, regardless of their accuracy. He asserted that:

> The general attitude of the Secretariat confirms my strong opposition to their being permitted to publish annual reviews of each country's aid. This would be most unlikely to help us and would cut across the confidence we have so far felt in working with the DAC. (NAA, 1967a)

The early DAC reviews evoked sensitivities in at least three ways. The first was the typical, individual and often negative human reaction to criticism, however well meant, in this case criticism of the aid policy, administration, outputs and outcomes for which a person or group was responsible. The second was the political sensitivity that could result if the critical segments of the reviews were made public and gained negative public attention, in turn providing 'political meat', for opposition parties and unsympathetic groups. The third, though a temporary sensitivity, was a concern as to the impact of adverse reviews on the extent of support for the hoped-for later moves to gain full OECD membership. DAC membership might well be a first step to such membership, but not if it resulted in increasing rising levels of irritation among senior officials, particularly if they became overly concerned as to the tenor and political impact of the peer review criticisms they might face with full membership.

OECD Ambassador Sir Ronald Walker was sufficiently concerned at the strength of Shann's views and, possibly, the damage they might cause to the move to persuade the government to seek full OECD membership, to immediately write to him stressing that there was no intention of publishing the reviews and that the Secretariat was not trying to be irritating and had a widespread appreciation of Australian aid. Moreover, as he pointed out, the DAC review was drafted before the year's Australian Budget had been released, and that it envisaged an increased rate of growth of aid appropriations, which would please DAC members (NAA, 1967b). Walker's assurances seem to have had the desired impact as less than two weeks later at a meeting to discuss the 1967 DAC review Shann remarked that at the end of the 1969 examination the DAC chair had warned him that its examiners were being rather kind to a new boy and not to expect such kindness in the future (NAA, 1967c). He also informed his Secretary that the review was generally positive (NAA, 1967d).

DAC's original and continuing mandate included the aim of consulting on ways of increasing and improving the flow of long-term funds and other development assistance to developing countries. Hence, its regular peer reviews of members' aid performance have always focused, in part, on trends in the volume of aid provided. As noted, this had been put forward repeatedly as a major reason for not applying for membership of the DAG/DAC in the 1960–65 period, in case there was unwelcome pressure to increase the volume of Australian aid. It is difficult to establish whether or not such pressure was actually perceived in this early period. When interviewed in the 1970s at least one official felt that DAC membership had been a factor in determining Australian aid volumes, but in two ways: (1) on occasion, the DEA was able to use DAC recommendations on the volume of aid to counter domestic pressures, notably from Treasury, to reduce aid; and (2) on the basis of DAC recommendations for increased aid volumes the DEA was able to successfully press for a regular, annual rate of increase in aid, at least until the middle 1970s, so Australia could hold its then favourable position in international comparisons of the volume of aid (Wilkinson, 1976: 236).

However, Australian aid volumes were already growing before membership of the DAC commenced and the reviews at this time, as they were generally positive in nature, would have been difficult, if not impossible to use in pressing a case for further increase in aid volumes in the annual budget process. Indeed, L.B. Engledow, later to become Secretary of the Department of Immigration, made this very point in a note to Shann regarding the 1968 DAC review, indicating, perhaps somewhat wistfully, that 'it is hardly critical enough to be used as a lever in forcing decisions about increased aid' (NAA, 1968b). Peer reviews were not only a learning experience, but a tool to be used in domestic budget negotiations by senior officials in departments.

Burden Sharing in DAC's 'Common Aid Effort': Aid Flows, Aid Targets and Their Measurement

The DAG had adopted a resolution establishing what was known as 'The Common Aid Effort', in March 1961, some months before it became the DAC in October that year. Among the resolution's key agreements were: (1) a recommendation to members that it should be a common objective to expand the aggregate volume of resources to less developed countries; (2) that they would periodically review the amount and nature of their contributions to aid programmes; and (3) that a study should be made of the 'principles on which governments might most equitably determine their respective contributions to the common aid effort, having regard to the circumstances of each country' (Fuhrer, 1994: 11).

When Australia joined the DAC in 1966 the 'burden sharing' task was well under way; the systematic collection of data had commenced, though it required further development; periodic reviews of members' aid also had commenced in the shape of the DAC peer reviews; and a DAC Recommendation on Financial Terms and Conditions for aid was agreed in 1963 (DAC, 1963). The latter set targets for the 'softness' or 'concessionality', of total assistance provided to developing countries calculated by reference to the grant element of total assistance, taking account of both grants and the 'grant element' of loans, based on a formula that took into consideration the loans' interest rates, grace periods, and maturities. This was an important step towards defining what would be considered aid or not, and later agreement on the use and definition of what became the concept of ODA, 'official development assistance'. The work was spurred on by rising pressure for increased concessional finance from developing countries in the competitive context of the Cold War. They were also pressing hard for the setting of aid targets, with the first ministerial meeting of the G77, at Algiers in 1967 calling for a minimum target for the official component of aid flows (Hynes and Scott, 2013). In 1964 UNCTAD had endorsed a recommended 1 per cent of national income aid target for developed countries and the DAC High Level Meeting that year agreed that its members would make their best possible efforts to comply with the recommended UNCTAD target.

The Menzies government was dubious about the 'Burden Sharing', objectives, the use of aid targets, the practicalities of the exercise and the likelihood of reaching an agreement, although Australia had earlier voted in favour of UNCTAD's 1964 1 per cent of national income aid target. This negative stance regarding aid targets has characterised the aid policies of Coalition governments from this time. In 2014, for example, nearly fifty years after Australia gained membership of the DAC, Foreign Minister Julie Bishop announced further sharp cuts to the aid budget, in a statement that indicated the concept of ODA (now measured as a per cent of gross national income), would no longer be immediately relevant in the Australian context (Tomar and Bruere, 2014).

In particular, it was felt, not unreasonably, that as the 1 per cent target included both official and private flows, with the Australian government having little control over private flows, the target was of little value (NAA, 1966d). The Australian position was much the same in relation to the revision of the UNCTAD 1 per cent of national income target in 1968, when it became one per cent of GNP, a measure that, in effect, represented an approximately 25 per cent increase in the volume of aid over the 1 per cent of national income measure.

Nevertheless, when DAC chair Edwin Martin started to push hard for the adoption of a separate target for official aid in 1969, Australian representatives were instructed to encourage the discussion of his views in DAC. While a number of motives might have been involved in this change of stance, the adoption of a separate target for official aid would be to Australia's advantage. This was because at this time private Australian overseas investment was very low, so that official aid was a very high proportion of Australia's total flow of resources to developing countries, and an official aid target might place it, comparatively, in a very favourable light (Wilkinson, 1976).

Meanwhile, the limitations of the 1 per cent of GNP target led to the 1969 recommendation by the Pearson Commission, based on the ODA work undertaken by DAC, that a 0.7 per cent of GNP target for ODA be set for 1975 and 'in no case' later than 1980 (DAC, 2010). In 1970 Australia, with some reservations, and along with all other DAC members, agreed to the adoption of the concept of ODA. Its focus was on the measurement of official transactions intended to be concessional in character and made with the primary objective of promoting economic and social development, rather than for commercial or military purposes. However, Cabinet decided not to commit itself 'in any way', to a formal commitment to a date for the target's achievement (NAA, 1970a). This was despite the urgings to do so from DAC chair Edwin Martin in his comments on DAC's 1970 review of Australian aid. He indicated that its adoption by the Australian government would encourage similar action by other DAC members who were hesitating to adopt the target (NAA, 1970b).

The political sensitivity of aid targets was to regularly become apparent. In 1972, for example, Deputy Secretary K.C.O. Shann reported to his ALP Minister Nigel Bowen, that the figures on aid were not encouraging. He went on to note that 'we have managed' to get away with assertions over the past year or so that the total flow of aid has gone over the 1 per cent target but 'the reasons are artificial' and 'border on the dishonest' (NAA, 1972a). As he pointed out, the figures included the Bougainville copper project in PNG, which was counted, as it could be under DAC rules, as an aid investment flow. Shann had suggested to Treasury that it not be counted but 'the temptation was too great'. Moreover, he wrote, most of the money for Bougainville came from foreign, not Australian capital, via holding companies in Australia. In addition, he asserted, the reverse flow of capital repayments would soon start, to Australia's disadvantage in regard to both future aid figures and Australia's image.

The Australian stance on the 0.7 per cent ODA target, as well as aid policy more generally, changed with the election of the ALP government of Gough Whitlam in 1972. At the 1971 ALP federal conference a new section on aid had been inserted into the ALP platform which accepted the UN aid target of 1 per cent of GNP, though it also recognised the limitations of such a target as a measure of aid effectiveness (ALP, 1971). In December 1972 in a report for Prime Minister Whitlam (who had taken on a number of portfolios in the first months in office, including Foreign Affairs), it was recommended that Australia accept the 0.7 per cent of GNP target by 1980 for ODA, pointing out that Australia had supported, with reservations, the UN's International Strategy for the Second Development Decade and its 1 per cent of GNP target, but had not committed itself to the 0.7 per cent ODA target (NAA, 1972b). The report noted that there had been increasing criticism of Australia's lack of support for the 0.7 per cent target, mostly domestic rather than international, such as the 'Action for World Development' campaign. Whitlam accepted the recommendation (NAA, 1973).

Australia and Tied Aid 1966–70: A Sanguine Stance

The DAC definition of tied aid is that it refers to loans or grants which are either in effect tied to the procurement of goods and services from the donor country or which are subject to procurement modalities implying limited geographic procurement eligibility. The period from 1960 to 1970 saw little substantive progress on the controversial issue of tied aid in DAC, though it was raised several times and a variety of draft texts were developed but did not reach fruition. Australian officials became aware that the issue might be discussed even before the DAG, DAC's predecessor, was established, and that if it reached an agreement on tied aid this would bring pressure to bear on the Colombo Plan countries such as Australia and New Zealand to follow suit (NAA, 1960).

The Australian stance regarding tied aid in this period was relatively sanguine. In the 1966 DAC Review of Australian aid, for example, it was noted that most Australian aid was already in the form of grants, which substantially reduced the cost of tied aid to recipients, so it was unlikely that Australia would have much to contribute to the proposed, international efforts to reduce such aid. At this time grant aid was not regarded as tied aid by the DAC. However, in a somewhat contradictory fashion, it was also noted that the current Australian procurement policy required aid-financed goods to have at least a 66 per cent Australian content, excluding aid to PNG, but asserted without explanation that the rule was not very onerous and exceptions were sometimes permitted

(NAA, 1969a: 7–9). A similar position was advanced in the 1969 DAC Review, where it was noted by Australian officials that 'Australian tying practices are relatively liberal and flexible', although this was largely because aid to PNG took the form of direct budget assistance, nominally untied (NAA, 1969b: 42). However, as K.C.O. Shann noted in 1970, while aid to PNG was not formally tied, a large part of it was used to purchase equipment from Australia and to pay Australian salaries. Moreover, while Australian multilateral aid was untied, he noted, about half of Australia's contribution to the new Asian Development Bank (ADB) was tied, and most of Australia's then limited bilateral aid was also tied, with a 66 per cent Australian content requirement. In conclusion, he noted that 'in practice', a high per cent of Australian aid was either tied to procurement in Australia or found its way back to Australia, and pointed out that there was pressure from the Associated Chambers of Manufactures (ACMA) to further increase tying (NAA, 1970c).

In 1969 Sweden proposed, unsuccessfully, a multilateral agreement on progressive untying of aid loans, with support from Germany, the Netherlands and Norway and, after some hesitation, Japan (Fuhrer, 1994: 22). The Australian stance was, for the most part, that of limited involvement, for three main reasons: (1) the perception that Australia would not benefit greatly, if at all, from increased untying of aid, given that the policy of 'protection all round', for Australian industry meant that most of its products were not internationally competitive, so untying would lead to a loss of current, but internationally uncompetitive Australian exports to more efficient competitors; (2) the perception that as Australia's tied grant aid could hardly be considered harmful, as it was a grant, not a loan, untying was not a major issue; and (3) the countries most in favour of untying would probably benefit most from untying as their products were in greatest demand and lower priced (NAA, 1970d). Hence, while Australia had supported recommendations in both the UN and the DAC on the general desirability of reducing the extent of untying as a matter of general principle, it was not keen to do so at this time. It was, however, willing to agree to a recommendation that contributions to multilateral organisations should generally be untied and that DAC should work out the rules necessary to implement such a recommendation (NAA, 1970e).

DAC agreed that contributions to multilateral institutions should be untied at its High Level Meeting in 1973. Australia was somewhat tardy in implementing this latter agreement, leading to the 'only serious comment', by DAC chair Edwin Martin in his comments on DAC's 1973 Review of Australian aid. Martin had noted that Australian contributions to the ADB were still tied and he urged that anything the Australian government could do to eliminate the procurement restrictions on Australian funds held by the ADB 'would be most welcome' (NAA, 1973).

In summary, the Australian experience of the DAC in the 1966–71 period was generally positive. It probably enhanced the strength of the views of those in the DEA and Treasury supporting a move to full membership and, from the point of view of Australian aid policy and administration, seems to have been a valuable, if not always positively received, learning experience. Phillip Flood, for example, became Director of the Aid Policy Section in the DEA from 1969 to 1971 on his return to Canberra from Paris, noting in retrospect that his new role 'offered the opportunity to put into practice some of the new ideas on aid policy that I had encountered in Paris, in the context of their adoption by OECD donor countries' (Flood, 2011: 60). In addition, the peer reviews may have played a minor role in domestic budget negotiations as to aid volumes.

AUSTRALIA IN THE DAC AFTER 1971: AID VOLUMES AND POLITICAL SENSITIVITY

DAC's peer reviews of aid continued to be politically sensitive after Australia gained full membership of the OECD in 1971, especially as its ODA volumes began to decline from 1976, under the first Fraser government. In the period 1976 to 1983, for example, as a per cent of Gross National Income (GNI) it fell to an average of 0.48 per cent, though this was still markedly higher than the DAC members' average of 0.33 per cent. However, as DAC chair Maurice Williams pointed out, it was 'at a significantly lower level than in the early years of the decade' and that it was:

> [a] source of concern to the Committee in view of the commitments to increase development assistance recently undertaken at CIEC, and reaffirmed by the 1977 OECD Ministerial Meeting. (OECD, 1977)

It should be noted that the relative decline in Australian ODA was also the case for the bulk of the members of the DAC in the 1970s following the two oil shocks, the decline of rates of economic growth in the Western economies and its replacement by 'stagflation'.

The critical DAC comments regarding aid volumes, combined with the decision to publish the bulk of DAC's reviews, may have played a part in encouraging the Fraser government to increase its aid allocations to 0.55 per cent in 1978 and 0.53 per cent in 1979, though they fell back to 0.48

per cent in 1980 and 0.41 per cent in 1981, before rising again to 0.56 per cent in 1982. This increase was well received, although DAC was critical of the absence (in common with most DAC members) of a timetable for Australia's progress towards the 0.7 per cent target, which had been pushed back to the end of the 1980s (OECD, 1981). It is unlikely that the Fraser government appreciated the chairman's advice that it might track its aid progress by determining a minimum yearly growth rate of aid volume or by adoption of intermediate targets. While ministers might have been sympathetic to the advice in private, the setting of precise, public targets, even if heavily qualified, would have provided ammunition for opposition parties if they failed to be achieved (see, for example, Uren, 1977: 1; Bowen, 1980). The typical government response to criticisms of its performance in relation to aid volumes was, not unreasonably, to point out that its performance was still better than the DAC average (see, for example, Minister Andrew Peacock, 1977: 1).

In the following 1983–96 period of Hawke and Keating ALP governments Australia's ODA fell even further, averaging 0.4 per cent, with a high of 0.49 per cent and a low of 0.27 per cent. The average for all DAC members in the period was 0.31 per cent. As had become the norm, opposition parties soon drew attention to this decline, especially Democrat Senator Michael Macklin (Macklin, 1987: 3411). He pointed to the December 1987 DAC aid review of Australia, noting that in its press release the Committee had:

> [R]egretted that the aid budget had suffered a disproportionately high share of the cuts in total public expenditure, and that as a consequence aid as a proportion of the total central government Budget had declined from 1.5% in the fiscal year 1985–86 to an estimated 1.3% in 1987–88. (Macklin, 1987: 3411)

Liberal Senator John Watson went further, formally submitting a petition to the Senate which requested the government to 'redirect' overseas aid to achieve the UN target of 0.7 per cent. He asserted that:

> Australia stands disgraced internationally. Despite global recessionary trends no other Western country has cut foreign aid to the same degree. The Development Assistance Committee of OECD has expressed regret at Australia's drastic cuts and urged it to resume real increases in aid. Of 141 member countries Australia is the only one to withdraw support from IFAD. (Watson, 1987: 112; see also OECD, 1987)

The decline in Australia's aid funding was also noted in the 1984 Jackson Committee Report and was discussed in Cabinet on a number of occasions (Australian Cabinet, 1985). As Foreign Minister Bill Hayden noted in a 1985 Cabinet submission that recommended an increase in aid volumes, not only was it at the lowest level ever recorded by DAC, it was in danger of falling below the average volume of DAC members for the first time. This would lead, he felt, to mounting domestic and international criticism and an adverse impact on foreign policy, especially as regards South East Asia, a priority region for trade and aid. In an observation that indicated the influence of DAC publications, he felt that the report of the recent DAC review of Australian aid, restricted to OECD members, would be critical of what it saw as a lack of commitment by the government to overseas aid. He concluded that 'These are unacceptable consequences: the decline in ODA/GNP must be halted and growth resumed' (Australian Cabinet, 1985).

Hayden's submission neither asked for a specific increase in funding for aid, nor did Cabinet agree any specific increase, other than to endorse moves towards achieving a target of 0.55 per cent by 1990–91, if at all possible. In justifying this move the Foreign Minister's submission argued that increased funds would result in a more effective aid programme both in humanitarian terms and in our 'ability to accommodate our political and commercial interests', going on to note that 'because of the nature of our aid program the increased funds available would largely be spent on Australian goods and services with consequent beneficial effects on employment'. By 'the nature of our aid program', was meant the increasingly tied nature of Australia's aid, with only two components of the aid programme not being directly tied, the budget support grant to PNG and the non-food multilateral aid. As the submission went on to note, a real growth in aid expenditures would make funds available for trade-linked initiatives such as the Development Import Financing Facility (DIFF), which could be rapidly increased (Australian Cabinet, 1985).

As Hayden had expected, the 1987 DAC review of Australian aid was expressed in very critical terms, far more so than had been customary in most of its earlier reviews, leading the Minister, unusually, to instruct his Director of the Australian International Development Assistance Bureau (AIDAB), Dr R. Dunn, to register an Australian protest with the chair and the members of DAC (Dunn, 1987). While not contesting the facts regarding its ODA performance, Dunn asserted in his letter that a 'balanced', review should have 'reflected the severe economic problems facing Australia, which led to reductions in aid funding', concluding that it adversely reflected on the credibility and authority of the DAC. However, the response of the DAC chair did not resile from the views that had been expressed by the peer review committee in its press release, nor the similar views expressed in his own customary letter to the head of the Australian delegation following the review (OECD, 1987). Moreover, similar criticisms continued to be made over the next few years in the DAC aid reviews and by the DAC chair, given the failure to achieve any significant growth in Australian aid levels in relation to the ODA 0.7 per cent target (see, for example, OECD, 1990).

Australia's aid performance as measured by ODA/GNI would have been even poorer had it not been for the successful proposal by Australian representatives to DAC following several years of effort, that the imputed costs of students from developing countries studying in a donor country should be included in ODA measures, which had not previously been the practice (OECD, 1996: 38). The proposal followed recommendations from both the Goldring and the Jackson Committee reports that free scholarships to international students should be charged to the Australian aid budget (amounting to more than $70 million in 1984, or approximately 12.9 per cent of Australia's ODA in that year, see OECD, 1985: 173). It should be noted that neither report argued that the amounts should be included in the calculations of Australia's ODA.

The advent of the first of the Howard governments in 1996 saw an even further decline in aid as measured against the 0.7 per cent target, averaging 0.26 per cent in the 1996–2007 period, despite the fact that, for the most part, the Australian economy grew strongly in the period, making Australian claims as to difficult economic conditions being at the root of the decline in its aid levels unconvincing to DAC members. The DAC's 1999 review, after noting that aid levels had been in a declining trend since 1975, further noted that as the Australian economy had entered its ninth year of expansion, it encouraged Australia to increase its ODA/GNI ratio by at least 0.01 per cent in 1999. Similar concerns were expressed in the 2004 review, where it was pointed out that Australia had now 'enjoyed thirteen years of economic expansion', but an expansion that had not been reflected in its ODA/GNI ratio, which had fallen to 0.25 per cent by 2003 (OECD, 2005: 14).

The review's recommendation that the Australian government 'revisit the issue of ODA commitments', seems initially to have fallen on deaf ears, as its ODA/GNI did not rise above 0.25 per cent until 2006, when it rose to 0.3 per cent. While Foreign Minister Alexander Downer did at times refer to the 1999 and 2004 DAC peer reviews, he chose usually not to highlight their concerns for the low levels of aid funding, instead focusing attention on the more positive aspects of the reviews (see, for example, Downer, 2000, 2005). This did not, however, escape the notice of the ALP members, with Opposition spokesman on Foreign Affairs Kevin Rudd drawing attention to that fact in a critique of the government's aid policy (Rudd, 2005).

Australian aid levels began to rise again in 2006, to 0.3 per cent, then 0.32 per cent in 2007, the last year of the Howard governments that had been in office since 1996. Australian aid averaged 0.32 per cent in the 2008–11 period under the Rudd and Gillard, ALP governments, compared to the DAC average of 0.31 per cent. DAC's 2007 aid review welcomed the increase in aid volumes and, in particular, the 2006 White Paper 'Australian Aid: Promoting Growth and Stability', that provided a detailed plan for Australia's aid policy over the next ten years. It also welcomed the pre-election commitment of all major parties to increase ODA to 0.5 per cent of GNI by 2015, a commitment reiterated, importantly, by Prime Minister Rudd after taking office (OECD, 2009: 23–4). As DAC pointed out, while welcoming the increase in aid, the planned rapid increase in volume would bring its own challenges, including: (1) effectively managing the scaling up process to ensure that aid quality was maintained; and (2) maintaining a strategic focus so as to avoid fragmenting the aid programme across an increased range of recipients and projects (OECD, 2009: 4).

The improvement in aid volumes was not to persist. A one year 'deferral' of the plan to achieve the 0.5 per cent target by 2015 was announced in the 2012–13 Commonwealth budget, as the impact of the global financial crisis increased, aimed at reducing expenses by $2.9 billion over four years, although it still entailed a doubling of aid in dollar terms from 2007–2008 to 2014–15. It was cut sharply again by the new government of Tony Abbot in 2013–14 and 2014–15 (Commonwealth Government, 2012).

While other elements of the regular DAC peer reviews might have offered valuable learning experiences, that regarding the volume of aid was not regarded as a learning experience, but as somewhat of an embarrassment and, at times, politically sensitive, for over thirty years. Unfortunately, the degree of influence that the reviews have had upon Australian aid volumes cannot be measured with any degree of precision. While DAC's increasingly critical views were, at least on occasion, presented to Cabinet, it seems that they had only a limited influence on decision making regarding aid volumes when Australia's economic performance was weak. In contrast, when the Australian economy was performing strongly, as it did for most of the period from 1996 to 2007, both ALP and conservative governments were willing to increase aid volumes, if not to the levels suggested in DAC reviews. Nevertheless, the regular publication of DAC's views regarding Australian aid volumes served at least to keep it on the agenda of successive governments so that in times of economic growth it would achieve at least a degree of attention.

'A REAL BLOODY PROBLEM FOR US': THE INCREASE IN USE OF TIED AID, EXPORT CREDITS AND MIXED CREDITS IN THE 1970S AND 1980S

As the volume of Australian aid began to decline in the 1970s following the two oil shocks and increasing economic difficulties, the per cent of Australian aid that was tied also increased, in large part to provide increased support for Australian business and its export performance. This was also a response to similar moves by most other DAC members. It included the rapidly increasing use of tied aid within the context of government-supported export credit, further complicating an already sensitive issue. In 1956 the Australian government had established the Export Payments Insurance Corporation to support Australian exporters, followed, in 1971, by a 'buyer's credit facility', to authorise the Corporation to guarantee repayment of loans by lending institutions to overseas buyers of Australian capital goods (Australian Cabinet, 1971). Further, in 1985, an amendment to *The Australian Trade Commission Act, 1985*, enabled the government to underwrite export credit risks in the national interest, as approved by Cabinet, covering all areas of risk, as well as export credit.

Tied aid had become increasingly entangled with the use of export credit from the later 1960s, as many OECD countries increasingly used subsidised export credit in support of domestic firms (Moravcsik, 1989: 178). Between 1960 and 1970, for example, the contract value of officially supported export credits rose from under SDR 1 billion to approximately SDR 8 billion. Export credit subsidies in the OECD member states increased from US$2 billion to US$5.5 billion in 1979, peaking at about US$7 billion in 1981 (Blair, 1993: 42–3). As noted in Chapter 5, the increased use and cost of export credit had led in 1963 to the establishment of the OECD's Group on Export Credits and Credit Guarantees (ECG) to attempt to manage competition by agreeing a set of guidelines for export credit and to assess national policies in that regard. It should be noted that it was the Trade Committee, not the DAC, that established the ECG, bringing into play in the development aid arena a wider range of actors from domestic trade departments, treasuries and export credit agencies. In turn, this necessitated at least a degree of information sharing and coordination between these 'new' players and those involved in the DAC and the related domestic aid agencies.

Treasury became a strong supporter of tied aid and was always reluctant to untie in this period, being often cynical as to members' motives in proposals for untying. In 1970, for example, at a meeting of

DAC's Working Party on Financial Aspects, Treasury's Mr B.W. Fraser (later Treasury Secretary), noted that a proposal to untie aid to multilateral organisations was strongly supported by all European members, Japan and the USA, with discussion confined to changes to the draft to ensure the 'resultant spoils would be reasonably evenly divided among the exporting countries concerned'. Fraser indicated at the meeting that he had had no instructions on the matter but it would cause difficulties. He noted that his remarks caused the chair, Bob Everts, to exclaim 'there goes our Declaration', followed by what was described somewhat euphemistically as a 'dialogue', between them. Fraser stated that there was no intention to 'torpedo', the aim to untie where tying resulted in higher prices, pointing out that Australian tying practices were as liberal as any other DAC member, that most of its bilateral aid was untied, while others allowed up to one third import content (NAA, 1970f). However, it was finally agreed that contributions to multilateral organisations should as a rule be untied and that the OECD would work out rules to implement it, with Fraser indicating that he would have to seek Canberra's views on the issue.

While the increased use of subsidised export credit could be (and often was) described as a form of aid to developing countries as it reduced the apparent costs of purchasing products and services from the donor country providing such aid, it was used primarily as a means of promoting the exports of the donor's firms by subsidising their price. The term 'mixed credit', often used interchangeably and confusingly with the term tied aid, or 'associated financing', refers to the practice of combining tied aid credits with standard export credits to reduce the overall cost of the financing offer from the donor country. In effect aid policy and trade policy became entangled, with a frequent tension between the two, caused by the differing objectives of aid and trade policy, which were by no means always compatible. Proponents of mixed credit financing argued that it reduced the costs of developing countries and enabled the 'stretching' of limited aid funds to cover a greater range of development projects. Critics argued that it was simply a predatory form of trade financing disguised as aid, a form of cheating and a violation of free trade norms, as well as being tied aid (Evans, 2005: 261–2). Moreover, empirical studies of tied aid, while still in their infancy in the 1970s, increasingly showed that it, in general, imposed increased costs on the recipients, often in the range of 15 per cent to 30 per cent (Clay et al., 2008: 36).

Between 1963 and 1975, international limitations on export credit subsidies were largely blocked by the United States, supported by Canada, which argued that credit terms were an element of normal competition. The EEC and the UK were in support of an agreement on credit restrictions, as was Australia (Blair, 1993: 60). Nevertheless there was some progress at the OECD, notably the 1972 introduction of an information exchange system and a prior consultation procedure, to which Australia signed up in 1974. The former agreement enabled members to request information from each other as to actual or proposed export credit operations. The latter required members to notify other members of any proposed extension of official support for export credit to developing countries. However, the USA, in company with Australia, Greece, Japan and Portugal chose not to participate in the consultation procedure (Ray, 1995: 46).

As the costs of subsidising credit grew, in 1976 the seven members of the Puerto Rico Summit reached an agreement on export credit and began meeting at the OECD in April 1977 (Blair, 1993: 45). While their meeting was technically separate from that of the already established Group on Export Credits, and was not, nor is, a formal agreement or decision of the OECD, the membership of the two groups was mostly the same, with the same chair and with the OECD Secretariat providing support, a situation which persists today. It was not, however, directly associated with the DAC, although their membership overlapped. In 1976 there was also the first comprehensive agreement on export credits, the 'Consensus on Converging Export Credit Policies of July 1976', often known as the 'Gentleman's Agreement', developed and managed within the confines of the OECD, though not formally an OECD Decision or Recommendation. Australia became a member of the 'Participants', in November 1976, attracted by the rules-based nature of the Agreement in a situation where it was able to compete to only a very limited extent with the growing subsidies provided by major actors, notably the USA and the EEC.

The key feature of the Gentleman's Agreement was the setting of minimum interest rates for credit offers and varying repayment periods for recipient countries. It also contained a set of procedures regarding mixed credits, whereby if the grant element of a credit arrangement was less than 15 per cent of the total finance, participants were required to give notice of seven days to other participants. Where the grant element was between 15 per cent and 25 per cent a prompt notice to the others was required and, if the grant element was above 25 per cent, it would be regarded as official aid and not subject to the Gentleman's Agreement. If a participant breached the Agreement it was required to give notice of seven days and the other members of the Agreement were permitted to match the terms of the offer. It did not apply to military equipment, aircraft, nuclear plant, new ocean going ships or, to the disappointment of the Australian government, to agricultural commodities.

The 1976 Agreement was replaced by the OECD Arrangement on Guidelines for Officially Supported Export Credits in 1978. The aim was, in part, to further stabilise the growing international competition in tied aid credits, though several DAC members soon began to circumvent the 1978 Arrangement, leading to a substantial increase in the number and value of export credits disbursed in the 1978–83 period. Most of the increase included relatively small amounts of aid, tied or untied, suggesting that it was being used primarily to stimulate exports (Moravcsik, 1989: 181–2). The 1978 Arrangement was not a formal treaty and it and its successors did not bind the members who were a party to it – it was a form of 'soft law', in contrast with traditional, international agreements, although there seems to have been a relatively high degree of compliance by its signatories, including Australia. This reduced, though by no means eliminated, the degree of competition that might otherwise have existed (Levit, 2004: 148).

While in the next few years Australian officials tended to flaunt what they regarded as their strict adherence to the 1978 Arrangement and in general supported a reduction in the extent of tied aid, in 1980 the Fraser government decided to introduce the DIFF, with the first loan under the scheme approved in 1982. DIFF was a tied aid, mixed credit scheme, operating within the bounds of the 1978 Arrangement and its aims were two-fold: (1) to deliver development benefits to developing countries; and (2) to bring substantial commercial benefits to Australia. It was adopted, in part, as a response to the introduction of other mixed credit schemes by other OECD members. When it was terminated in 1996 it accounted for about 8–10 per cent of the total aid budget, at AUD $120 million per annum (McLeod and Cuthbertson, 1996). DIFF financing for a project combined an AusAID grant (generally 35 per cent of the contract value for developing countries) with non-concessional export financing provided by the government's Export Finance Insurance Company (EFIC). While Australian officials were concerned that the introduction of DIFF could be embarrassing, at least to members of the Delegation in Paris, it was hoped that the recent Canadian introduction of a similar, but more generously funded scheme would warrant much greater interest (NAA, 1981). Expenditure under the scheme rose rapidly, although it was subject to growing criticism from domestic sources and aid recipients (Simons Committee, 1997: 200–205).

Despite increasing domestic criticism of the DIFF scheme, the ALP governments of the 1980s made no move to dismantle the scheme, but rapidly expanded its funding, in contrast to the overall volume of

Australian aid as measured by the DAC's ODA/GNI measure, which the government had reduced to its lowest ever level by 1985. The 1984 Jackson Report on Australian aid was very critical of the DIFF, asserting that it distorted competition and had become a threat to the developmental objectives of aid. It recommended that it should be seen as an interim measure pending the development of better international trade rules (Jackson Committee Report, 1984: 124–5). However, the Report had little or no impact in regard to the government's stance on DIFF, whose funding for it rose from AUD $12.5 million in 1984–85 to AUD $93 million in 1991–92, an increase of nearly 400 per cent at a time when the total Australian aid programme shrank by 14 per cent (Sherlock, 1991).

In 1985 the Reagan Administration, under pressure from the US Congress, announced that it would create a US$300 million Tied Aid Credit Fund, soon to be known as the 'War Chest', within its Eximbank. The funds were to provide additional leverage for the US delegation to the OECD negotiations on tied aid credit practices, with Eximbank using the War Chest against countries whose practices were felt to be obstructing the negotiations process (Rosefsky, 1993: 448). Despite its growing use of the DIFF facility, the Australian position at the DAC and in the Arrangement in the 1980s was to urge for the end, or at least the reduction of the use of mixed credits, which, in Minister Hayden's view, were undermining the effective operation of the Arrangement (NAA, 1984a). At a press conference following the Council meeting Hayden's ambivalent views regarding the DIFF surfaced when, in response to questions about the DIFF and his support for the ending of mixed credits, he stated:

> I am not unstitching it, I don't like it, we don't have much choice as I said this morning. I feel we would be better off without it but with everyone else into it we don't have much choice. What we've got to do is to get some controls on it … it is a real bloody problem for us. (NAA, 1984b)

The Gradual Untying of Aid and the End of DIFF

The continued pressure by the USA and other members for a reduction in, and greater control of tied aid credits led to the 'Helsinki Package' agreement, substantially modifying the Arrangement, which came into operation in February 1992. US pressure took, in particular, the shape of a joint US$500 million pool of funds for capital goods financing in Indonesia, the Philippines, Thailand and Pakistan, in effect an even larger 'War Chest' than had been established in 1985 and one that was more threatening from the Australian perspective, given its rapidly growing trade with each of those countries (Rosefsky, 1993: 449). In turn, this led to the adoption by the DAC of its 'Guiding Principles for Associated Financing and Tied and Partially Untied Official Development Assistance', based on the Helsinki Package, markedly strengthening provisions for transparency and discipline in relation to export credits and tied aid. Perhaps most importantly, the Helsinki Package specified that tied or partially tied ODA would only be counted as official aid if the grant element was set at a minimum level of 80 per cent, or if bilateral donors wanted to use it for projects which were 'commercially unviable'.

The Australian government strongly supported the Helsinki Package, which markedly increased the costs of using tied aid for export promotion, hoping for a substantial reduction in the practice. This was despite the fact that the new rules meant that DIFF would no longer be available for projects considered commercially viable, reducing its utility (DFAT, 1994a: 208). Coincidentally, the government had extended DIFF financing to Vietnam in 1992, despite the generally accepted wisdom that severely indebted low income countries such as Vietnam should not be encouraged to increase their debt (Simons Committee, 1997: 200). Moreover, as the Simons Committee noted, by 1994 Australia had become the fourth largest provider of tied aid credits, the third largest as a proportion of its aid programme, which made it difficult to argue that Australia was a reluctant participant in the tied aid mixed credit business and somewhat contradicting its strong support for the Helsinki Package and the new DAC Guiding Principles (Simons Committee, 1997: 201).

Despite the changes brought about by the Helsinki Package the DIFF continued to be popular with Australian businesses and AusAID, even though approximately 50 per cent of the proposed projects in the energy sector and 60 per cent in telecommunications were found to be commercially viable and, hence, no longer eligible (Tomar, 1996: 5). Such popularity suggested that any attempt to disband the scheme would meet with considerable resistance, although the Liberal–National Party coalition in Opposition opposed the scheme. This proved to be the case when the scheme was dropped by the first Howard government in 1996, leading to intense criticism in *The Australian* newspaper and from a number of ambassadors and ministers in countries receiving DIFF financing (McLeod and Cuthbertson, 1996: 517).

The Simons Committee went so far as to recommend that tied aid mixed credit schemes such as DIFF should not be reintroduced into the Australian aid programme (Simons Committee, 1997). Moreover, it argued that given that the DAC had attempted over several decades to persuade its members to reduce the incidence of aid tying, plus the fact that the new UK government was proceeding to reduce its own tied aid and to encourage other DAC members to do likewise, then:

> [T]he Committee recommends that Australia respond to the challenge offered by Britain; and two, as specified in Recommendation 10.2, Australia should work with the Netherlands, Britain, Japan and like-minded members in the DAC to encourage the untying of aid. (Simons Committee, 1997: 191)

No scheme similar to DIFF has since been used by later Australian governments.

DAC: A RELATIVELY LOW AUSTRALIAN PRIORITY

The consequences of the Helsinki Package, especially the monitoring of the signatories' performance, the new DAC Guidelines and continuing budget stringency in the middle 1990s, saw a number of developments that indicated a relatively low priority for Australia's engagement with the DAC in this period. Four sources indicate that this was the case: (1) an unsuccessful proposal for additional Australian staff capacity at the OECD for DAC-related work; (2) the government's rejection of the Simons Committee proposal that AIDAB have its own representative at the DAC; (3) the relatively low priority accorded to DAC-related work that emerged in a review of Australia's engagement with the OECD undertaken in 1994–95; and (4) departmental responses to a survey by the OECD Secretariat asking for members' priorities in relation to OECD work.

One outcome of the Helsinki Package and the new DAC Guidelines was an increase in the workload of the member of the Australian OECD Delegation responsible for DAC matters and, in addition, a range of other, non-DAC related duties. This prompted a proposal from Phillip Flood, now Director of AIDAB, to DFAT's Secretary, Mr Michael Costello, that the responsibility for funding the First Secretary position at the Delegation be transferred to AIDAB and for it to focus wholly on DAC and DAC-related matters (AIDAB, 1993). In support of his proposal Flood argued that in general the development-related work of the position had increased and would increase further, at a time when the workload of the current officer at the Delegation already meant that he could not attend or be involved in many DAC-related matters. In particular, the workload related to aid quality, aid and the environment, aid and good governance and the work of the OECD's Export Credits Group was rising. In regard to the latter he noted that proposals for DIFF funding:

> [a]re increasingly being assessed with an eye to their likely reception in the Export Credits Group. A number of Australian proposals have had to be defended in the ECG against charges that the projects concerned were capable of attracting financing on market terms, and two such proposals were recently found to be ineligible for mixed credit financing. The defence of proposals in the ECG is a new, specialised and quite resource-intensive responsibility. (AIDAB, 1993)

Flood went on to note that in the recent DFAT Post Evaluation Report on the OECD the Delegation indicated that its resources were 'visibly overstretched' and that the Ambassador, Trevor Boucher, supported a new position at the Delegation. Similarly, AIDAB's recent Overseas Staffing Review had found there were substantial benefits to be gained from a direct AIDAB representative in Paris. However, Flood's proposal was not accepted. Secretary Costello, in replying to Flood, noted that on the advice of Ambassador Boucher, if the position was transferred to AIDAB its non-DAC work would have to be dropped or done by the other two DFAT officers in the Delegation, who were already overstretched. While Costello was prepared to reconsider Flood's proposal if AIDAB itself could fund a new, additional position, the files indicate that no further action was taken (AIDAB, 1994a).

The 1997 Simons Committee Report recommended that AusAID should have its own permanent representative at the DAC as part of its more general recommendation that AusAID should participate more actively in international development debates (Simons Committee, 1997: 167). The recommendation was not accepted, in large part on the basis of a Treasury paper (AIDAB, 1994b). The paper noted that AusAID already conducted an extensive dialogue with other donors in a variety of locations, and the DAC links formed only a part of this dialogue. It went on to note that senior AusAID officials regularly attended the DAC annual HLM and Senior Level meetings and, also, that Australia and Europe-based AusAID specialists were active in a range of DAC forums, including the DAC reviews, with the First Secretary at the Paris Delegation attending 'most', regular meetings of the DAC.

In noting that the Simons Committee Report argued that a DAC posting would provide greater access to the experiences and insights of other donors, the Treasury paper was dismissive of this view, pointing out that most permanent DAC delegates were mid-ranking officers not in the 'policy loops', of their aid agencies and a number were not aid specialists at all but were from foreign ministries. Moreover, it asserted, the regular DAC meetings focused more on housekeeping matters rather than on 'cutting edge policy discussions', which took place in DAC's annual HLM and SLM meetings. Hence, given that a new position would cost about $400,000 annually, it was felt that such funds might be better spent on: (1) increased Australia-based attendance at DAC meetings; (2) the improved dissemination of key DAC outputs in AusAID; and (3) improved AusAID briefings for members of the Delegation in advance of the regular DAC meetings, enabling them to better target its efforts and fine tune reporting to AusAID's particular needs. The paper concluded by suggesting that a thorough evaluation of DAC's efficiency and effectiveness was needed if a decision for a new post was to go ahead, pointing out that despite its 'long and prestigious history':

> [I]t would not be unfair to say that it is now at a cross-roads. A number of members are unhappy with the recent performance of this body and there is an undercurrent of questioning its role in the OECD. (AIDAB, 1994b)

The Treasury paper's rather negative view of the importance of DAC was echoed in a broad-ranging review of Australia's OECD involvement that was conducted in 1994–95 to assess the benefits and costs of OECD membership in the light of the creation of APEC and the WTO. It was the first government-wide review since Australia joined the OECD in 1971. The review concluded that the OECD remained a key international organisation of great value for Australia, despite concerns with various aspects of its operations, the advent of APEC and the WTO, and the costs associated with membership. The priority it accorded to DAC-related work was, however, very low (DFAT, 1995a: 101). Departments and agencies had been asked to rank how well the OECD met their objectives, or that part of them that they largely engaged with, on a three point scale, ranging from fully effective, to adequate, or inadequate (DFAT, 1994b). AIDAB ranked the OECD as 'Adequate', in relation to its key objectives of obtaining comparative statistics and qualitative material, including that related to ODA trends and to that examining the links between development cooperation policy and other policy sectors.

Further, in June 1995, in the first stage of a two stage process, OECD members were asked by the Secretariat to identify their top and bottom ten priorities for OECD work from a list which divided the OECD's work into fifty-two categories. List A was for the top priority items, List B was the bottom ten priorities and List C were an intermediate priority (DFAT, 1995b). No AIDAB items were in List A. In September 1995 OECD members were asked to reply to the second stage of the process, this time being required to nominate fifteen activities in each category listed in the survey. Again, following discussions of an early draft at an interdepartmental committee, aid-related items were contained in either the bottom or middle list, with no items in the top fifteen priorities. The

Ministerial Submission summarising departments' responses noted that the AusAID representative was reported as indicating that it would have preferred the item 'Horizontal Efforts to Integrate "Coherent" Attention to Development Issues', to be promoted to the middle list but agreed at the interdepartmental committee meeting to leave it in the bottom list. It also noted that while they agreed that the item 'Surveillance and Coordination of Member Countries' Development Cooperation Policies' (including peer reviews), was an important activity within OECD, it was 'not sufficiently to displace any of the activities we have included at Attachment A', adding that 'AusAid are unlikely to press strongly' for such inclusion.

The Agreement on Guidelines for Officially Supported Export Credits, then the responsibility of the Department of Industry, Science and Technology (DIST), in which AIDAB had a strong interest, as noted above, was ranked in the middle group of priorities. DIST officials were reported as having preferred it to be in the list of top priorities, but that they would not insist on this ranking (DFAT, 1995b). In the later list of the top fifteen priorities drawn up by the OECD Secretariat on the basis of the members' responses to the survey, only one item related to development or aid. This was priority number eleven, 'Surveillance and Coordination of Member Countries' Development Cooperation Policies', which had not been included in the Australian top ten. In the list of the OECD's bottom fifteen priorities was item fifty-two, horizontal efforts to integrate 'coherent' attention to development issues and their development cooperation implications in the work of OECD mainstream committees. It was also in the bottom fifteen of Australia's list (DFAT, 1998). All of which tended to confirm the 1994 Treasury views as to the low priority OECD members' gave to DAC's work.

CONCLUSION

Australia's engagement with the DAC commenced at a relatively high level of intensity, but more because of the view that it would be a valuable first step to full OECD membership, as had been the case for Japan, than for its value in relation to foreign aid policy and administration. Once membership had been achieved then its status and priority gradually fell to a lower level, which remains the case at the time of writing. This did not, nor does not mean that DAC's activities were of no value, for participation in its activities, while selective, was seen as a valuable learning experience, particularly in the early years of membership when Australian aid policy and administration were less sophisticated and effective.

Perhaps the most obvious and certainly most frequent evidence of Australian decision makers learning from the work of the DAC and its directorate lies in the area of aid statistics, recommendations, reports and guidelines. These are drawn upon almost on a daily basis for purposes of identifying trends in aid volumes, aid types, trends, sources and comparison of Australia's aid performance with other states, both over time and in relation to international aid targets such as the Millennium Development Goals. All of the Australia public servants interviewed for this study stressed the value of this learning activity.

The learning that took place was accompanied by, for the most part, the acceptance of the classifications, meanings and norms developed by the OECD and its members. In addition, the DAC's regular reviews of members' aid policies and programmes enabled them to further learn from each other and, as was intended as the key objective of the peer review process, to put relatively gentle pressure on members to conform, in whole or in part, to new standards and practices. This is not to argue that any member, including Australia, simply and slavishly accepted what was developed by DAC, but that it was a likely outcome of membership, one that grew slowly in significance over time as the process of acculturation took place. While much of the Australian learning based on DAC's statistics, recommendations, reports and guidelines has been relatively straightforward, some of it has been, at times, more difficult and politically sensitive. This has been most notable in relation to the regular DAC peer reviews, especially their comparative and sometimes critical assessment of the volume of Australia's aid, tied aid and mixed credit policies and administration.

BIBLIOGRAPHY

AIDAB 1993. A memo dated 18 December 1993 from Director Phillip Flood to DFAT Secretary Costello, regarding the funding of a position at the OECD Delegation, AIDAB File No 94/0152 'AIDAB Representation at Paris OECD'.

AIDAB 1994a. A memo dated 11 February 1994 from DFAT Secretary Costello to AIDAB Director Flood, AIDAB File No 94/0152 'AIDAB Representation at Paris OECD'.

AIDAB 1994b. 'Simons Review recommendation that an AusAID officer should be posted to the Development Assistance Committee', an undated Treasury paper for AusAID, AIDAB File No 94/0152 'AIDAB Representation at Paris OECD'.

ALP 1971. 'Federal Platform and Policy', Section XIX, p. 14.

Australian Cabinet 1971. 'Cabinet Minute – 25 May 1971 – Decision No. 187, Submission No 105 – Export Finance – Buyer's Credit', accessed 12 April

2015 at http://recordsearch.naa.gov.au/SearchNRetrieve/Interface/ViewImage.aspx?B=4290847.
Australian Cabinet 1985. 'Cabinet Submission 3391 – Australian overseas aid – Decision 6828, National Archives, Series No A14039, accessed 12 April 2015 at http://recordsearch.naa.gov.au/SearchNRetrieve/Interface/ViewImage.aspx?B=31427775.
Blair, D. 1993. *Trade Negotiations in the OECD*, London: Kegan Paul International.
Bowen, L. 1980. 'Speech', House of Representatives Hansard, 20 March 1980, p. 2.
Clay, E., Geddes, M., Natali, L. and te Velde, D. 2008. 'Thematic Study, The Developmental Effectiveness of Untied Aid: Evaluation of the Implementation of the Paris Declaration and of the 2001 DAC Recommendation on Untying ODA To The LDCs, Phase I Report', Copenhagen, December 2008.
Commonwealth Government 2012. 'Budget 2012–2013: Budget Paper No. 1: Statement 6: Expenses and Net Capital Investment', Parliamentary Library Publications, accessed on 10 August 2012 at http://parlinfo.aph.gov.au/parlInfo/download/library/budget/2012_10/upload_binary/bp1_bst6.pdf;fileType=application%2Fpdf#search=%22ODA%20target%22.
DAC 1962. 'Development Assistance Efforts and Policies in 1961 of the Members of the Development Assistance Committee', Report by the chairman of the DAC on the Annual Review', September 1962, Paris: OECD.
DAC 1963. 'Development Assistance Efforts and Policies in 1963 of the Members of the Development Assistance Committee', Report by the chairman of the DAC on the Annual Review', September 1963, Paris: OECD.
DAC 2010. 'History of the 0.7% ODA Target', DAC Journal 2002, 3(4): III-9–III-11, revised June 2010.
DFAT 1994a. 'Australian Department of Foreign Affairs and Trade Annual Report 1993–94', AGPS.
DFAT 1994b. 'Review of Australia's Interests in the Organisation for Economic Co-operation and Development (OECD)', Cabinet Memorandum No. 2082, from DFAT, on behalf of the Minister for Trade. The Review, led by an interdepartmental committee, aimed at evaluating the value of OECD membership and at identifying key priorities for the future. Attachment A provides a summary of the responses from the departments, DFAT File No 94/060329 Part 3 Review of Australia's OECD Membership.
DFAT 1995a. 'Australian Department of Foreign Affairs and Trade Annual Report 1994–95', AGPS.
DFAT 1995b. 5 Oct 95 DFAT Ministerial Submission File No 90/9741, dated 5 October 1995, from John Crighton, Assistant Secretary, Multilateral Trade Organisations Branch to Senator McMullan, Senator Evans and Mr Bilney, seeking their response regarding the proposed Australian response to the OECD Priorities Questionnaire, DFAT File No 94/060329 Part 6 Review of Australia's OECD Membership.
DFAT 1998. 'Priorities', a briefing paper dated 10 February 1998. It noted the 1995 OECD survey and indicated that it had not in practice led to changes in programmes or activities, that it had been a difficult exercise as domestic agencies sought to have high rankings placed on those OECD activities in

which they were engaged and to resist inclusion in the bottom list, DFAT File No 94/060329 Part 6 Review of Australia's OECD Membership.
Dillon, D. 1960. 'International Partnership for Economic Growth', *Department of State Bulletin* XLIII, No 1101 (1 August), p. 186.
Downer, A. 2000. 'Speech', House of Representatives Hansard, 29 November 2000, p. 23010.
Downer, A. 2005. 'Speech', House of Representatives Hansard, 10 March 2005, pp. 85–88.
Dunn, R. 1987. 'Director General', a copy of a letter from Dunn to the DAC chair, 9 February 1988, OECD Archives, Paris: OECD.
Evans, P. 2005. 'International Regulation of Official Trade Finance: Competition and Collusion in Export Credits and Foreign Aid', a doctoral thesis submitted to the Department of Political Science on 23 May 2005 at the Massachusetts Institute of Technology, accessed on 20 January 2017 at http://dspace.mit.edu/handle/1721.1/33684.
Flood, P. 2011. *Dancing with Warriors – A Diplomatic Memoir*, North Melbourne: Australian Scholarly Publishing.
Fuhrer, H. 1994. 'The Story of Official Development Assistance: A History of the Development Assistance Committee and the Development Co-Operation Directorate in Dates, Names and Figures', OCDE/GD(94)67, Paris: OECD.
Hynes, W. and Scott, S. 2013. 'The Evolution of Official Development Assistance: Achievements, Criticisms and a Way Forward', OECD Development Co-operation Working Papers, No. 12, OECD Publishing, accessed on 20 January 2017 at http://dx.doi.org/10.1787/5k3v1dv3f024-en.
Jackson Committee Report 1984. 'Report of the Committee to Review the Australian Overseas Aid Program 1984', AGPS, Canberra.
Levit, J. 2004. 'The Dynamics of International Trade Finance Regulation: The Arrangement on Officially Supported Export Credits', *Harvard International Law Journal*, 45: 65–182.
Macklin, M. 1987. 'Asian Development Fund Bill 1987, 1987 International Development Association Association Bill, International Fund for Agricultural Development Bill 1987 Second Readings', 17 December 1987, p. 3411, Senate Hansard.
McLeod, R. and Cuthbertson, S. 1996. 'The DIFF: An Obituary', *Agenda*, 3(4): 517–528.
Moravcsik, A. 1989. 'Disciplining Trade Finance: The OECD Export Credit Arrangement', *International Organization*, 43(1): 173–205.
NAA 1960. 'European Economic Conference Committee on Aid', dated 29 January 1960, a cable from K.C.O. Shann in the Australian High Commission in London to the DEA regarding the Committee and its implications, following a meeting with Mr Rumbold, a UK official, in company with John Stone of the Australian Treasury, then based at the High Commission, NAA Series No: A3092 Title: 'Development Assistance Group'.
NAA 1960a. 'Organisation for Economic Co-operation and Development', Outward Cablegram, 12 May 1960, For Crawford from Trade, NAA A987/4.
NAA 1960b. Cabinet Decision 615, 4 February 1960, NAA A3092.

NAA 1965. 'Report to the Minister of External Affairs by the Inter-departmental Committee to Review Australian External Aid', 25 March, 1965, A4311, 147/2.

NAA 1965a. 'OECD and DAC – Australian Relations With'. The file contains a copy of Cabinet Submission No 1194, 1965, which rejected the proposal for possible membership of the OECD, but agreed to an application for membership of the DAC and left open for later consideration the question of an application for full membership. A1838, File No 724/5 Part 4.

NAA 1966a. 'Development Assistance Committee', Memo No 214 from First Secretary G.C. Lewis at the Australian Embassy in Paris to the Secretary, DEA, noting that it was typical of DAC working parties that documents were circulated less than a week before a meeting. NAA Series 1838 724/5/5 Part 1 DAC Working Party on Assistance Requirements.

NAA 1966b. A letter dated 18 May 1967 from K.C.O. Shann in the DEA to Mr Frank Pryor in Treasury, asking for his views on which department had principal executive responsibility for meeting the Australian government's obligations regarding the DAC. Shann understood this to be DEA's, responsibility, noting a difficulty that had arisen, DEA File No 724/5/3 PT 2, Subject: 'DAC – 1966 – 1967 Review of Australian Aid'.

NAA 1966c. '1966 Review of Australian Aid by the DAC', a memo from acting DEA Secretary Laurance McIntyre, dated 28 October 1966, to the Minister noting that the government's decision to join DAC was 'fully justified' by the positive and helpful 1966 DAC review of aid, DEA File No 724/5/3 PT 1.

NAA 1966d. Summary of HLM of 20–21 July 1966 regarding the 'Report of WP on Assistance Requirements' DAC(66) 22, NAA, Series 1838 724/5/5 Part 1 DAC Working Party on Assistance Requirements.

NAA 1967a. In a cable to the DEA in Canberra dated 29 September 1967 K.C.O. Shann noted that he was not happy with the 1967 DAC review of Australian aid, DEA File No 724/5/3 PT 2 Subject: 'DAC – 1966 – 1967 Review of Australian Aid'.

NAA 1967b. In a cable dated 30 September 1967 to K.C.O. Shann, from the Australian Embassy in Paris, Sir Ronald Walker reassured Shann regarding the 1967 DAC review, also noting that it was accepted at the OECD that unpublished confidential reports on aid programmes should aim at criticism rather than praise, in part to stimulate discussion at the DAC, DEA File No 724/5/3 PT 2 Subject: 'DAC – 1966 – 1967 Review of Australian Aid'.

NAA 1967c. 'Informal record of Proceedings', dated 10 October 1967 on the 1967 DAC examination of Australia. In his introductory remarks K.C.O. Shann commented that last year the chair warned him at the end of the examination that they were being rather kind to a new boy and not to expect such kindness in the future, DEA File No 724/5/3 PT 2 Subject: 'DAC – 1966 – 1967 Review of Australian Aid'.

NAA 1967d. 'DAC Review of Australian Aid – 1967'. A memo from K.C.O. Shann to the Secretary of the DFA noting that the review went quite well and 'too gloomy a view should not be taken of Mr Thorp's concluding remarks', for he told me privately later he was well pleased and when I see him again tomorrow I propose to make the point that 'in some quarters, searching for things to criticize might not be taken too well and could be counter-productive', DEA File No 724/5/3 PT 3 Subject: 'DAC – 1966 – 1967 Review of Australian Aid'.

NAA 1968a. 'DAC: Representation at Meetings', a memo dated 17 April 1968 from the head of the Aid Policy Section, G.J. Price, to the Secretary of the DEA. In a hand written P.S. to the memo Price noted that Flood had indicated that the Treasury's representative, based at the Australian High Commission in London, had only attended one DAC special topic meeting in two years, DEA File No 724/5/6 Part No 1 'OECD DAC Calendar of meetings, work program etc'.

NAA 1968b. A note dated 24 January 1968 L.B. Engledow to K.C.O. Shann regarding the 1967 DAC review, apologising that it was not possible to have an interdepartmental committee for the 23 January about the report. Engledow noted that the report was not controversial and that 'it is hardly critical enough to be used as a lever in forcing decisions about increased aid', DEA File No 724/5/3 PT 3 Subject: 'DAC – 1966 – 1967 Review of Australian Aid'.

NAA 1969a. 'DAC – 1966 – 1967 Review of Australian Aid', DEA File No 724/5/3 PT 3.

NAA 1969b. 'Australia's International Development Assistance', 1969 DAC Review of Australia, OECD.

NAA 1970a. 3 September 1970 Cabinet Minute Decision No 657 Sub Nos 509, 511, DEA File No 724/5/3 PT 13 Subject: 'DAC – 1968 Review etc'.

NAA 1970b. 'Memorandum Submitted for Review of Australian Aid 1970', undated, p. 3, DEA File No 724/5/3 PT 13 Subject: 'DAC – 1968 Review etc'.

NAA 1970c. A letter from K.C.O. Shann, dated 8 April 1970 to the Secretary, Prime Minister's Department regarding Australian aid, A1838 File No 724/5/48 Part No 1 'DAC Untying of Aid'.

NAA 1970d. Cable from DEA to OECD Delegation, dated 28 April 1970, with a briefing on aid tying, File No 724/5/6 Part No 1 'OECD DAC Calendar of meetings, work prog etc'.

NAA 1970e. Memorandum dated 10 April 1970 from Mr B.W. Fraser (a Treasury member of the OECD delegation) to FAS Overseas Economic Relations Division in Canberra, A1838 File No 724/5/48 Part No 1 'DAC Untying of Aid'.

NAA 1970f. A memorandum dated 10 April 1970 from B.W. Fraser at the OECD delegation in Paris to the Treasury's First Assistant Secretary responsible for the Overseas Economic Relations Division, A1838 File No 724/5/48 Part No 1 'DAC Untying of Aid'.

NAA 1971. 'Financial Implications of Untying Australia's Contributions to Certain Multilateral Organisations', 23 August 1971, A1838 File No 724/5/48 Part No 3 'DAC Untying of Aid'.

NAA 1972a. A memo from Deputy Secretary K.C.O. Shann to the Minister, date 28 April 1972, DEA File No 724/5/3 PT 14 Subject: 'DAC – Review etc'.

NAA 1972b. 'Targets for Australian Aid', a report for the Minister, December 1972, NAA Series 1838 724/5/5 Part 4 DAC Working Party on Assistance Requirements.

NAA 1973. Comments by chairman Martin on the 1973 DAC Review of Australian aid, DEA File No 724/5/3 PT 18 Subject: 'DAC – Review etc'.

NAA 1981. A cable from the Australian Development Assistance Agency in Canberra to the OECD Delegation, with a copy of the Australian Development Agency Bureau's brief by A.J. Kelloway 'Consensus Arrangement: Brief on Tied Aid Credits', ADAA File No 81/3424 'OECD Arrangement on Export Credits – Part 1'.

NAA 1984a. A cable from the OECD Delegation dated 17 May 1984 to DFAT in Canberra with the text of Minister Hayden's statement to the OECD's 1984 Ministerial Council meeting on the international trade item, DFA File No 84/0703 'OECD Arrangement on Export Credits and DAC Associated Finance Part 5'.

NAA 1984b. A copy of the Press Release following the OECD Ministerial Council meeting 17 May 1984, in DFA File No 84/1450 'OECD Arrangement on Export Credits and DAC Associated Finance Part 6'.

OECD 1969. 'Australia's International Development Assistance', Paris: OECD.

OECD 1973. 'Comments by the Chairman of the Development Assistance Committee on the 1973 Aid Review of Australia', a copy of a letter from Edwin M. Martin to the Australian Ambassador to the OECD, R.J. Cameron. OECD Archives, 18 December 1973, Paris: OECD.

OECD 1977. 'Comments by the Chairman of the Development Assistance Committee on the annual Aid Review of Australia', a copy of a letter from M. Williams to the Australian Ambassador to the OECD, F.P. Donovan. OECD Archives, 29 November 1977, Paris: OECD.

OECD 1981. 'Aid Review of Australia – DAC Chairman's Comments', a copy of a letter from the new chair, John P. Lewis, to the Australian Ambassador to the OECD, J.C. Humphreys. OECD Archives, 28 December 1981, Paris: OECD.

OECD 1985. 'Twenty-Five Years of Development Co-operation – A Review, Efforts and Policies of the Members of the Development Assistance Committee', Paris: OECD.

OECD 1987. 'Comments by the Chairman on the Aid Review of Australia 4th December 1987', a copy of a letter from DAC chair Joseph Wheeler, to the Australian Ambassador to the OECD, A. McGoldrick, OECD Archives, 10 December 1987, Paris: OECD.

OECD 1990. 'Comments by the Chairman on the Aid Review of Australia 30th November 1989', a copy of a letter from DAC chair Joseph Wheeler, to the Australian Ambassador to the OECD, Ed Visbord, OECD Archives, 12 January 1990, Paris: OECD.

OECD 1996. 'Shaping the 21st Century: The Contribution of Development Co-operation', Paris: OECD.

OECD 2005. 'DAC Peer Review of Australia 2005', Paris: OECD.

OECD 2009. 'Australia Development Assistance Committee Peer Review', Paris: OECD.

Peacock, A. 1977. 'Official Development Assistance: Aid Target (Question No. 1124)', 18 August 1977, p. 1 House of Representatives Hansard.

Ray, J. 1995. *Managing Official Export Credits: The Quest for a Global Regime*, Washington, DC: Institute for International Economics.

Rosefsky, K. 1993. 'Tied Aid Credits and the New OECD Agreement', *Journal of International Law*, 14(3): 437–467.

Rudd, K. 2005. 'Speech', House of Representatives Hansard, 10 March 2005, p. 89.

Sherlock, S. 1991. 'A Guide to the Australian Overseas Aid Program and Issues in Development Assistance', Parliamentary Research Service Background Paper, Department of the Parliamentary Library, Australian Parliament.

Simons Committee 1997. 'One Clear Objective Poverty Reduction through Sustainable Development', Report of the Committee of Review, April 1997, AusAID, Canberra.

Tomar, R. 1996. 'A Difference of Opinion: Cancellation of the Development Import Finance Facility', Current Issues Brief 20, 1995–6, Parliamentary Library, Canberra.

Tomar, R. and Bruere, W. 2014. 'Official Development Assistance – the Future of Australian Aid', Budget Review 2014–15 Index, Research Papers, Parliamentary Library, Canberra, accessed on 20 January 2017 at www.aph.gov.au/About_Parliament/Parliamentary_Departments/Parliamentary_Library/pubs/rp/BudgetReview201415/ODA.

Uren, T. 1977. 'Official Development Assistance: Aid Target (Question No. 1124)', 18 August 1977, p. 1 House of Representatives Hansard.

Watson, J. 1987. 'Petitions Overseas Aid', 24 August 1988, p. 112, Senate Hansard.

Wilkinson, A. 1976. 'The Politics of Australian Foreign Aid Policy 1950–1972', PhD thesis, Research School of Pacific Studies, ANU.

8. An extensive involvement: the Treasury Portfolio and the OECD

The aim of this chapter is to describe and examine the involvement of the Treasury Portfolio in the work of the OECD, the most extensive involvement of all government portfolios. As a result only a limited selection of the Portfolio's often very active involvement with the work of the organisation can be examined in this chapter. It commences with an examination of Treasury's role in promoting Australian membership of the OECD, before moving on to provide an outline of the varying extent and intensity of the Treasury Department's involvement with OECD committees. This is followed by a brief description of the involvement of the major agencies in the Treasury Portfolio, which is too extensive to fully document in this chapter. The final section provides a more in-depth examination of Treasury involvement with the Economic Development Review Committee (EDRC), the reviews of which have often provided considerable challenges for the Department, largely as regards their political sensitivity when they are critical of current economic policy. Chapter 9 provides a detailed examination of Australia's involvement with the OECD's tax work, in which Treasury and, in particular, the Australian Tax Office has been increasingly involved.

GAINING ACCESS AND POSSIBLE INFLUENCE IN INTERNATIONAL CIRCLES: THE VIEWS OF TREASURY OFFICIALS

As a small to medium power Australia in the 1960s had a limited capacity to influence international economic discussion and activities, a fact of which its public servants and ministers were well aware. However, a number of developments had driven this realisation even further home in that decade, awakening a search for avenues of influence by the DEA and Treasury, particularly the latter, which was largely responsible for international economic policy and represented Australia at the IMF, World Bank and the ADB. The first development, commencing in the later 1950s, was a growing dissatisfaction with the capacity of the United

Nations and its specialised agencies to provide effective channels by which Australian representatives could exercise the little influence they possessed. In that context Australia had attempted to portray itself as something of a 'midway country', at least in terms of economic development and not part of the what came to be known as the wealthy, Group B countries in the UNCTAD talks, but had not been successful in getting that position accepted by the members of the Group of 77 (NAA, 1969a).

The second development was the declining value of the Commonwealth as a means of Australian access to British decision making circles as the 'end of empire' loomed, with Britain focused increasingly on gaining membership of the EEC. This had been driven home at the highest levels of Australian government by the discovery of the British guarantee of the sterling holdings of members of the European Payments Union (later the European Monetary Agreement), a guarantee not offered to Commonwealth members and kept secret from them. It was reinforced by the realisation that Britain was unlikely to gain much in the way of consideration of Australian economic interests when it gained EEC membership.

The third development was Australia's exclusion from the General Agreement to Borrow (GAB), established in 1962. The GAB was an agreement between the USA, UK, Japan, France, Italy, Canada, the Netherlands and Belgium, plus the central banks of Germany and Sweden, to make borrowings available to the IMF in times of international monetary crisis. Switzerland was invited to associate with the GAB, or Group of Ten as it became known, in 1964 and the Bank for International Settlements, IMF, European Commission and the OECD became official observers. The establishment of such a group, outside the IMF but with substantial power within it, caused considerable resentment among non-G10 members, including Australia, with the Australian Executive Director at the IMF reportedly complaining that the G10 was 'a very exclusive group', and unsuccessfully demanding admission (Mountford, 2008: 9). It was a sharp reminder of Australia's relatively minor status in international relations. It also suggested at the time that the IMF was becoming less influential and might become increasingly reliant on the views of its GAB members, perhaps reducing the value of the IMF for the pursuit of Australian interests.

The fourth development was the growing signs that the Bretton Woods system was in increasingly rapid decline, a decline that came rapidly to the fore of international monetary relations in the 1968 to 1971 period, culminating in President Nixon's unilateral suspension of the US dollar's convertibility into gold, a move that led to substantial uncertainty in economic and political arenas. It was a growing uncertainty that was felt most keenly in Treasury, mindful of its responsibilities for Australia's international economic policy and increasingly concerned with the state of the Australian economy (Whitwell, 1986: 176–7).

These were developments that were conducive to forum shopping, with both Treasury and DEA officials searching for organisations that offered at least the prospect of maintaining the limited influence that Australia then possessed. The OECD was such a prospect as it contained the world's wealthiest nations, including all of those in the EEC and EFTA and the Group of Ten, as well as Japan. Indeed, the Group of Ten, with the initial exception of Japan, constituted the membership of the OECD's influential Working Party 3 (WP3) of the Economic Policy Committee, with strong links to the Bank for International Settlements (BIS) and the IMF, and whose first chairs were Emile van Lennep and Otto Emminger, both also senior members of the EEC's Monetary Committee. Van Lennep became the OECD's second Secretary-General in 1969 and Emminger was the President of the Bundesbank, 1977–79, having been the West German Executive Director at the IMF from 1953 to 1959. Some have argued that WP3 became the de facto 'crisis manager' of the capitalist world for much of the 1970s and, in addition, that it paved the way for the structural adjustment reforms of the 1980s, though its influence then declined (Kazuhiko, 2012; Galeazzi, 2015).

Not only was the OECD a key focus for international economic policy, its reports and publications were becoming widely respected and, while many of them were openly available to non-members, this was not always the case. Moreover, where publication did take place it typically occurred several months, sometimes years, after the reports had been considered by OECD members, with non-members normally not participating in OECD committee discussions about the reports, discussions that could reveal useful detail regarding the positions and policies of members.

Despite the above developments, not all Treasury officials or ministers initially were positive about OECD membership. Treasurer Harold Holt, for example, initially strongly opposed DEA Minister Barwick's proposal that Australia should take up a US invitation for membership of an ad hoc OECD consultative group regarding Thailand in 1962, although his opposition was unsuccessful (NAA, 1962). However, within a year Holt was more positive in not opposing a proposal for OECD membership, suggesting it should not be dismissed without further study, but deferred for a year or so, when a later opportunity might arise (NAA, 1963).

Hence, by 1969, while, as senior Treasury official Robert Whitelaw noted, 'Treasury corridors were not full of people running about screaming for membership of OECD', there was general and growing support for membership (NAA, 1969a). From the Treasury perspective membership offered: (1) increased access to key decision makers in the great powers, especially regarding the major reserve currencies, the US dollar and the British pound, and decision making in the IMF, BIS and EEC; (2) the opportunity to make Australian interests better known; (3) more timely access to OECD reports, publications and discussions – it had been reported, for example, that Australia had suffered a disadvantage from not being a member as it was not informed as to what export subsidies the OECD members were developing (NAA, 1965); and (4) to a limited extent, the opportunity to exercise a greater degree of influence. As indicated in an internal Treasury memorandum following the decision to work towards accession to the OECD, maximum benefit would come if Australia could get into WP3 and there was some optimism that this could be achieved, despite the fact that WP3 was then one of the OECD's few restricted membership committees, the memorandum noting:

> We could reasonably expect to gain entry after a waiting period during which time we might find it possible to attend meetings as part of another members' delegation. Japan was admitted after almost 12 months full membership of OECD. (NAA, 1968)

The memorandum expressed some concern about possible, adverse results that might follow after the publication of the Economic Development Review Committee's (EDRC) regular review of the Australian economy, should Australia gain membership, and as regards the annual cost of membership, estimated at approximately $500,000, but it was felt doubtful that these would outweigh the benefits of membership. A similar concern was voiced in regard to the possible adverse impact of the OECD Codes of Liberalization and Current Invisible Operations and Capital Movements, which did not look favourably on strict regulation of capital movements and restrictions on invisible transactions, such as those used at this time by Australia. However, upon examination of Australia's position under the Codes, it was found, initially, that only six items were in breach of the Codes and that a reservation could be lodged that would enable them to continue in place. It was found that there were:

> [F]ew grounds for concern that any serious attempt by Australia to secure full membership of the OECD would be held up by Australia's inability to meet the obligations imposed by the Codes of Liberalization. (NAA, 1969b)

While Treasury felt that there were distinct economic advantages to be gained from OECD membership, senior officials in the DEA tended to also emphasise the political advantages. DEA Deputy Secretary, K.C.O.

Shann, for example, in a letter to the Minister, noted that 'The case for joining has never been one of commercial or trade advantage – it is essentially financial and political' (NAA, 1970a). Similarly, E.J. Bunting, Secretary to the Prime Minister's Department, felt that both political and economic motives were of importance, noting that the OECD had become the major effective organ for cooperation between countries of the Western world, and that the United Nations had ceased to deal with serious major practical economic issues of concern to the more developed countries, 'it concentrates largely on the problems of the less-developed' (NAA, 1970b). These differences of view were typical of those that led to interdepartmental disputes as to which department should be the lead agency responsible for the OECD and that led to the decision to rotate the OECD ambassadorship on a three-yearly basis between the DEA and Treasury, as discussed in earlier chapters.

Treasury officials were not unrealistic about gaining membership of, or influence in, the WP3. It was felt that because of Australia's role in the sterling area and the importance to Australia of many of the matters coming before WP3, it could expect to become a member in due course and that, in the meantime, the UK had indicated the Australian representative would probably be able to attend as an observer (NAA, 1965: 12). Three years later, in 1968, another Treasury official, in a detailed assessment of the advantages and disadvantage that membership of the OECD might bring, felt that Australia would not be able to exert great influence (NAA, 1968).

Treasury views were increasingly supported by senior officials in the Cabinet Office, which, while initially cautious, by 1970 were very positive. Cabinet Office Secretary Bunting, in a copy of a note he had prepared for Prime Minister Gorton about the arguments for OECD membership, indicated that it: (1) had become the major effective organ for cooperation between countries of the Western world; (2) that the United Nations had ceased to deal with serious major practical economic issues of concern to the more developed countries, concentrating largely on the problems of the less-developed countries; (3) that, in not being a member of OECD, Australia was cut off from a mainstream of economic thought and from the formation of policy attitudes; and (4) that Australian participation in the OECD would produce a new awareness of Australia in European countries, which would assist our relations with Europe, 'which are largely economic' (NAA, 1970b).

In summary, Treasury officials played a persistent, leading role in persuading the Australian government that membership of the OECD was in Australia's best economic interests. It proved to be a difficult task, spread over ten years, one marked by the strong and, for the most part, effective opposition of Black Jack McEwen and his department.

THE TREASURY DEPARTMENT AND THE OECD

The involvement of the Treasury Portfolio in the OECD is substantial and the Treasury Department generally shares with DFAT, on a three-yearly, rotational basis, the nomination for the position of the Australian Ambassador to the OECD, who heads the Delegation in Paris and sits on the OECD Council. The Ambassador also frequently is a member, chair or vice chair of other standing and ad hoc Council committees and groups, with a number of Australian ambassadors having been chair of the Council's Executive Committee. While, initially, the Treasury Department had two full-time staff members based in the Delegation, in the last decade this was reduced to only one, a Minister-Counsellor, although the frequency of staff visits to attend committees has risen over the decades as air transport has become less costly.

Decisions as to whether to participate, or not, in the work of an OECD committee or ad hoc group are sometimes routine, but at other times can have sensitive, symbolic and/or political implications. In 1978, for example, the MCM adopted a declaration and associated general guidelines on 'Policies for Adjustment: Some General Orientations', with a strong, microeconomic reform emphasis, which Australia strongly supported. This was emphasised again at the 1979 MCM, which led to the establishment of a Special Group on Positive Adjustment Policies under the Economic Policy Committee. Its major objective was to conduct a series of reviews aimed at improving understanding of members' policies and how they related to the objective of positive adjustment. Aware of the political sensitivities involved, there were to be no published reports or 'formal' judgements regarding country policies, although they were to provide background for an eventual, general report on positive adjustment policies.

The Treasury representatives were asked if Australia wished to be reviewed and the views of interested departments were sought and, initially, none of those consulted were opposed. However, shortly afterwards a senior official in Industry and Commerce, Fred Bennett, indicated his opposition to participation. Treasury officials noted that:

> Bennett is said to be sensitive to possible criticism of Australia within the Organisation regarding decisions that will be taken in the next few months in

> relation to the clothing, footwear and textile industries and motor vehicle industries. (Treasury, 1980)

Treasury Secretary John Stone was informed of the situation and contacted N.S. Currie, Secretary of the Department of Industry and Commerce, noting that Treasury had strongly supported OECD work on positive adjustment, enclosing a copy of a draft letter from Treasurer John Howard to Prime Minister Malcolm Fraser (copied to all other interested ministers), that indicated Howard's strong support for Australian participation. Fraser supported Howard's proposal, which was ultimately designed to enable market forces to operate more effectively and break down perceived rigidities to economic structures that hindered economic change. The Prime Minister had earlier stressed the importance of such policies in addresses to UNCTAD in Manila and at the CHOGM in Lusaka in 1979 (Treasury, 1980).

Membership of the major OECD standing committees has been less controversial and was and is expected by other members, though the extent and intensity of participation varies. At the least it usually involves a watching brief over potential and actual developments and consideration of their implications for Australian interests, both domestic and international, but can, less frequently, involve more positive activities to pursue specific objectives. In 2000, for example, a proposal from the Committee on International Investment and Multinational Enterprises (CIME) that it should conduct peer reviews of its members performance, especially that of National Contact Points (NCP), was opposed as it was felt that no NCP should have to justify its activities and role to CIME. A negative CIME review, it was felt:

> [d]irected at one particular country could have repercussions domestically that would be difficult to contain politically. (Treasury, 2000a)

In contrast and more positively, later that same year Treasury's representative in Paris was briefed to the effect that a major effort was required to ensure and promote CIME's leadership in investment matters following the failure of the Multilateral Agreement on Investment (MAI). This should include, it was proposed, cooperation with BIAC and TUAC and dialogue with non-members and other members of civil society who had strongly opposed the MAI (Treasury, 2000b).

In the early years after membership Treasury focused its efforts primarily on the Economic Policy and the Economic Development Review committees and their subcommittees. It then expanded its involvement to include a range of other key committees, for example, the

Committee of Fiscal Affairs (CFA) and, working closely with the Australian Tax Office (ATO), several of the CFA's working parties involved with tax issues, an involvement that has grown significantly over the last two decades and is regarded as of considerable importance. Treasury and ATO officials, for example, held the following positions on CFA working parties at the time of writing, reflecting positive views as to their importance:

- Co-chair of the Joint Meetings of Tax and Environment Experts.
- Chair of Working Party No 2 on Tax Policy Analysis and Tax Statistics.
- Vice chair of the Forum on Tax Administration.
- Vice chair of Working Party No 9 on Consumption Taxes.
- Bureau member of Working Party No 11 on Aggressive Tax Planning.
- Vice chair of the Task Force on the Digital Economy.

Treasury officials, working closely with the Australian Competition and Consumer Commission (ACCC), also participate in the work of the Competition Committee, where a member of the ACCC is currently a vice chair. An ACCC official is also the Chair of the Committee on Consumer Policy's Working Party on Consumer Product Safety. Treasury officials also participate in the work of the Investment Committee and the Insurance and Private Pensions Committee. Dr Malcolm Edey, Assistant Governor of the Reserve Bank, was elected chair of the Committee of Financial Markets in 2010, having previously been seconded to work as a senior economist in the OECD's Money and Finance Division. He is also a vice chair of the OECD's Advisory Task Force on the OECD Codes of Liberalisation. As a signatory to the OECD's voluntary Guidelines for Multinational Enterprises, supervised by its Corporate Governance Committee, in which Australia participates, a Treasury official from the Foreign Investment and Trade Policy Division acts as the Australian National Contact Point.

In general terms Treasury officials on the various committees are drawn from the relevant Division of the Department, with the extent and intensity of involvement varying over time as the relevance and importance of issues varies. The Revenue Group, for example, had only a limited international engagement including sporadic involvement with the OECD for most of the 1980s and 1990s, with its focus being on domestic tax and revenue reforms. In 2004, as concern regarding the rate of avoidance of Australian tax by multinational enterprises began to grow, it was decided that a process should be put in place for increasing its international engagement, including the identification of the Revenue Group's priorities as regards the OECD, and that a coordinated strategy for OECD engagement should be developed (Treasury, 2004). It was agreed that relevant staff should meet four times per annum, twice prior to, and twice post the meetings of the CFA. In addition, representatives of specialised subgroups would brief the CFA representative prior to each CFA meeting and, in turn, the CFA representative would debrief the group after each CFA meeting. Once a year the group would identify or reconfirm its priority areas. In addition, it was agreed that a clearer delineation of responsibilities between Treasury and the ATO as regards tax work at the OECD was needed and that a better coordinated Australian position needed more effective consultation with the ATO, DFAT and Prime Minister and Cabinet.

As indicated above and in the following section, following this strategic review and better coordination, Australian involvement in OECD tax work, already significant, grew more rapidly and, at least as judged by the number of Australians elected to key positions on committee bureaux, became more influential. Recently, for example, the Revenue Group, working closely with the ATO, has played a significant role in the development of the joint OECD-G20 Base Erosion and Profit Shifting (BEPS) project, especially the development and implementation of its action plan. The importance of the OECD in this context can be seen in a 2013 scoping paper prepared by Treasury at the request of the Assistant Treasurer, 'Risks to the Sustainability of Australia's Corporate Tax Base' (Commonwealth of Australia, 2013).

The paper examined the risks posed by multinational profit shifting and aggressive tax minimisation and found that the rise of the digital economy and the increased importance of intangibles presented challenges to the corporate tax bases of countries, including Australia, that required multilateral efforts if it was to be effectively managed. It recommended that the focus of Australia's efforts should be on shaping and leading efforts to improve multilateral reform and that it should endorse the Action Plan establishing the joint OECD and G20 project with a comprehensive work programme to address the major causes of base erosion and profit shifting. It further noted that, as G20 chair in 2014, Australia could play a prominent role in determining and driving this agenda (Commonwealth of Australia, 2013). The government accepted the recommendation and the Action Plan was endorsed by world leaders at the next G20 Summit.

THE AGENCIES IN THE TREASURY PORTFOLIO AND THE OECD

A number of other agencies in the Treasury Portfolio also play an active role of varying extents as regards the OECD, notably the Australian Bureau of Statistics (ABS), Australian Competition and Consumer Commission (ACCC), Australian Prudential Regulation Authority (APRA), Australian Reinsurance Pool Corporation (ARPC), the Productivity Commission and, most of all, the ATO. This extent of involvement poses a continuous need for coordination by Treasury officials, particularly as regards the ATO and its involvement in the growing tax work of the OECD.

The ABS, the official statistical agency, has had a representative on the OECD's Committee on Statistics and Statistical Policy for many years and Brian Pink, the Government Statistician from 2007 to 2014, was the chair of the Committee from 2008 to 2012. At present, ABS representatives are the vice chairs of at least two of the Committee's key working parties, the Working Party on Financial Statistics and the Working Party on National Accounts. The ABS is the official source of a great deal of statistical data that Australia provides to the OECD and, not only is a significant portion of that data based on standards promulgated by the OECD, in 2014 the ABS commenced trialling the use of the OECD's data warehouse technology to enable Australian users to better access and use the data on the ABS website. The ABS involvement with the OECD is an active one that, over time, has seen it play a substantive role in a variety of projects including, for example, that driven by the Expert Group on micro statistics on household income, consumption and wealth (ABS, 2014).

The ACCC is an independent statutory authority which administers the Competition and Consumer Act 2010 and performs a variety of functions under other Commonwealth legislation and State and Territory Competition Policy Reform Acts. It undertakes a range of activities with similar bodies overseas and participates actively in the OECD's Competition Committee and the closely related International Competition Network (ICN). Professor Alan Fels, for example, was co-chair of the Joint Group on Trade and Competition at the OECD from 1996 until 2003, as well as a member of the Competition Committee. Currently, one of its commissioners, Dr Jill Walker, is a member of the bureau of the Competition Committee. In addition, an ACC representative often attends meetings of the OECD's Regulatory Policy Committee (currently chaired by Professor Gary Banks, previously the Chair of the Productivity

Commission), one of its subsidiary bodies, the Network of Economic Regulators and, in 2013, Mark Pearson, the ACCC's Deputy CEO for Regulation, was voted on to the bureau of the latter, later becoming its chair.

The ACCC also maintains a close relationship with the OECD Consumer Product Safety Working Party and has hosted a virtual symposium with the OECD in relation to online issues. In 2012, for example, the ACCC strongly supported the introduction of the OECD's Global Recall portal, developed by the Consumer Product Safety Working Party, which brings together recall of product data from the US, Europe, Canada and Australia. While not examined here, the OECD has been particularly influential regarding cartels and their impact in restricting competition. In 2008, for example, the *Trade Practices Amendment (Cartel Conduct and Other Measures) Act, 2008* put into effect in Australia the OECD's 1998 Recommendation of the Council Concerning Effective Action against Hard Core Cartels that its members put in place laws that more effectively deter, detect and punish hard core cartel conduct. The amendment meant that individuals engaging in cartel conduct faced the prospect of up to ten years imprisonment (OECD, 1998).

APRA, established in 1998 following the collapse of HIH, Australia's second largest general insurer, is the financial supervisor responsible for the prudential regulation of banking, other deposit taking, insurance and superannuation industries in Australia. It has been a member of the OECD Insurance and Private Pensions Committee (IPPC) since its inception, providing standardised data on an annual basis. It is also a founder member of the International Network of Pensions Regulators and Supervisors, formed under OECD auspices in 2000, and its representative was elected to its technical committee, with a member of APRA's staff also co-chairing its first conference. APRA has been perhaps most active on the Insurance Committee's Working Party on Private Pensions (ICWPPP), with its Deputy Chair, Kerry Jones, having acted as a vice chair until 2013. The Working Party surveys and monitors private pensions systems, analyses related policy and technical issues, and formulates policy recommendations for the regulation and supervision of such systems.

APRA has been involved in a number of projects with the ICWPP, including a joint OECD/International Organisation of Pension Supervisors good practices paper on risk management. At present it is contributing to a major project on annuities involving a stocktake of types of annuity products and their guarantees, and an examination of the regulatory framework governing different types of annuity products and of their fiscal treatment, jointly undertaken by the IPPC, the WPPP and IOPS.

It is not only APRA that is involved in the OECD's work on insurance and private pensions. In 2012, for example, the WPP issued a ten-point roadmap outlining what was needed for the good design of superannuation systems. This was applied by the Charter Group, established by the Treasurer and Minister Assisting for Financial Services and Superannuation to help assess the adequacy of the Australian superannuation system. The Group suggested that on that basis it ranked about six or seven out of ten on the measures used by the roadmap, with some way to go before it met the OECD standard (Charter Group, 2013: 22). However, the incoming Abbott government decided in 2013 not to proceed with the Charter or proposed Council.

The ARPC is a statutory authority established under the *Terrorism Insurance Act 2003*, following the 11 September 2001 terrorism attack in New York. The scale of the attack led to the widespread withdrawal of terrorism insurance and an adverse impact on the commercial property sector. The Howard government responded by establishing the ARPC to administer a scheme to provide insurance cover for eligible terrorism losses, and its involvement with the OECD in its work on terrorism insurance dates back to 2003. Board member Ms Lorraine Allan, for example, then a member of the Superannuation and Insurance Unit of the Treasury, was Australia's representative on the initial OECD task force on terrorism insurance. In the early years of the ARPC its CEO was also a member of the Advisory Board to the OECD Network on the Financial Management of Large-scale Catastrophes, which provided the CEO with valuable insights into current trends in catastrophe management. ARPC representatives always participate in the meetings of the Network, and it initiated and sponsored the OECD's first terrorism insurance conferences in 2010 and 2012 (OECD, 2011: 3).

The Productivity Commission is the Commonwealth government's independent research and advisory body on a range of economic, social and environmental issues, fulfilling a similar role at the national level to that performed by the OECD internationally, with which it has maintained close contacts over several decades. Its own research often draws heavily on OECD data in order to enable international comparisons of Australian public policy and its impact, as can be seen, for example, in 'Aspects of Structural Change in Australia', 'Mechanism for Improving the Quality of Regulations: Australia in an International Context', 'Regulatory Impact Analysis: Benchmarking Research Report' (Productivity Commission, 1998, 2003, 2012). The Commission has also used OECD models to assist in analysing data for its own reports, such as its adaptation of the WALRAS general equilibrium model (McDougall and Sugden, 1991). Several Productivity Commission commissioners have worked with or at the OECD, for example, current Commissioners Jonathan Coppel and Paul Lindwall, and its former chair, Gary Banks, is now the Chair of the OECD's Regulatory Policy Committee.

The ATO is the subject of more detailed examination in Chapter 9. It is the largest of the agencies in the Treasury portfolio and, as its Annual Report notes, it takes an active leadership role to combat global tax problems. In particular, currently it is focusing on the implementation of the OECD's Action Plan on Base Erosion and Profit Shifting, a key issue for the G20, with its Deputy Commissioner (Large Business and International), Jim Killaly, on secondment to the OECD (ATO, 2014: 3, 9). Killaly was previously a participant at the Committee for Fiscal Affairs, highly involved in its tax work. ATO representatives sit on several of the tax-related OECD committees and working parties, an area of work that has expanded rapidly over the last decade, and its main focus has been on developing multilateral cooperation between tax administrations, such as its significant contribution to the OECD Forum on Tax Administration. The ATO also led a team of six other tax administrations to investigate global tax planning of multinational enterprises in the digital economy, and analysis from the project's pilot was used to inform the OECD Task Force on the Digital Economy (ATO, 2014: 28). The OECD's Model Tax Convention also forms the basis for Australia's double taxation agreements.

THE EDRC REVIEWS OF AUSTRALIA

The OECD's Economic Development Review Committee process is one of peer review in which the performance of a member's economy is subject to detailed examination by other members with the overall aim of helping to improve that performance. As such, it is a politically sensitive process for all governments as its reviews frequently question, explicitly and implicitly, economic policies, institutions and related activities. Treasury officials were acutely aware of the potential political sensitivity of the EDRC reviews of the Australian economy in the years leading up to membership (NAA, 1971).

While the EDRC review aims at objectivity, this does not mean that it is always a critically 'gentle' process, particularly when major differences in economic thought and theory develop, as was the case from the later 1970s to the early 1990s, when more firmly market-based, monetarist policy prescriptions became more influential and Keynesian demand management approaches became less influential. In 1991, for example, a senior Treasury official wrote to Dr Stephen Potter, the Director of the Country Studies Branch of the Economic Department of the OECD regarding the first draft of the latest EDRC review, or survey as it is commonly described, noting that a number of sections of the draft 'do not appear to be as balanced as they could be in outlining policy developments in Australia'. The note went on to indicate that Treasury was particularly struck by the draft's focus on the alleged 'short-termism' of Australian monetary policies in the 1980s, claiming they brought about Australia's relatively poor inflation performance in that period, which he felt was a 'little extreme' and contrasted unfavourably with earlier, more positive EDRC reviews. The Reserve Bank, in particular, felt the draft reflected the 'enchantment' of the OECD review team, or at least some members of it, with 'the New Zealand model' (NAA, 1990a).

The dynamic force behind the EDRC process is what loosely may be described as peer pressure, taking the shape of a fluctuating mix of questions and comments from: (1) the members of the OECD Secretariat who make up the membership of the survey team drawing up the survey; (2) from the two or three committee members who conduct what was originally known as the face-to-face 'confrontation' with the Australian representatives (largely senior officials from Treasury and a representative of the Reserve Bank), in Paris about the contents of the draft survey; (3) the formal recommendations contained in the draft and final reports; (4) importantly, the sometimes critical comments from the media and opposition parties when the report is released, though these are not, strictly speaking, a form of peer pressure; and (5) the potential for the review to have a negative economic impact upon Australian business. In addition, the OECD reviews can be drawn upon by IMF staff for information in their annual, 'Article IV', reviews of Australia's obligations under the terms of the article (see, for example, NAA, 1992).

While the process has varied somewhat over time, it commences with a detailed questionnaire from the OECD to Treasury, usually received with rather less than enthusiasm by those responsible for its completion given the extent of the task involved (most of the branches of Treasury have input, as well as the Reserve Bank), plus a request for a 'calendar' of main Australian economic events for the period since the last survey. A draft questionnaire has, at times, been made available in Paris for scrutiny by a Treasury member of the Australian delegation, largely to ensure there is a common and accurate understanding of the meaning of the questions and what is desired in the answers to be provided.

A completed questionnaire is then returned to the OECD by Treasury, forming an important part of the basis for a first, draft survey of the economy by OECD officials in its Economics Department. This is followed by a three to five day mission to Australia by a small OECD team (the 'mission'), of officials who meet with a variety of Treasury and Reserve Bank officials, officials from a limited range of other departments, particularly from the department involved in any detailed review of a selected policy area that might be undertaken as part of the review, such as education or health, and representatives from peak business and trade union bodies and a small number of academics. The members of the OECD team have, at least from the perspective of the Australian Treasury, varied in the extent of their knowledge of the Australian economy over time, a variation that has the potential to influence the accuracy and quality of their report.

A lack of knowledge was not a major issue with the first, 1972 EDRC survey of Australia, largely written by Professor Heinz Arndt of the Australian National University, while he was on secondment to the OECD's Economics Department as Deputy Head of its Country Studies Branch (NAA, 1983). The OECD team also included Peter Farren, an Australian who had worked in the Australian Treasury in the 1960s (NAA, 1972). Indeed, Arndt later indicated that he had been surprised when the visiting Treasury team, led by John Stone, an old friend of his, insisted on only one change being made to the draft report, requesting a modification to Arndt's recommendation to abolish Australia's capital controls (Coleman et al., 2007: 252). This first EDRC review was also approved by the outgoing McMahon government, though incoming Prime Minister, Gough Whitlam, at first expressed reservations about the report, perhaps based on no more than the fact that it had been approved by the outgoing government. However, as Arndt later related:

> [W]hen his attention was drawn to the paragraph advocating an across-the-board cut in tariffs, he changed his mind: 'This is how I can dish Jim [Cairns, his protectionist party colleague].' (Coleman et al., 2007: 252)

Arndt was also of the view that his review contributed to Whitlam's surprise decision to cut Australian tariffs by 25 per cent, a cut recommended by the Tariff Board, as well as to appreciate the dollar, shortly after taking office (Coleman et al., 2007: 252–3).

A further, detailed draft survey and associated recommendations is then provided for Treasury by the OECD, nowadays by means of its On-Line Information Service (OLIS) system. It is, as one can imagine, subject to a detailed examination as to its accuracy, the soundness of its arguments and, of course, as to politically sensitive issues that might arise. The Treasury provides its views on the draft survey to the OECD team in something of an iterative process, the length of which depends primarily on the extent of any differences it might have and any reservations and political sensitivities identified by Treasury. While the quality and recommendations of Arndt's first survey were largely acceptable, this is not always the case. John Stone, later to become Secretary of the Treasury, in discussions he had in November 1976 with Emile van Lennep, the Secretary-General, expressed considerable dissatisfaction with the quality of the preliminary draft of that year's survey, and requested improved procedures and a longer period of investigation in Australia by the members of the OECD's survey team (NAA, 1977c).

Similarly, the 1992 survey, for example, was strongly criticised by both Treasury and Reserve Bank officials, resulting in relatively large changes to the draft, though this extent of change is not common, at least for surveys of Australia. At the other extreme, the 2003 EDRC Survey was described by a senior Treasury official as 'probably the most supportive of an examined country in EDRC history', going on to point out that its commendations of Australia were driven, in part, by the OECD's desire to use Australia as a desirable model for reform by European members, a desire that apparently was not well received by those members and which resulted in criticism of OECD officials by several EDRC members (Treasury, 2003).

The next stage is the formal examination of the revised draft by EDRC members in Paris, with Australia represented by senior Treasury and Reserve Bank officials, supported by one or two members of the permanent Australian Delegation. In addition, in recent years 'Questions for Discussion' are posted on OLIS by the OECD in the week before the meeting. A list of briefing topics is provided for the Australian delegation by the Treasury coordinator for the survey, who meets with delegation members in Paris and goes through the material in detail, including lists of suggested revisions to the draft report. At the 'confrontation', or examination meeting, the morning is devoted to macroeconomic and more general structural issues, with the afternoon devoted to the special topic selected for the review (if any). In between the sessions it has become the tradition for the Australian Ambassador to host a lunch for the EDRC chair, including the delegates from the examining countries (most frequently Japan and the Netherlands in the 2000s), members of the Secretariat and the Australian delegation. It provides an opportunity for more relaxed discussion in a non-adversarial context.

In the examination the senior Australian member presents an opening statement, usually presenting an overview of the survey and major issues the team have identified, and each examining country then asks a series of questions, most of which are, if not known in detail, then expected on the basis of discussions on earlier drafts. Responsibility for answering specific types of questions is normally divided among the Australian representatives in advance. The chair of the EDRC, one of only two full time positions for chairs of OECD committees, then opens the floor to questions from other delegates. The Australian coordinator takes notes on the questions being asked for later attention, if necessary.

The day after the examination the Australian delegation meets with Secretariat officials to discuss proposed revisions, taking into account the recommendations made by the EDRC chair and the Australian representatives. It is unusual for major changes to be made at this point and discussion focuses largely on the 'Summary and Recommendations' section of the survey. The final version then goes back to the Committee for approval in what is largely a rubber stamping process. It is possible that if major, unresolved issues are sufficiently serious at this stage the member being examined might refuse to agree to the survey document going forward to the EDRC, by voting against the proposal, though this has rarely, if ever, occurred. It was reported in 1983, however, that Alan Renouf, formerly Secretary of the Department of Foreign Affairs, had indicated that the Fraser government had once threatened to withdraw from the OECD if a particular section of an EDRC survey was not deleted, possibly in 1976. Renouf was also reported as saying that such 'bullying' had not occurred under the McMahon or Whitlam governments (Summers, 1983).

The revised draft, which takes into account comments made during the examination meeting and any more recent, relevant information from Australia, is then circulated to the members of the EDRC for approval. The amendments are considered approved if there are no comments received by a set date and the survey is then published. The timing of the publication has been a sensitive issue from the onset. In 1971, for example, John Stone, in providing the Treasury Secretary, Sir Frederick Wheeler (who had only been in the position for 16 days) with the schedule for the first EDRC survey of Australia, pointed out that the proposed publication timetable of about mid-June 1971 would make it a matter of public debate just prior to the annual Premiers' Conference and a month or so prior to the Budget Cabinet discussions. As Stone went on to note, the report would certainly be the subject of close attention by the media:

> [W]hose general support for Australia's entry to the OECD has, I gather, been not uninfluenced by the very consideration that one effect would be some 'independent' assessment of our economic policies in published form. (NAA, 1971)

He further noted that political controversy could not be ruled out and that 'If that fear should prove correct, I doubt if the Treasury would earn many marks from our Ministerial masters for letting that situation develop.' Given how long it has taken to persuade the government to accede to the OECD, he concluded, 'it would be a tremendous pity if Ministers' views regarding it were soured from the outset by their initial experience of the country review procedure'(NAA, 1971). Some six years later, following discussions with his senior staff, Sir Frederick, in a note to Treasurer 'Billy' Snedden, about the timing of the next EDRC survey, noted that 'It is a matter of political judgement but it would seem that the week ending 17 December would be safer.' This was a week after the forthcoming federal election, when its release would be too late to influence election outcomes (Treasury, 1977).

It might have been a somewhat safer timing, from a political perspective, but it did not protect the government from criticism. The Leader of the ALP Opposition, Bill Hayden, for example, in 1977 asserted in a question for the Treasurer, in the context of a debate on the Australian economy, that the publication of the next EDRC review had been suppressed from its normal December publication to avoid negative comments on the economy during the election (Hayden, 1977a). He followed it up with another, similar question to Prime Minister Fraser, which excited a vehement denial (Hayden, 1977b; Fraser, 1977). The government felt that several details from this draft EDRC review had been leaked from the OECD to the ALP, with the Australian ambassador to the OECD expressing the government's displeasure to the Secretary-General (NAA, 1977d). As might be expected, the issue was taken up by the Australian media, with *The Age*'s Kenneth Davidson alleging (incorrectly) that the 'PM bars economic study' (Davidson, 1977).

A further example of the use of EDRC reviews in domestic political debate occurred in the lead up to the 1983 national elections, won by the ALP under Bob Hawke. Hawke alleged that the Treasury had 'doctored' an EDRC review, to the advantage of the Fraser government. The Treasurer, John Howard, challenged (unsuccessfully) Hawke to a debate on the issue. *The Bulletin*'s Max Walsh then alleged that a Treasury team, presumably authorised by Treasurer Howard, had had deleted from a draft EDRC review its somewhat favourable conclusions about the virtues of a return to a centralised wage fixing system, a central plank of the ALP's proposed incomes and prices policy and one very much opposed by the Fraser government (Walsh, 1983). Walsh indicated his claims were based on a copy of a confidential memo from Treasury Deputy Secretary Richard Rye that showed how Treasury had manipulated the OECD to push Treasury's own point of view, which was hostile to incomes and prices policies. The issue was taken up strongly by the ALP's Senator Peter Walsh, leading, unusually, to a Treasury Press Release from Secretary John Stone, defending his department from the allegations of its misuse of OECD data (NAA, 1983).

The extent to which Treasury uses, or is influenced by, EDRC reviews is difficult to assess with any degree of precision, as are Treasury attitudes to the reviews, for there is relatively little of substance in departmental files or archives that throw light upon the reviews. After membership was gained in 1971 it was felt by Treasury officials that they were useful in helping other OECD members to better understand the nature of the Australian economy and government policies (NAA, 1976: 8). However, by 1981, a review of Australian participation at the OECD felt that the EDRC reviews, while of some value, should be undertaken only every two years, rather than annually, noting that Australia had had seven reviews in the previous ten years (NAA, 1981: 64). In a 1995 review of Australian priorities for work to be undertaken by the OECD, Treasury officials noted that one of its highest priorities in regard to OECD work was the access it provided to country-specific analyses of macroeconomic and structural policy interactions, especially as embodied in EDRC reviews, though, again, the latter were needed at less than an annual frequency (DFAT, 1995a).

A 1998 statement of Australian priorities for work at the OECD again listed the EDRC reviews as a high priority (DFAT, 1995b). A Treasury response to a request for information regarding its views regarding the value of OECD participation noted that it played an active and constructive role in surveillance in the EDRC process, aimed, in particular, at ensuring that the conclusions of EDRC reviews represented a balanced assessment of issues. Treasury's response also noted that its active role was aimed at ensuring that the emphasis of many European countries on 'social cohesion' did not obscure the need for further work on structural reform issues. While EDRC reviews were regarded as a high priority, it was also felt that the EDRC would be more effective if the members of the OECD teams sent to Australia were more prepared and in a position to more actively discuss policy settings, as they tended to focus on understanding the Australian situation rather than outlining their thinking (DFAT, 1995b). It was also felt that the reviews should be more targeted.

In a series of recent interviews with current and ex-Treasury officials who had participated in one or more reviews there was a general feeling that the reviews continued to be of value, but a value that had declined over time as other sources of information regarding major economies had become available. Similarly, it was felt that the recommendations contained in EDRC reviews did have an impact on policy development, though it was only one of several such sources of advice, a view confirmed by a recent, comparative study of the effectiveness of EDRC review recommendations for the years 2008 and 2011, which found that Australia had adopted 58 per cent of the sixty EDRC recommendations made in the two reports, with 37 per cent pending (Alva-Araya et al., 2012).

CONCLUSION

The Australian Treasury and the members of its portfolio of agencies have had a long-standing interest in, and involvement with, the OECD that grew over time to involve a wide range of committees and related activities. In cooperation with DFAT, it was primarily responsible for driving Australian interest in OECD membership throughout the 1960s, keen to gain access to an OECD that it saw as an increasingly important actor in international economic activity, especially after the creation of the G10. While ultimately successful in persuading the Australian government to gain membership of the OECD, the two departments only gradually overcame the resistance of the Department of Trade and its powerful minister, McEwan.

After membership had been achieved Treasury gradually expanded its interests to involve all of the major OECD economic committees, including the Economic Policy Committee, the EDRC, the Committee on Fiscal Affairs and the Centre for Tax Policy and Administration. Somewhat more slowly, a growing range of other agencies in the Treasury Portfolio also entered into and expanded their involvement with the OECD, with the ATO, for example, playing an increasingly important role in the activities of the Centre for Tax Policy and Administration. It was an expansion of involvement that increased the coordination responsibilities of the Treasury and a period as a member of the OECD Delegation came to be regarded as important for those likely to gain senior positions within the Treasury Department, along with a period as an Executive Director at the IMF and World Bank. It helped 'high flyers' develop a wide range of influential contacts and an entrée to international economic networks that of considerable use as their career progressed.

The OECD was perhaps most influential as regards Australian economic policy from the later 1970s to the early 1990s, as can be seen in the attention paid to its EDRC reviews of the Australian economy, with its championing of the need for structural reform in the major Western economies providing an important and credible source of support for Treasury recommendations for both Coalition and ALP governments. In recent years, while still of importance, the OECD has been regarded as rather less influential, with greater attention focused on the IMF and, since the global financial crisis, upon the G20, a trend signified by the reduction in number of Treasury officials being posted to the Delegation in Paris.

BIBLIOGRAPHY

ABS 2014. 'Australian Bureau of Statistics Role in International Relations', accessed on 5 January 2015 at www.abs.gov.au/ausstats/abs@.nsf/Lookup/1301.0Main+Features2192012.

Alva-Araya, V., Katsukawa, T., Andrew, R., Marte, J., Armstrong, R., McGillis, J., Baxter, C., Messina, J., Bezerra, P., Oztoprak, O., Bolton, G., Pantel del Cueto, S., Carroll, J., Prempeh, A., Christianson, K., Roods, S., Einhaus, J., Rosario, N., Hampton, E., Saha, S., Teale, H., Shong, K., Ijichi, J., Soukas, C. and Edwards, M. 2012. 'Evaluating the Effectiveness of OECD Economic Surveillance', John C. Whitehead School of Diplomacy and International Relations, Seton Hall University, accessed 31 December 2014 at http://streitcouncil.org/uploads/OECDreport.pdf.

ATO 2014. 'Commissioner of Taxation Annual Report 2013–14', accessed 8 January 2015 at http://annualreport.ato.gov.au/sites/default/files/downloads/n0995-10-2014_js32662_w.pdf.

Charter Group 2013. 'A Super Charter: Fewer Changes, Better Outcomes', A report to the Treasurer and Minister Assisting for Financial Services and Superannuation by the Charter Group, accessed on 5 January 2015, at www.treasury.gov.au/Policytopics/SuperannuationAndRetirement/supercharter/~/media/Treasury/Policy%20Topics/Superannuation/supercharter/Downloads/PDF/super_charter_report.ashx.

Coleman, P., Cornish, S. and Drake, P. 2007. *Arndt's Story the Life of an Australian Economist*, Canberra: ANU E Press.

Commonwealth of Australia 2013. 'Risks to the Sustainability of Australia's Corporate Tax Base', Scoping Paper, July, accessed 11 January 2015 at www.treasury.gov.au/~/media/Treasury/Publications%20and%20Media/Publications/2013/Aus%20Corporate%20Tax%20Base%20Sustainability/Downloads/PDF/BEPSscoping_paper.ashx.

Davidson, K. 1977. 'PM Bars Economy Study', *The Age*, 5 November.

DFAT 1995a. Department of Foreign Affairs and Trade Ministerial Submission, File No 90/9741, 5 October 1995, by John Crighton, Assistant Secretary, Multilateral Trade Organisations Branch, to Senator McMullan, Senator Evans and Mr Bilney, seeking their response regarding a draft, proposed Australian response to the OECD Priorities Questionnaire, DFAT File No 94/060329 Part 6 Review of Australia's OECD Membership.

DFAT 1995b. 'Priorities', a briefing paper dated 10 February 1998, updating the priorities indicated in a 1995 review of Australian participation at the OECD. It also contains a copy of the Treasury response to a request for information about the value of participation at the OECD, dated 26 June 1998, provided by the Assistant Secretary of Treasury's International Economic Issues Branch. DFAT File No 94/060329 Part 6 Review of Australia's OECD Membership.

Fraser, M. 1977. 'Speech', House of Representatives, 4 November, p. 1.

Galeazzi, F. 2015. 'The WP3 Gatekeeper of International Payments? 1961–1987', a Paper presented at the 'Warden of the West: OECD and the Global Political Economy 1948 to Present', University of Zurich, Zurich, August.

Hayden, W. 1977a. 'Speech', House of Representatives, 26 October, p. 1.

Hayden, W. 1977b. 'Speech', House of Representatives, 3 November, p. 1.

Kazuhiko, Y. 2012. 'Crisis Management in the International Monetary and Financial System: OECD Working Party 3 (1961–1979)', Waseda University, Japan, accessed on 18 February 2014 at www.unige.ch/ses/ihise/research/sar/Yago_Geneva_paper.pdf.

McDougall, R. and Sugden, C. 1991. 'Implementation of the WALRAS Model of the Australian Economy', SALTER Working Paper No 3, 1991 p. 1.

Mountford, A. 2008. 'The Historical Development of IMF Governance', IMF Independent Evaluation Office Background Paper BP/08/02, rev. May 2008.

NAA 1962. 'OECD-DAC Development Assistance Committee (including Ad Hoc Committee)', 17 May 1962, copy of a letter from Treasurer Holt to External Affairs Minister Garfield Barwick, Prime Minister's Department, File A1029, File No. 62/992.

NAA 1963. 'Notes of Meetings', p 28 of Secretary Bunting's notes on Cabinet Meetings, 27 February 1963, A11099, accessed on 12 February 2013 at http://recordsearch.naa.gov.au/scripts/Imagine.asp.

NAA 1965. 'Australian Relations with OECD', a 23 February 1965 copy of the record of an interdepartmental meeting to identify what the Australian position should be regarding an OECD invitation to attend a meeting of the Trade Committee, NAA File No 69 2095 Part 1 Reconsideration of Possible Australian Membership of OECD.

NAA 1968. A memorandum from A.F. Pryor to a Treasury official in response to the latter's request for an assessment of the advantages and disadvantages of OECD membership, dated 16 September 1968, NAA File No 69 2095 Part 1 Reconsideration of Possible Australian Membership of OECD.

NAA 1969a. 'Australia and the OECD Summary of Meeting held on Friday 10 January 1969 at 10 am', a Minute Paper regarding a meeting called by the DEA to reassess Australia's relationship with the OECD, chaired by DEA's Ed Shann, with Corkery, Price and Hield from DEA, Fogarty and Wolters from DTI, Deane from PM's, and Robert Whitelaw, from Treasury, NAA File No 69 2095 Part 1 Reconsideration of Possible Australian Membership of OECD.

NAA 1969b. 'Australia and the OECD Codes of Liberalization and Current Invisible Operations and Capital Movements', 24 March 1969, a memo to the

acting Assistant Secretary in Treasury, NAA File No 69 2095 Part 1 Reconsideration of Possible Australian Membership of OECD.
NAA 1970a. 'Reconsideration of Possible Australian Membership of OECD'. A memo 'OECD', from K.C.O. Shann to the Minister dated 31 March 1970, regarding a forthcoming Cabinet submission on OECD membership and Minister McEwan's separate letter to Cabinet, NAA File No 69 2095 Part 5.
NAA 1970b. 'Reconsideration of Possible Australian Membership of OECD'. A memo dated 6 April 1970 from E.J. Bunting to the Secretary of Treasury and Secretary of the DEA with a copy of a note that Bunting had provided to Prime Minister Gorton in response to the latter's queries regarding the Cabinet submissions urging OECD membership, NAA File No 69 2095 Part 5.
NAA 1971. 'OECD – Economic Development Review Committee'. A minute dated 17 November 1971 from acting Deputy Secretary John Stone to the Secretary, Sir Frederick Wheeler, Treasury File No File No 71/2740 Part 1.
NAA 1972. 'OECD – Economic and Development Review Committee Part 2', File No 71/2740. A note from the Australian Delegation to Treasury, dated 23 June 1972.
NAA 1976. 'OECD – Development Assistance Committee' NYE. The file contains a copy of the then annual, 'Australian Delegation to the OECD Annual Review for 1976', a report summarising Australian activities at the OECD for the year.
NAA 1977a. 'OECD: EDRC Survey of Australia 1977'. Minute from a First Assistant Secretary to the Treasurer regarding possible dates for the next EDRC survey in which he indicated the dissatisfaction Treasury had had with the 1976 review, leading to face-to-face discussions between the OECD's Secretary-General and Treasury's John Stone, Treasury File No 77/1275 Part 2.
NAA 1977b. 'OECD: EDRC Survey of Australia 1977'. A note from Sir Frederick Wheeler to the Treasurer, Treasury File No 77/1275 Part 2.
NAA 1977c. 'OECD – EDRC – Survey of Australia – 1977 Part No 4', File No 77/1275. A 1 December 1977 Minute Paper from Deputy Secretary John Stone, 'Consultations with the OECD'. An attachment 'Notes for Discussion with Mr van Lennep, 26 Nov 1976', outlines Treasury's concerns regarding the process and quality of the EDRC reviews of the Australian economy.
NAA 1977d. 'OECD: EDRC Survey of Australia 1977 Part 2', File No 77/1275. A note dated 10 November 1977 from the Australian Delegation at the OECD to Canberra indicating that Ambassador Donovan had seen Secretary-General van Lennep regarding the Hansard of 4 November and an alleged leak from OECD. Van Lennep indicated he viewed the matter very seriously and would investigate the matter at once. Donovan indicated to van Lennep that some of Hayden's figures were very close to those included in a confidential document prepared by the OECD Secretariat for a forthcoming meeting of the Working Group on Short Term Economic Prospects, to be distributed in a few days and it seemed likely the figures could have come only from OECD.
NAA 1981. 'OECD: Review of Australian Participation June, 1981 DOT B81/000162', NAA File No A6343 A6343/4.
NAA 1983. 'OECD – EDRC – Economic Survey of Australia – 1982'. As noted in correspondence between Professor John Freebairn, Editor of the 'Economic

Record', and Treasury Secretary John Stone, dated 8 March 1983, NAA File No 0 83/649. In a note dated 8 March 1983, Arndt indicated that while employed at the OECD in 1972 he wrote most of the first EDRC survey of Australia as Deputy Director of the Country Studies Division, as asserted to by journalist Paddy McGuiness in the December 1982 issue of the Economic Record. However, Arndt noted that McGuiness was incorrect in stating that some critical comment in the survey was deleted or softened at the behest of Treasury officials. Rather, in discussions with the Treasury review team, including John Stone, after the meeting, some changes were made, involving no points of substance. Stone vouched for the correctness of Arndt's view.

NAA 1990a. 'Review of Australia 1991–92', File No 90/1623 Part No 5. A letter dated 3 January 1992 from G.R. Stevens, Chief Economist in the Reserve Bank of Australia to Treasury with very detailed and critical comments on the draft EDRC review of Australia.

NAA 1990b. 'IEB/IEC: Organisation for Economic Co-operation and Development – EDRC Review of Australia 1991–92', File No 90/1623 Part No 5. A note dated 20 December 1991 from the Deputy Secretary (Economic), to Dr Stephen Potter, Director, Country Studies Branch of OECD, regarding the recently received, first draft of the EDRC review.

NAA 1992. 'IEB/IEC: Organisation for Economic Co-operation and Development – EDRC Review of Australia 1991–92', File No 90/1623 Part No 6. In a letter dated 2 January 1992, Australia's Executive Director at the IMF, E.A. 'Ted' Evans (later to become Secretary of the Treasury), to Treasury's Deputy Secretary regarding problems with the current EDRC draft review of Australia, noted that IMF staff were likely to have a copy of the draft for the forthcoming Article IV mission to Australia for consultation regarding its obligations.

OECD 1998. 'Recommendation of the Council Concerning Effective Action against Hard Core Cartels', accessed 5 January 2014 at http://webnet.oecd.org/OECDACTS/Instruments/ListByInstrumentDateView.aspx.

OECD 2011. 'Terrorism Insurance in 2010: Where do we stand?' Proceedings, Paris: OECD.

Productivity Commission 1998. 'Aspects of Structural Change in Australia', Productivity Commission, Canberra, accessed on 8 January 2015 at www.pc.gov.au/research/completed/structuralchange.

Productivity Commission 2003. 'Mechanisms for Improving the Quality of Regulations: Australia in an International Context', Productivity Commission Staff Working Paper by Steven Argy and Matthew Johnson.

Productivity Commission 2012. 'Regulatory Impact Analysis: Benchmarking', a Research report, Productivity Commission, Canberra, accessed 8 January 2015 at www.pc.gov.au/__data/assets/pdf_file/0003/120675/ria-benchmarking.pdf.

Summers, A. 1983. 'Renouf's OECD allegation', 28 February 1983, an article by Ann Summers in the Australian Financial Review. The article reports former head of the Department of Foreign Affairs, Alan Renouf, as saying that the Fraser government once threatened to withdraw from the OECD if a particular section of a draft EDRC survey was not deleted, possibly in 1976. Renouf said that such 'bullying', of the OECD did not occur under the McMahon or Whitlam governments.

Treasury 1977. 'OECD: EDRC Survey of Australia 1977', File No 77/1275 Part 2. A Note for the Treasurer, dated 8 November 1977 from Secretary F.H. Wheeler, indicating that 'It is a matter of political judgement but it would seem that the week ending 17 December would be safer.' The week beginning 12 December 1977, a week after the election, was finally agreed.

Treasury 1980. 'Information Supplied to OECD by Economic Conditions Branch', File No 77/1021. A Treasury Minute 'OECD's Special Group on Positive Adjustment Policies: Country Review Program', dated 6 June 1980 from the Acting First Assistant Secretary to Secretary John Stone.

Treasury 1992. A note dated 3 January 1992 from G.R. Stephens, Chief Economist at the Reserve Bank to Treasury regarding the draft EDRC review. In particular, as regards Section II Stephens asserted that the chapter gave a very misleading picture of the main developments in monetary policy and inflation during the 1980s, and was something of a caricature 'and an extreme one at that'. The note went on to give several pages of specific examples of generalisations, inaccuracies, omissions and unsupported assertions. Treasury File No N88/748 Part 5 IEB/BOP OECD Mission to Australia – Balance of Payments (BOP) Aspects – re EDRC visit.

Treasury 2000a. 'Briefing for CIME Meeting 19–20 April 2000, Paris', File No 2000/02207 'Committee on International Investment and Multinational Enterprises (CIME) Meeting – Paris, 19–20 April 2000'.

Treasury 2000b. A briefing paper from Canberra to the Treasury representative in the Delegation to the OECD in Paris, dated 19 September 2000, File No 2000/06596 'Committee on International Investment and Multinational Enterprises (CIME) Meeting – Paris, September 2000'.

Treasury 2003. Executive Minute to the Treasurer, Peter Costello, dated 26 February 2003, Treasury File No 2003/02215 'International Economic Affairs – Reporting – Examination and Report including preparation and release material for the OECD Economic Survey of Australia 2002–2003'. The minute noted 'This Report is probably the most supportive of an examined country in EDRC history. The explicit nature of the Report's commendations of Australia – which were in part driven by a desire to hold out Australia as a desirable model for reform to European numbers (sic) – resulted in criticism of the Secretariat by EDRC members'.

Treasury 2004. 'Taxation and Income Support – Analysis – Strategy for OECD Engagement', File No 2004/01283.

Walsh, M. 1983. 'Secret Paper: How Treasury Nobbled Hawke', *The Bulletin*, 1 March, pp. 18–19.

Whitwell, G. 1986. *The Treasury Line*, London: Allen and Unwin.

9. Australia and OECD tax work

The OECD has played an important role in the development of international tax policy, first developing a Model Double Taxation Convention in 1963 (revised in 1977) that served as a basis for both the development of a United Nations Model Double Taxation Convention between Developed and Developing Countries in 1980 and the development of 'East West' tax treaties during the Cold War, the first of which was concluded between the US and the USSR in 1973 (Doman, 1982: 162). The Model Tax Convention (MTC) has been remarkably influential, with an estimated 2,000 bilateral tax treaties having been based on it (Eccleston, 2013: 65–9). The OECD also developed in 1995 guidelines for addressing the problem of transfer pricing, or the sale of goods and services between related corporations in different jurisdictions so that profits are minimised where taxes are highest and maximised where they are lowest. These guidelines were updated in 1996 and 2010.

This work in addressing 'harmful tax practices' (HTP) continued to build, with limited success, to the present, when a major project addressing 'Base Erosion and Profit Shifting' (BEPS) is under way. Australia received relatively little from its early engagement with the OECD on tax, as this chapter shows: it relied primarily on bilateral diplomacy to try to deal with the threat of tax havens in its region (but drew increasingly on the Model Tax Convention); and it was able to provide insights to the OECD members from its early taxation of fringe benefits.

This was perhaps not surprising. When long-serving Director of the Centre for Tax Policy and Administration (CTPA), Jeffrey Owens, joined the OECD at about the time of Australian accession, 'tax was three people and the main work [they] did was principally on double taxation treaties and tax statistics'. When he retired in 2012, after the CTPA was budded off from the Directorate for Financial, Fiscal and Enterprise Affairs (which then became the Directorate for Financial and Enterprise Affairs in 2012), it had a staff of more than 100, from 25 countries, including staff from non-member countries (International Tax Review, 2012). The OECD has played an increasing role in the development of international tax policy, largely because it was a useful arena for work in this area, undertaking both analytical work on numerous domestic tax problems and serving as a venue where largely like-minded members could address international tax issues, like-mindedness however being limited by the operation of functional tax havens by some members, or (in the case of the United Kingdom) some of its territories.

This chapter first examines some issues related to tax that arose at the time of Australian accession and indicates briefly where it has concentrated its engagement. It then examines its participation in a number of focused issues: taxation of fringe benefits (where it learned bilaterally and then was able to share insights with other members); the growing importance of tax avoidance and evasion, particularly in Australia's region, that stimulated greater interest in both Australia and the OECD, and Australia's interest in the working party established to deal with it. It also examines the use of the OECD to develop the Multilateral Convention on Mutual Administrative Assistance proposed by the Council of Europe, which briefly caused problems for improvements to the integrity of the Australian tax system but to which Australia eventually acceded, and some problems arising from the Harmful Tax Competition Initiative, particularly because of the intersection of the OECD initiative and Commonwealth interests. Both these issues draw attention to the initial, though weakened, Eurocentric nature of the OECD and Australia's location in the Asia-Pacific, particularly its relations with small Pacific nations. It concludes by looking briefly at some administrative matters and more recent priorities for work on tax, up to about a decade before the time of writing.[1]

The decision by Australia to take up OECD membership if offered, involved, among other matters, consideration of whether or not it wanted to accede to the various OECD acts, Decisions and Recommendations. As was commonly the case, Australia decided it wanted to abstain from several, including the OECD's Double Tax Convention number 84, a Recommendation, developed earlier by the OEEC. In essence, double taxation was seen as an obstacle to the free movement of goods, services, capital and manpower between members and the Convention recommended members conclude bilateral Conventions for the avoidance of double taxation, where not already in place, and, when doing so, 'to conform to the Draft Convention set out in the Annex, as interpreted by the Commentaries and the Report of the Fiscal Committee'. The Convention also recommended that members who were members of regional groups (for example, the EC) examine the feasibility of concluding similar agreements within such regional groups, based on the OECD's draft Convention, and to inform the OECD of new or modified agreements.

As with other OECD Decisions and Recommendations the relevant documentation was sent to the Commissioner of Taxation. An undated reply from the Assistant Commissioner to the Secretary of Treasury indicates that a number of features of the Convention were 'unacceptable to Australia', such as the requirement for a revised UK tax agreement and an agreement with Japan. This raised the question of the extent to which, as a member of the OECD, Australia would be free to continue present policies, though it was soon resolved (NAA, 1970).

The bilateral delegation in Paris was handling these transitional matters and communicating in detail was problematic, with the diplomatic bag containing the preliminary reactions regarding the Double Taxation issue not arriving after some three weeks, and so a cable had to include a summary (NAA, 1970). The logistics of engagement with the Committee on Fiscal Affairs in general were also, at the time of accession, rather problematic. For example, the CFA was covered initially by a representative from the High Commission in London, and a Note on the CFA by a Treasury officer on 15 July 1971 included a fifteen page transcription of a report of Working Party 1 on Double Taxation that had been published in French (OECD, 1971; NAA, 1971). The only options for written communication at this stage were diplomatic cables (via telex) or the diplomatic bag. There were even occasions when letters were sent by mail and (in these days when photocopying was not widespread practice) carbon copies kept on file.

On 12 October 1970 the Delegation cabled on the issue of double taxation following a meeting with M. Gilmer, Chief of Financial Section of the Financial Affairs Division of OECD, in considerable useful detail regarding the status of the recommendation, after an 'investigatory delegation' from Australia to the OECD to clarify various issues, gain advice, and so on (NAA, 1970). A subsequent cable a few days later from the Delegation summarising discussions with senior advisors in the OECD Secretariat, indicated that in their view was there were no 'insurmountable problems' concerning the OECD acts as they were Recommendations rather than Decisions (NAA, 1970). The OECD was hoping that members would gradually harmonise their agreements in line with the draft Convention but in the meantime would not pressure any members.

On 27 November 1970 a draft list of abstentions and remarks Australia intended to seek as part of a possible membership package was drawn up following an interdepartmental committee meeting held on 17 November, and this list was accepted by all Departments by 21 December (NAA, 1970). A cable from Ambassador Renouf on 28 December 1970 confirmed that all was well with the abstentions, but he noted:

> I should add that the Secretary General and his staff are not (repeat not) keen on telephone calls from officials in Canberra to particular members of the Secretariat. Moreover, it is a bit embarrassing for us in the Embassy to be politely 'ticked off', about them. (NAA, 1970)

With specific reference to tax, brief explanations for the OECD as to why Australia was abstaining concerning aspects of double taxation were provided in March 1971 (NAA, 1971).

After this tentative beginning, Australia's interest and involvement in the taxation work of the OECD grew, particularly in areas such as tax avoidance and evasion, where it has persisted. But the OECD's work (and Australia's engagement) has been broader than this. There has been substantial work in the OECD on taxation as an instrument of environmental policy, for example, and Australia was an active participant in these activities. Issues such as transfer pricing in the 1990s were of obvious interest to a resource-exporting country, and much could be learned from OECD members, especially those who were members of the EEC, about their experience with domestic taxation issues such as consumption taxes. From 1980, the OECD produced numerous reports dealing with economic instruments to address environmental issues (some on climate change supporting the work in the International Negotiating Committee developing the climate regime in the UN system).

A joint Environment Directorate and Directorate for Financial, Fiscal and Enterprise Affairs Task Force on Taxation and Environment finished its work in October 1992 (OECD, 1993). Work on taxation and the environment was then carried out through 'Joint Sessions on Taxation and Environment' gathering together environmental and fiscal experts. The joint meetings were part of a larger Group on Economic and Environment Policy Integration (GEEPI) (OECD, 1993), and they were held back to back with the meetings of the Group on Economic and Environment Policy Integration, or meetings of the Working Party No. 2 of the CFA, 'thereby promoting a more efficient use of Member countries and secretariat resources' (NAA, 1993). The first meeting was held in June 1992.

These Joint Sessions on Environment and Taxation necessitated considerable coordination of work between Treasury and the Department of the Arts Sport the Environment Tourism and Territories (DASETT), but it also brought additional benefits to those directly related to its outputs. A handwritten note attached to the file copy of a fax from the Delegation attaching the agenda for a forthcoming Joint EPOC/CFA Joint Session on Taxation and the Environment indicated the kind of serendipitous benefit that participation in OECD work programmes could bring, indicating that

'This paper flow is worth watching re prospective PRISMOD work on energy taxes' (PRISMOD was Treasury's Price Revenue Incidence Simulation Model, that had been developed in 1991 (NAA, 1993)).

Australia has been selectively active in the various subsidiary bodies of the Committee on Fiscal Affairs (CFA), particularly in Working Party 8 (WP8) on Tax Avoidance and Evasion which we examine in more detail below. Other subsidiary bodies where Australia has been active are the WP1 on Double Taxation and Related Questions, WP2 on Tax Analysis and Tax Statistics (and its Statistical Group on Estimating Methodology of WP2), WP6 on the Taxation of Multi-National Enterprises, and after the adoption of a Goods and Services Tax in 1999, WP9 on Consumption Taxes. Australian taxation policy has not just been informed by sharing of best practice in the OECD, however, and (as a brief case study of the taxation of fringe benefits shows) it has at times been able to share its expertise with other members.

TAXING FRINGE BENEFITS: THE OECD LEARNS FROM AUSTRALIA

One area where Australia both received little benefit from OECD work and then later shared its experience through the OECD was the taxation of fringe benefits. Australia identified the issue and engaged in some bilateral learning from New Zealand and the US, but was close to the vanguard on such taxes and, rather than learning from the OECD, was able to share its experience with other members through the Organisation.

Fringe benefits were an issue because a non-salary benefit was both a deduction for employers, and mostly tax free for employees. Treasurer Paul Keating told the newly-formed Economic Planning Advisory Council (EPAC) in December 1983 that the government was targeting fringe benefits, along with the cash economy, tax shelters, and 'the perennial issue of capital gains' (Veyret, 1984: 12). The issue had received some impetus from a legal ruling that had held that if the receipt of an item saved a taxpayer from incurring expenditure, the saving was not income; 'income is what comes in, it is not what is saved from going out'.[2]

Then on 11 January, Acting Treasurer, John Dawkins, wrote to the Secretary of the Treasury raising the issue and asking 'Is there a growing trend towards non salary remuneration and if so, what are the current and emerging consequences?' (NAA, 1984). Dawkins' office followed the matter up by telephone a mere two days after, indicating that the minister 'was very keen to have a substantive response as soon as possible'. There followed extensive media coverage of the issue (Meagher, 1984; Short, 1984; Veyret, 1984).

The Australian Bureau of Statistics had been publishing an irregular statistical series (ABS, 1980) (of which Treasury was previously unaware) and now made this an annual publication. A report, in this series prepared in August 1983, but released in January 1984 (ABS, 1984) found that 57.9 per cent of employees received some kind of benefit, 67.0 per cent by males, and 43.4 per cent by females. Some form of salary packaging involving fringe benefits to minimise tax was clearly becoming widespread.

But while a 1968 OECD report had first defined fringe benefits (NAA, 1989), there was little information gained from that source. Rather, there was evidence of bilateral policy learning, particularly from the US and New Zealand. US moves on taxing fringe benefits were noted (US Department of Treasury, 1984), as were developments in New Zealand arising from a policy review there that examined 'The Case for Taxing Fringe Benefits' (New Zealand, 1982).

The issue was reviewed by the Commissioner of Taxation and a high level Tax Reform Task Force was established, comprising Mr E.M.W. Visbord (Deputy Secretary, PM&C), the Private Secretary (Taxation) in the Treasurer's Office, Dr Ross Garnaut (Adviser, Economic, Prime Minister's Office), and representatives from the Australian Tax Office (ATO) and EPAC (NAA, 1984a). A meeting was also held with Bernie Galvin (Secretary of the Treasury, New Zealand), and a Minute Paper from the ATO to Secretary of Treasury provided a summary of FBT arrangements in the UK, USA, Canada, and New Zealand.

A fringe benefits tax was then developed and announced in a press release by the Treasurer on 4 February 1985 (which cited *Commissioner v Cooke and Sherden*). This experience was eventually shared in a report developed within the OECD in 1986 by WP8 of CFA. By 1986 Australia, Ireland, New Zealand and the USA had recently adopted new legislation or amended administrative practice to tax fringe benefits, New Zealand from 1 April 1985, Australia from 1 July 1986 (under the *Fringe Benefits Tax Assessment Act 1986*), and the USA with new rules in the *Tax Reform Act 1984*. The Report prepared for the WP8 for a meeting in March 1986 shared information on matters such as definition, valuation, approaches in member countries, and administration.

In this instance, therefore, Australia was close to the vanguard of tax reform, and drew upon bilateral policy learning, but, as with the concerns over tax havens at the time of accession, drew little on the OECD. Rather, it contributed its experience to the OECD as part of what was, in effect, an ongoing exchange relationship. There was interest within WP8 in Australia's tax reforms as set out in the Treasurer's Tax Statement on 19 September 1985, and the issue was also of interest to WP2 which 'would be interested in, and probably expand upon, the quantitative section of the report dealing with the valuation of fringe benefits' (OECD, 1985b).

THE GROWING SALIENCE OF TAX AVOIDANCE AND EVASION

One issue that has been constant throughout the history of Australia's involvement in taxation matters in the OECD has been that of addressing the avoidance and evasion of tax (see Boucher, 2010). Concerns were raised, for example, when Treasury learned via a news item in the *Financial Review* in December 1971 that the British Residency in the New Hebrides (now Vanuatu, then a British–French condominium, but with murmurings of an independence movement that came to fruition in 1980) was attempting to develop it as a tax haven using the company law of Bermuda and Caymans as a base (NAA, 1973). While it was hoped that the OECD might provide a forum for addressing this issue, it was later dealt with by bilateral means, and Australia was unable to prevent the New Hebrides from establishing a tax haven.

It was not known whether the French Administration in the New Hebrides was taking similar steps, but the French had expressed concern over Norfolk Island's constitutional status and a clause had been inserted in a draft double tax agreement (at France's request) to stop Norfolk Island being used as a tax haven to France's detriment. Australia sought French reciprocity, and Treasury asked the DFA to approach the French authorities to request their assistance in restricting the use of the New Hebrides as a tax haven by Australian firms (NAA, 1973b). The Reserve Bank also imposed currency controls on travel to the New Hebrides.

Australia sent a note to the United Kingdom government and the Australian High Commission in London took up the question of the New Hebrides tax haven proposal with the Head of the Pacific Dependent Territories Department, Foreign and Commonwealth Office, on 10 August 1973. The FCO advised that the British High Commission in Canberra would soon be instructed to reply to the Australian note along the following lines:

> The British intended to control the development of the tax haven/investment centre to ensure that no doubtful practices were introduced. Their aims were to try to gain maximum advantage for the NH but at the same time would not

> wish to see it develop in a direction that would prejudice the interests of their neighbours including, of course, Australia. (NAA, 1973b)

The FCO interlocutor was reported as saying that 'the British did not have much experience in the operation of tax havens ... although there have been some developments in this direction in the West Indies'. The words 'did not have much experience in the operation of tax havens' contained in the file document were underlined in pen, with the margin note: 'Rot. Cf. B.W.I., Isle of Man, Channel Islands & Gibraltar!' It was also revealed that the proposal had been developed only because the French had refused British requests for the introduction of an income tax (NAA, 1973c).

The Second Commissioner at the ATO was critical of UK attitude in a memorandum to the Secretary of the Treasury, expressing the view that the situation was not zero-sum, but that the losses to Australia would be out of all proportion to the benefits flowing to the New Hebrides. He noted that the British attitude was at odds with what appeared to be an inevitable movement towards international cooperation to reduce revenue losses to governments through the use of tax havens, and saw the OECD as providing a forum where these issues could be addressed:

> In this context reference can be made to the consideration being given by the O.E.C.D. to such things as the abuse of double tax agreements, the tax position of multinational corporations and the use of bearer debentures to evade tax and to studies by the United Nations ad hoc group of taxation experts on co-operation to control international tax avoidance and evasion. (NAA, 1973c)

The Commissioner for Taxation wrote directly to Inland Revenue in the UK expressing concern over the New Hebrides tax haven, but received a rather bland reply, stating that they 'fully share' Australian concerns 'about tax havens, existing or proposed, and I suspect that we also share problems. We shall do what we can about this one and let you have a note in due course' (NAA, 1973d).

Australia faced the threat of tax havens much closer to home, including one within an offshore territory under its sovereignty on Norfolk Island. Other initiatives arose with the Cocos Islands and with Nauru (*Australian Financial Review*, 18 September 1972). Australia withheld a Draft Treaty of Friendship with Nauru over its tax free status and proceeded to develop a bilateral agreement based on the OECD Model Tax Agreement. Ultimately, the High Court of Australia upheld the application of Commonwealth tax jurisdiction to Norfolk Island in 1976 (*Berwick v*

Gray, 1976). Significantly, while the Commissioner was hopeful for the role the OECD might play, the issues were essentially resolved through bilateral means.

Working Party No. 8 on Tax Avoidance and Evasion

The issues of Tax Avoidance and Evasion eventually merited the establishment of a more formalised body within the CFA to address these issues: Working Party No. 8 on Tax Avoidance and Evasion, which first met in March 1977. Australia began to use WP8 the following year (NAA, 1977). The *Income Tax Assessment Amendment Bill 1978* introduced a clampdown on tax avoidance schemes such as prepaid interest, dividend stripping, and the issuing of bonus shares, and WP8 was an important means of sharing information on such issues as the taxation of itinerant activities (artists and sportsmen), methods of audit (techniques for audit selection), and methods used to estimate the extent of tax evasion. In addition to the formal proceedings of the Committee on Fiscal Affairs and its Working Parties, the OECD provided a point of contact where information could be sought from other Member Countries. For example, in August 1978 the Australian Taxation Office wrote to the Delegation seeking to obtain UK, French and German lists of 'light tax' countries (NAA, 1978).

The Committee on Fiscal Affairs has provided a means of monitoring tax developments, not just in member countries but in other international arenas. The agenda for the 16th session in January 1979, for example, surveyed recent taxation issues in other international fora: the GATT; UNESCO; Council of Europe; the UN Group of Experts on Tax Treaties with Developing Countries; Recent Developments in the European Communities; and even the UN Conference on the Law of the Sea (OECD, 1979). The discussion of UNCLOS was a good example of the value in bringing to the attention of taxation agencies in Australia matters of which they were not necessarily aware, for it indicated that 'Open Registry Shipping' (flags of convenience) raised tax issues, with Liberia and Panama, for example, providing tax free or virtually tax free registries, and Treasury was apparently unaware of this. The CFA then addressed the issue through liaison with the OECD's Maritime Transport Committee.

While the benefits of OECD participation were growing, the burdens were not inconsiderable. For example, in order to produce a note by the Secretariat on Tax Evasion and Avoidance (OECD, 1979a), a questionnaire on the Exchange of Information Between OECD Member Countries was distributed, but its timely completion proved beyond the Australian authorities. The 52-page questionnaire, in which question 22 alone had 43 sub-questions, necessitated a cable to the Delegation indicating that an early response was not possible, and they were expecting to respond 'within the next few weeks' (NAA, 1979).

Multilateral Convention on Mutual Administrative Assistance

In 1978, the Council of Europe's Parliamentary Assembly had adopted Recommendation 833 (1978) on cooperation among Council of Europe states against international tax avoidance and evasion (NAA, 1978a). The Council of Europe then decided to organise a colloquy in Strasbourg in 1980, seeking broader multilateral assistance than that provided by either the Nordic Convention on Administrative Assistance in Tax Matters or a European Community Directive on mutual assistance between fiscal authorities. The Council of Europe considered existing European Conventions were inadequate, had limited scope, did not apply to information held in confidence (an essential element), excluded use of compulsory powers, and prevented evidence being requested if not intended for use in judicial proceedings.

It was considered that a Joint Council of Europe–OECD approach to tax avoidance and evasion was preferable, and a draft Multilateral Convention on Cooperation Between the Council of Europe and OECD Concerning Mutual Assistance in Tax Matters was considered at the 14th Meeting of WP8 held 9–11 February 1982, and in April a Draft OECD Council Recommendation Concerning Mutual Administrative Assistance in Tax Matters was prepared, instructing the Committee on Fiscal Affairs to cooperate with the Council of Europe in finalising a multilateral convention (OECD, 1982). A draft of the Convention was submitted to WP8 for its consideration at its meeting 25–27 May 1982. WP8 was also at this time surveying members on bank secrecy provisions (OECD, 1981).

The negotiation of the Draft Convention took some time (OECD, 1982a). It was not until 1985 that the text of the draft was approved by a majority vote (on 5 December 1985) by the European Committee for Legal Cooperation, meeting in Strasbourg. If approved by competent organs of the Council of Europe and the OECD, it was then to be open to signature by member countries of both, with the OECD and its Secretary-General, included along with the Council of Europe, as the depositaries of the Convention. BIAC opposed the proposal, considering the matter should be one for bilateral agreements (OECD, 1985a). Also concerned was Switzerland, which took exception to the prospect of being named as a tax haven in two reports, threatening to oppose their derestriction, and wanting some tables annexed to a report deleted (OECD, 1985). The Report by WP8 on 'Tax Havens: measures to prevent abuse by taxpayers' (DAFFE/CFA/85.10) and a Report by WP1 on 'Double Taxation conventions and international tax avoidance through "base companies"' were substantially approved at a session of the Committee on Fiscal Affairs on 11–12 July.

The International Chamber of Commerce (ICC) was also critical of the proposed Convention, citing unnecessary secrecy and questioning the need for a new Convention. In its lobbying efforts against the draft, the ICC joined forces with BIAC, with the ICC primarily focused on the Council of Europe and a lobbying 'blitz' in Germany which resulted in repeated German requests to delay the vote in the Council of Europe (Waters, 1987). When put to the vote in April 1987, the FDR voted against the text, joined by Switzerland, Luxembourg and Liechtenstein; eleven voted in favour and three (including Austria and Portugal) abstained.

There was a degree of public controversy over the proposal, with a *Wall Street Journal* editorial even questioning whether the OECD had a mandate to be involved in minimising tax avoidance, arguing that if the OECD was to 'support the ability of markets to efficiently allocate resources it should be working to make it *easier* for individuals and businesses to avoid taxes where it is legal to do so' (*Wall Street Journal*, 1988).

Australia decided against supporting the proposal from an early stage. On 8 May 1984, the Commissioner for Taxation reported to the Treasurer on the outcome of a recent meeting convened by the ATO of Prime Minister and Cabinet, Treasury, Attorney-General's, and Foreign Affairs. The consensus view was:

> [T]hat Australia should not, at this stage, become a party to the Convention, but should monitor its further development and leave open the question of becoming a member at a later date. (NAA, 1988)

A handwritten note on the file copy of the cable seeking confirmation that Australia still had no intention of becoming a signatory to the draft convention indicated a degree of buck passing between Treasury and the ATO, noting that 'ATO say that this is our responsibility' with a 'Reply: 'ATO should handle' (NAA, 1985b).

Later, after the failed attempt in 1985–87 by the Hawke government to introduce an 'Australia Card' (a Tax File Number identification system was introduced instead) there was some sensitivity over the multilateral convention, which financial journalist Padraic P. McGuinness wrote would require governments to share tax files, not just Tax File Numbers. McGuinness noted that 'So far the Australian government has not decided whether it should sign the convention, although it is favourably disposed towards it'. Germany and Switzerland, he noted, had indicated they would not (McGuinness, 1988).

The ATO objections to signing the Multilateral Convention related to it being perceived as an attempt to implement the Australia Card in another way and left a cloud hanging over the Tax File Number (TFN) system that was being introduced to replace it as a means of improving the integrity of the tax system. There was clearly a concern over how the reaction to the proposed multilateral convention might impact on support for the tax file number, as expressed by the Treasurer, Paul Keating, in a letter to the Attorney-General: 'While the claims are unfounded they could, if unchecked, prejudice the tax file number project' (NAA, 1987). Treasury was 'not overly impressed' by ATO's objections, though granting that it might not know the full extent of some of the ATO's 'more technical' concerns. 'Nevertheless, the benefits from signing might only be marginal and we are not inclined to push hard for signature at this stage' (NAA, 1988).

The Treasurer issued a press release on 18 October 1988 announcing that the government had decided not to become a signatory to the Convention, 'consistent with the recommendation of the Australian Tax Office'. It assured there would be no central global data base (NAA, 1988b). The decision was not universally supported, however, with DFAT Minister Gareth Evans writing to the Treasurer the day after the announcement pointing out the Convention's advantages and wanting to keep open the possibility of acceding. However, this 19 October 1988 response to a letter of 16 September seeking views on the matter was too late to be considered (NAA, 1988b).

Australia eventually finally signed the (amended) Convention on Mutual Administrative Assistance in Tax Matters on 3 November 2011 and ratified it on 30 August 2012, after the United Kingdom had also acceded to it in 2011 and extended it to its tax havens: Anguila, Bermuda, Cayman Islands, Gibraltar, Isle of Man, Jersey, Montserrat and the Turks and Caicos Islands. Luxembourg subsequently acceded in 2014, while Switzerland signed in 2013, but at the time of writing is yet to ratify.

The Council of Europe using the OECD to develop a convention with wide coverage was but one example of others employing the OECD as a venue, and using other venues and bilateral interaction to progress their agendas within the OECD. For example, the US Internal Revenue Service wrote to the ATO in October 1985 advising it that the Group of

Four (UK, US, Germany and France) was nearing completion of a 'Statement of Principles' setting out principles countries should adopt 'as a means of achieving greater justice for their tax systems, protecting taxpayers' rights, and countering international tax avoidance and evasion' (NAA, 1985b). The Statement of Principles set out some actions that should be taken by countries:

1. Not grant tax exemptions or privileges which facilitate and promote tax avoidance and evasion;
2. Amend domestic bank secrecy laws to increase the availability of information for use by tax administrations and develop exchanges of bank information;
3. Enact withholding law and other law which counters avoidance and evasion; and
4. Enter into tax treaties with other countries to provide a means for avoiding double taxation, exchanging information, and resolving problems.

Besides adoption by member countries, the Group of Four planned to submit the document to the CFA in the OECD, and the German delegation (the project coordinator) requested members of the Four to seek comments from members of other international organisations. The US was specifically asked to contact the member countries in the Pacific Association of Tax Administrators (PATA). Support within the CFA was sought by this means, with it 'requested that the comments including views on whether their delegate who attends the OECD Committee on Fiscal Affairs Meeting could support referral of the document to the appropriate working party for adoption' (NAA, 1985b).

As this example shows, Australia was important in extending the reach of the OECD beyond Europe and North America, and it continued to beat the drum for attention to be given to the Asia-Pacific in the area of tax. Australia, for example, hosted a seminar on tax and investment flows in Sydney in November 1992, and the OECD convened a workshop covering FDI in Paris 12–13 July 1993 as part of the OECD's ongoing dialogue with the Dynamic Asian Economies (DAEs) (NAA, 1992, 1992a). Australia was approached by the OECD Secretariat, which asked for input and specifically that Australia present a paper, but time constraints meant that it was not possible to present a paper, and the best that could be offered was 'A-based' attendance at the meeting. The emphasis Australia placed on Asia created expectations:

> In seeking our participation at the DAEs workshops the Secretariat constantly refers to Australia's criticism of the Eurocentric tendencies in the OECD and the importance we place on the Asia Pacific region. (NAA, 1992a)

WP8 also discussed issues such as withholding taxes on interest payments, and the cable on a meeting in 1989 indicated that greater use of exchange agreements might be the preferred option, and that 'generalised withholding tax regimes might be a second best solution' (NAA, 1989). The issue again demonstrated the possibility that deliberations within the OECD could become embroiled in issues of politics within the European Communities.

Much of the discussion of withholding taxes was taken up by a special presentation by the European Commission, which led to considerable discussion of the Mutual Assistance Procedures, with a number of European delegations, especially France, questioning Luxembourg as to why it had in the last week passed 'very strict legislation via an emergency procedure which would effectively prevent them passing information to other EC tax administrations' (NAA, 1989). The Commission was apparently very concerned about the Luxembourg legislation, which they saw as having effectively declared that state as a tax haven within the EEC, a situation exacerbated because it was anticipated that the withholding tax proposal might 'also flounder on Luxembourg's vote in Council' (NAA, 1989). This would mean it would be very difficult, after liberalisation of capital flows, to monitor capital flows to Luxembourg and likely lead to significant revenue losses to governments, a situation the French Treasury was already very concerned about.

THE HARMFUL TAX COMPETITION INITIATIVE, AUSTRALIA AND THE COMMONWEALTH

In 1996, on the initiative of the US, the G8 requested the OECD to address the issue of harmful tax competition. The G8 lacked the capacity to progress the initiative, but the OECD's long history of involvement with tax made it a sensible choice of arena to address the problem.

'Harmful' tax competition (HTC) among countries to lure corporations and wealthy individuals using low rates of taxation and lax financial regulation had not universally been regarded as a problem beyond the EU. The Clinton Administration called for work on HTC, and the *Communiqué* from the 1996 G8 Meeting in Lyon passed to the OECD a mandate for work in this area (G8 1996). At the 1996 MCM the OECD established a work programme under the Committee on Fiscal Affairs which led to a report in April 1998, *Harmful Tax Competition: An Emerging Global Issue*. This identified two types of HTC: tax havens and preferential tax regimes (PTRs). The former were deemed to be harmful when they lacked transparency (especially in the exchange of information with tax authorities in other jurisdictions). PTRs were jurisdictions which 'ring fenced' their domestic tax base and offered low tax rates to non-citizens, also with a lack of transparency and information exchange between tax authorities (see Eccleston, 2013; Woodward, 2009). To carry the issue beyond the OECD, a Global Forum on Transparency and Exchange of Information for Tax Purposes was established in 2000.

The Harmful Tax Competition Initiative (HTCI) raised some problems for Australia, particularly because the issue aroused small island tax havens who used the Commonwealth to advance their concerns, and Australia was scheduled to host the Commonwealth Heads of Government Meeting (CHOGM) in the latter part of 2001. The Commonwealth became involved in the HTCI because 25 of the 35 countries that were listed by the OECD in 2000 and five of the six jurisdictions that had entered into commitments before the list was published were past or present British colonies (see Sharman, 2006: 58). The HTCI was later discussed at the Commonwealth Finance Ministers Meeting in Malta September 2002. In late 2000 the Secretary-General of the Commonwealth invited the OECD to co-chair a meeting on the initiative in Barbados in January 2001, at which the OECD agreed to establish a Joint Working Group. The OECD members lacked enthusiasm for the Joint Working Group and at its Second Meeting in Paris on 2 March 2001 it was clear that agreement would be difficult, and it was also clear to Australian representatives that OECD members did not want further JWG meetings (DFAT, 2001).

Many Developing Country tax havens were less than happy with the OECD HTC initiative and raised the matter in other fora such as the WTO. WTO Director-General Michael Moore told a London audience in response to a question concerning taxation arrangements for financial services that some were 'enraged' that the OECD could blacken their name and undermine investment without consulting them. A major concern was that the matter might be raised for discussion at the Commonwealth Heads of Government Meeting to be hosted by Australia later that year. In early April St Kitts and St Lucia joined Bahamas and Grenada in putting the OECD's harmful tax policies at the top of the list of subjects that they would like to see discussed at the Brisbane CHOGM. A series of bilateral meetings was arranged for the tax havens with Australia, Japan and New Zealand at the Pacific Islands Secretariat in Suva on 25–27 April 2001, followed by a joint meeting between the OECD and the seven listed countries on the 28th (DFAT, 2001).

The OECD HTCI had set a deadline of 30 November 2001 for commitment by non-OECD tax havens to agree to comply with the measure (OECD Members were given longer). The desire to avoid the embarrassment of the Commonwealth tax havens raising the matter at CHOGM, rather than opposition to the intent of the initiative, drove Australian strategy (DFAT, 2001). Australia tried hard to move the deadline back by five months and considered blocking release of the OECD Report on HTP if it was proposed to release key documents before the CHOGM in Brisbane on 6 October 2001. There were some moves at conciliation. The OECD members offered technical assistance to tax havens to help them meet transparency requirements, and Vanuatu suggested to Australia that aid might be increased to offset lost revenue through compliance with the initiative. The HTP Bureau (France, Ireland, US) met again on 26 September 2001, with Australia present, to discuss the proposed draft statement on the commitment date which was then to be considered by Council. There was no consensus on the wording of the draft statement, and Australia's proposals for additional text were not supported by any participant. Nevertheless, the deadline was moved back by four months to 28 February, which Australia 'could live with', at the OECD Council Meeting on Thursday 27 September (DFAT, 2001).

Australia's quest for a deferral in the HTP deadline was assisted for other reasons by Spain, which entered a reservation and was threatening to block release over the perennial issue of Gibraltar, a tax haven under the jurisdiction of the United Kingdom. There was a possibility that Spain would lift its reservation on release in time for a special Council Meeting on Monday 1 October to ask the CFA to revise the 30 November deadline with a view to releasing the report with a new date by Wednesday 3 October. As a fall-back, the Council meeting also agreed the Secretariat would work with several delegations on the text of a statement that could be made by the Secretary-General on 1 October making it clear the OECD was no longer considering the 30 November deadline. Australia was thus able to achieve a slightly shorter delay, assisted by the Spanish reluctance (DFAT, 2001a).

Unfortunately, on 28 September 2001 CHOGM was postponed until the first quarter of the next year, because of security concerns after the terrorist attacks on 11 September, and was held at Coolum Resort between 2 and 5 March 2002, putting the OECD deadline back in the frame for inclusion on the CHOGM agenda. There was pressure from the Prime Minister's Office to dampen down any issues which might be controversial at CHOGM, but postponement meant CHOGM was 'no longer a scene setter', and it did not emerge as a visible issue when CHOGM was eventually held (DFAT, 2001a).

By 19 October, there was discussion in the CFA of an 'exit strategy', because the HTP was taking up much of the CFA's time to the exclusion of other important work. Australian representatives on the CFA were giving consideration to raising the issue of the OECD's long-term role on tax competition at the next CFA meeting (in January 2002) with thought being given, for example, to the work being spun off somehow. Options included the UN – 'but only if you wanted to kill it off', as one officer put it in an email – or a new global tax body, or linking this work to World Bank or IMF governance work. 'Thinking on this [was] embryonic' (DFAT, 2001a).

There was concern that further delay in issuing the 2001 progress report would jeopardise the continuation of the OECD HTC project, with the credibility of the OECD at stake if the 2001 report was not released. As Martin Quinn, Manager of the OECD Policy Unit in DFAT put it to Ambassador Ian Forsyth:

> The successes of the project in bringing to commitment the most significant havens (including now the Bahamas) will be lost if the report is not released. Existing commitments will be rethought and potential commitments, including Pacific nations, will not materialise. Further delays could also result in unresolved issues emerging at CHOGM. (DFAT, 2001a)

By early November, the Delegation had learned that the UK and Spain had found a basis for Spain to lift its veto on the release of the report on HTPs, and the Delegation sought urgent advice on whether they could still go along with the amended deadline of 28 February, knowing by now the new problem with the rescheduled CHOGM. It was thought that there would be a reluctance to change that date, and that to do so would require a substantial lobbying effort (DFAT, 2001).

Both the OECD Secretariat and Spain approached the Delegation on the issue of the deadline, advocating that the Council agree to stick with the 28 February 2002 deadline and that the report be released on the afternoon of 14 November. The Delegation advised they were awaiting instructions on the issue and that 'the further, unfortunate delays in the release of the report had again raised the need for some sensitive judgements' (DFAT, 2001). The Secretariat was reportedly up-beat on the prospects for the listed Pacific island countries signing onto the initiative and had expressed a desire to work with the Commonwealth Secretariat on the issue (the Caribbean commitment was conditional on the release of the report) (DFAT, 2001). PM&C wanted an extension to five months, having settled on this position without consultation with Treasury/ATO or DFAT, and wanted to accept the 28 February deadline subject only to conditions – if Australia were isolated and the UK could guarantee all the Caribbean states signed on before 28 February and Treasury and ATO guarantee all the Pacific Island countries signed on by then (see a note from Senator Bill Heffernan to Foreign Minister Alexander Downer on behalf of the Prime Minister, DFAT, 2001a). This was clearly impractical, as Council could hardly commit to such a deadline subject to conditions that had to be met by that date.

The Bureau of the CFA and the Secretariat had circulated their view that the deadline of 28 February was reasonable and should be confirmed. They were keen to maintain that date so that the forum on HTPs would be able to take stock of the situation at its meeting in mid-March. They also wanted to give the Bahamas no reason to slip in its commitment to action following the release of the report. Australia decided to live with the 28 February deadline, and deal with 'CHOGM heat' by the device of moving the meeting of the Ministerial Group on Small States (MGSS)[3] – where the tax havens were most likely to raise the issue – to a date one month before CHOGM, rather than the usual day before, and focusing MGSS firmly on implementation of UNSC Resolution 1373 on terrorism, which extended to terrorist financing. This was clearly intended to displace consideration of tax havens by means of an issue that would trump it in importance. As one officer put it, 'UNSCR 1373 makes the griping about the OECD initiative irrelevant' (DFAT, 2001a).

By July 2003 a progress report on HTPs was ready for approval, though with some outstanding issues (Treasury, 2004). Switzerland and Luxembourg were given until October to modify their ring-fencing regimes (Treasury, 2004). The Progress Report on Bank Secrecy was also considered in July (Treasury, 2004). No consensus on Harmful Tax Practices proved possible at the meeting of CFA 1–2 July, and there was pressure on Switzerland, Luxembourg, Belgium and Austria to comply (Treasury, 2004). The 2003 Progress Report indicated that 13 regimes had been modified, 18 abolished and another 13 found not to be harmful, including Australia's offshore banking unit (OBU) regime. Four regimes (one in Luxembourg and three in Switzerland) were found to be actually harmful because they were not transparent. Of 36 regimes, all but six had given commitments to enter into agreements to exchange information on tax matters which would substantially reduce harm, but these were contingent on OECD countries dealing with harmful regimes within their own countries so that there was a level playing field – a key demand of the small tax havens represented by the International Tax and Investment

Organisation. Progress towards the success of the project was therefore very much dependent on progress on the Swiss and Luxembourg regimes.

Switzerland had abstained in 1998 from the decision establishing the project, and although it had since cooperated, it maintained it was not bound by it and thus objected to the finding that its regimes were harmful. Other countries maintained that it was within their right to assess the Swiss regimes and take coordinated counter-measures against them, including outside the OECD if necessary. Switzerland was reluctantly given more time but it was now recognised that terrorism financing, money laundering and tax evasion/avoidance were linked and addressing bank secrecy was seen as a key step in addressing these issues. If this could not be achieved through the OECD, there was a willingness by key countries to establish new institutional arrangements to progress cooperative implementation of this project among the countries that supported it. Only with the global financial crisis in 2008, with the added impetus of its origins of unregulated off-shore financial centres, did the mechanism of bilateral Information Exchange Agreements achieve widespread success.

ADMINISTRATIVE MATTERS

In recent times, Australians have occupied prominent positions in the Centre for Tax Policy and Administration. For example, David Bradbury, a former tax lawyer and junior Minister until the defeat of the ALP government in 2013, was appointed Head of the Tax Policy and Statistics Division within the CTPA from April 2014. Richard Highfield, a former Second Commissioner of the ATO served as Head of the Tax Administration Division, in the CTPA, where he played a major role in the creation of the OECD's Forum on Tax Administration, now widely regarded as the pre-eminent forum grouping for heads of national revenue bodies. He continued as a Senior Advisor to the CTPA until 2015.

The Treasury was the lead agency for tax matters from the time of accession, with the involvement of its subordinate agency, the Australian Taxation Office, but the ATO assumed the lead role in 2002. The division of labour between Treasury and the ATO was an ongoing issue requiring coordination. For example, a 'Post It' note attached to the Agenda for the 29th meeting of WP8 stated: 'Pls note. Most of the briefing on this should be ATO's responsibility' (NAA, 1989). Similarly, responsibility for providing the briefing for the meeting being held on 29–30 March 1989 lay with the ATO for items V, VII, and VIII, and coordination between Treasury, the ATO and the Delegation was not always perfect, even though by the mid-1980s the use of facsimile transmission was beginning to supplement considerably cables and the diplomatic bag as the only means of communication. While faster and able to send images and letters, fax provided no failsafe substitute.

For example, the International and Indirect Taxation Branch of Treasury faxed the following letter to the Delegation on 23 March 1989:

> With regard to item IV, we do not understand why the Secretariat is still awaiting a country chapter from Australia. The chapter was sent by ATO to you on 13 October. Norway's comments on the chapter were received from you on 23 November; our response was faxed to you on 6 December.
>
> Neither we nor ATO have received copies of DAFFE/CFA/WP8/88.2 (1st Revision) or DAFFE/CFA/WP8/89.2. (NAA, 1989a)

These were then faxed by the Delegation to Treasury on 27 March, with the note:

> Because of communication problems over Easter it appears that you might not have received WP8/89.2 with my fax FP03318 (of 23 March). While it is now probably too late to provide comments in time for the meeting, any reactions from the Tax Office would still be able to be passed to the Secretariat. (NAA, 1989a)

A hand-written note on the fax in Treasury read: 'pls. send to ATO this morning BY HAND'. A reply from the ATO was then sent to the Communications Room, DFAT for transmission on 28 March. It stated that, while the agenda for the meeting on 29–30 March stated 'Country chapters are awaited from Australia ...'. 'Our complete response to the questionnaire was forwarded to you on 13 October 1988' (NAA, 1989a).

In terms of the organisation of OECD tax work within Treasury, this evolved over time. In 1989, WP8 was being handled by the Personal Taxation Branch within Treasury and responsibility for the overall relationship with the OECD rested with the International Economy Branch (NAA, 1990). In response to a Minute seeking the interest of Branches in Committees and asking for a contact officer, the Personal Taxation Branch indicated that it would like to receive papers from the Committee on Consumer Policy, the Committee on Fiscal Affairs, and the Manpower and Social Affairs Committee. Its interests lay in the Committee on Fiscal Affairs, including its WP1 on Double Taxation and Related Questions, WP2 on Tax Analysis and Tax Statistics, the Statistical Group on Estimating Methodology of WP2, WP6 on the Taxation of MNEs, and WP8 on Tax Avoidance and Evasion.

The organisation of Treasury in 2003 involved a Macroeconomic Group, a Fiscal and Corporate Group, a Revenue Group, and a Markets Group. Interaction with the OECD was largely organised through the Revenue Group, which had an International Tax and Treaties Division, a Tax Analysis Division, a Business Tax Division, a Tax Design Division, a Personal and Retirement Income Division, and an Indirect Tax Division. The agenda for a strategy meeting in 2003 gives some insight as to how the engagement of the Revenue Group with the OECD was organised (Treasury, 2004). A Deputy Secretary, head of the Revenue Branch, who had worked at the OECD from 1997 to 2002, represented Australia at the CFA.

Much of the detailed work was undertaken in the various Working Groups, and much value derived from this. For example, major achievements of WP1 were seen as the development and regular updating of the OECD Model Tax Convention, which is used as the basis for all bilateral tax treaties, including Australia's, and major recent reports on such matters as: treatment of partnerships in tax treaties; application of the permanent establishment concept; entitlement to treaty benefits; inclusion of an article on assistance in collection; and treaty characterisation of various e-commerce transactions. The level of engagement consisted of the main delegate to WP1 (where 'Australia [was] recognised as a key player …'), who was an officer at SES Band 1, who attended biannual meetings and, where possible, meetings of key subgroups. This work occupied the delegate for approximately six weeks annually, plus the work of an officer at Executive Level 2 for a similar period and one at Executive Level 1 for approximately two weeks annually. For WP2 on Tax Policy Analysis and Tax Statistics, an officer at SES Band 1 attended, with no delegate from the ATO attending. For WP9, an officer at SES Band 1 chaired an Informal Working Group on Services, while another at SES Band 1 from the ATO also attended and was also on the WP9 bureau, and the ATO often sent a second delegate at SES to Executive Level 1 (Treasury, 2004).

The level of engagement has increased as the OECD's Base Erosion and Profit Shifting initiative (BEPS) has developed, with the ATO posting a permanent representative to Paris from 2014, who attends the Working Parties and works with the Secretariat to advance Australia's position.

THE RECENT AGENDA

A high-level delegation from the CTPA (Director Jeffrey Owens and Jacques Sasseville) visited Canberra on 5 September 2003, spending the morning at Treasury and the afternoon at the ATO. These discussions informed the meeting at the end of October that considered Australia's strategy for OECD engagement (Treasury, 2004), and demonstrated the value of engagement with the OECD for the development of tax policy in Australia. The agenda by now was quite extensive and the record of the meeting shows a deep and productive relationship between Australia and the OECD.

The appropriateness of the CFA Agenda was discussed, with questions raised such as whether the CFA was more interested in the mechanics of the tax system or policy. It was thought the CFA needed more of a strategic focus rather than an approach that 'plugs holes' (which should be left to subsidiary bodies). A number of emerging tax issues were identified: a shift in tax bases to Developing Countries; transfer pricing; environment; competition for human capital; and extending work on Harmful Tax Practices to an Investment Agreement. The mobility of the tax base was noted, with an increased emphasis on the taxation of less mobile property and consumption taxes.

The opportunity was taken to reflect on where the global tax environment was heading, focusing, for example, on the concept of principle-based law. Treasury wanted to move to a simpler principle-based approach to tax law design, and away from the US approach of detailed legislation. The introduction of the GST was seen as an example of principle-based law, with the conceptual principle stated up front and detail following. Australia's transfer pricing laws were also principle-based and the ATO had a large role in interpreting them. There was considered to be a risk in simplifying the law in that it left the interpretation open to the Courts. An increase in tax planning was noted, which had been pushed from the corporate level to the retail level and it was considered that tax offices around the world should be targeting the promoters of aggressive tax planning. Nevertheless, tax avoidance was regarded as a relatively small percentage of the factors driving tax policy. Corporate tax shelters were considered to be likely to always adapt their products to circumvent anti-avoidance measures. Jacques Sasseville advised that other countries appeared to have lost the battle to implement principle-based law.

Australia's corporate tax base was considered to be strong as most exports were tangible, and therefore more easily taxed than intangibles (Treasury, 2004). Moreover, the Australian imputation system of granting tax credits to shareholders for corporate tax already paid provided an incentive for business to recognise profits in order to ensure that the tax credits were forthcoming. Questions were being raised as to the benefits of tax treaties in the context of the current global environment, and it was thought that a bilateral treaty approach had benefits over international law because the two different tax systems could be taken into account and it also avoided the political problems related to enacting international law. But there were also challenging issues discussed. The OECD Model Tax Convention, for example, was seen as depending on a shared vision and currently there did not appear to be agreement on such a vision. Also, there was a varying lag between revisions to the OECD Model and their inclusion in treaties by member states. Jacques Sasseville noted increasing pressure from taxpayers and authorities to increase detail in treaties because uncertainty benefits the 'high end of town' (Treasury, 2004).

The perennial issue of Europe was also discussed, because the view was that EU tax policy was being decided in the European Court of Justice, and that 'the Court [was] undermining well-established treaty concepts' (Treasury, 2004) The ECJ, in *Lankhorst-Hohorst GmbH v Finanzamt Steinfurt* (C-324/00), for example, had held that German thin capitalisation laws (which facilitated shifting of profits by servicing high levels of debt to related foreign companies at higher than commercial rates) were contrary to European Community law. This led to a review of such laws in Germany, France and the UK, and there were implications for treaties with non-EU countries. A question therefore arose as to whether this should become an OECD issue. The 'political reality' was that many OECD members did not want it discussed, and there was likely to be more discrimination between EU and non-EU countries.

This meeting ranged across numerous taxation matters, allowing the insights of Owens and Sasseville to be shared with Treasury (with a similar meeting at the ATO), and illustrates the benefits of engagement with the OECD, especially in allowing international experience and best practice to inform Australian policy, as with other member states.

CONCLUSION

Australia was cautious in its initial engagement with tax activities in the OECD at the time of accession, but engagement grew significantly over time, to the extent that it now plays a strategically focused and significant role in its work, deriving value from its engagement, but also sharing its own experiences in a mutually beneficial exchange relationship.

The OECD's special characteristics have made it a useful arena in which to develop tax policy for the Council of Europe and the United Nations, to which some of the initiatives of the HTCI have been exported. But the intersection between these arenas is imprecise, and gave rise to some problems for Australia, particularly because of its hosting of CHOGM and the significance of action against tax havens for small Commonwealth nations, especially those in the Pacific.

More recent work, such as that on BEPS, continues to interest Australia, and found a prominent place on the agenda for the G20 heads of government summit hosted by Australia in 2014. The lack of enthusiasm for action on tax minimisation among some OECD members has in the past limited the success of similar initiatives, and it remains to be seen if BEPS meets a similar fate.

NOTES

1. The Australian Taxation Office has had greater involvement in OECD tax work since that time, but, despite considerable efforts, the authors were unable to secure Special Access from the ATO for this project. This has limited the ability to bring this chapter up to the present day.
2. *Commissioner of Taxation v Cooke and Sherden* 80 ATC 4140.
3. The MGSS traditionally meets just before CHOGM, and is chaired by the foreign minister of the host nation and is to help the 32 of the 54 Commonwealth members that are Small States (populations less than 1.5 million) advance their common interests.

BIBLIOGRAPHY

Australian Bureau of Statistics (ABS) 1980. Employment Benefits, Australia, February to May 1979 (Preliminary) 6332.0 (9 January 1980).

Australian Bureau of Statistics (ABS) 1984. Employment Benefits, Australia, August 1983 6332.0 (25 January 1984).

Australian Financial Review 1972. 'Cocos Islands' financial options under study', *Australian Financial Review*, 18 September.

Bentley, D. 2003. 'Influence from the Shadows: the OECD, the Shape of Domestic Tax Policy and Lessons for Federal Systems', *Revenue Law Journal*, 13(1): 128–146.

Boucher, T. 2010. *Blatant, Artificial and Contrived: Tax Schemes of the 70s and 80s*, Canberra: Australian Taxation Office.

Cockfield, A. 2006. 'The Rise of the OECD as Informal "World Tax Organization" through National Responses to E-Commerce Tax Challenges', *Yale Journal of Law and Technology*, 8: 136–187.

DFAT 2001. Trade Policy – Committees – OECD – Committee on Fiscal Affairs. File 01/050233.

DFAT 2001a. Trade Policy – Committees – OECD – Committee on Fiscal Affairs – OEU. 01/050801.

Doman, N. 1982. 'East–West Tax Treaties', *International Business Law*, 10(5): 162–167.

Eccleston, R. 2013. *The Dynamics of Global Economic Governance: The Financial Crisis, the OECD, and the Politics of International Tax Cooperation*, Cheltenham, UK and Northampton, MA, USA: Edward Elgar Publishing.

Fax from Counsellor, Economic and Financial Affairs, Delegation to Treasury, 7 June 1992.

Helfrich-Laubrock, J. 1987. 'Critical review of the OECD/Council of Europe Multilateral (Draft) Convention on Mutual Administrative Assistance in Tax Matters', *Bulletin (of the International Bureau of Fiscal Documentation)*, August/September: 410–413.

International Tax Review 2012. 'Owens looks back on his time in office', *International Tax Review*, 1 February, accessed on 6 February 2015 at www.internationaltaxreview.com/Article/2967120/Owens-looks-back-on-his-time-in-office.html.

McGuinness, P. 1988. 'Your Second Tax File in Paris', *Australian Financial Review*, 1 March.

Meagher, M. 1984. 'Executive Salaries: Hour Does *Yours* Compare?', *The Bulletin*, January 10: 76–79.

NAA 1970. Commonwealth Treasury. OECD Taxation aspects of Australia's Accession (including privileges and immunities). Series Number A571 Item Number 1970/6528 Part 1.

NAA 1971. Taxation Policy – OECD CFA WP No1 WG No. 4 – non-discrimination: 1971–3. A3720/12 1979/404.

NAA 1972. A1985/219 IIT/INT: Organisation for Economic Co-operation and Development (OECD) – Committee On Fiscal Affairs (CFA) – Working Party No.2 – Double Taxation.

NAA 1973. 73/564 Part 7 Taxation Policy – 'Tax Havens' & The Avoidance of Australian Taxation.

NAA 1973a. 73/564 Part 8 Taxation Policy – 'Tax Havens' & The Avoidance of Australian Taxation.

NAA 1973b. Taxation Policy – 'Tax Havens' & The Avoidance of Australian Taxation. 73/564 Part 9.

NAA 1973c. 73/564 Part 10 Taxation Policy – 'Tax Havens' & The Avoidance of Australian Taxation.

NAA 1973d. 73/564 Part 11 Taxation Policy – 'Tax Havens' & The Avoidance of Australian Taxation.

NAA 1976. 76/4668 OECD – CFA Working Party on Double Taxation and Related Questions.

NAA 1977. J245/73/71 Pt2 Working Party No8 on Tax Avoidance and Evasion Meeting 22–24 June 1977.

NAA 1978. J245/73/71 Pt4 Working Party No8 on Tax Avoidance and Evasion Meeting 15–16 February 1978.

NAA 1978a. Working Party No8 on Tax Avoidance and Evasion Meeting 14–15 November 1978. J245/73/71 Pt6.

NAA 1979. Working Party No8 on Tax Avoidance and Evasion Meeting Series. J245/73/71 Pt7.

NAA 1982. OECD – Working Party No8 on Tax Avoidance and Evasion – Meeting Series. J245/73/71 Pt16.

NAA 1984. A 84/271 Part 1 – Income Tax – Fringe Benefits – Policy.
NAA 1984a. A84/271 Part 4 – Income Tax – Fringe Benefits – Policy.
NAA 1985. A1985/219 IIT/INT: Organisation for Economic Co-operation and Development (OECD) – Committee on Fiscal Affairs (CFA) – Working Party Number 2 – Double Taxation.
NAA 1985a. A85/201 Part 1 IIT/INT: Organisation for Economic Co-operation and Development (OECD) – Committee on Fiscal Affairs – Working Party Number 8 – Tax Avoidance and Evasion.
NAA 1985b. A85/201 Part 2 IIT/INT: Organisation for Economic Co-operation and Development (OECD) – Committee on Fiscal Affairs – Working Party Number 8 – Tax Avoidance and Evasion.
NAA 1985c. A85/201 Part 3 IIT/INT: Organisation for Economic Co-operation and Development (OECD) – Committee on Fiscal Affairs – Working Party Number 8 – Tax Avoidance and Evasion.
NAA 1986. A85/201 Part 4 IIT/INT: Organisation for Economic Co-operation and Development (OECD) – Committee on Fiscal Affairs – Working Party Number 8 – Tax Avoidance and Evasion.
NAA 1986a. A85/201 Part 5 IIT/INT: Organisation for Economic Co-operation and Development (OECD) – Committee on Fiscal Affairs – Working Party Number 8 – Tax Avoidance and Evasion.
NAA 1987. A85/201 Part 6 IIT/INT: Organisation for Economic Co-operation and Development (OECD) – Committee on Fiscal Affairs – Working Party Number 8 – Tax Avoidance and Evasion.
NAA 1988. A85/201 Part 7 IIT/INT: Organisation for Economic Co-operation and Development (OECD) – Committee on Fiscal Affairs – Working Party Number 8 – Tax Avoidance and Evasion. W. J. O'Reilly Commissioner of Taxation to Treasurer, 8 May 1984, Letter, Draft Convention on Mutual Administrative Assistance in Tax Matters.
NAA 1988a. A85/201 Part 8 IIT/INT: Organisation for Economic Co-operation and Development (OECD) – Committee on Fiscal Affairs – Working Party Number 8 – Tax Avoidance and Evasion.
NAA 1988b. A85/201 Part 10 IIT/INT: Organisation for Economic Co-operation and Development (OECD) – Committee on Fiscal Affairs – Working Party Number 8 – Tax Avoidance and Evasion.
NAA 1989. A85/201 Part 11 IIT/INT: Organisation for Economic Co-operation and Development (OECD) – Committee on Fiscal Affairs – Working Party Number 8 – Tax Avoidance and Evasion.
NAA 1989a. A85/201 Part 12 IIT/INT: Organisation for Economic Co-operation and Development (OECD) – Committee on Fiscal Affairs – Working Party Number 8 – Tax Avoidance and Evasion.
NAA 1989b. A85/201 Part 13 IIT/INT: Organisation for Economic Co-operation and Development (OECD) – Committee on Fiscal Affairs – Working Party Number 8 – Tax Avoidance and Evasion.
NAA 1989c. A85/201 Part 14 IIT/INT: Organisation for Economic Co-operation and Development (OECD) – Committee on Fiscal Affairs – Working Party Number 8 – Tax Avoidance and Evasion.

NAA 1989d. A85/201 Part 15 IIT/INT: Organisation for Economic Co-operation and Development (OECD) – Committee on Fiscal Affairs – Working Party Number 8 – Tax Avoidance and Evasion.

NAA 1990. A85/201 Part 16 IIT/INT: Organisation for Economic Co-operation and Development (OECD) – Committee on Fiscal Affairs – Working Party Number 8 – Tax Avoidance and Evasion.

NAA 1992. 92/03131 Workshop on OECD/DAEs Foreign Direct Investment Relations. OECD: Committee on Fiscal Affairs (CFA) – Tax Investment Flows – Meeting with Dynamic Asian Economies (DAE) 1992 – Background Information.

NAA 1992a. N1992/2609 IEB/IEC: OECD – Dynamic Asian Economies (DAES) Seminar On Tax and Investment Flows – Sydney – November 1992.

NAA 1993. 93/01722 Organisation for Economic Co-operation and Development (oecd) – Joint Sessions on Taxation and the Environment – Briefing For 24 and 25 June 1993 Meeting.

New Zealand 1982. *Report of the Task Force on Tax Reform in New Zealand*, Wellington: Government Printer.

Norfolk Island (n.d.) http://norfolkisland.gov.nf/governmentgazette, accessed 28 January 2015.

OECD 1971. Working Party No. 1 on Double Taxation. Study Group No. 4 Annex to the Fourth Report on Amendments to be Made to Article 24 of the Draft Convention Relating to Non-Discrimination. 14 December 1971 [DAF/CFA/WP1/71.10].

OECD 1977. Recommendation of Council on tax avoidance and tax evasion of 21 September 1977 [C(77)149].

OECD 1978. CFA/A(78)2 CFA 16th Session 17–18 January 1979 Agenda.

OECD 1979. Committee on Fiscal Affairs, 16th Session 17–18 January 1979 Agenda. [CFA/A(78)2].

OECD 1979a. Committee on Fiscal Affairs. Tax Evasion and Avoidance (Note by the Secretariat) 31 May 1979 [CFA(79)4].

OECD 1979b. DAF/CFA/WP8/79.2 Unacceptable Tax Avoidance: Its Scope, Courts' Attitudes and Legislative Approaches (Note by the Secretariat).

OECD 1981. Bank Secrecy; An analysis of the Replies to the Questionnaire [DAF/CFA/WP8/81.8].

OECD 1981a. Multilateral Convention on Mutual Administrative Assistance in Tax Matters. DAF/CFA/WP8/81.3 Part 1 (2nd revision).

OECD 1982. Draft Council Recommendation Concerning Mutual Administrative Assistance in Tax Matters 21 April 1982 [DAFFE/CFA/WP8/82.9].

OECD 1982a. DAFFE/CFA/86.3 23 January 1982 Draft Multilateral Convention on Mutual Assistance in Tax Matters: General Procedural and Legal Aspects (A Note by the Legal Directorate).

OECD 1982b. Cooperation Between The Council of Europe and OECD Concerning Mutual Assistance in Tax Matters [DAFFE/CFA/WP8/82.4].

OECD 1985. Committee on Fiscal Affairs. Tax Havens and Related Questions: Finalising of Report and Draft Publication. Addendum. 1 October 1985 [DAFFE/CFA/WP8/85.4].

OECD 1985a. Joint Meeting of Working Party No. 8 With BIAC Representatives 9 September 1985 [DAFFE/CFA/WP8/85.4].

OECD 1985b. Summary Record of the 22nd Meeting of Working Party No. 8 (held from 1 to 4 October 1985) [DAFFE/CFA/WP8/85.9].
OECD 1986. Draft Multilateral Convention on Mutual Assistance in Tax Matters: General Procedural and Legal Aspects (A Note by the Legal Directorate) 23 January 1986 [DAFFE/CFA/86.3].
OECD 1986a. The Taxation of Fringe Benefits. Draft Report for meeting on 4–6 March 1986 [DAFFE/CFA/WP8/86.1].
OECD 1988. 8 February 1988 Draft: Future Work of Working Party No. 8 (Note by the Secretariat) [DAFFE/CFA/WP8.88.3].
OECD 1993. Environment Policy Committee and Committee on Fiscal Affairs Task Force on Taxation and Environment. Draft Mandate and Work Program for Joint Sessions on Taxation and Environment. 17 March 1993 [COM/ENV/EPOC/DAFFE/CFA (92) 102/REV2].
OECD 1993a. ENV/EPOC/GEEI/(93) 6 19 MAY 1993. Group on Economic and Environment Policy Integration (GEEPI). Overview of OECD/IEA Work Related to Climate Change.
Sharman, J.C. 2006. *Havens in a Storm: The Struggle for Global Tax Regulation*, Ithaca: Cornell University Press.
Short, J. 1984. 'Perks Could Bring On a New Tax', *Sydney Morning Herald*, 26 January.
Taylor, J. 2011. 'Some Distinctive Features of Australian Tax Treaty Practice: An Examination of their Origins and Interpretation', *eJournal of Tax Research*, 9(3): 294–338.
Treasury 2004. Taxation & Income Support – Analysis – Strategy for OECD Engagement. Treasury File 2004/01283.
United Nations 1980. Model Double Taxation Convention between Developed and Developing Countries.
US Department of Treasury 1984. 'Highlights of 1984 Tax Changes', IRS Publication 553 (revised November 84).
Veyret, M. 1984. 'Fringe Benefits Face Tax Chop', *Australian Business*, 1 February: 12–15.
Wall Street Journal 1988. 'The OECD Tax Revival' (Editorial), *Wall Street Journal*, 17 November.
Waters, R. 1987. 'Business turns its guns on OECD tax plan', *Financial Times*, 9 October.
Woodward, R. 2009. *The Organisation for Economic Co-operation and Development (OECD)*, London: Routledge.

Cases

Berwick Ltd v Gray [1976] HCA 12; (1976) 133 CLR 603.
Commissioner of Taxation v Cooke and Sherden 80 ATC 4140.
Lankhorst-Hohorst GmbH v Finanzamt Steinfurt (C-324/00).

10. The OECD's work on the environment

The Environment Committee of the OECD (later the Environmental Policy Committee, or EPOC) was established in 1970, the year before Australian accession, which allowed Australia to play a formative role in its evolution (OECD, 1970). The work of EPOC has been important, not least because by the end of 2014 it had given rise to around 30 per cent of the 284 formal legal instruments of the OECD (Council Acts) – although only 16 of these were Decisions or Decision-Recommendations. The Council Acts were in the areas of waste (9), nuclear energy (8), 'green growth' (1), environment (44), energy (1), and chemicals (22).

Since Decisions are binding on Members, this international regulation has been significant, and Australia as a vast island continent with considerable open spaces and an economy more oriented to resource extraction and processing than most existing Members has often found itself somewhat out of alignment with the environmental concerns of many other members, especially those of Europe. This was very much in evidence with the proposal by the US and the EU for the OECD to adopt a Council Act on lead, which is the subject of a case study later in this chapter. First, however, a general overview of some of the main issues relating to Australia's involvement in the Environment Committee is provided.[1]

THE EARLY DAYS

The Australian Ambassador Sir Ronald Walker attended the first post-accession meeting of the Environment Committee in 1971, probably because there was no dedicated staff member responsible for the environment in the Delegation, rather than because of any importance initially attached to it (NAA, 1971). The deliberations of the Committee very much reflected concerns over transboundary air pollution in North America and Europe, with the approval of a project to measure Long Range Transportation of Air Pollution, to be funded under Part II of the Budget (OECD, 2011). Australia did not see this work to be a priority, but was later aware that it had ramifications for the French nuclear testing issue (a case over which was then being heard at the International Court of Justice). Australia alerted New Zealand to these implications, but was careful not to alert France. The Delegation was instructed by Canberra to support a US–Canada amendment including, if appropriate:

> [M]aking a statement that states have a legal obligation not to infringe the sovereignty of other states by carrying out activities within their territory that result in pollutants impinging on the territory of others. (NAA, 1973)

The environmental activities of the OECD were clearly of low priority, even to the Department, with C.L. (Sir Lenox) Hewitt, Secretary of the Department of the Environment, Aborigines and the Arts (DEAA) writing to the Secretary of the Department of Foreign Affairs on 24 November 1971:

> We would not think that it is necessary for Australia to participate in the meeting of the Group of Experts on Research on Measurement of Air Pollution to be held from 6–9 December 1971. (NAA, 1971)

Australia was still feeling its way, and taking guidance from the Secretariat as to what kind of representation was appropriate. For example, Ralph Hillman (Third Secretary, later to serve as Ambassador to the OECD) wrote to the Secretary of the Department of Foreign Affairs on 18 November 1971 concerning representation at the Sector Group on Unintended Consequences of Chemicals in the Environment, scheduled to meet in Berlin in January 1972:

> The Secretariat advised that representation at previous meetings was generally by a technical expert of a fairly senior level. However, since broader issues are also to be discussed at this meeting, it is likely that countries will send a less specialized representative as well. (NAA, 1971)

While Sir Ronald Walker was the sole representative at the 3rd session of EPOC in September 1971, representation was increased to three at the 4th session, four at the 5th, and five at the 6th, when Sir Lenox Hewitt (Secretary of the Department) made the journey from Canberra in November 1972. The Committee was still developing a set of Guiding Principles, and received the report of a Berlin meeting of the Sector Group on Unintended Consequence of Chemicals in the Environment, which was considering issues such as PCBs and DDT. It settled back to a delegation of three at the 7th session in February 1973, however (NAA, 1973).

Attendance of Meetings of EPOC at Ministerial Level has typically been by larger delegations, including both the minister's staff and representatives of state governments, as well as the growing importance of the environment for the Australian government. For example, at the 3rd Ministerial EPOC, Ralph Willis, Minister for Employment and Industrial Relations, attended representing environment minister Barry Cohen in a delegation totalling fourteen, including the Ambassador, Fred Argy, P.J. Galvin, Secretary, DAHE, departmental staff from Canberra, state representatives, the Minister (Energy) from the Delegation, and the Trade Counsellor (Agriculture) from the Australian High Commission in London.

Early work on environment in the OECD led to the development of a Recommendation on *Guiding Principles Concerning the International Economic Aspects of Environmental Policies* (OECD, 1972) in May 1972, perhaps encouraged by the convening of the UN Conference on the Human Environment in June of that year (OECD, 1972). These principles included (a) the harmonisation of environmental standards to improve the effectiveness and efficiency of environmental policies while preventing trade distortions; (b) national treatment and non-discrimination to ensure conformity of environmental policies with GATT rules; (c) procedures to promote conformity of product standards; and (d) compensatory import levies and export rebates. By far the best known of these, however, was the 'Polluter Pays Principle', which set out the idea that polluters should not be subsidised and should be charged for the costs of their action. Most of these matters required consultations with the states and therefore required Australia to consider entering a Reservation, potentially isolating Australia on the issue (NAA, 1972).

Australia suggested an amendment but found no support among the other members. The European members were taking a hard line on the preservation of the Polluter Pays Principle, intending to adopt domestic regulations on the basis of it, and attempting to minimise any 'exceptions'. France subsequently mentioned that the EEC was working towards a programme that would provide exemptions from the PPP only for existing industrial plants (NAA, 1974). Japan similarly pushed for a strict limitation on exceptions, especially for new plants, but indicated a willingness to compromise in order to get a resolution. The chair invited Australia to reflect further, and the Secretariat was concerned that the text not be made 'too abstract' in order to accommodate Australia's position (NAA, 1974). Australia foreshadowed making a general Reservation, and sought instructions from Canberra. Canberra, however, relented, cabling that 'Although it would have been helpful to have obtained minor drafting changes … we regard the present draft as broadly acceptable'

(NAA, 1974). The instruction was given that Australia should not pursue amendments, not wishing to go against the consensus.

The Whitlam government sought assistance from the OECD in 1973 in establishing its new Department of Urban and Regional Development, seeking the services of a member of the Urban Division of the Environment Directorate for 4–6 weeks from March 1973 to offer advice, informed by the unique position of the Secretariat in reviewing the experience of member countries. The government saw the OECD as being an important disseminator of international best practice in determining the structure and functions of DURD, stating that Australia was 'naturally very anxious to draw on the best advice available. We are particularly interested to avail ourselves of the opportunity of drawing on the experience of other countries in establishing the new Department' (NAA, 1972a).

Initially, however, and in contrast, Australia did not have a particularly high opinion of the Environment Committee, as compared to the Secretariat, but they were not alone in this. Dr D.F. McMichael, Secretary, Department of the Environment and Conservation, discussed the Committee with Alan Renouf, Secretary of Foreign Affairs and Mr P. Furlonger, Science Advisers Office (Department of Foreign Affairs) in February 1975 (NAA, 1974). Dr McMichael noted that during a visit to New York in December he had discussed the OECD Environment Committee with Christian Herter (Deputy Assistant Secretary of State, US State Department) and representatives of a number of other countries, including Norway and the FRG, 'who agreed with his view that the Committee was a fairly ineffective body'. Dr McMichael had some ideas on how make it into a more useful body and agreed to prepare a paper setting out those ideas, with the blessing of Foreign Affairs. A paper was subsequently presented to the Environment Committee by Deputy Secretary Mr H.J. Higgs in March 1975, advocating that the Committee become more policy oriented and was apparently well received, but 'no firm decisions were made, since the Committee's program for 1975 [was] already firm' (NAA, 1974). Ultimately, however, the Australian view prevailed and the name of the Committee was changed to Environment Policy Committee to reflect its new emphasis, but not until 1992 (Long, 2000: 86).

The environment activities were not well supported, at least as reflected by government budgetary decisions, and its place in a small Delegation had to be defended only six years after accession. In 1977 Cabinet had decided (Decision No. 3873 (Ad Hoc)) to amalgamate the positions of Counsellor (Education and Social Affairs) and Counsellor (Scientific and Environmental Affairs), thus leaving one position to cover these four areas of activity in the OECD. The OECD Delegation at that time consisted only of representatives of Treasury, Foreign Affairs, Trade, and the Counsellor (Education and Social Affairs) and Counsellor (Scientific and Environmental Affairs).

The tensions between Delegation size and the difficulties in sending Australia-based staff to meetings in Paris were highlighted in 1972 by the issue of biodegradable detergents. The Department of Foreign Affairs had to request that a member of the Delegation attend all or part of a meeting on Non-ionic Synthetic Detergents on 15–16 January 1973, with a briefing to be provided by the Departments of Science and Environment and Conservation. The problem arose in part because the meeting had not been mentioned in the routine 'Meetings Cable' setting out forthcoming meeting commitments (NAA, 1972a). There had been informal correspondence between Dr Peter Crawford, Counsellor (Scientific and Environmental Affairs) and Science in Canberra, and discussion between Science and Environment on the importance of the meeting. As a result Crawford was able to attend on the first day only.

Australian personnel in the environment area were well regarded. Dr Crawford, for example, later at one stage the most senior Australian in the Secretariat, was seconded to the OECD in 1983 as a chemicals expert to assist with the Environmental Performance Review of Yugoslavia. Similarly, Dr Don McMichael was elected to the chair of EPOC in April 1981 for two years, the first of two Australians to fill that role, with Kevin O'Keeffe elected to the chair in 2008, serving for four years. McMichael was a distinguished public servant, having served in both the New South Wales and Commonwealth governments. After McMichael was asked to serve for a further year, he sought an extension from his minister. The Minister, Tom McVeigh, in turn had to seek the approval of the Prime Minister, through Ian Sinclair (as Acting Minister of Foreign Affairs). This was agreed to in view of a wish to 'play a positive role in environmental matters'. But there was some reluctance over the commitment required: 'The Prime Minister remains concerned, however, at frequent or lengthy absences from Australia by Permanent Heads and particular proposals for visits by Dr McMichael in connection with his OECD duties should be carefully examined' (NAA, 1983).

THE FIRST MINISTERIAL MEETING

At its 8th Session on 27–29 June 1973 EPOC agreed to hold a meeting at Ministerial Level. The Bureau then selected November 1974 as the preferred time. Consideration was given to an Australian nomination for a vice chairmanship of Environment Committee at Ministerial level, but it was later decided that this was unlikely to succeed and should not be proceeded with (NAA, 1973). Dr Moss Cass, the Australian minister, did, however, initiate his nomination as 'appropriate', and H.J. Higgs, Deputy Secretary, Department of the Environment and Conservation wrote to the Secretary, DFA that 'unless soundings in Paris indicate that his nomination is likely to prove unsuccessful it would be appreciated if Dr. Cass' name could go forward for one of the positions of Vice Chairman' (NAA, 1973). Apparently, some delegations had sought a nomination from Australia at the previous meeting of the Environment Committee. While not going so far as advocating opposition to Cass' nomination, the Department was hopeful that 'more appropriate' nominations would come forward as Spain and Norway had 'not been the most progressive delegations on the Environment Committee …'. With respect to the chairmanship of the meeting, the DFA felt, and 'in keeping with our views on the global nature of the Organisation we would prefer that the Chairman not come from an EEC country' (NAA, 1973).

However, a Heads of Delegation Meeting held on 8 October agreed unanimously to a Norwegian chair, Mrs Gro Harlem Brundtland (later to chair the production of the eponymous report on sustainable development and Secretary-General of the WHO) and Spanish and Japanese vice chairs, but the Netherlands (also a candidate) unexpectedly and for unknown reasons withdrew its candidacy. At Australia's request, the Secretariat then canvassed an Australian nomination for vice chair and then informed Australia that all delegations were happy to accept an Australian candidacy (NAA, 1973).

Environment Minister Moss Cass attended the first Ministerial on 13–14 November 1974, and released to the *Canberra Times* a copy of the speech he gave (*Canberra Times*, 15 November 1974), which echoed the neo-Malthusian themes popularised by the likes of Paul Ehrlich and the Club of Rome and raised issues with other portfolios that had not been consulted. It was reported that Cass said at the Paris Ministerial 'that the industrial-consumer society could not go on for ever, but must be replaced by a steady-state society with birth control'. He continued: 'The poor nations cannot expect continuing help to overcome food shortages if they continue to permit and even encourage population growth making them still more dependent on the surplus food producers.'

Cass' speech sent the government into damage control, and a cable was immediately sent to Foreign Affairs in Canberra (NAA, 1973). This pointed out that the speech traversed the Club of Rome, Kenneth Boulding's critique of the 'cowboy economy', and Malthus, stating 'Malthus was aware of it in 1798 and will be proved correct in everything but timing unless Man changes course.' A handwritten annotation on a copy of the cable reads: '*Mr Rodgers*!! I look forward to comparing this with the statements of other Ministers' (NAA, 1973).

A full copy of the speech was not provided to Foreign Affairs until 20 November, but a 'Possible Parliamentary Question' response was prepared for the Minister of Foreign Affairs on 18 November 1974. Cass' full speech contained text that would have been alarming to the developing world, which found the neo-Malthusianism and 'lifeboat ethics' being espoused by some in the global North at this time to be deeply concerning (Lucas and Ogletree, 1976). Cass stated in the copy of the speech provided to DFA:

> The rich nations are ignorant and foolish because of their continuing excessive resource consumption per capita and will be evil if they pursue their general intention to increase this still further. The poor nations are ignorant and foolish because, whilst often depending on the rich to save them from the extremes of famine, they fail to take firm enough action to control their population growth, which aggravates their food shortages despite valiant efforts to grow more food themselves. (NAA, 1973)

Cass, as noted above, promoted the cause of Zero Population Growth:

> The poor nations cannot expect continuing help to overcome food shortages if they continue to permit and even encourage population growth making them still more dependent on the surplus food producers.

To which he added:

> The rich must continue to help feed the poor and indeed must deprive themselves in order to increase that support – not because they are generous, but because they have no other choice. (NAA, 1973)

Similar rhetoric for the North played an important part in raising the concern of the South, leading ultimately to the emergence of the agenda of 'sustainable development'.

A review of Australia's participation in the OECD was conducted in 1981 (NAA, 1981). Australia at this stage had not been subjected to peer review by EPOC and its participation was found to be 'selective and focused', not having participated in activities on issues such as water quality and waste management, except in relation to priority topics such as hazardous chemicals. Hazardous chemicals were seen as of high priority for Australia because of possible future legislation in this area. Council was at this time considering draft Decisions and Recommendations on hazardous chemicals for the May 1981 MCM, although difficulties arose in arriving at an Australian position on the draft Council Act because of the time required to obtain agreement from the states, making it likely that Australia would to have to abstain. The Review noted federalism was an ongoing issue for Australia in EPOC: 'While State Governments bear almost all of the costs of environmental participation, the Government is involved in the control of coordination and international aspects.'

Perhaps indicating an increase in interest from the time immediately after accession, the Review noted Australia had 'generally been at the forefront in OECD environment activities'. Australia was relatively well represented in the Environment Directorate at this time, with one officer classified at A5, one at A4, one A3, and one consultant. The principal Secretariat officer (A5) was Dr Crawford, formerly Australian Counsellor (Scientific and Environmental Affairs). The Review recorded that the most recent Environment Committee meeting (1–3 April 1981) had elected Dr D.F. McMichael, Secretary of the Department of Home Affairs and Environment as chairman for a two year term, noting 'It is to be expected that Dr McMichael's success in obtaining this prestigious position will result in considerable benefits for Australia' (NAA, 1981).

THE FEDERAL FACTOR

From the outset, the Commonwealth needed to consult with the states on environmental matters, as was perhaps to be expected, since the expansion of the *compétence* of the Commonwealth regarding environmental policy did not begin until the mid-1980s. For example, the concept of the Polluter Pays Principle was put before states through the Standing Committee of the Australian Environmental Council meeting on 7 April 1972.

An OECD Decision on PCBs in 1973 had both federal and inter-agency implications, as the actions necessary to give effect to the Decision could only be undertaken by the states. The Commonwealth again, earlier, had consulted the Australian Environment Council (NAA, 1972a). The formal position was that the Australian participation in the Decision was 'subject to implementation'. This was not seen as constituting sufficient grounds for entering a reservation, and it was assumed that other member states would find themselves in a similar position, but it was thought wise to have the Australian position 'recorded by a suitable entry in the minutes of the Council Meeting at which the Decision is taken'.

Sir Ronald Walker then drafted a short statement at the Council Meeting on 13 February:

In agreeing to participate in this Council Decision the Australian Government intends to take appropriate measures within its jurisdiction to give effect to the Decision as far as practicable.

[Under] the Australian Constitution, some aspects of the implementation of this Decision are not within the jurisdiction of the Federal Government, but are matters for the individual State Government.

The Federal Government will take up such matters with the State Governments through the Australian Environment Council which is a joint Federal–State body. No difficulties in State implementation of appropriate measures are anticipated. (NAA, 1972a)

Similar sensitivities in intergovernmental relations arose in areas of predominantly state jurisdiction, such as education (see Chapter 11). But environment matters were additionally complicated by the fact that the area was a fresh concern to governments, later raising issues that were to cause the High Court to redefine the Constitution, but with most environment agencies being established only from about 1969 onwards, as was reflected in a file note for Philip Flood on the PCB issue:

Until the advent of Environment departments all environmental style matters were dealt with principally by health departments (exceptions include water conservation which was usually an irrigation style department).

Health departments (Commonwealth and state) are currently engaged in a series of running battles on jurisdiction questions.

The principal combatants in the Commonwealth field is Health Department and the NHMRC – the latter having a number of environmental subcommittees, Dr Mitchell of Health in Canberra is involved as convenor/secretary of those dealing with, *inter alia*, PCB's and non-ionic (i.e. biodegradable soft) detergents.

The 'Warning on PCB's' published in the Financial Review today is one of the first public utterances by NHMRC on a matter in dispute. The warning is very similar to the OECD PCB recommendations just completed by OECD's Environment Committee. (NAA, 1972a)

The inter-agency rivalry Flood noted was so entrenched it proved impossible to get a satisfactory compromise draft reply to a cable from the Delegation from either Health or Science. The nature of the turf war was captured in a Note on the issue of non-ionic synthetic detergents:

While Environment & Conservation have an overriding interest in non-ionic synthetic detergents the fight as to who should test the samples is between Mitchell (Health) and Peters (Science).

> I would suggest that the matter be taken up at a senior level – perhaps Mr Rogers or even Mr Flood.* I have ensured in my contact with both Science & Health that F.A.'s opinion has been kept out of the argument.
>
> *A margin note (by Mr Simon) noted: 'Mr Flood does not want to get involved'. (NAA, 1972a)

Health and the National Health and Medical Research Council (NHMRC) apparently wanted Shell Chemical (Australia) and ICI of Australia to be the two reference laboratories for the development work adopted by NHMRC. The Australian detergents industry had entered into a voluntary agreement with Commonwealth and state Health ministers to cease using biologically hard surfactants by 31 December 1971, and administration had been entrusted to the NHMRC.

There was even a dispute over the test methods to be used. NHMRC had chosen its own (German) Husman Test, which had been adopted as a confirmatory test by the OECD. An alternative proposal was for the Commonwealth Analyst to use the Wickbold Analytic Procedure. The Health Department appealed to the Department of Prime Minister and Cabinet on 26 January, recommending ICI and Shell's Industrial Chemicals Laboratory in Geelong as reference laboratories 'as the most competent in Australia' (NAA, 1972a). PM&C simply referred this to Foreign Affairs, and provided a briefing note to them, on which the recipient wrote: 'I'm not sure what we're supposed to do with this, although Health seem to have backed down somewhat from their original intention of Min. to Min. correspondence' (NAA, 1972a).

This demarcation problem was not unusual for this time, because many environmental issues in many jurisdictions globally had been within the jurisdiction of health departments as matters of public health. As the environment issue expanded from the late 1960s, new agencies were established to deal with environmental regulation. The matter of biodegradable detergents (and to a lesser extent PCBs) were primarily matters of pollution of the natural environment rather than simply public health, and jusrisdiction over natural resources at this stage lay very much with state governments. In the end, DFAT cabled the Ambassador with the message that these governments would ultimately be responsible for implementing these matters (NAA, 1972a).

The complexities of the federal nature of the Australian state were again demonstrated by the need to abstain from the first OECD Council Act dealing with trade in hazardous waste considered in 1983 and adopted by Council on 1 February 1984 (OECD, 1984). Australia was the only member country to abstain from the Council resolution on control of hazardous wastes, a move seen as necessary because control of hazardous wastes had been almost exclusively a matter for state governments (NAA, 1983). There had been no nationally accepted definition of hazardous wastes, and no national system (and generally no state systems) for monitoring the generation and movement of wastes. Consequently there needed to be substantial development work and Commonwealth–state consultation and agreement before Australia's abstention could be withdrawn. The Department pursued the matter via the Australian Environment Council's Hazardous Industrial Wastes Working Group on technical aspects, but ultimately there also had to be consultation with the states at the political level. The Ambassador, Mr Argy reported that Australia's 'continuing abstention has been raised informally with him by representatives of other Member countries' (NAA, 1983). The issue was of some practical importance for Australia, which at this time was increasingly exporting intractable chemical wastes to Europe for incineration. The Department saw some value in the OECD measure in increasing its influence over state governments, however, noting that 'the OECD agreement gives the Commonwealth Government some leverage in encouraging the States to be more thorough in the management of wastes' (NAA, 1983). Australia eventually associated itself with the Decision.

BILATERALS AND OTHER ARENAS: WHALING AND CLIMATE CHANGE

Meetings of EPOC at Ministerial level and other meetings attended by ministers offered substantial opportunities for bilateral consultations at the margins of the meetings. When in 1991 Maurice Strong, Secretary-General of the forthcoming UNCED conference in Rio attended the EPOC Ministerial, for example, Minister Ros Kelly sought him out for a side meeting. The Ministerial and a Round Table on Sustainable Development in April 2008 demonstrated both the value and the pitfalls of such 'pull-asides', as they are called. These opportunities were not always confined to other members, but also extended to NGOs, with Greenpeace seeking a meeting with the Minister Peter Garrett, on whaling while he was in Paris for these meetings.

At the time of Garrett's 2008 visit, 22 bilateral meetings were organised for the Minister, including with ministers from non-members engaged through the OECD's programme of 'Enhanced Engagement'. One such bilateral 'pull-aside' with the Chinese gave rise to some considerable embarrassment for the Minister regarding a paper provided to the Chinese minister on the Australian whaling position:

> [W]hich we thought was in Chinese was actually in Japanese; the Chinese delegation was very gracious about it but the Minister was not happy as you can imagine. (DSEWPC, 2008)

The Delegation took responsibility for the 'stuff-up', but understandably wanted to know 'how we came to be carrying a Japanese version of the paper at all …'. It turned out that the document was made available in languages other than English (French, Spanish and Japanese) only on the afternoon of the Minister's departure. 'The Japanese document was included as a contingency, in case the Minister engaged with his Japanese counterpart at some stage during the OECD meeting.' Its purpose was not made clear in writing, and it appears the Minister and his staff therefore provided it to the Chinese minister in ignorance.

Minister Garrett's bilateral programme in the margins of the EPOC Ministerial covered whaling, climate change, biodiversity, coral reef protection, cooperation in the South Pacific and World Heritage issues (DSEWPC, 2008). Ministers were reportedly favourably disposed to Australian proposals to modernise the International Whaling Commission and universally welcomed Australia's increased engagement in international fora. France raised the prospect of a small group of countries, including Australia, working together to 'pilot' UN climate change discussions.

Such direct communication between ministers can help advance mutual understanding of issues at a political level, but it is, of course, not without its risks, not least because officials are not always present and thus are not always aware of what was discussed. An example of this came from a 'substantial pull-aside' between Minister Garrett and Austrian Minister Josef Pröll that the brief shows was scheduled for the Minister for 11am on 29 April 2008. A flurry of emails in June 2008 saw the Austrian Embassy in Canberra seeking from the Environment Department any information on the meeting (DSEWPC, 2008).

The request was made to Kimberley Terrell (Acting Director – International Section, Department of the Environment, Water, Heritage and the Arts) and came from Constance Churchill, an employee in the Austrian Embassy Canberra (and ironically, wife of Ben Churchill, Policy Adviser in the Department). It seemed from the cable that 'nothing substantial' was discussed and, while an offer was made to check with the author of the cable if there was anything more on Austria, although 'there probably isn't as we were really scratching to find any topics for discussion when we did the briefing' (DSEWPC, 2008). However, it was subsequently confirmed by Minister Garrett 'that he raised issues as per the brief, i.e. international Whaling, a quick discussion on climate change, etc' (DSEWPC, 2008).

The OECD has also been a useful venue for airing concerns and developing architecture for wider multilateral action on global environmental problems. As noted above, work on long-range transportation of air pollutants and trade in hazardous waste began in the OECD, and initial concern over the ozone-depleting capabilities of chlorofluorocarbons were first raised there, when the Secretary of the Environment Committee sent to Delegations a copy of a US report, *Fluorocarbons and the Environment* (USCEQ, 1975). This led to these concerns outweighing those over climate change in Australia at the time, and the briefing notes for the 17th Session of EPOC in March 1976 recorded regret that those attending 'the largest conference on climatology yet held in the Southern Hemisphere' in December 1975 'almost completely failed to address themselves to the possibility of anthropogenic changes to the distribution of stratospheric ozone' (DSEWPC, 1976).

Considerable work on climate change was later conducted in the OECD, well before the issue came to public prominence, and Australia often played a significant part in this. This work on climate change was particularly important before the Framework Convention on Climate Change (concluded in 1992) entered into force in 1994, and has taken on renewed importance more recently and the OECD sought to play a role in the period before the key climate change meeting in Paris in December 2015. As the Organisation often takes referrals of issues from forums such as the G8 summit in Helligendamm in 2007 (which referred work on biotechnology to the OECD), so it continues to be both a means of becoming involved in such debates and forums, but can be potentially distracted by the priorities of other forums such as the G8 and EU. The latter was significant in the case of the proposed Council Act on lead (see below), but it has continually been a significant factor in the intersection between environment and trade, especially agricultural trade, and particularly in the Joint Working Party on Agriculture and Environment and Joint Working Party on Trade and Environment.

These examples of attempts to use the OECD as a venue to develop concepts for export have included attempts to import the precautionary principle into the trade regime as a basis for weakening the scientific requirements of measures such as the Sanitary and Phytosanitary Agreement in the WTO, and the development of the concept of multifunctionality by the European Union, as a means of supporting its Common Agriculture Policy in the face of moves to liberalise trade in agriculture.

Australia has been consistent in its concern that environmental reasons might be used to justify trade restrictive actions and, for example, registered 'strong concerns' over the selection of case studies commissioned by the secretary of the Joint Working Party on Trade and

Environment that examined Australia's phytosanitary measures applied to Durian fruit exports from Thailand and the ANZFA food standard on GMO labelling. It considered the relevance of the Durian study to be highly questionable, but for 'strategic purposes' it decided not to try to block development of this paper (DSEWPC, 2002). It was 'however strongly of the view that the GM labelling case study is not within the mandate and should not proceed'. The view was that it 'was not an environmental or food safety measure. It does not and cannot restrict exports from developing countries on that basis'.

Multifunctionality essentially involved subsidies to farmers, rather than to their products, so that they could maintain a more traditional rural landscape and traditional rural society (see, for example, Potter and Burney, 2002). The matter was of particular concern to Australia, which had done much of the work to develop the concept of Producer Subsidy Equivalents as a measure of the level of agricultural subsidy (OECD, 2003). Another issue was that of 'geographical designations' or 'indications', which identify a good as originating in a particular region where a given quality or reputation is essentially attributable to its geographical origin (see Goldberg, 2001).

The challenges of addressing these concerns in a largely Eurocentric OECD were highlighted by Ambassador Ian Forsyth in preparation for the MCM to be held on 29–30 April 2003:

> Some European and other ministers will probably stress social cohesion and sustainable development in their interventions – agendas that are, unfortunately, loaded with protectionist objectives and that are essentially anti-growth rather than pro-growth. There are ongoing attempts to elevate the importance of work on sustainable development in the OECD, much of which is driven by voluntary contributions from European countries. [New Zealand] PM Clark is sympathetic to this focus. In our view much of this work is of dubious quality and value and we are resisting attempts to shift the focus of the OECD from sustainable economic growth, in which its real expertise and mission lies, to the European agendas on sustainable development and social cohesion. (DSEWPC, 2003)

The Ambassador was well aware of the significance developments in the OECD that might have for the wider trade agenda, noting that:

> We are also battling attempts by the same countries to re-instate trade restricting agendas for the Doha Round through the OECD, including on the environment, geographical indicators and multifunctionality (DSEWPC, 2003).

ENVIRONMENTAL PERFORMANCE REVIEWS

The use of the peer review process familiar in other areas of the OECD was rather more slowly to be adopted in EPOC, and the first Environmental Performance Review of Australia did not take place until 1997–98. It was proposed, originally, in 1985 for 1988, at which point five members had been reviewed: Sweden (1973); Japan (1976); New Zealand (1980); Greece (1982); and Yugoslavia (1985). Erick Lykke, head of the Environment Directorate, expressed considerable interest in reviewing Australia (DSEWPC, 1986).

The Secretary of the Department sought approval for a review in 1988, but the proposal ran into opposition from the Department of Finance. Numerous arguments against the idea were advanced: a likely lack of state government involvement; it was 'unlikely to earn kudos for the Government either internationally or within Australia'; it would require considerable staff resources and funding; it was unlikely to provide significant additional leverage for any substantial government action; also, other OECD reviews (Education, Science, Youth) apparently had not been considered to be of major impact or lasting value to these functional areas in Australia; 1988 was already overcrowded with events (such as the Bicentennial) (DSEWPC, 2005). The conclusion was reached:

> [T]hat unless particularly compelling reasons can be advanced for continuing the proposal, either by departmental officers or by the Director of the Environment Committee in Paris, it should go no further.

A review eventually came in November 1997, conducted by the OECD Group on Environmental Performance (GEP) on 19 November 1997. It wrote to the Minister on 4 December outlining outcomes as well as possible strategies to handle the release of the report, scheduled for early April 1998.

The Review included four phases and was broadly similar to those conducted in other policy areas, involving: data gathering; a visit to Australia by an OECD Review Team (Norway, New Zealand, Canada, Germany, plus members of the OECD Environment Directorate) in April/May 1997; consultation with stakeholders (Commonwealth, state and territory governments, industry groups, environment groups and academics); field trips to Queensland, New South Wales, and Victoria. A draft report was then prepared and discussed at the Peer Review Meeting in Paris, attended by a high level delegation led by the Department of Environment, and including five Commonwealth and three state government representatives. As is typical of such reviews, the report made some 52 recommendations for improvement (DSEWPC, 1997).

The next Review was held in 2006, and this time it was planned for there to be up to eight reviewers from the Secretariat and the USA, Austria, United Kingdom and New Zealand. There were three phases in the Review:

1. Pre-review negotiations and provision of material to the OECD (November 2005 to May 2006);
2. Support to Review Team during the in-country visit (July 2006); and
3. Response to draft review prior to finalisation (September 2006 to May 2007).

The Review looked at the 1998 Review and the document *OECD Environmental Strategy for the First Decade of the 21st Century* (OECD, 2000). The meeting of the OECD Working Party on Environmental Policy conducting the EPR of Australia was held on 26–28 June 2007 in Paris (DSEWPC, 2005, 2005a). A high-level delegation of seven attended the meeting, including two from state governments: David Borthwick, Secretary of DEWR (and a former OECD Ambassador); Anthea Tinney, Deputy Secretary of DEWR (and Head of Delegation for the previous Australian EPR in 1998); Kevin O'Keeffe, Assistant Secretary, Communications and International, DEWR.

The briefing document also provided some points to note from previous reviews of other members. Australia had attended for the reviews of Belgium, Switzerland and New Zealand in September 2006 and the following insights were provided for the delegation:

- The proceedings were not officially recorded (which was unusual).
- Frank and honest discussion appears to impress members and suppress further questions on sensitive or political issues.
- Australia should assertively address any attempts by third parties to alter recommendations or text in the Australian EPR that do not reflect the views of Australia (the chairman and Secretariat will side with the reviewed country if there is a disagreement).
- It is useful to attend the peer review the previous day to get a feel for the process. 'Similarly, attending the cocktail event of the previous reviewed country provides an opportunity to network and build relationships with delegates who may be active in Australia's review. (DSEWPC, 2005)

The Australian presentation to the Working Party on Environmental Policy involved showing a slide that underscored some of the challenges for Australia compared to the European members of the OECD: a map of the continent of Europe that fitted inside that of Australia, with room to spare. The very different nature of the Australian continent was something most Europeans simply did not understand and so there was clearly value, too, in having OECD Environment Director Joke Waller-Hunter visit Australia in March 1999. A similar tour was arranged for EU personnel around this time. There were also problems of Eurocentrism with participation in the OECD by environment NGOs being channelled through the European Environmental Bureau (EEB), which had even sought funding support from Australia in November 1998. The EEB is supported financially by the European Commission and 13 member states, and there are Australian concerns about its priorities being those of Europe, rather than Australia.

The differences between Australia and many other (especially European) members were highlighted by a significant issue in the 1990s, a proposal for a Council Act on lead which emerged from the Risk Reduction Program for Existing Chemicals. This also raised issues for the OECD's commitment to open trade and saw Australia isolated initially, but playing an important role in protecting both its interests and principles of trade and environmental policy, and ultimately setting out principles to govern future risk management in the OECD.

THE PROPOSED LEAD COUNCIL ACT

Work on the risks of existing chemicals commenced in the OECD in the 1980s, with the adoption of a Decision-Recommendation (OECD, 1987) turning the attention of the Chemicals Program from new to existing chemicals, largely because the US saw the focus on new chemicals as harming the competitiveness of its industry compared with Europe, which had greater reliance on existing chemicals (Schweitzer, 1991). After a Workshop in Ottawa in November 1987, an Initial Action Plan on existing chemicals was developed, including 12 chemicals, of which only zinc and tributyl tin were metals. When the OECD Risk Reduction Program started in 1990 however, three of the five 'pilot substances' were metals (lead, cadmium, mercury) while two were synthetic chemicals (methylene chloride, a paint stripper, and brominated flame retardants, both readily substitutable) of little value to the chemical industry, perhaps reflecting the success of the chemicals industry in steering the agenda to chemicals away from substances that were a threat to its interests (OECD, 1990).

The Council Act establishing the Risk Reduction Program called primarily for action at the domestic level, but the Program focused on achieving harmonised international action that would have had the effect of exporting regulatory standards already current in Sweden (semi-lead crystal) and the US (plumbing and canning) that would have advantaged their industries (Vogel, 1997). Not surprisingly, this was viewed by the mining industry in Australia as a threat to its interests. Many ores were silver-lead-zinc, and restrictions on lead would affect the viability of mines with these co-products. Two of the largest companies, MIM and Pasminco, were politically active from an early stage, preferring regulation of lead exposure to be a national, rather than an international matter. At an early stage the industry communicated to the Australian government the implications of any restrictions on lead, which MIM stated would also eliminate the production of zinc and silver and also render their copper production uneconomical (DSEWPC, 1991). On 15 April 1991 Rob Hulls, Federal Member for Kennedy, requested a meeting with Environment Minister Ros Kelly on behalf of Ken Dredge, General Manager (Lead and Zinc) MIM, who had 'expressed concern over recent OECD initiatives to "ban" lead production and would like to discuss the same' (DSEWPC, 1991).

Industry considered that the risks of lead were not transboundary, and therefore did not require international action. The government also consulted the Lead Education and Abatement Design Group (LEAD), a group that had emerged in 1991 that was seeking bans on lead, and a local group, Lakes Environmental Action Defence (No-LEAD) in Newcastle. These groups had obtained a copy of the second draft of the lead monograph (dated 21 May 1991) and, inter alia, were pleased that it indicated that 'an international co-operative strategy could be developed, one similar to the Montreal Protocol for CFCs' (LEAD, 1993). Minister Kelly convened a day-long Round Table Conference on Lead in Petrol on 29 July 1993, and, while Australia was eventually to move to a lower standard for lead exposure and a phasing out of leaded gasoline, the industry view prevailed in the formulation of the Australian position, that risk management at the international level should involve harmonisation of technical issues such as procedures, tests, the types of data needed and the manner of their collection, while leaving the *level* of acceptable risk to be set by sovereign states (Stonehouse and Mumford, 1994: 68; Repetto, 1994: 40).

The production of a monograph on lead as part of the Risk Reduction Program (OECD, 1993) revealed a declining incidence of environmental lead in members and provided little rationale for international regulatory action, but the OECD pressed on with a proposal for a Council Act (Dal

Bon, 2001: 138). At a workshop held in Sweden in 1992, the chairman's report had stated that, for a chemical to be selected for risk reduction activities, at least two OECD Member countries should be in agreement on the need for co-operative risk reduction activities, and that, should a significant number (25 per cent) of OECD Members wish to pursue a co-operative programme, this would trigger participation of the Secretariat subject to approval by the Joint Meeting. To ensure that the work was adequately resourced, at least three countries were required to be willing to contribute resources to support the project (see Dal Bon, 2001).

This relatively low threshold allowed a few members to push all others towards a Council Act. The minutes of an Interdepartmental Working Group on OECD Lead Risk Reduction noted that 'the move towards development of an OECD Council Act on lead was being driven by the OECD Secretariat, USA, Nordic Countries and Netherlands' (DSEWPC, 1994a). Australia was supported by Canada, the UK, Japan, France, and Austria, although it was considered Japan was unlikely to take a strong stand on lead, as cadmium and mercury were of more concern there. Despite this support for Australia, the European Commission favoured a Council Act and public support for Australia was rather muted, allowing the Secretariat to try to paint it as totally isolated on the issue. The Australian Delegation reported that when they raised with the Chemicals Program why the OECD should be involved in setting international standards as proposed in the Council Act, the response 'delivered most forcefully' was that 'the OECD should have a role because 24 of its 25 Member Countries wanted it to have a role' (DSEWPC, 1994).

The OECD position at this stage largely reflected the views of the USA. Domestic regulation in the USA had already addressed major exposures such as lead in gasoline and paint and lead solder in the canning industry. A Council Act 'exporting' US standards would have assisted US producers by exposing international competitors to those that US industry had already met, and it had to resort to justifications for international action such as the risks from lead leaching out of crystal glassware (Barbee and Constantine, 1994; Graziano and Blum, 1991). Aside from being a decidedly 'First World' problem, the risks were rather trivial and easily addressed by an initial washing of new glasses and decanters (DSEWPC, 1994).

Australia lobbied other governments (especially economic agencies), through bilateral missions emphasising that a workshop in Toronto in 1994 concluded that lead risks were best dealt with by current domestic, bilateral and regional agreements compatible with multilateral trade rules. Of 10 products and uses examined, only three were identified as needing some international action: lead shot, fishing sinkers and leaded petrol. It added that it concluded that there was no evidence to justify a Council Act, and that it had highlighted the 'protectionist motivations behind US and Nordic support for an Act …' (DSEWPC, 1994a).

Australia was nevertheless concerned that the outcomes of the Toronto Workshop were not being accepted, nor reported accurately. A cable from Canberra to the OECD Delegation stated:

> Notwithstanding the findings, the Nordics, the US and the Workshop Chair (Buccini, Environment Canada), maintained the need for OECD-wide action, including a Council Act, to reduce lead risk. The 'Working Group on the Development of a Council Act Lead Risk Reduction', which met at the end of the Workshop, also re-wrote some of the findings of the Workshop sessions. We are also concerned that OECD Secretariat documentation does not accurately reflect what took place at the Working Group meeting. (DSEWPC, 1994a)

After the Toronto workshop, Canada, the United Kingdom, the US and Australia advanced proposals for OECD action on lead. The US proposed a Council Act involving a prescriptive (and binding) Decision, the UK a relatively non-prescriptive Recommendation, Canada a Voluntary Action Plan and Australia a Ministerial Declaration. A fear was expressed that the US, the Nordics and Canada might 'sideline' the workshop's findings at future meetings. As the cable reported, Canada initially neither supported nor opposed a Council Act because of divisions between Environment Canada (which supported the proposal) and Natural Resources Canada (which was opposed to it) (DSEWPC, 1994a). Natural Resources Canada had informed Australia privately that they opposed the proposal because it would lower lead prices and there would thus be a lower percentage of lead recycled. They were opposed to a 'motherhood' Act in the form of a non-binding Recommendation 'as the issue might end up in the UN and become "another Basel"'.

A fortnight later, however, the Ottawa mission cabled news from Gary Nash, Secretary-General of the International Council on Metals and the Environment concerning a Canadian proposal for a voluntary lead Risk Reduction Program that would be definitely supported by Australia, Turkey, and New Zealand and likely by Spain, Mexico, Italy, Ireland, Japan, Switzerland and Germany (DSEWPC, 1994). Opposition was expected from the Nordics, US, Belgium, the Netherlands and the UK.

Arenas outside the OECD also proved useful. At a meeting in Dortmund of a working group developing guidance on risk reduction and risk-benefit analysis in connection with the EC Regulation on existing chemicals, useful intelligence relating to the Council Act was obtained and passed by industry contacts through to the Commonwealth EPA (CEPA). The Lead Industry Association lobbied the US EPA, and sought assurances that the US would vote against a Council Act inconsistent with or contrary to US laws and regulations. Canberra asked all delegations in member countries to test host government views on the Council Act and ask them to oppose it in the likelihood it would be discussed at the margins of the Intergovernmental Forum on Chemical Safety (IFCS) in Belgium 20–23 March 1995 (DSEWPC, 1994).

The IFCS meeting also provided the opportunity for meetings on the Council Act, and a meeting to discuss the US/EC proposal was scheduled for Friday 24 March, with the Heads of Delegations of the members of the Joint Meeting of the Chemicals Group and Management Committee invited. The Secretariat had a preference for the proposed Canadian Voluntary Action Programme to be merged into the Council Act, and used logistical factors to try to achieve this end, raising problems in scheduling a meeting of an Action Programme Working Group around the same time because of the travel commitments of key participants from 25 March onwards. It was therefore considered whether the meetings should be combined on 24 March, but the room available only held 35. It was suggested that a possible combined meeting, if it took place, would not merely consider the two proposals, but be used to explore whether the two approaches could be merged into a single programme. Significantly, BIAC was not invited to the meeting (DSEWPC, 1994).

The European Commission, rather than its member states, was taking the lead in pushing for the Council Act, and was not discouraging its members from attending the 24 March meeting, which it saw as being primarily for the benefit of the non-EU OECD members, and an opportunity to try to change the views of Canada and Australia. It came as something of a surprise to the Commission that some of its members, such as Italy (which was strongly supportive of the Canada/industry initiative), were not supportive of the Council Act.

Australia and Canada eventually pre-empted the US/EU proposal for a Council Act by the development of an alternative proposal for an industry Voluntary Action Plan developed by industry (ICME) and Canada, and an Australian proposal for a Ministerial Declaration. By June 1995, Australia was examining the rules of the OECD, including those governing Ministerial Declarations (the first of which had been made in December 1974) and sounding out other Members on the issue.

The UK was 'not attracted' to a Council Act, but could 'live with' one that imposed no requirements additional to existing EU Directives. They could not support the US/European Commission proposal as currently drafted but were 'not inclined to take the running in opposing it' (DSEWPC, 1994). Mexico was also opposed to the proposal after Australia had lobbied it directly as well as through Chile and Peru. New Zealand chose not to be represented at the key meeting in Paris, because the Ministry for the Environment was pushing for a review of that country's opposition to a Council Act and had concerns over the action plan/industry initiative approach. Its Ministry of Foreign Affairs and Trade was 'on side' but decided not to attend so as not to draw domestic attention to the issue (DSEWPC, 1994).

The 23rd Joint Meeting of the Chemicals Group and Management Committee 21–23 June 1995 considered both the US/EU proposal for a Council Act and the Canadian Action Plan incorporating a Voluntary Industry Program funded by industry. There were three significant outcomes from an Australian perspective, recorded subsequently (DSEWPC, 1994a):

> (A) The U.S./E.U. failed to force agreement to a prescriptive OECD Council Act on Lead Risk Reduction. Australian opposition to the Act was based on the belief that the Act would deliver few if any practical environmental outcomes, and it would set an undesirable precedent for future risk management approaches.
>
> (B) The issue was not resolved at Joint Meeting but agreed that consideration be given to a revised Council Act and the new option of a Ministerial Declaration proposed by Australia. If consensus could not be reached in the short term the OECD would abandon attempts to develop an instrument for lead risk reduction. (Although the U.S. was initially giving serious consideration to the MD it was an out of hand rejection of this proposal by the E.C. which prevented an early resolution of the lead issue at the Joint Meeting.)
>
> (C) The most significant result was the acceptance by the Joint Meeting that the process followed by the OECD Risk Reduction Program was heavily flawed. This outcome recognised that a chemical by chemical approach to risk reduction is not effective. The U.S. agreed to join Australia in co-sponsoring a review of this program. To this end an ad hoc working group was to meet in Rome from 6–7 November 1995.

An Australian discussion paper, 'Principles for Future International Risk Reduction', was presented at the Joint Meeting, having been developed after consultations with the key Australian departments, the states, industry and environment NGOs. At a meeting of the Bureau after the Joint Meeting the leader of the US delegation (Dr Lynn Goldman) proposed (and Australia agreed) that unless there was consensus on a single proposal for consideration by the extended Bureau Meeting in October, the US would abandon the issue. 'She indicated at a restricted meeting that the U.S. could reluctantly accept a Ministerial Declaration so that there would at least be something to show for all the effort' (DSEWPC, 1994).

Goldman had argued that only a Council Act would 'send the right signals' and attempted to have the Secretariat confirm that a Ministerial Declaration would not involve binding commitments. 'The Legal Directorate responded that on the contrary Ministerial Declarations "Constitute an important means of expressing the political will of governments of member countries, and to preserve their value they are limited to major statements on important topics"' (DSEWPC, 1994).

Italy not only continued to oppose the revised Council Act, viewing the revisions as a 'proactive tactic', but rejected and resented the European Commission's claims of the unanimous support of EU member states, being especially displeased with the issuing of a joint EC/US press release to this effect on 28 June after the Joint Meeting (DSEWPC, 1995). Italy was not alone in failing to support the EU consensus. Austria, for example, thought the draft Act was poorly drafted, but was not prepared to break EU solidarity on an issue of little domestic importance (DSEWPC, 1994). Similarly, Spain had no enthusiasm for the measure, but was prepared to 'go along with the EU line for reasons of EU solidarity'. Belgium considered that a Council Act and a Voluntary Action Programme were not mutually exclusive. The Nordic members remained resolute in their support for a Council Act embodying the Swedish 'substitution principle', with a statement to that effect having been made on 15 November 1994 by the Nordic Council of Ministers, Ministers for the Environment. The UK could live with either the Council Act or the Ministerial Declaration, with the environment ministry supporting the former but the Department of Trade and Industry not inclined to support it.

The US began to waver a little, and was aware the European Commission had 'heavied' a number of member states in order to claim that they had full backing on the proposal (DSEWPC, 1994). Nevertheless, it still preferred a Council Act, and considered the revised draft now reflected the 'concerns expressed by Australia'. Australia indicated to the US that while it was prepared to look seriously at a Council Act, US/EU 'pressure to force an agreement to an unacceptable prescriptive instrument may result in no OECD consensus on lead'. New Zealand remained opposed, while Mexico considered the Council Act should be a Recommendation not a Decision.

Australia produced a proposal for a Ministerial Declaration on Lead on 20 July 1995, and a revised EC/US draft proposal for a Council Act was provided on 1 August, attempting to incorporate many of the elements of the Australian proposed Declaration in the form of a Council Act but subsequent discussions between the core countries demonstrated there was still considerable distance between the two approaches. A further US draft was produced on 20 August, but the tide was by now running in favour of the Australian and Canadian position.

An Australian proposal (developed in consultation with Canada) for a Ministerial Declaration was faxed to the Heads of Delegations of participants in the Joint Meeting on 21 July 1995. The fax noted both Australian support for the Canadian Action Plan still stood and a US acknowledgment that there would be no outcome if there was no consensus at the meeting in February. But it also took issue with what seemed to be signs that consideration of options other than a Council Act was being foreclosed:

> While the process agreed by the Bureau envisaged limited consultation to core countries in the first instance, I note that copies of the revised EC/US proposal have been circulated more widely. There was also agreement that there be no public comment on the outcome of the meeting. Subsequently, under pressure from proponents of the Council Act I agreed to a brief reference to lead in the communiqué. It was therefore with some disquiet that I learned of the US/EC joint press statement of 28 June. (DSEWPC, 1994)

The fax also expressed disappointment that the US/EC press statement and a subsequent letter 'appear to extinguish any hope of proper consideration of anything but the preferred U.S./E.C. position, although a recent conversation with Lynn Goldman suggests the door has not been entirely closed'.

The *New Scientist* reported on the blocking of the Council Act in July 1995 by Australia and Canada, and quoted Ellen Silbergeld as saying that 'If the OECD can't take action on lead then it is unlikely it can take action on anything.' Silbergeld clearly did not appreciate the point that exposures could be best dealt with by domestic regulation, and ironically the same page of *New Scientist* reported that the European Commission had decided upon a relaxation of regulation at that level, reporting a loophole in a new draft Directive from the European Commission which at the last minute exempted water companies and governments from meeting a tightened standard for excessive lead levels in tap water because of the costs of removing lead plumbing (Pearce, 1995; Patel, 1995).

An ABARE analysis estimated that the negative economic impact of the proposed Council Act on lead on Australian industry would be in the range of $170–300m per annum. There was some reluctance in DFAT to use the ABARE analysis, on the grounds that it drew attention to

Australia's domestic economic interests and might detract from its principled arguments based on trade agreements and sound environmental policy. The concern perhaps summed up the enthusiasm of some for international action: 'Even if it is not noticed overseas, it is likely to stimulate adverse comment from NGO's in Australia which generally see international treaties as a preferred indicator of government concern and commitment' (DSEWPC, 1994).

There was a suggestion that the US and EC might try taking an earlier, more prescriptive text directly to EPOC, circumventing the Joint Meeting. A reference to joint US/EU initiatives on lead in the 'New Transatlantic Agenda' signed by US President Clinton and EU President Santer in Madrid on 3 December 1995 was not reassuring, but 'intensive discussions at a special meeting on 6 and 7 February … resulted in broad consensus on a text for a Ministerial Declaration on lead' (DSEWPC, 1994).

A compromise text for a Declaration was then drafted at the margins of the 24th Joint Meeting on 7–9 February and discussed, along with the Council Act proposal, at a Steering Groups meeting on 15 February. It was then accepted at the Meeting of Environment Ministers on 19–20 February. Both the US and EC delegations stated they would prefer a Council Act, but saw the consensus text as a good outcome that they would recommend to their governments. The mood at the meeting was reported to be one of relief (DSEWPC, 1994).

The experience with lead gave rise to the development of a set of draft principles for future international risk reduction approaches. These were developed in a Workshop in Rome in November 1995 sponsored by Australia, Italy, Mexico, Turkey and the US, the purpose of which was to:

- Evaluate current OECD RRP for Existing Chemicals;
- Develop a proposal (or proposals) for principles for a revised RRP, based on the Australian and OECD Secretariat discussion papers;
- Develop a proposal for a voluntary risk reduction framework to be conducted jointly with industry groups;
- Develop alternatives to the 'chemical by chemical' approach to risk reduction; and
- Propose to the February 1996 Joint Meeting new directions for the OECD Risk Reduction Programme. (DSEWPC, 1994)

After further work at a subsequent Workshop in September 1996, what became known as the 'Rome Principles' were adopted after a major role was played by Australia in ensuring risk management work in the OECD would be consistent with its commitment to an open trading system.

Somewhat distrustful of the Secretariat after previous summary records did not accord in all respects with Australian recollections of meetings, Australia produced many key papers which the delegation kept on their laptop, revising them as the meeting wished, but maintaining close control of the revisions.[2] Despite daily caucusing by the European Commission, Australia received considerable support at the margins of these meetings from some EU members, concerned at the use of the OECD by Nordic members to influence EU policies at a time when Sweden had recently acceded to the EU and was undergoing a five-year period of harmonisation of policies. (Some thought there was rather too much adjustment of EU standards to Swedish approaches, rather than vice versa.)

The Rome Workshop led to the establishment of a generic approach to risk management in the OECD and the establishment of an Advisory Group on Risk Management. Assisted by the real budget cuts imposed on the Organisation after 1995, this effectively put an end to ambitions by other members to use the OECD as a forum to develop restrictive regulations for possible export to other arenas, such as the EU or the UN. As an indicative measure, only three Council Acts on chemicals have been adopted by the OECD since the adoption of the Ministerial Declaration.

CONCLUSION

Australia was initially a somewhat unenthusiastic participant in environment matters in the OECD, although the enthusiasm of Whitlam's minister, Moss Cass, went rather too far and led to the activation of damage control. The limited role for the Commonwealth in environmental policy at the time of accession was one reason for this, with the need for consultation with the states often leading to Australian hesitancy at the OECD 'table', although as Commonwealth jurisdiction increased this issue abated in importance. While there was still little enthusiasm for an OECD environmental policy review in 1988, there was growing, if selective, interest in the work of the Environmental Policy Committee.

Participation grew and offered opportunities, not just in the OECD, but through 'pull aside' meetings with Members and non-members alike, and not just in the environmental policy domain, but also on environmental policy issues that had the potential to impact in areas of interest to Australia such as agricultural trade. The proposed development of a Council Act on lead threatened Australia's interests and promised to have ramifications in other arenas, prompting it to play an active role, not just in a defensive matter, but also by playing a positive role in developing broader principles for risk management that would have importance in other areas of risk management in the OECD and beyond.

NOTES

1. Department of the Environment, Aborigines and the Arts (May 1971 to December 1972); Department of Environment and Conservation (December 1972 to April 1975); Department of the Environment (April 1975 to December 1975); Department of Employment and Industrial Relations (December 1975 to December 1978); Department of Science and the Environment (December 1978 to November 1980); Department of Home Affairs and Environment (November 1980 to December 1984); Department of Arts, Heritage and Environment (December 1984 to July 1987); Department of the Arts, Sport, the Environment, Tourism and Territories (July 1987 to December 1991); Department of the Arts, Sport, the Environment and Territories (December 1991 to March 1993); Department of the Environment, Sport and Territories (March 1993 to October 1997); Department of the Environment (October 1997 to October 1998); Department of the Environment and Heritage (October 1998 to December 2007); Department of the Environment and Water Resources (January to December 2007); Department of the Environment, Water, Heritage and the Arts (December 2007 to September 2010); Department of Sustainability, Environment, Water, Population and Communities (September 2010 to September 2013); Department of the Environment (September 2013–). Any reference to 'the Department' refers to the entity at the time. References to files are to the Department of Sustainability, Environment, Water, Population and Communities (DSEWPC), which was the legal entity that granted access to them.
2. One of the present authors (Kellow) was a member of the Australian delegation to both Rome Workshops.

BIBLIOGRAPHY

Barbee, S. and Constantine, L. 1994. 'Release of Lead from Crystal Decanters Under Conditions of Normal Use', *Food and Chemical Toxicology*, 32(3): 285–288.

Canberra Times 15 November 1974.

Dal Bon, K. 2001. 'Reducing Chemical Risks: OECD and Lead' in David Robertson and Aynsley Kellow (eds), *Globalization and the Environment: Risk Assessment and the WTO*, Cheltenham, UK and Northampton, MA, USA: Edward Elgar Publishing, pp. 135–151.

DSEWPC 1976. OECD ENV Committee 17th Session March 1976 File 76/1285.

DSEWPC 1986. Proposed EC Review of Australia 1988 (Briefing Note for EPOC) File 86/00305-01 National and International Relations Section – OECD – 42nd Environment Committee Meeting 28–30 April 1986.

DSEWPC 1991. Chemicals Assessment Section – Organisation for Economic Co-operation and Development (OECD) – Cooperative Risk Reduction Activities Directed at Chemicals of Current Concern – Lead. 91/00996.

DSEWPC 1994. Commonwealth Environmental Protection Agency (CEPA) – Lead Abatement Section – Organisation for Economic Co-operation and

Development (OECD) – Cooperative Risk Reduction Activities Directed At Chemicals of Current Concern – Lead. 94/02015.

DSEWPC 1994a. Commonwealth Environmental Protection Agency (CEPA) – Organisation for Economic Co-operation and Development (OECD) Lead Workshop – Toronto – September 1994 – Briefing. 94/03945.

DSEWPC 1994b. Cable CBR to Delegations 14 October 1994 OECD: Proposed Council Act on Lead: Toronto Workshop, File 94/03945 Commonwealth Environmental Protection Agency (CEPA) – Organisation for Economic Co-operation and Development (OECD) Lead Workshop – Toronto – September 1994 – Briefing.

DSEWPC 1995. Cable Rome to CBR 12 July 1995 OECD Risk Reduction: Italy, File 95/06345 EPA – ESB – EXE – Organisation for Economic Co-operation and Development (OECD) Risk Reduction – Rome – November 1995.

DSEWPC 1997. EPC – ILC – IGU – Organisation for Economic Co-operation and Development (OECD) Environment Performance Review of Australia 1997 97/04224.

DSEWPC 2002. CBR TO PAR CABLE 6 June 2002 RR Bangkok/Brussels/Geneva WTO/NZMFAT/Ottawa/Tokyo/Wellington OECD: Joint Working Party on Trade and Environment File 2002/07394 International Relations – Liaison – Organisation for Economic Co-operation and Development (OECD) – Joint Working Party on Trade and Environment.

DSEWPC 2003. International Relations – Liaison – Organisation for Economic Co-operation and Development (OECD) – Joint Working Party on Trade and Environment. 2003/09595.

DSEWPC 2005. Environment Division – Environmental Studies Branch – OECD Review of Australia's Environmental Policies. 85/00563.

DSEWPC 2005a. International Relations – Advice – International Liaison – Organisation for Economic Co-operation and Development (OECD) Environment Performance Review of Australia 2005/2006. 2005/06743.

DSEWPC 2008. Department of Sustainability, Environment, Water, Population and Communities. International Relations – Committees – OECD – Meetings – Organisation for Economic Co-operation and Development – Environment Policy Committee (EPOC) – Meeting at Ministerial Level – 28–29 April 2008. File 2008/14227.

Goldberg, S. 2001. 'Who Will Raise the White Flag – The Battle between the United States and the European Union over the Protection of Geographical Indications', *University of Pennsylvania Journal of International Economic Law*, 22(1): 107–151.

Graziano, J. and Blum, C. 1991. 'Lead exposure from lead crystal', *The Lancet*, 337(8734): 141–142.

Kellow, A. 1999. *International Toxic Risk Management: Ideals, Interests and Implementation*, Cambridge: Cambridge University Press.

LEAD 1993. LEAD Action News 1(2), accessed 5 January 2015 at www.lead.org.au/lanv1n2/lanv1n2-9.html.

LEAD 2000. LEAD Action News 7(4), accessed 5 January 2015 at www.lead.org.au/lanv7n4/L74-23.html.

Long, B.L. (ed.) 2000. *International Environmental Issues and the OECD 1950–2000: An Historical Perspective*, Paris: OECD Publishing.

Lucas, G. and Ogletree, T. (eds) 1976. *Lifeboat Ethics: The Moral Dilemmas of World Hunger*, New York: Harper & Row.
NAA 1971. Memo to Secretary, Department of Foreign Affairs from Ronald Walker, Ambassador. 18 October 1971, re Environment Committee Meeting 29 September – 1 October. A1838 724/4/20 Part 2 Organisation for Economic Co-operation and Development – Study Group on the Environment. 1971 – 556681.
NAA 1972. A1838 724/4/20 Part 4 Organisation for Economic Co-operation and Development – Study Group on the Environment – 1972 – 556687.
NAA 1972a. A1838 724/4/17 Part 9 Organisation for Economic Co-operation and Development – Environment Committee, 1972–1973, 556563.
NAA 1973. A1838 724/4/17/6 Part 1 Organisation for Economic Co-operation and Development – Meeting of Environment Committee at Ministerial level 1973–1975 – 556585.
NAA 1974. Delegation to Canberra. A1838, 724/4/17 Part 12 Organisation for Economic Co-operation and Development – Environment Committee 1974–1975, 55657.
NAA 1981. A6343 B1981/162 Organisation for Economic Co-operation and Development – Review of Australian Participation – June 1981. 5834712.
NAA 1983. A5343/18 82/309 Part 2 National and International Relations Section – OECD – Australian Representation.
OECD 1970. Resolution of the Council of 22 July 1970, Establishing an Environment Committee [C(70)135].
OECD 1972. Guiding Principles concerning International Economic Aspects of Environmental Policies [C(72)128].
OECD 1984. Decision-Recommendation of the Council on Transfrontier Movements of Hazardous Waste 1 February 1984 [C(83)180/Final].
OECD 1987. Decision-Recommendation on the Systematic Investigation of Existing Chemicals [C(87)90/Final].
OECD 1990. Decision-Recommendation on the Co-operative Investigation and Risk Reduction of Existing Chemicals [C(90)163/Final].
OECD 1990a. Decision-Recommendation on the Systematic Investigation of Existing Chemicals [C(87)90/Final].
OECD 1993. Lead: Background and National Experience With Reducing Risk (Risk Reduction Monograph No.1) [OCDE/GD(93)67].
OECD 1996. Resolution of the Council Concerning the Declaration on Risk Reduction for Lead [C(96)42/Final].
OECD 1997. Environment Directorate, Chemicals Group and Management Committee. Advisory Group on Risk Management. Draft Summary Record of the 1st Meeting of the Advisory Group on Risk Management. Ottawa 15 February 1997 [ENV/MC/CHEM/RM/M(97)1].
OECD 2000. OECD Environmental Strategy for the First Decade of the 21st Century. [ENV/EPOC(2000)13/REV4].
OECD 2003. Directorate of Food, Agriculture and Fisheries, Environment Directorate, Joint Working Party on Agriculture and the Environment. *Lessons Learned from OECD work on Agriculture and the Environment*, COM/AGR/CA/ENV/EPOC(2003)103/REV1.

OECD 2011. *Celebrating 40 years of the OECD Environment Policy Committee 1971–2011*, Paris: OECD Publishing, p. 44.
Patel, T. 1995. '… While Industry Blocks International Ban', *New Scientist*, 147(1986): 10.
Pearce, F. 1995. 'Lead Trickles through European Loophole …', *New Scientist*, 147(1986): 10.
Potter, C. and Burney, J. 2002. 'Agricultural Multifunctionality in the WTO – Legitimate Non-trade Concern or Disguised Protectionism?', *Journal of Rural Studies*, 18(1): 35–47.
Repetto, R. 1994. *Trade and Sustainable Development*, Geneva: UNEP.
Schweitzer, G. 1991. *Borrowed Earth, Borrowed Time; Healing America's Chemical Wounds*, New York: Plenum Press.
Stonehouse, J. and Mumford, J. 1994. *Science, Risk Analysis and Environmental Policy Decisions*, Geneva: UNEP.
Thorpe, S., Kilijn, N. and Cox, A. 1995. *Economic Effects on the Lead-Zinc Industry of Possible OECD Risk Reduction Measures for Lead*, Canberra: Australian Bureau of Agricultural and Resource Economics (ABARE).
US Council on Environmental Quality and Federal Council for Science and Technology (USCEQ) 1975. Report of the Federal Task Force on Inadvertent Modification of the Stratosphere June.
Vogel, D. 1997. 'Trading up and Governing Across: Transnational Governance and Environmental Protection', *Journal of European Public Policy*, 4(4): 556–571.

11. Australia and the OECD work on education

Education was not an activity within the OECD when it was established, yet its roots precede the formation of the organisation, going back to the OEEC when Sir Alexander King, formerly Director of the British Department of Scientific and Technical Research was charged with supporting work on the economic benefits of scientific training, pursued through the Governing Committee for Scientific and Technical Personnel (CTSP). King recruited his compatriot James Ronald (Ron) Gass, who played a significant role in the later development within the OECD of work on social, educational and labour affairs, from which a separate Education Directorate was eventually to emerge (Eide, 1990: 8).

As Eide put it, 'Educational policy became interesting for the OECD because of its assumed importance for economic growth and development' (1990: 15). An early part of education activities was a project on planning, the Educational Investment Programme (EIP), but educational statistics also became a focus with the establishment of a working party on Educational Statistics for Planning. Throughout the 1960s education slowly became the object of greater attention in the OECD, more out of intrinsic interest, rather than out of economic interest, thanks in large part to the work of Ron Gass in soliciting support among education agencies in members' states.

Work on education matured at just the time Australia acceded to the OECD, with the establishment first of the Centre for Educational Research and Innovation (CERI) on 28 July 1967 as a semi-autonomous centre (similar to the IEA (1974), NEA (1958), the Development Centre (1962), and Club du Sahel (1976)), and funded through Part II of the budget and initiated by industry funding, with a grant of $100,000 from the Ford Foundation, followed by a more substantial $750,000 from the Shell Group of Companies. CERI carries out studies and promotes an international dialogue about education across OECD countries. Non-members are able to become participants or observers on the recommendation of the Governing Council in the framework of its global relations strategy, and subject to approval by the OECD Council. In 1970 the CTSP was transformed into the Education Committee (Eide, 1990: 24).

The Education Directorate has numerous work programmes, and these are governed by five bodies, each with its own mandate and budget. Work on education statistics and indicators is overseen by the Education Policy Committee (EDPC) and CERI meeting in joint session, with the work undertaken through a series of working groups and networks. The work of EDPC is funded from the core budget, while CERI (as noted above) is funded from Part II, as are the Programme for International Student Assessment (PISA, an international assessment of the abilities of 15-year-olds), the Programme on Institutional Management in Higher Education (IMHE), and the Programme on Educational Building (PEB), for which participating countries and organisations make contributions.

The Education programme areas include Education Training and Policy (ETP), in which Australia has only been involved in the *Improving School Leadership* programme, and Indicators of Education Systems (INES), which is primarily concerned with the methodology behind the production of valid internationally comparable education statistics. INES and PISA work is undertaken by the Education Indicators and Analysis Division of the Education Directorate, and INES is governed by EDPC and CERI meeting in joint session. IMHE and PEB have their own governing boards and their work is undertaken by the Education Management and Infrastructure Division. (There is also a Unit for Cooperation with Non-Member Economies, but Australia has been largely uninvolved with this.)

This chapter sets out Australia's engagement with education matters in the OECD, providing some detail of that relationship, including its assessment of the value of education activity. It is fair to say, as we show below, that Australia has had a very close relationship with the Secretariat in education, although, as the chapter shows, this relationship began extremely modestly, with the Secretariat and especially Ron Gass (Director of CERI) working hard to secure Australian participation. Australia sees PISA as being the most important education programme in the OECD, and the chapter sets out its substantial commitment to the development of this programme, including the process of securing the necessary participation of state government education departments. First, however, we set out some indicators of the importance of education for Australia.

DEST has found most activities in the OECD to be of considerable value, with the exception of the Programme on Educational Buildings, which dealt with matters of concern to state and territory governments, and sought to shift costs for this on to them (DEST, 2006: 5). Total expenditure by DEST on OECD activities in 2006 was $5.625m, not including staff costs for 10 FTE positions, of which $1.075m (and 2.75 FTE) was for the member of the Delegation in Paris. The Part I contribution allocated to the Education Directorate was estimated at only $91,750, with most coming from the Part II budget. The most resource-intensive activity was PISA, to which was devoted $1.287m and 1.1 FTE staff, with $2.5m allocated to the Adult Literacy and Lifeskills Survey (ALLS), together with $2m from the Australian Bureau of Statistics. The latter administers the ALLS in Australia, undertaken only every decade, commencing in 1996. DEST has recently sought to encourage greater involvement by state and territory governments in OECD activities by, for example, inviting them through the Australian Education Systems Officials Committee (AESOC) to nominate a representative to attend CERI and Education Committee meetings.

In 2006, Australian activities in the OECD related to education were coordinated through the International Education Group in DEST and the key ongoing programmes were regarded as PISA and INES (DEST, 2006: 14). The Schools Group had carriage of PISA and INES Network A, which helps provide internationally comparable information and data, and was involved in the development of PISA and the Programme for International Assessment of Adult Competencies (PIAAC). The Higher Education group in DEST was involved in the OECD's Thematic Review of Tertiary Education and the Higher Education Policy Portal. The Strategic Analysis and Evaluation Group was responsible for the balance of INES work, including Networks B and C, with B looking at the impact of education on socioeconomic outcomes, and C (of which Australia is not a full member) at school features and processes.

Australia had little interest in (or knowledge of) education matters in the OECD at the time of accession, and was somewhat nervous about what peer-review might entail. In contrast, it has more recently played a prominent role in its education activities providing, for example, the inaugural Director of Education, Professor Barry McGaw, who had been Deputy Director for Education of the Directorate for Education, Employment, Labour and Social Affairs, and was appointed to head the new Directorate when it was separated out from DEELSA in 2002. Prior to this, he had been Executive Director of the Australian Council for Educational Research (ACER)[1] between 1985 and 1998 and Professor of Education at Murdoch University. A chemistry graduate from the University of Queensland, he later studied psychology, completing a PhD in educational psychology and psychometrics at the University of Illinois. But Australia's (and McGaw's) involvement with the OECD Secretariat went back a decade before this, with his predecessor being Professor Malcolm Skilbeck, Vice-Chancellor of Deakin University (1986–91), who had been a consultant to CERI in the 1970s.

The Department of Employment, Education and Training[2] had funded a study in the Spring of 1993 aimed at developing indicators of educational R&D, and ACER's McGaw and Phillip McKenzie undertook the project (ACER's work was known to the OECD Secretariat even prior to Australia's accession). McKenzie also worked at the OECD (from 1996 to 1998), serving as Principal Administrator in the Education and Training Policy Division, and working on the Transition from Initial Education to Working Life study (1996–98) and later on the Attracting, Developing and Retaining Effective Teachers project (2002–2004) (OECD, 2014). In 2002–2003 he was Editor of the OECD's annual Education Policy Analysis series. McGaw joined DEELSA as Deputy Director in 1998, and was appointed Director of the new Education Directorate by Secretary-General Johnston in July 2002.

The close links between Australia and education activities in the OECD include the current Director of what is now the Directorate of Education and Skills, Andreas Schleicher, a German national, who graduated with an MSc in mathematics and statistics in 1992 from Deakin University, where Skilbeck had been Vice-Chancellor until 1991. Schleicher became project manager at CERI in 1994 and began to develop the PISA study there in 1995, becoming leader of the Indicators and Analysis Division in DEELSA in 1997. In 2001 he presented the first PISA results and from 2002 took responsibility for PISA.

EARLY AUSTRALIAN PARTICIPATION IN OECD EDUCATION ACTIVITIES

Australia's interest in education matters in the OECD had not initially been particularly high. As the briefing paper for the first meeting of the Education Committee at which Australia would be represented noted, 'the nature of the agenda suggests that it is unlikely that issues will arise on which an Australian position will need to be stated formally' (NAA, 1971).

Reservations had emerged around the value of education in the OECD even before the Australian decision was taken to accede. Contact in June 1969 with officials in the UK Department of Education and Science had revealed they had reservations about OECD membership and there was some thought membership could not be justified simply on the grounds of practical benefits for British education (NAA, 1969). While the OECD

Secretariat was held in quite a high regard compared to UNESCO, the UK found few of its areas of work of interest and there was an associated burden placed on staff in providing it with detailed statistics; they considered value could be improved by getting publications produced earlier. CERI was not considered to have achieved much at this time.

While Australia played a prominent role in education activities such as the development of PISA, as described below, it has been selective in its commitment of resources and attention. Indeed, it was drawn into the education field only reluctantly from the outset as education at that time was largely a matter for the states, with the Commonwealth role increasing only over time, especially after the election of the Whitlam government in 1972. Australia was not, at the time of accession, a participant in CERI, but it was courted by CERI and eventually succumbed to its overtures after a little over a year.

Ron Gass, CERI Director, wrote to Ambassador Sir Ronald Walker, on 13 September 1971 seeking approval for CERI to enter into further discussion with Keith Jennings, an official of the department then at the LSE on a Public Service Postgraduate Fellowship, and expressing the view that this might lead to improved information on the two sides which could facilitate later Australian–OECD cooperation. Jennings was later appointed (by the OECD on the nomination of Australia) as Australia's first member of the CERI Governing Board (NAA, 1973).[3]

Gass wrote to the Counsellor at the Delegation on 12 November 1971 agreeing to provide papers from a meeting on Institutional Management in Higher Education held recently in Paris, but also making a definite play for Australia to join CERI:

> You will, of course, realise that we must place some limitations on the provision to non-Member countries of CERI of the results of CERI's work. We shall continue to take a broad-minded attitude to this but we hope very much that the Australian position in relation to CERI will be gone into as soon as possible.

And additional inducement was provided in the form of an invitation to those not yet participating in CERI, but which were intending to do so from 1972, to send observers to the second meeting of the Governing Board in December 1971. A handwritten note on the file correctly observed that this invitation assumed that Australia had decided to participate in 1972, but the invitation was declined until this 'threshold question' had been resolved, after some indication from the Department of Education and Science, which had not at that stage responded with its views. The Acting Director of CERI then proposed that a senior member of CERI staff visit Australia in order to identify specific CERI projects of interest to the Australian authorities.

Australia was included in the distribution of material on the prospective work programme, and CERI corresponded with Professor B. Williams, Vice-Chancellor of the University of Sydney, on Institutional Management in Higher Education, with the DFA informed. The chair of CERI's Governing Board Mr Kjell Eide was visiting Australia and New Zealand on private business between 10 May and 15 June and Gass suggested it would be opportune for him to discuss possible CERI membership while he was in the country.

The Program on Institutional Management in Higher Education was used as an incentive for Australia to join, with it pitched to Universities, but met with caution within the Department and DFA as to whether participation would be possible without Australia joining CERI, a decision which was deferred until at least 1973. This decision was conveyed to the Delegation and to CERI in a letter on 18 April. Gass' response indicated that Mr Eide could no longer visit Australia, as his programme in New Zealand (at a UNESCO seminar) was filled and he was required to return to Norway immediately thereafter, though it was possible Australian attendees at the seminar might be able to meet with him. In a letter to the Counsellor on 8 May, Gass left open the possibility that individual universities might be able to participate in the absence of Australian membership of CERI, depending on whether the programme was established as a part of CERI or as an activity separate from it.

The push for full CERI membership came from the Minister for Education and Science, Malcolm Fraser, who wrote to the Minister for Foreign Affairs, Nigel Bowen (himself a former minister in Fraser's portfolio) on 14 July recommending that Australia join CERI, pointing out that it was the only OECD member that was not a member. The response, drafted by DFAT, was for caution and it recommended the advice of Treasury be sought. Fraser had already consulted the states and the university sector on the issue (NAA, 1973).

The Science Counsellor, P.J. Crawford, briefed the Director, International Relations in the Department of Education and Science in a long Memorandum (OECD Memo. No. 447) on a discussion of CERI membership with Gass and his deputy Papadopolous that he had had on 26 July 1972. Gass indicated Australia should identify three or four areas of particular interest where it would be prepared to participate in either the CERI programmes or those of the Education Committee. He reported that:

> I believe that Gass was indicating that a positive initiative from Australia would result in strong positive responses from the Secretariat. Gass went on to say that this approach had been adopted with some success in both Canada and Japan. (NAA, 1973)

Gass also suggested that Counsellor Crawford could attend meetings of the Governing Board as an observer for consideration of those items identified, in lieu of an Australian Governing Board representative.

The deliberations were not helped by CERI inviting an expert from ACER (Fitzgerald) to participate in a meeting in Paris without advising the Delegation of the invitation, but on 15 September the Acting Minister of Foreign Affairs, Ian Sinclair, wrote to Fraser agreeing that the financial costs would be small and supporting Australian membership, on the understanding that travel to attend CERI meetings be kept to a minimum. Fraser then wrote to Minister Bowen on 25 October, stating that he was following Sinclair's advice an arranging for his Department to consult with DFA and Treasury on how this might be arranged. Consequently, the Ambassador R.J. Cameron wrote to Secretary-General van Lennep on 6 November conveying Australia's wish to participate in CERI from 1 January 1973. This required the Council to amend the Decision extending the initial mandate of CERI until 1976, which it did on 13 December 1972.

After consultation with the states, the Department indicated an interest in six CERI projects: Early Childhood Education, New Functions and Structures of the School, Guidelines for Curriculum Development, Creativity in the School, Curriculum Development in Universities, and Recurrent Education. A final decision on which three or four in which it would wish to participate was reserved pending discussions with the proposed CERI Director Ron Gass later in the year. This was a quite strategic selection from 21 projects that had been listed in the Draft Programme of Work for 1974 (see OECD, 1973, Annex II), reflecting Australia's early caution on involvement in education matters.

THE CONTINUING RELATIONSHIP

Australia's careful, strategic engagement in OECD education activities has continued, keeping a watchful eye on the value to be gained from the costs of participating. It was agreed in 2003 for example, that Australia should not seek an elected position on the INES Strategic Management Group 'at this time'. It was noted that INES was a highly technical body with at least two meetings annually in Paris, that INES was highly dependent on Part II USA funding and that the USA had reduced its funding support by about a third (DEEWR, 2004). But the OECD is valued more highly than UNESCO, particularly because of the focus of the latter primarily on the needs of developing countries (DEST, 2006a). As discussed below, Australia supported the development of international student assessment in the OECD in preference to UNESCO, in much the same way that it selected the OECD for substantial health performance work, rather than the WHO (see Chapter 12).

As noted above, activities in the OECD have been coordinated through the International Education Group in the Department, and (until recently) had a Minister Counsellor (Education and Employment) and a Senior Adviser to the Minister Counsellor (Education and Employment) in the Delegation. There is now only a locally engaged Education Manager. This represents a marked advance on initial representation, which was handled through a Counsellor (Scientific Affairs). Australia was represented at its first Session of the Education Committee by the Education Liaison Officer at the High Commission in London, rather than by a delegate from Canberra.

Australia has been cautious about its level of engagement. In 1999 Australia was not represented on the INES Steering Group (which produced *Education at a Glance*), but was on the Board of Participating Countries (BPC) for PISA. It had been a leading member of Network B, although this met very rarely between 1995 and 1998. Permission was sought to join Network A, which held its meetings back to back with BPC meetings. The cost was estimated at $7,000–9,000 per visit, for 5–6 meetings each year. This was rejected initially by the Secretary but later agreed to (DEEWR, 1999).

Participation in the Education Committee has not always run smoothly, as reflected in a Briefing from the Delegation provided by Paul Cowan (Counsellor Employment, Education and Training) for the 65th Session in March 2000. Cowan reported that the Secretariat held the 'now regular briefing for delegations' on the upcoming meetings, the first conducted by John Martin, the new Director of DEELSA. He noted that 'The meeting commenced with an, unfortunately also regular, apology for the lateness of the papers. We were advised that the following papers would be available on OLIS by the end of today' (DEEWR, 1999).

It is worth noting just how large the OECD's work on education was by this stage: CERI alone had a similar budget to the OECD's entire Trade Directorate, though very little of this was in Part I of the Budget. The establishment of a separate Education Directorate under Barry McGaw was seen as providing a strategic opportunity for Australia, as recognised in a briefing note in October 2002:

> The … agenda for the OECD's work on education appears to be largely driven by the Secretariat. If you put this to them they would no doubt deny this arguing that the work plan comes out of ministerial mandates etc. While this is true, these mandates, and the member countries, give the Secretariat a lot of scope to develop work proposals. This is not a problem as the OECD's education people are very good. However, it does highlight the fact that we could have a larger say on the work program. The establishment of the Education Directorate provides an opportunity to do this. (DEEWR, 2002b)

It was proposed to come up with some medium-term ideas for the programme of work, discussed with McGaw and at a lunch with Abrar Hasan (Head of Education and Training Policy Division, OECD). There was a conscious caucusing of like-minded members on this issue, with a meeting arranged for 20 October at the Canadian delegation with a non-European group (Australia, Canada, Ireland, New Zealand, the UK and the US). It was thought this could be expanded to include the Netherlands – a 'non-Anglo' member but seen to have innovative labour market policies.

Frictions were also occasionally evident in the workings of the subsidiary bodies within Education. There were concerns by Australian representatives of the direction taken by some of the INES networks, for example, with one delegate to a 2005 meeting of INES Network C noting:

> I must admit that I emerged from the event strengthened in the conviction that there needs to be a thorough overhaul of the INES structures in order to ensure that the work that goes on reflects the priorities decided through the Education Committee and CERI Governing Board. As far as I can see, there is a high degree of 'capture' of the work of the INES networks (most obviously Networks A and C) by the Network Chairs. Most effort goes into work of interest to the Chairs and their coterie. This does not necessarily reflect either the INES mission or the priorities agreed by member countries. In the case of Network C, this is flagrant. (DEEWR, 2005)

An example given was work on indicators of instructional effectiveness that required funds of €200,000. Some funding was to come from the US, the Netherlands and Germany, but the chair had expressed disappointment that the proposal had not been supported by the INES Senior Management Group (SMG) nor the Joint Meeting of Education Committee and CERI Governing Board. The delegate reported:

> I indicated that the SMG (of which I am a member) had not seen this work as a priority in terms of indicator development … and that it seemed to be more of a research project of an open ended nature which was not in the Education Directorate work program. Sweden indicated that it had no interest in this

> work. The UK delegate stated that it looked very much as if the proposal was 'driven by the personal interests of the proponents rather than the needs of member countries' (a comment which was subsequently withdrawn following strong objections from the Chair). Few other countries spoke which was taken as encouragement by the Chair. (DEEWR, 2005)

The delegate added that some work was likely to continue, but then added the comment:

> This is symptomatic of the main problem with the INES Networks – work is driven by interested individuals or countries with particular interest that are prepared to devote resources to achieve their particular goals rather than any defined strategy related to the overall priorities of OECD work in education. (DEEWR, 2005)

The brief for the October 2003 Joint Session of the Education Committee and CERI Governing Board contained a report on Joint Session Paris 8 April 2003, which revealed some concerns with limitations on the scope for participation in these meetings. It noted that (regarding PISA) Andreas Schleicher 'gave one of his usual excellent PowerPoint presentations but no time was left for discussion. This caused considerable disappointment for several delegates and raised issues about the time allocated for the meeting' (DEEWR, 2004).

Meetings of the Education Committee at Ministerial Level elicited varying responses from Australian Ministers. Ministerials were usually held every five years, although the formation of a separate Directorate for Education prompted the OECD Secretariat to re-schedule the one due in 2006, bringing it forward to 2004 (DEEWR, 2002a). Education Minister Simon Crean chaired the 1996 Ministerial, but Minister David Kemp merely addressed the 2001 Meeting (2–4 April) by video, thus missing the treat of a 'brief, stimulating' presentation during dinner by the French Minister, M. Jack Lang on 'The human brain: New discoveries and possibilities for education'. Ministerials also provided opportunities for consultations with BIAC and TUAC, and on 18 March 2004 an Informal Forum was organised on the topic 'Education and Social Cohesion', with the media, civil society organisations and invited experts present.

THE VALUE OF OECD EDUCATION ACTIVITIES TO AUSTRALIA

In addition to the outputs of work programmes and the value of networks within the OECD, participation also provides a means for direct interaction with other governments on education matters. For example, at a meeting of OECD Education Ministers on the future of higher education held in Athens on 27–28 June 2006, bilateral meetings were arranged with American, British, Greek and German counterparts (during what was intended as consultation with BIAC and TUAC, which perhaps reflected the low value placed on those consultations). Corridor briefs were also provided in case the Minister had the opportunity to exchange a few words with the Japanese, South Korean, Chilean, Mexican and Dutch education ministers in the meetings (DEEWR, 2006). Such meetings also provide a point of contact with groups such as the G8 members, with a Report on the G8 meeting of Ministers of Education provided.

The briefing document provided for the Minister for the Athens Meeting contained a document 'DEST Involvement in the OECD', which provided a useful summation of the views of the Department on involvement in the OECD at that time (DEEWR, 2006). This was summarised as follows:

> DEST's involvement with the OECD has three overarching benefits:
>
> - It provides an important resource for the Department's policy development;
> - It enhances Departmental analysis and research; and
> - It provides an opportunity for Australia to highlight its areas of achievement in education, training and the sciences.
>
> The key objectives of involvement in the OECD were seen as:
>
> - To contribute to the development of comparative descriptors of education and training participation and performance indicators, including the *Education at a Glance* and PISA learning outcomes standards;
> - To form networks for international scientific collaboration;
> - To influence the formation of international policy frameworks and standards, such as for qualifications recognition and educational quality assurance; and
> - To benefit from the exchange of innovative ideas and 'what works' experiences.

DEST was also responsible for the work conducted in the OECD by the Directorate for Science, Technology and Industry (DSTI). DEST saw value in the Centre for Science and Technology Policy, especially in activities such as: the Global Science Forum; the Working Group of National Experts on Science and Technology Indicators (NESTI); the Working Group on Innovation and Technology Policy (TIP); the Working

Party on Biotechnology (WPB); and the Ad Hoc Group on Steering and Funding of Research Institutions (SFRI).

The OECD performs a valued role in collecting and publishing comparative statistics on education, so that informed policy deliberation and debate can be conducted on issues such as tertiary education funding. While the Commonwealth and state departments use such information, their value in providing a shared basis for public debate was called into question by the publication in 2009 of an article by Brendan O'Reilly, formerly Director in charge of Australia's reporting of education statistics to the OECD and UNESCO at the Department and Australian representative on the OECD Technical Group on Education and Training Statistics (O'Reilly, 2009). O'Reilly pointed out that misunderstandings of how the OECD statistics were collected, especially in relation to the innovative HECS and HELP deferred partial payment and government loan schemes operating in Australia led to both Coalition and Labor politicians (including then Prime Minister John Howard in 2007 and then Education Minister Julia Gillard in 2008) misinterpreting OECD statistics to make political points. Moreover, the misuse was not confined to politicians, with the same confusion arising in much of the press and in the work of academic analysts, including both Simon Marginson and former OECD Director Barry McGaw. O'Reilly concluded:

> Overall, much of the public debate on the funding of tertiary education in Australia has been very ill-informed. This is largely because the OECD's *Education at a Glance*, from which key statistics are sourced, is a technical document and contains only summary tables in the hard copy text. Casual users generally lack an adequate understanding of the basic concepts underlying it and often try to interpret technically complex educational expenditure data intuitively.
>
> Since more than one Minister, as well as a sitting PM, has provided Parliament with clearly misleading interpretations of OECD educational statistics, questions arise about the quality of advice provided to them in the first instance and about why the public record has never been corrected. (O'Reilly, 2009)

The most significant education activity in recent years has perhaps been PISA, and Australia played a prominent role in its development, as outlined below. It should be noted that Australia now also participates in the OECD's Teaching and Learning International Survey (TALIS), which began in 2008 with 24 countries participating, increasing to 34 in 2013. TALIS focuses on lower secondary education, but also surveys students in their primary and upper secondary schools. Some countries also sought to gain additional insights by conducting the survey on schools that participated in the 2012 PISA.

It should be noted that Australia also participates in other studies outside the OECD, specifically the studies Trends in International Mathematics and Science Study (TIMSS) and Progress in International Reading Literacy Study (PIRLS) which are organised by the International Association for the Evaluation of Educational Achievement (IEA).[4] But PISA is perhaps the most notable such international assessment project, and is applied beyond the OECD membership, though its history is related to the predecessors of TIMSS, and Australia played a significant part in its development.

THE PROGRAMME FOR INTERNATIONAL STUDENT ASSESSMENT

PISA is an international survey, conducted triennially on 15-year-old students in more than 65 countries. It is seen as a response to countries' desire for high quality and regular comparative data on both the knowledge and skills of their students and the performance of their education systems. The intention was to evaluate education systems by testing the skills and knowledge of a sample of students at a common point in time, close to the point where some might exit the education system (OECD, 2014). PISA was developed in the OECD from the mid-1990s, and launched in 1997, with the first survey in 2000. It has been conducted triennially since, and has been adopted by many non-OECD members. In 2012, 510,000 students of an estimated 28 million of that age globally participated, being tested on reading, mathematics and science. In total, 44 'economies' (including places like Hong Kong and Taiwan, not considered countries) took part in an assessment of creative problem solving and 18 in an assessment of financial literacy.[5] PISA does not assess the curriculum, but how students can apply knowledge, understanding and skills to meet real situations encountered in adult life.

PISA's origins emerged from an example of forum shopping by the USA and UK, which had tried to establish a similar project in UNESCO, but were frustrated in their efforts and then turned to the OECD. After the Second International Mathematics Study (SIMS) and 1980–82 Second International Science Study (SISS) 1983–84 (both conducted by the IEA)[6] revealed a poor result for USA students, the USA and UK wanted UNESCO to carry out research on educational indicators, but UNESCO refused. The US subsequently withdrew from UNESCO in 1984, followed by the UK in 1985, amid concerns about the accountability and direction of UNESCO under the administration of Director-General Amadou-Mahtar M'Bow (Kuehn, 2004). The US was also critical of some aspects (including their methodology) of the IEA studies, which were conducted with limited resources (Medrich and Griffith, 1992).

PISA had its origins in the OECD's Educational Indicators Program (INES), which addresses many of the technical aspects related to OECD education activities. It develops and analyses indicators and data collection instruments for application regarding school performance (students and teachers) through to adult competencies, as well as the publication *Education at a Glance*. In addition, the World Education Indicators (WEI) project was run jointly by UNESCO, the OECD and the World Bank. Further, an annual report, 'Education at a Glance' (EAG), was produced from 1992, containing largely standardised chapters covering core indicator areas: context of education; expenditure on education; participation and access to education; issues related to teachers (salaries, teaching time, staff/student ratios); labour market outcomes of education; learning outcomes of education (DEEWR, 2006). The policy direction of each EAG was set at a UNESCO General Assembly every five years, with the OECD Secretariat having administrative responsibility for preparing the EAG. National coordinators had responsibility for the data input for each country and for contributions to the overall project.

Both Germany and France apparently initially opposed the development of such work in the OECD, but the USA and UK then threatened to withdraw from the Education Committee, and they capitulated. The USA then provided Part II funds to support Network A to develop the PISA tests. Rivalry between the OECD and UNESCO re-emerged in 1997 when UNESCO proposed establishing a World Education Indicators project at a time when PISA was being developed, but this was halted when funding for it from the World Bank (where the US enjoys a dominant position) was diverted to the OECD. The USA then pushed PISA to non-OECD members, especially in the Asia-Pacific, inviting members of the new APEC Education Forum to Washington in 1997 to be briefed on the OECD indicators project (Kuehn, 2004).

A prominent role was played in PISA by Barry McGaw's former organisation, ACER. In a letter to Ms Linda Lipp, Assistant Secretary, DEET dated 21 November 1994, for example, Professor Skilbeck (CERI) considered 'the cooperation between ACER and CERI a total success'. Skilbeck expressed 'the hope that the co-operation between DEET, the ACER and OECD can be maintained and strengthened' (DEEWR, 1994).

In 1995 the OECD was undertaking new work to examine changes in business strategies, enterprise structure, work organisation, and production practices, and their implications for human resources, including qualifications requirements. This was to follow up an OECD Jobs Study and a request by the G7 for the Organisation to further investigate the relationship between technology, productivity and employment (DEEWR, 1995a). The INES General Assembly held in Lahti, Finland 12–15 June 1995, the first General Assembly in four years, agreed that the growing importance of the international dimension in education would further increase the need for statistics and indicators on education and training (OECD, 1995). The General Assembly recommended continuation of the INES project (which had commenced in 1988) for another five years starting in 1997 (OECD, 1995). Peter Grant, Acting Deputy Secretary, briefed the Secretary who headed the three-person Australian delegation, and reported on the outcomes in a Minute to the Secretary (DEEWR, 1995).

There was seen to be a need 'to rectify the most glaring gap in the current set of INES outputs', being the lack of any reliable international data on student outcomes and achievement. A lack of progress by NEA was noted and the question was how to remedy this: IEA surveys? Country-specific testing within an agreed international framework? Or through international studies coordinated and directly managed by the OECD? There was also a need recognised for revision of the International Standard Classification of Education (ISCED), which was a UNESCO priority, but a UNESCO representative spoke to the procedures and timetable governing the revision process, and, as Grant put it, 'inspired little confidence that the work was proceeding with the urgency and commitment that it deserves' (DEEWR 1995).

INES also raised challenges for Commonwealth-state relations for Australia, and the opportunities for using it for extending Commonwealth control over the states was not lost. State education departments were somewhat fearful that PISA would allow interstate comparisons, exposing any poor performing states, and education unions were similarly concerned that comparisons might be possible between state schools and private schools. Grant raised the issue, considering whether:

> [W]e should broaden the base of our INES involvement by engaging the more active interest of bodies such as MCEETYA and ACVETS, while still maintaining effective Commonwealth control. … More substantively, a potential benefit of this approach would be to highlight the illogicality of the States' reluctance to expose their own educational systems to comparative analysis and scrutiny. They would be hard put to maintain that stance in the face of the INES work. (DEEWR, 1995)

Australia was playing a prominent role in education generally at this time, not just in the development of PISA. Education Minister Simon

Crean chaired the meeting of the Education Committee at Ministerial Level on 16–17 January 1996, although the decision that he should do so was only made belatedly on 10 January and only after a ministerial reshuffle in Norway that saw its Minister Hernes moved to another portfolio, and only after some 'initial resistance by the French' was overcome (DEEWR, 1995). This came at a time when Australia also chaired the non-ministerial Education Committee, with Deputy Secretary Alan Ruby elected unopposed as chair at the 55th Session held on 18–20 September 1995 for an initial term of two years. This term covered the January 1996 Ministerial and the introduction of a new mandate for the Committee, and saw the establishment of PISA.

In his minute reporting on the November 1996 meetings of the Education Committee and the Governing Board of CERI, Ruby stated his view that this 'was one of the most substantial meetings of both committees, bringing to completion 5 years' work and beginning preparation for the next 5 years' work'. As he put it, 'After nearly 10 years of definitional work and complex international politics around measuring student achievement INES (the indicator project) has finally brought forward a proposal for an international survey of student outcomes.' Ruby noted that the survey was to be contracted out, that the USA government was underwriting the costs but there would be costs for participating countries. He noted that ACER was likely to be a bidder for some of this work (DEEWR, 1995).

It was clear that these developments would impact negatively on the International Association for the Evaluation of Educational Achievement (IEA), an international cooperative of national research institutions and governmental research agencies that had been conducting large-scale comparative studies of educational achievement since 1958. The OECD and Statistics Canada had also conducted an International Adult Literacy Survey (IALS) between 1994 and 1998. Ruby noted that the OECD initiative was likely to either force IEA out of the field, or to be the contractor to the OECD, leaving the OECD as the main player on international comparisons of student achievement. Ruby therefore recommended that Australia, to advance its interests, should get involved with Network A, the part of the INES project that would oversee the survey development. He flagged that this would involve some international travel and some time for an SES officer, and that the Department might also need 'to look at involving ACER on a consultancy basis to give us some expertise'. There were some domestic sensitivities attached to this. He noted: 'There will be difficulties with the states on this exercise and we will need to make a judgement about when and how to involve them in this work', as their cooperation was needed to administer PISA in their classrooms. He saw that it might be desirable to involve them in Network A 'but I do not see this as essential'. Costs of around $300,000 per annum were thought to be involved, and for this reason the approval of the Minister, Dr Kemp, needed to be sought.

The Minister, Dr Kemp, was clearly enthusiastic about Australia participating, as a Minute to the Secretary on 5 August 1997 noted:

> Dr Kemp is very keen for Australia to be involved in these surveys, and, following a letter from the OECD asking for firm commitments from countries, he has recently written to his State and Territory counterparts seeking their support for and agreement to Australia's participation. This is a prerequisite for full Australian participation, as we would need the agreement of school systems to approach schools and students. (The Minister will also need to write to non-government sector authorities once we have responses from the government sector.) (DEEWR, 1997)

In June 1997, Minister Kemp agreed to the Ambassador advising the OECD of Australia's strong interest, noting the need to seek the agreement of states and territories. He also noted Australia's keen interest in the participation of other countries in our region. On 17 July he then wrote to state and territory ministers. The ACT agreed, but had some concerns on costs. Peter Adamson, the Northern Territory Minster for Education and Training expressed some displeasure with the haste with which the Commonwealth was proceeding:

> This is the second such agreement sought by the Commonwealth within a week. On the first occasion we were asked to commit the NT to a national civics survey (IEA) with only a few days' notice and inadequate information. This survey is a much bigger and more costly operation, and the implications are more complex, yet only one week was allowed for a response. It could be argued that a major decision such as this needs to be discussed by MCEETYA [Ministerial Council on Education, Employment and Youth Affairs] after adequate examination. (DEEWR, 1997a)

Adamson was concerned that the small numbers in the Territory might mean a proportionately large sample, and the impact this might have on schools and students. He was interested, but expressed a desire to have an opportunity to discuss some practical aspects at the next MCEETYA meeting.

The Tasmanian Minister, Sue Napier, also raised similar concerns stating that:

> [T]his proposal is also being driven by a time line which is too short for proper consultation with my colleagues in other States. As well, I am growing

> increasingly concerned at the large volume of student learning outcome data that is being required at local, national and international levels. (DEEWR, 1997a)

She too wished to discuss the matter at Minister or official level, and, while not rejecting the proposal, was 'unwilling to agree to Tasmania's participation until such discussions have occurred'.

South Australia expressed concerns on costs and scope, and opposed the possible inclusion of 13-year-olds. Western Australian Minister, Colin Barnett (later to be Premier), supported the thrust of the proposal, but was also concerned with the timetable:

> It is unfortunate that this issue is being addressed in a hurried fashion. I would prefer that Australia's reply to the OECD be delayed to allow the chief executive officers to consider the issue. If that is not possible, I am prepared to support Australia's involvement in the first phase, however funding arrangements would still be needed to be discussed among the states. (DEEWR, 1997a)

For Queensland, Minister Bob Quinn expressed support and suggested a 50/50 sharing of costs between the Commonwealth and states and territories. Victorian Minister Phil Gude supported the proposal in general terms, but noted the need to monitor potential participation by OECD countries and particularly Pacific-rim countries, suggesting this should be taken into account prior to a final decision by Australia and that he would like to be kept informed on this. He agreed on cost sharing and wanted comparability of data. For New South Wales, Minister John Aquilina expressed support in principle on 4 August, but wanted the sample size increased to allow for interstate comparisons, a sensitive issue. Stating that NSW's participation was dependent on its involvement in the process, including test construction and interpretation and analysis of the data, he added:

> It is also important that any analysis of the data is not published before full details of the results are made available to the New South Wales Government. Furthermore data collected in New South Wales belongs to the New South Wales Government and is not to be used for any purpose without the express permission of this Government. (DEEWR, 1997a)

Despite the request by several states, there was no consideration of the issue by MCEETYA. Instead, the Commonwealth pressed on without receiving the agreement of all the states, with a 17 September Minute seeking by 26 September a decision on Australia's participation, which was (somewhat belatedly) agreed to by Minister Kemp on 30 September

(DEEWR, 1997a). The urgency was, perhaps, provoked by the fact that the next BPC Meeting was being held on 6–7 October.

The Minute noted that most state and territory Ministers had been supportive of participation, with NSW, Victoria and South Australia being very positive. Tasmania and the North Territory, it was noted, had been less enthusiastic and had held back on giving their agreement, and they (and Western Australia) had expressed a preference for discussion at Ministerial or official level prior to any firm decision being taken on participation'. The Minute added:

> My view is that there is sufficient State support to warrant a positive decision on participation. To obtain a representative sample of Australian schools/students, it is not necessary to have all States involved. However, non-participation of some States would reduce the possibility of interstate comparisons (thereby reducing the usefulness of the surveys). It is also the case that making a formal decision at Commonwealth level to commit Australia to participate without having had further consultations with the States, may cause concern to some States. The decision will need to be conveyed sensitively to the States. (DEEWR, 1997a)

The CEOs of the state and territory departments were informed in advance by telephone, but they were not pleased, with the chair of the Conference of Education Systems Chief Executive Officers (CESCEO) Michael Fong (NT), writing to Mr Bill Daniels, First Assistant Secretary, Schools and Curriculum Division on 27 September 1997 expressing concern over the process, and indicating that the Commonwealth had expended some political capital with the course it had followed:

> CESCEO is concerned at the short time frame given to systems to consider participation in international surveys. A case in point is the OECD Survey of Student Achievement Outcomes and the IEA's Study of Civic Education.
>
> CESCEO's position is that any future involvement in international student surveys or studies by school education systems will need to be preceded by discussion involving all States and Territories and the Commonwealth. (DEEWR, 1997a)

While Fong had written on 27 September, it was only stamped as 'Received' by the Department on 7 October. By that time, in principle support had been obtained on 2 October from the National Catholic Education Commission (in response to a letter dated 15 September) and Australia had indicated to the OECD that it had agreed to participate, with Ambassador Hillman writing to the DEELSA Director on 3 October, noting that while he had informed him of Australia's inability to commit in a letter of 4 July, 'I am now pleased to be able to advise that the

Australian Minister for Schools, Vocational Education and Training, having consulted with his State and Territory colleagues, has approved Australia's participation' (DEEWR, 1997a).

DEETYA was aware (in a minute dated 12 September) that many states and territories would be 'extremely concerned should Dr Kemp make a final decision without any discussion having taken place at either Ministerial or officer level'. They were also aware that their reaction might be to refuse access to their schools, and while they did not need all states and territories to get a nationally representative sample, they would not be able to achieve comparisons across all states. It was considered that this would reduce the benefits of being in the OECD survey and might also jeopardise future such projects (DEEWR, 1997a).

The opportunities for discussions between the Commonwealth and the states were extremely limited in the immediate future, with no MCEETYA meeting scheduled, and the Commonwealth not invited to the CESCEO meeting the following week. It was therefore proposed that the First Assistant Secretary, Schools Division, Bill Daniels speak to each of the state Directors General over the following week, with a view to 'discussing/removing their concerns'. Having been tipped off by a state source, the Department was aware that the OECD surveys were on the agenda for the forthcoming CESCEO meeting. A margin note a few days later ('WSW 16/9') indicates that 'Bill was concerned about ringing DsG at this time' and that Evans advised 'WSW' to proceed with a minute to the Minister recommending that Australia participate (DEEWR, 1997a).

The deliberations of CESCEO were conveyed to Canberra by Graham Harrington, Tasmanian Director-General, who reported that the item on international surveys (OECD and IEA) was dealt with briefly (recorded in a Minute on 26 September). While there was no formal decision taken on participation, most states and territories seemed to be of the view that they could not refuse to participate. Nevertheless, states were concerned about the approaches and the timing of the two recent invitations and they passed a resolution to the effect that future such invitations should be directed to the Ministers via MCEETYA, and sufficient time should be allowed for thorough consideration (DEEWR, 1997a).

Harrington was less convinced than the other state ministers about the need to participate, being concerned about excessive amounts of testing and the potential for teachers in Tasmania to take industrial action. He reported that the states were generally 'crabby' with DEETYA in relation to OECD matters, because there apparently had been an agreement between Alan Ruby and state Directors General under which they would participate in OECD meetings and be kept informed of OECD projects and developments, but they felt this had lapsed in the previous twelve months or so. There was also reportedly 'huge antagonism' to ACER (to the extent that some states were talking about not paying their share of its core grant) and they would not welcome ACER being employed to perform the PISA surveys in Australia. The antagonism had more to do with the threat of publication of data by ACER than with the organisation itself.

A further problem with the time line was that consultations had not been held with the National Catholic Education Commission (NCEC) and the National Council of Independent Schools Australia (NCISA). The Department drafted letters for Minister Kemp to send to NCEC and NCISA, but these were returned to the Department with an annotation (margin note 'Molly 3/9' – Molly Decini in Kemp's office) that 'After discussion with John Roskam, these letters can be signed by the Dept.' (DEEWR, 1997). DETYA had known in May that it was intending to participate in PISA, and yet it found itself under time pressure because it had not consulted the states and territories and the non-government schools earlier.

Given the time pressures, the option of seeking a deferral of the first BPC meeting was canvassed, but quickly ruled out. A letter from DEELSA dated 22 August was faxed from Shelagh Whittleston in the Delegation on 3 September to Wendy Whitham in the Department in Canberra, with Whittleston ruling out the possibility of Australia asking for the dates of the first BPC Meeting to be further changed, as the dates were fixed within the OECD meeting schedules and letters had gone out to Ambassadors. 'Also as you know we have not indicated our participation in the project – wouldn't look too good.' The first meeting of BPC had initially been scheduled for Paris on 7–8 September 1997, with Australia to be invited as an intending full participant, but on 22 August this was rescheduled by DEELSA to 6–7 October.

After the event, in December 1997 the Commonwealth put a paper to Ministers at the 8th MCEETYA meeting regarding OECD's proposed surveys of student achievement (now referred to as PISA). The Commonwealth Department therefore forced the somewhat reluctant state and territory governments to go along with the PISA proposal, thus making it possible, but it also played a significant role in the region in securing buy-in from OECD members and non-members alike.

As noted above, ACER was not unreservedly popular with the state education departments, though it did administer the first application of PISA according to a Minute dated 13 September 2000 (DEEWR, 2001). Later, in March 2001 CESCEO decided to review the future of the core grant to ACER (DEEWR, 2001a). Nevertheless, ACER was the only organisation invited to tender for the conduct of the second round, as it was considered unlikely that any other organisation in Australia could satisfactorily conduct the project. An application was therefore made for Exemption from the Minimum Standard of Procurement and ACER was sent a request for tender, but it was not informed they were the only tenderer.

The states and territories accepted an invitation to participate in PISA 2000. In Australia 6,000 students were to participate and 15-year-olds from 231 schools were randomly selected. Australia was one of the highest performers in PISA in all three domains, ranking second to Finland in reading, second to Japan in maths, and third to Japan and Korea in scientific literacy.

Australia notified DEELSA that it would participate, with a Note by the Secretary-General dated 10 September 1997 (recommending Council adopt the draft Resolution on a Programme for Producing Student Achievement Indicators on a Regular Basis set out in appendix) indicating that Australia was among the 22 countries that had 'informed the Secretariat of their intention to participate … and their wish to be represented on the Board of Participating Countries that would govern the programme (OECD, 1997: 3) (Australia, most of Europe, the US and UK – but not Canada – had given a positive indication).

Internationally the study was implemented by a consortium of educational research organisations headed by ACER, and the Australian Department assisted ACER in its securing of the work (DEEWR, 2001b). The OECD, in accordance with Rule 17 of the Financial Rules of the Organisation, issued an international invitation to tender for the implementation of the first survey cycle of the programme. Australia was clearly keen for ACER to be well positioned to secure some of the PISA consultancy work. Wendy Whitham emailed Ray Adams at ACER on 5 September 1997, in response to Barry McGaw speaking with Bill Daniels that day:

> I am writing to confirm that OECD has advised that the closing date for bids for the Network A surveys is now 18 November 1997. I will fax you a copy of the letter from the OECD that sets this out. Will you also let Barry know please? (DEEWR, 1997a)

ACER helped put together and led an international PISA Project Consortium that was successful in securing the contract, together with the Netherlands National Institute of Educational Measurement (CITO group), Educational Testing Services (ETS, US), the National Institute for Educational Policy Research (NIER, Japan), and Westat (US). A competing consortium was led by Boston College (Centre for the Study of Testing, Evaluation and Educational Policy) and included the International Association for the Evaluation of Educational Achievement, Statistics Canada, National Foundation for Educational Research, and Educational Testing Service. Boston College had previously administered the Trends in International Mathematics and Science Study (TIMSS) study.

The OECD's relationship with ACER was not always without problems but the consortium continued to secure the PISA contract beyond 2000. In 2003, for example, work to finalise the thematic report on social backgrounds and student achievement, being prepared by ACER, for example, finally was undertaken by the OECD Secretariat because members of the Editorial Group were not prepared to give ACER further time to produce the report. ACER (and an earlier team including an ACER staff member), had failed 'to respond appropriately to Board and Editorial Group comments or to keep to agreed timetables' (DEEWR, 2003a). Nevertheless, the consortium led by ACER was to be appointed as international contractor for PISA 2006.

The first cycle of PISA was conducted in 2000 with results reported on 4 December 2001 in three domains: reading, mathematical and scientific literacy. The Commonwealth bore the international cost and split national costs with the states and territories. The costs to the Commonwealth were approximately $1m. The Commonwealth paid 50 per cent of the costs of PISA and the states and territories the other 50 per cent allocated according to population, with the Commonwealth also paying some special costs. In 2001–2, the Commonwealth expenditure was $327,800 and the states and territories $74,700. In the 2003 PISA cycle, the sample size was increased to enable a longitudinal follow up, and the Commonwealth contribution increased to $562,300 and that of the states and territories to $175,800 (the Commonwealth bore the costs of the extended sample) (DEEWR, 2002c).

Meetings of the BPC were normally bi-annual, but an extra meeting was held for the release of the PISA 2000 results. The OECD required BPC Members to sign a confidentiality contract with OECD, and each reviewer was required to sign a non-disclosure agreement with their BPC member. It was reported that 'draft national reports will employ secure country codes to ensure confidentiality of international data in the process of writing national reports' (DEEWR, 2001c). There was nevertheless some cooperation between Australia and Canada on PISA, with (for example) a sharing of the PISA 2000 national report with Canada. Australia sent a copy of the Australian national report to a Canadian official, who responded 'I want to let you know that your report is the best PISA report I never saw' (DEEWR, 2003).

Australian officials also played an important role in securing participation in the Asia-Pacific, concerned at limited participation in the region, especially with the IEA ceasing its work. In late January 1997, for example, the First Secretary (Cultural Affairs) at the Japanese Embassy (Mr Nagayama) sought the Australian government's views on the survey proposal, as Japan was apparently reluctant to take part in PISA. Mr Nagayama was advised that the Japanese Minister for Education might approach the Australian Minister for his views, but Mr Nagayama indicated that there was no time to do so as their Minister wanted to have Australian views before the Japanese OECD representative called on the Ministry in early February to discuss the issue. As an Asia-Pacific member of the BPC, Australia was later asked by the OECD to write to China at Ministerial level encouraging participation (DEEWR, 1998). Minister Kemp duly wrote to the Ministers of Japan, Korea, Singapore and China encouraging their participation.

Issues with the states persisted as PISA was operationalised over issues such as the ownership of the results and conditions governing their release. New South Wales, for example, agreed to participate on the understanding that no material would be released publicly without the agreement of the signatories to the contract (DEEWR, 2002c). Western Australia had some problems because 15-year-olds could be in any one of three high school grades, an issue that persisted, with that state reluctant to pay for an increased sample size for PISA 2012 because this complication meant, arguably, that it could see little benefit for the additional cost.

In Network A in 2004 some concerns were expressed about the withdrawal of a number of OECD countries from the ongoing Trends in International Mathematics and Science Study (TIMSS) surveys (DEEWR, 2004a). The proposed release date for the PISA 2003 results was just a week ahead of the IEA's proposed release date for the results of TIMSS 2002/03 in which Australia and some other PISA countries had participated. To avoid confusion over the two sets of results, the OECD was asked to work closely with the IEA in developing a statement about the similarities and differences between the two surveys, especially because of the possibility that some countries might perform differently in the two studies (DEEWR, 2003a).

The modalities of PISA came under discussion in 2003, with the Europeans wanting PISA to be conducted every four to five years and the UK suggesting it be conducted annually. Australia opposed both these suggestions and it strongly opposed the proposal of some Europeans to move the administration of PISA to age 17 or 18. Australia considered 15 to be a good point, as only 62.5 per cent of the estimated resident population of 17-year-olds were still at school in 2002, and it was considered that 17-year-olds – 77 per cent of whom were in their final year at high school (Year 12) – would be reluctant to participate in an international assessment that did not count towards their final assessments. Australia also opposed moves to change the core domains of PISA (DEEWR, 2004c).

PISA data inform policy debates in Australia, and have recently revealed falling educational performance despite increased funding, for example (Ferrari, 2013; Marginson, 2013). But public discussion of key comparisons between states and between students in public and independent schools has been limited because of the insistence by the states (supported by the education unions) that such comparisons should not be permitted, much to the chagrin of Barry McGaw, who had returned to Australia and took up the position of Director of the Melbourne Education Research Institute (McGaw, 2007; Trounson, 2009). This opposition has rather been in vain, as the National Assessment Program – Literacy and Numeracy (NAPLAN), an annual assessment for students in Years 3, 5, 7 and 9 introduced in 2008, allows comparisons between schools and states.

CONCLUSION

As this chapter shows, Australia has been a significant player in OECD Education activities, reflected both in levels of engagement and commitment of resources, and in the senior roles played by Australians (Skilbeck and McGaw) or those with an Australian connection (Schleicher), which is not matched by Australia in any other OECD directorate. Australia was rather slow and reluctant to engage in this space; it might be said that they were 'CERI-naded' by Gass (if a bad pun might be permitted).

This reluctance was undoubtedly partly the result of the limited role for the Commonwealth government as regards education in the Australian federation at the time of accession, but this was also exacerbated by the rather negative assessment conveyed by the United Kingdom. It also stemmed at least partly from the fact that much of the activity at this time occurred in CERI, a Part II activity initiated and funded initially (and even after its 1971 renewal) by industry. At this time, Australia had only recently decided to participate in the Development Centre – its first Part II activity – and was in no mood to commit voluntary funds to activities about which it was still learning.

From that modest beginning, Australian involvement has grown. It is strategic in deciding where it will engage, but it has become a significant player in education at the OECD.

NOTES

1. ACER was established in 1930 as an independent not for profit company.
2. The Commonwealth department responsible for education has undergone numerous changes since Australia joined the OECD. These various names are: the Department of Education and Science between December 1966 and December 1972; the Department of Education between December 1972 and March 1983; the Department of Education and Youth Affairs between March 1983 and December 1984; the Department of Education between December 1984 and July 1987; the Department of Employment, Education and Training (DEET) between July 1987 and March 1996; the Department of Employment, Education, Training and Youth Affairs (DEETYA) between March 1996 and October 1998; the Department of Education, Training and Youth Affairs (DETYA) between October 1998 and November 2001; the Department of Education, Science and Training (DEST) between November 2001 and December 2007; the Department of Education, Employment and Workplace Relations (DEEWR) between December 2007 and September 2013; from September 2013, the Department of Education. For convenience, any references to 'the Department' will be to the name of the entity current at that time. As the files consulted were held by DEEWR at the time, they have been referenced to that entity.
3. The documents cited in this section are held in NAA, 1973.
4. The IEA commenced in 1958 when a group of scholars met at the UNESCO Institute for Education in Hamburg to discuss problems of school and student evaluation. Its secretariat is located in Amsterdam.
5. Between McGaw and Schleicher, the Director was Dr Barbara Ischinger (from 1 January 2006).
6. Kuehn (2004: 61) wrongly states that the trigger was the Second International Mathematics and Science Study (SIMSS). In fact, the two studies (mathematics and science) were separate and combined only in the Third International Mathematics and Science Study (now Trends in IMSS) in 1995.

BIBLIOGRAPHY

Blackmur, D. 2007. 'A Critical Analysis of the UNESCO/OECD Guidelines for Quality Provision of Cross-Border Higher Education', *Quality in Higher Education*, 13(2): 117–130.

Connell, W. 1980. *The Australian Council for Educational Research 1930–80*, Melbourne: ACER.

DEEWR 1994. C94/12637 RB – DSS – Input into OECD International Education Indicators Projects – 1994. Letter Malcolm Skilbeck (CERI) to Ms Linda Lipp, Assistant Secretary, DEET 21 November 1994.

DEEWR 1995. NO95/02671. OECD – International Educational Indicators (INES) Project – General Assembly of the INES Project – Lahti Finland – 12–15 June 1995.

DEEWR 1995a. NO95/28434 OECD International Education Indicators Project – Network B – 1995.

DEEWR 1996. NO96/23693 OECD (OECD) Education Committee Meeting, 25–27 November 1996 and OECD CERI (CERI) Governing Board Meeting, 28–29 November 1996 – Divisional Contributions.
DEEWR 1997. NO97/22127 Minute 5 August 1997 to Secretary from Bill Daniels FAS, Schools Division, 5 August 1997.
DEEWR 1997a. NO97/22423 Section Involvement in OECD – International Education Indicators Project (INES). Network A. Surveys of Student Achievement Outcomes – 1997.
DEEWR 1998. NO98/09430 Section Involvement in OECD – International Education Indicators Project (INES). Network A. Surveys of Student Achievement Outcomes – 1998.
DEEWR 1999. ET99/098353 RNR Section Involvement in OECD INES Network A – 1999.
DEEWR 2001. ET01/02361 OECD (OECD) – Programme for ISA (PISA) – Appointment of an Australian National Project Manager for PISA – 2003.
DEEWR 2001a. ET01/05625 OECD Surveys of Student Achievement – Divisional Involvement with National Advisory Committee – 2001.
DEEWR 2001b. ET01/16081 OECD PISA 2000 Policy and Reporting 2001.
DEEWR 2001c. ET01/10736 BPC 11 Ottawa July 2001. Report by Wendy Whitham to Secretary, 20 August 2001.
DEEWR 2002. ES02/00986 'A Brief Summary of Current Australian Involvement in OECD Educational Indicators'.
DEEWR 2002a. ES02/15585 OECD – Centre for Education Research & Innovation (CERI) Activities – Briefing Material and Section Liaison.
DEEWR 2002b. ES03/00145 'Briefing Points for the Education Committee and CERI Meetings Autumn 2002', Matthew James, October 2002.
DEEWR 2002c. ESO2/11695 PISA – Program for International Student Assessment.
DEEWR 2003. ES03/01674 OECD PISA 2000 – Policy and Reporting 2003.
DEEWR 2003a. ES03/25425 BPC 16 – Lisbon October 2003. Report on PISA Board of Participating Countries and Network A Meetings, Lisbon October 2003.
DEEWR 2004. ES04/09513 Joint Session of EC and CERI Governing Board – October 2003. Conclusions from the Meeting of the INES Strategic Management Group on 8–9 September.
DEEWR 2004a. ES04/00789 BPC Lucerne March 2004 (14–19 with Network A), Wendy Whitham Report to Sec 21 April 2004.
DEEWR 2004b. ES04/09464 OECD – DEELSA Educ. Committee – 65th Session March 2000.
DEEWR 2004c. ES04/09509 EC 72nd Session – October 2003 Part I and ES04/09508 Part II.
DEEWR 2004d. ES04/09513 Joint Session of EC and CERI Governing Board – October 2003.
DEEWR 2004e. File ES04/28455. Draft Agenda of the 74th Session 25 October 2004 EDU/EC/A(2004)5/REV1.
DEEWR 2005. ES05/01428 DEST Involvement in OECD Education Activities, 2005. 'Report on Network C Meeting: Montreux, Switzerland, 30 November – 2 December 2005'.

DEEWR 2006. ES06/03704 Meeting of OECD Education Ministers, Athens 27–28 June 2006.

DEST 2006. Overview of the Department of Education, Science and Training's Involvement in the Education Activities of the Organisation for Economic Co-operation and Development. October 2006. In DEEWR File E506/19273 OECD – Overview of DEST Involvement in the OECD – 2006–2007.

DEST 2006a. Briefing for Minister (Ms Bishop). International Education: DEST's Multilateral Engagement. 16 February 2006. In DEEWR File E506/19273 OECD – Overview of DEST Involvement in the OECD – 2006–2007.

Eide, K. 1990. '30 Years of Educational Collaboration in the OECD', Paper presented at the International Congress 'Planning and Management of Educational Development', Mexico, 26–30 March.

Ferrari, J. 2013. 'Billions fail to stop slide in world student rankings', *The Australian*, 4 December.

Istance, D. 2011. 'Education at OECD: Recent Themes and Recommendations', *European Journal of Education*, 46(1): 87–100.

Kuehn, L. 2004. 'Leaning between Conspiracy and Hegemony: OECD, UNESCO and the Tower of PISA', in Marita Moll (ed.), *Passing the Test The False Promises of Standardised Testing*, Ottawa: Canadian Centre for Policy Alternatives, pp. 57–66.

Lokan, J., Greenwood, L. and Cresswell, J. 2001. *15 Up and Counting, Reading, Writing, Reasoning: How Literate are Australia's Students? The PISA 2000 Survey of Students' Reading, Mathematical and Scientific Literacy Skills*, Camberwell, VIC: ACER Press.

Marginson, S. 2013. 'Australia falls further behind in PISA test of basic education skills', *The Australian*, 16 December.

Martens, K., Balzer, C., Sackmann, R. and Weymann, A. 2004. 'Comparing Governance of International Organisations – The EU, the OECD and Educational Policy' (*TranState Working Papers, 7*), Bremen: Universitat Bremen.

McGaw, B. 2007. 'Resourced for a world of difference', *The Australian*, 1 August.

Medrich, E. and Griffith, J. 1992. *International Mathematics and Science Assessment: What Have We Learned?* Washington: National Center for Education Statistics, US Department of Education, Office of Educational Research and Improvement (*Research and Development Report*, NCES 92-011), January.

NAA 1969. File No 69 2095 Part 3 Reconsideration of Possible Australian Membership of OECD.

NAA 1971. A1838 OECD – Education. Fourth Session of OECD Education Committee. 29 November – 1 December 1971.

NAA 1973. A1838 1724/4/19/2 PART 1 Organisation for Economic Co-operation and Development – Centre for Educational Research and Innovation 1971–1973.

Norton, A. 2008. 'The OECD Cringe', *Policy*, 24(2): 5–6.

O'Reilly, B. 2009. 'Misinformed Debate on Public Funding of Universities', *Australian Review of Public Affairs*, June, accessed on 23 January 2017 at www.australianreview.net/digest/2009/06/oreilly.html.

OECD 1973. CERI Governing Board. Draft Programme of Work for 1974 (Note by the Secretariat). CERI/CD(73)5.
OECD 1995. International Education Statistics and Indicators (INES) Outcomes of the Third General Assembly of the INES Project. DEELSA/ED/CERI/CD/RD(95)1.
OECD 1995a. The INES Project (1988–1995) – Historical Brief. PRAG(95)2] (English).
OECD 1997. Decentralised Programme for Producing Indicators on Student Achievement on a Regular Basis (Note by the Secretary-General) 10 September 1997 C(97)176.
OECD 2011. Directorate for Education. Education Policy Committee. OECD Reviews of Evaluation and Assessment in Education: Australia. EDU/EDPC/EA(2011)10.
OECD 2014. www.oecd.org/pisa/aboutpisa/. Accessed 23 November 2014 at www.oecd.org/edu/innovation-education/newoecdeducationdirectoratetohelpdevelophumancapitalsocialcohesion.htm.
Papadopoulos, G. 2011. 'The OECD Approach to Education in Retrospect: 1960–1990', *European Journal of Education*, 46(1): 85–86.
Schuller, T. 2005. 'Constructing International Policy Research: the Role of CERI/OECD', *European Educational Research Journal*, 4(3): 170–180.
Sellar, S. and Lingard, B. 2013. 'The OECD and Global Governance in Education', *Journal of Education Policy*, DOI: 10.1080/02680939.2013.779791.
Sellar, S. and Lingard, B. 2013. 'The OECD and the Expansion of PISA: New Global Modes of Governance in Education', *British Educational Research Journal*, DOI: 10.1002/berj.3120.
Thomson, S., Cresswell, J. and Bortoli, L. 2004. *Facing the Future: A Focus on Mathematical Literacy Among Australian 15-year-old Students in PISA 2003*, Camberwell: ACER.
Trounson, A. 2009. 'Results of School Testing Hidden', *The Australian*, 19 January.
Walberg, H. and Guoxiong, Z. 1998. 'Analyzing the OECD Indicators Model', *Comparative Education*, 34(1): 55–70.
Williams, B. 1994. *Education With its Eyes Open: A Biography of Dr K.S. Cunningham*, Melbourne: ACER.

12. A leading role for Australia: health work at the OECD

The aim of this chapter is to describe and assess Australia's involvement in the health work of the OECD, an involvement that was only of 'minor interest' for over twenty years but that increased sharply from 1997 to 1998. It was not only a rapidly increased but a successful involvement, resulting in a programme of health work that, at least in part, was in Australia's interests and that brought it substantial influence. Moreover, it was an influence that persisted for over a decade, focused on the Department of Health and Ageing's (DHA) then Secretary, Jane Halton. The chapter commences with a brief description of Australia's place in the global health regime, a regime of increasing complexity that posed increasing management and organisational challenges for officials within the DHA. It then examines the change of strategy that took place in the period of the first Howard government and the reasons for the 'forum shopping', that resulted in the selection of the OECD as the forum for an expansion of health work in which the DHA was interested. The chapter then moves on to illustrate the difficulties faced in promoting increased health work at the OECD at a time of severe budgetary constraint and the desire of successive Australian ambassadors to the OECD to curtail the growth in the breadth and cost of its work. The last two sections focus on Australia's success in promoting a major expansion of health work that came to be known as the Health Project, a project that was widely perceived as a major success and that led to a firmly embedded place on the OECD's agenda in the years after the end of the Health Project.

FROM 'ONLY A MINOR INTEREST' TO MAJOR INVOLVEMENT

The governance of health at the national, regional and global levels changed rapidly in the period from 1945 to the end of the 1970s. The 1940s were marked by significant changes at the national level in the more developed countries, with the exception of the USA, as the provision of health care became an increasingly important function of the new welfare states that arose after 1945, although there was still substantial national variation in how it was organised and financed (Leichter, 1979). In Australia, initial constitutional authority for health rested largely with the state governments, making the Commonwealth government's involvement in, and management of, its international health activities more challenging than for a unitary state. This changed rapidly in the 1940s, following a constitutional referendum in 1946, the introduction of a series of five-year funding agreements with the state governments for health, the 1947 Pharmaceutical Benefits Act and the 1948 National Health Service Act, although the delivery of health services remained with the states.

At the global level the later 1940s also saw rapid change with the establishment of the major UN specialised agencies concerned with health, focused on the World Health Organization (WHO) and the United Nations Children's Fund (UNICEF), sometimes working in cooperation with the United Nations Relief and Rehabilitation Administration (UNRRA) (until 1948, when most of its functions were transferred to the International Refugee Organization or the WHO), FAO, ILO, ICAO and UNESCO, as well as the various offices of the UN (Staples, 2006; WHO, 1958: 129–45). The specialised agencies soon developed extensive, operational networks of regional offices, as well as associated national offices, the latter established as non-governmental organisations concerned largely with fundraising. The WHO, for example, was required by its Constitution to establish and maintain 'effective collaboration', with the UN, specialised agencies, government health administrations, professional groups and other appropriate organisations. Such collaborations developed quite rapidly and, by the end of 1957, for example, forty non-governmental organisations had a recognised relationship with the WHO, including the World Medical Association and the Red Cross (WHO, 1958: 143). In particular, WHO's Director-General was authorised to have direct access to national health departments, governmental or non-governmental, as well as international bodies operating in the field of health.

While the establishment of the WHO and the associated UN specialised agencies represented a considerable centralisation of international work on health, the rapidly developing Cold War introduced a sharp divide in the actual extent of centralisation in the new networks and control over the bulk of health related work was retained within national systems. However, national control did not necessarily result in nationally coordinated policies in relation to international health, whether at the WHO or the associated, specialised agencies and there is little sign, for example, that the three Commonwealth agencies with major health responsibilities, the DEA (in regard to the overall coordination of Australia's external affairs), Health and what became AusAid (regarding health in the development context), systematically or regularly co-ordinated their international health efforts.

Australia's main focus as regards the international dimensions of health was, not surprisingly, for several decades directed at the WHO, in which it played an active role (Carroll, 2013). Also, given that at the time of Australia's accession to the OECD in 1971 there was little in the way of work on health care being undertaken at that organisation, it is not surprising that, in response to a call for departmental expressions of interest in OECD membership and involvement in its activities a senior health official could state that:

> The Department has only a minor interest in the working of the OECD but areas such as tourism and quarantine requirements for entry into Australia were relevant. (NAA, 1970)

A further indication of the difference in emphasis at this time between the Department of Health's interest in the WHO and the OECD can be seen in the fact that Australia's membership contribution to the WHO in 1974–75 was $1,023,000 and to the OECD was $790,000, the latter covering all areas of the OECD's work, very little of which was focused on health (Australian Parliament, 1974). Similarly, there is no reference to the OECD's health work in the Australian Hansard for the 1970s and 1980s, despite a marked growth in references to OECD data and publications, largely regarding the state of the Australian economy, the 'health', of which was a matter of frequent concern.

This Australian focus on the WHO was complicated from the early 1980s by the increasing role of the World Bank in the area of health, the decision by the World Health Assembly to freeze WHO's budget in 1982, the 1985 US decision to pay only 20 per cent of its assessed contribution to all UN agencies, including the WHO, followed shortly afterwards by a further US decision to withhold all of its assessed contribution to the WHO budget, sparked off by its opposition to WHO's 'Essential Drug Program'. Also, there had been a rapid growth in voluntary, non-budget, or 'extra-budgetary', funding of the WHO by its richer members, similar to that experienced by most of the UN's specialised agencies in this period. Such voluntary funds overtook the size of the WHO's regular budget by the early 1990s, amounting to 54 per cent of its total budget.

In essence, the growth in voluntary funding meant that the policies and priorities of the World Health Assembly, with its majority of developing countries, for the most part only related to the items in the regular budget, while policies and priorities supported by the wealthier members were funded by the voluntary funds. The WHO was, in effect, declining in relative importance and prestige, so that by the 1990s a situation had emerged in which the World Bank had become, at least in financial terms, the major actor in international health affairs, with its annual loans for health purposes greater than the WHO's entire budget.

From the perspective of Australian decision makers the global health regime had thus become increasingly more complex, with a greater variety of actors involved, both public and private, requiring an increasingly sophisticated response in a range of international institutions, not only the WHO. This complexity was even more challenging as by the middle 1990s there had been no systematic review of health policy in Australia for several years (Baume, 1995: 97). However, Australian decision makers gradually became more interested in the health work of the OECD, so that by 1995, in response to a review of Australia's OECD's membership conducted by DFAT, Don Cameron-Stephen, then the Cabinet Liaison Officer for the Department of Human Services and Health (DHSH), noted 'that Australia benefits significantly from membership of the OECD', and that the DHSH supports the promotion of social issues, including health policy analysis, as among Australia's priorities for the work of the OECD (DFAT, 1995).

Signs of Life: Australian Participation in OECD Health Work in the 1990s

The 1990s were characterised by a slowly increasing Australian participation in four streams of OECD health work, outlined below. Three were directly related to the Department of Health and Family Services (DHFS): the OECD's health data and health accounts work, work on the health implication of an ageing population and the increased involvement of the Therapeutic Goods Administration (TGA) with the OECD, largely as regards its use of the OECD's Principles of Good Laboratory Practice. The fourth was related far more to the Treasury, in the shape of the 1995–96 review of the Australian economy by the Economic and Development Review Committee (EDRC).

The increased involvement can be seen, for example, in the shape of the gradually increasing participation in OECD work of the Therapeutic Goods Administration (TGA) and the Australian Institute of Health and Welfare (AIHW), federal government agencies in the health portfolio. The TGA was particularly interested in the OECD's Mutual Acceptance of DATA (MAD), agreed in 1981. MADs core agreement was that test data generated in any member country in accordance with the OECD Test

Guidelines and Principles of Good Laboratory Practice should be accepted in other member countries for assessment purposes and other uses relating to the protection of human health and the environment. It was accompanied by a set of procedures for monitoring compliance by government inspections and study audits, as well as a framework for international liaison among monitoring and data-receiving national authorities (OECD, 2014).

The AIHW became involved in the OECD's health data work from the later 1980s and in its health accounts work from 1997 to 1998. The OECD data regarding health, now published annually, was useful for national decision makers in helping identify the gap between the desired state of affairs and the current or likely future state of affairs as it provided comparative trend data over time regarding a wide range of standardised health and health system indicators. In summary, it provided data that could be used to help determine the performance of current and planned health policies on the nation's health, for example, data on life expectancy, maternal and infant mortality, non-medical determinants of health, health care resources and their utilisation, pharmaceutical consumption and sales, health expenditure and more general data on demographic and economic trends related to health (OECD, 2013).

The AIHW was allocated responsibility for providing Australian health data for the OECD health database and developed a continuing, close relationship with the OECD in this area, with an OECD official, for example, becoming a Visiting Fellow at the AIHW in the second half of 1994–95 (AIHW, 1995: 13). In addition, the AIHW made increasing use of the health data to compare Australia's health performance for its domestic audience, for example, 'Indicators of Public Health in Australia', which reported trends in public health in Australia, comparing them with seven OECD countries (AIHW, 1997: 17). It also contributed the occasional report to the OECD's newly-established, Health Statistics Working Party (AIHW, 1997: 24).

Similarly, the AIHW became involved during the later 1990s in the health accounts work that resulted in the OECD's 'System of Health Accounts' (SHA) in 2000. The SHA was aimed at developing a standardised system of health accounts that would enable systematic, accurate comparisons of health revenues and expenditures and, with a number of modifications it was adopted in Australia (OECD, 2000a, 2011; AIHW, 2003: 6 and Chapter 3). The AIHW regarded the SHA as 'A most important initiative' (AIHW, 2003: 6, and Chapter 3). A further indication of the value placed on the SHA and related expenditure data was demonstrated by the AIHW's regret that there was no similar framework for welfare services expenditures, although it had decided to move to adopt the OECD's less detailed framework for social expenditures (AIHW, 2003: 8). The AIHW also participated in the later revision of the SHA again indicating its perceived value (AIHW, 2010: iii).

There was also a gradually increasing involvement in the OECD's growing work on ageing and its health implications, especially ageing's escalating cost for OECD members from the early 1990s though, for the most part, it was undertaken by officials in the human and community services divisions of the Department in the 1990s, not by those in health. Participation was complicated by the fact that the bulk of the health work at the OECD took place in the Directorate for Education, Labour and Social Affairs (DELSA), so that meetings of its main Education, Labour and Social Affairs Committee (ELSAC) covered four areas: education, labour (employment and industrial relations), health and social welfare.

This involved the need for considerable coordination within the Australian Department, with Australian representatives to ELSAC often not including officials from the health side of the Department. ELSAC itself had spawned a wide range of more specialised subcommittees and working groups, although several of these covered a wide range of policy areas, several not related to health matters. Health initially was a responsibility of its Working Party on Social Policy (WPSP), in which it had to compete to gain space on a crowded agenda with many non-health items, reflecting health work's low priority in the OECD at this time. WPSP also had responsibility for issues concerning the long-term care of the elderly, where advice was provided by an associated meeting of experts, which a representative from the Australian Office of the Aged attended (DHA, 1992).

Rather more attention began to be devoted to the health implications of ageing as the 1990s progressed following a USA proposal, with strong support from Japan and Germany, for a major OECD project on ageing, including a range of health issues (DHA, 1994). It resulted in the commencement in 1995 of the OECD's Ageing Populations Study, modelled on its earlier, 1994 Jobs Study. The Study had two work phases with the first reviewing the policy implications of ageing in the areas of pensions, health and long-term care, the labour market, fiscal policy and financial markets, concluding with a report 'Ageing in OECD Countries: A Critical Policy Challenge'. This led a broader study, sponsored by the Japanese in 1996, 'Initiative for a Caring World', to promote cross-national policy learning regarding both social security and health that, in turn, led to a number of reports in the later 1990s, including 'The Caring World: National Achievements', and 'The Caring World: An Analysis', which were assessments of important social policy developments. The

DHA regarded them as of a high quality, providing extensive and valuable information (DHA, 1999a).

The regular EDRC reviews of members' economies are well regarded and influential, as discussed in Chapter 7. In the later 1980s, following their greater focus on microeconomic reform, they began to include one or more reviews of specific sectors, particularly health, in large part because of the rapid growth of health expenditures that was putting an increasing strain on members' budgets. After discussion with the Australian Treasury it was agreed that the 1995–96 review of Australia would contain a review of the health sector and, though the DHFS was consulted, it played a relatively small part in the review, providing information regarding health policy and practices and helping check on the accuracy of data. The Report was generally positive, both as regards Australia's overall economic performance and the state of the health sector.

The Report pointed out that, in common with most OECD states, Australia's health-care expenditures had grown rapidly, with the GDP share increasing from 4.9 per cent in 1960 to 8.5 per cent in 1993, close to the OECD average. Further, that while successive governments had largely restrained further growth in health expenditures in the later 1980s by capping budgets for public sector hospitals, introducing measures to reduce the dissemination of new and expensive technologies, and restraining price increases for medical services and pharmaceutical goods, the Report noted such restraint needed to be supplemented with a range of more sophisticated incentives for the efficient production of hospital services. In particular, an emphasis was needed, it was felt, on reducing the incentives for the over-supply of medical services and on empowering purchasers of health care to obtain better value for their expenditures (OECD, 1995: 71–2).

The health chapter in the EDRC review concluded with a number of recommendations, several of them radical in the Australian context. The first was for an extension of case-mix funding to out-patient services, based on the model introduced in Victoria. The second was distinctly more radical, the possible 'broad-banding' of all public health funding into a single budget at either the Commonwealth or state level, together with a full purchaser–provider split in health expenditure on lines similar to those introduced in New Zealand and the UK. The third was also radical, at least as far as Australia's medical practitioners were concerned, the introduction of 'blended' payment for GPs, who would receive part of their incomes as capitation payments for specified health outcomes, aimed at reducing the extent of fee for service payments and their incentive to oversupply medical services (OECD, 1995: 114–17).

The broad-banding and purchaser–provider split recommendation, assuming the proposed single health budget was to rest in the hands of the Commonwealth government, would have meant a major reform, had it been accepted, especially if it was also to be responsible for setting national health policy objectives, with the state governments responsible for the purchase of health services, accountable to the Commonwealth. This recommendation trod heavily into the politically sensitive area of federal–state relations and might have been stimulated by the Commonwealth in order to gauge reaction from the state governments to such a proposal without having to shoulder the responsibility for making the recommendation. Even further, the report suggested that funds could be provided directly to a new system of district health authorities, by-passing state governments, with the new authorities being responsible for the purchase of health care for their local populations on a contract basis. While such views might have been welcome to an ALP Commonwealth government and to the Treasury, it is unlikely that they would have been so welcome to state governments, especially those dominated by Liberal–National coalition governments. It was not for another twelve years and the ALP government of Kevin Rudd that elements of this proposal were implemented.

While the above activities indicate a slowly growing Australian role in the OECD's health work it was still of a limited nature. As First Assistant Secretary Briggs noted in regard to OECD health work, until the beginning of 1997–98, 'minimal resources were devoted by the portfolio to OECD engagement' and the 'broader area of ongoing health policy analysis has not received substantive attention' (DFAT, 1998). This was soon to change, in the shape of the department's new international engagement strategy.

A NEW INTERNATIONAL ENGAGEMENT STRATEGY, FORUM SHOPPING AND ENCOURAGING GREATER WORK ON HEALTH AT THE OECD

This section describes and explains the factors that led to a rapid expansion in the Department's involvement in the health work of the OECD. It commences with a brief examination of the development of a new strategy of greater international engagement before moving on to consider why the OECD was selected for greater involvement and how the Department pushed, successfully, for greater health work to be conducted at the OECD.

In the period up to and including 1996 there was rarely any mention of the Department's international activities in its annual reports or other publications, including the OECD. The only unit within the Department with an explicitly international role was the Public Affairs and International Branch within the Information Services Division. This changed in 1997, following a review of the Department's aims and strategies under the first Howard government. It was decided that the broad and ambitious new goal of 'within three years being the leader in promoting, developing and funding world class health and family services for all Australians', would require the substantial strengthening of the Department's international relationships, particularly with the WHO and the OECD.

It was also noted that a Memorandum of Understanding had been established with Japan regarding health matters and that membership of the 'Four Nations Conference of Health Experts' (US, Canada, Germany and Holland) had been sought (DHFS, 1998: 4). Any future claim that the ambitious goal of world class health services had been achieved, in order to be credible, would require the identification and comparative analysis of what was world class and a more active participation in the WHO, OECD and the Four Nations Conference, with their increasing emphasis on the comparative efficiency of health systems. The Department's efforts in this regard were to be organised by a new Industry and Development Branch within the Portfolio Strategies Group and it was claimed that already it had been successful in promoting Australia's objective to focus the work of the WHO and the OECD on cost-effective strategies for 'improving health research, policy development, information activities and service delivery' (DHFS, 1998: 16, 32). Such work was to be a 'Priority Outcome' of the Department (DHFS, 1998: 257).

Forum Shopping and the Selection of the OECD

While the new international engagement strategy encompassed the WHO and the OECD, it was the OECD that soon gained a greater priority, following a period of forum shopping, although its Secretary Andrew Podger was keen to ensure that the connections between both were strengthened (DHA, 1997a). There were several reasons for the increased focus on the OECD, the first of which was the nature of the work that was desired, comparative health policy analysis. All of the international organisations interested in health had a degree of expertise in this area, but in the case of the WHO and the World Bank it had been work that focused primarily on developing countries, whereas Secretary Podger was keen to see a comparative focus on more developed countries similar to Australia, such as Canada, where comparative policy learning was likely to be more useful. As he noted:

> The skills of the World Bank were acknowledged, but the OECD was seen as the more natural centre of excellence in cooperative health policies in developed countries. (DHA, 1997b)

In addition, the Department had felt for some years that at least some of the related work being done in the WHO was 'academic', a fatal sin in the eyes of most public servants (DHA, 1995). Further, senior departmental officials had not been impressed by the distinct lack of progress within WHO in implementing a 'Program for Research on Ageing and Health' (PRAH), to which their Minister had agreed to provide a voluntary contribution of $250,000. Following a meeting with WHO officials from its Social Change and Mental Health Cluster to discuss the situation, a departmental official concluded that it was:

> [N]ot one of the WHO's better divisions, with its ageing and health work program unclear and unstructured and with poorly developed links to other organisations undertaking related activities, for example, the OECD. (DHA, 1999b)

DHA's view of at least this section of the WHO did not improve when, in 2000, following a continued lack of progress on the project and considerable delays in responses to requests for progress reports from DHA, it was announced that the project had been discontinued as the 'time was not right', and the Department commenced the recovery of $250,000 for the research not undertaken (DHA, 2000a).

The second factor considered was in which of the WHO, the OECD or the World Bank was Australia most likely to get the necessary support from other members for a significant, increased programme of health work. It would be most difficult in both the WHO and the World Bank, with their far larger memberships and a greater range of national interests, although the judicious use of voluntary contributions could be used as an incentive to gather sufficient support for a project. However, given the already fairly close relationships with senior health officials in the UK, Canada and the USA, all of whom were major players in the OECD, plus its far smaller membership, greater homogeneity and familiarity with the use of voluntary contributions to fund projects, then the OECD seemed a more attractive option. Indeed, Secretary Podger had taken pains to discuss the Australian interest in promoting increased international work on health with officials in both Canada and the UK and had received a positive response, including the view that the OECD would be an appropriate location. In a frank admission of the realities of the situation, he'd also noted that 'to get the most out of the OECD, we must make a real contribution (effort and/or money)' (DHA, 1997c).

Detailed advice was also, of course, provided by a variety of Commonwealth government officials from within and outside of the Department, especially those with direct experience of the OECD. Deputy Secretary David Borthwick, an economist, for example, recently arrived from Treasury, had been Australia's ambassador to the OECD from 1991 to 1993 and was very familiar with its workings. Perhaps the most detailed and useful advice was in a lengthy paper provided for Secretary Podger in 1998 by the head of the Industry Development and International Branch within the Department's Policy and Strategy Group, Susan Ingram. It noted that the OECD was a single source that provided useful health data on a range of countries and that, in particular, its peer analysis process could provide an evaluation of Australia's health policies in a 'fairly confidential and non-threatening environment', with evaluations published only with the consent of the country concerned – but rather disappointingly noticing that peer reviews of member health systems were not a regular or frequent item on the OECD's agenda. Another drawback was that peer evaluations had a heavy emphasis on economic and managerial issues, sometimes to the detriment of social or cultural factors important in shaping health policy (DHA, 1998a).

The paper also stressed that as with most international organisations, the OECD had recently experienced an increasingly severe budget cutback, restricting its ability to conduct research, with some members pushing for a greater focus on fewer topics. This had brought about a painful re-prioritisation of its work that had identified seven core work areas, including, fortunately, health. In addition, it had identified nine emerging areas of work, again including health. The author had also discovered, from informal discussion with DFAT officials, that a conservative and influential view of the OECD's future work agenda was emanating from the Australian Treasury, with an emphasis on restricting the OECD's work to its traditional, core area of economic analysis, a view that was influential within the Australian delegation at the OECD. While this would not necessarily lead to Treasury officials opposing an increase in the OECD's health work, it was a possibility that needed to be considered, especially as the Australian delegation had been one of the major supporters of the recent OECD budget cutbacks.

Encouraging Greater Work on Health at the OECD

Given the OECD's difficult budgetary situation, it was thus likely that the department would need to fight on two fronts if it was to successfully promote an increase in health work at the OECD: the first on the domestic front with Treasury to gain an Australian endorsement of an increased health agenda; the second with those other members of the OECD keen to restrict its costs, notably the USA (DHA, 1998a). The former would not be easy, it was advised, as, in addition to the budgetary situation, health work had received 'little attention' at the OECD for some years, as demonstrated, it was noted, 'by the rather lowly organisational ranking of the health sector, hidden away in a "Health Unit", which in turn forms only a small part of the vast Directorate for Employment, Labour and Social Affairs (DELSA)' (DHA, 1998a).

It might also have been noted that while it might be possible to gain the eager support of the few officials working on health projects, their morale was low and career prospects in doubt following the cutbacks and the loss of their head, Jean-Pierre Poullier, who had been recently been replaced by Peter Scherer as head of the Social Policy and Health Division of DELSA. Scherer was an Australian who had been working with the OECD for ten years. It would be necessary, hence, to gain not only Scherer's support but support at more senior levels, both within DELSA, in the shape of its Director, Tom Alexander, and Deputy Director, John Martin, and, ideally, at the level of the Secretary-General, Donald Johnston and his deputies. Similarly, it would be necessary to ensure effective communication with, and the support of, the key figures in the Australian delegation to the OECD, particularly the Ambassador, Ralph Hillman and the Counsellor responsible for social policy and health matters, David Kalisch, an official from the Department of Family and Community Services. It would also be necessary to gain the support of the health minister, Michael Wooldridge.

As well as developing important contacts and support, it was felt necessary to reorganise responsibilities for the OECD within the Department. Until July 1997 responsibility for coordinating responses regarding requests for information from the OECD had been with the Health Service Outcomes Branch within the Health Services Development Division. It was decided that this responsibility should be transferred to the Industry Development and International Branch of the more powerful Policy and Strategy Group (PSG), with more senior officers involved in, and responsible for, its work relating to the OECD. The coordination of department-wide responses would be cleared by the First Assistant

Secretary of the PSG, with those related to policy having to be cleared by a member of the Department's Executive or, where appropriate, the Minister. As a sign of the great interest of Secretary Podger in this area, copies of the coordinated responses would be forwarded to his Senior Executive Assistant for information (DHA, 1997e).

Interdepartmental 'turf battles' also had to be overcome, but with the Department of Social Security (DSS) rather than, as expected, Treasury, to the extent that the secretaries of the two departments became involved in resolving a dispute. What was described by Secretary Podger as a 'highly provocative cable', had been sent to the Australian representative to a March 1998 OECD preparatory committee meeting instructing the OECD delegation 'not to press the health agenda', relegating a health topic that earlier had been proposed by the DHA for the lunch discussion between Ministers to the lowest priority. It also stipulated that the DSS officer in the delegation would be the delegation leader, over a more senior official from DHA, advising that the DSS officer would:

> [c]onsult with the DEETYA and HFS members in relation to those interventions **she decides** (sic) that it is appropriate for Australia to make at the meeting. (DHA, 1998b)

Given the priority that the DHA was giving to its efforts to upgrade health work at the OECD, the content of the cable in question did not go down well with Secretary Podger, who informed Dr Rosalsky, Secretary of the DSS that he saw:

> [a] resistance on the part of DSS to our closer interest in the OECD which, disturbingly, is being acted out in thoroughly unprofessional turf battles. (DHA, 1998b)

Moreover, Podger noted that the cable had been sent without consultation with the DHA, in the weeks leading up to the important June 1998 OECD Ministerial meeting. At the heart of the issue was the fact that the DHA had not normally been represented at such meetings in the past, simply providing any relevant material to the DSS, which was then responsible for coordinating inputs to the meeting. As was pointed out in the letter:

> Once we provide material, DSS exercises editorial control with little or no consultation, and copies the final brief to us only after its despatch. (DHA, 1998b)

After further discussions it was agreed that there would be: the joint clearance of instruction cables; joint clearance of final briefs; and, where both departments were represented on a delegation, each would speak to their own portfolio issues; also, where only one department was represented on a delegation covering the responsibilities of both portfolios, that member 'will pursue in a professional manner the range of policy matters covered by the consolidated Australian brief' (DHA, 1998b).

On a more positive note, Secretary Podger visited the OECD in 1997, following an earlier meeting with Mr Clive Smee in the UK's Department of Health. Smee had been chair of the OECD's WPSP, with its health responsibilities, was still a member and was very familiar with its workings. At the OECD Podger met with Ambassador Hillman, Director Tom Alexander and Deputy Director John Martin (to become Director in 2000), as well as Peter Scherer, outlining his strong interest in seeing the OECD increase the extent of its health work. In order to add weight to his proposal, he later proposed that a senior member of his department be seconded to the health unit of the OECD for an initial period of twelve months to work on health projects, and that he was considering providing a voluntary contribution to support health work (DHA, 1998c). The offer was gratefully accepted.

Deputy Director Martin then visited Podger in Canberra on 12 June 1998, as did Peter Scherer later that year, to further discuss developments. Martin was informed that the Department now had funding for a voluntary contribution to the OECD of up to $150,000 in 1998–99 and $300,000 each year thereafter and asked how it could be used to best effect in improving OECD health and long-term care policy research (DHA, 1998d). As, for example, the budget for OECD expenditure on health work for 1999 was slightly less than FF8 million with about 50 per cent coming from Part I of the budget and the rest from Part II, this was a significant contribution and would have proved most attractive to Alexander and Martin, not to mention Peter Scherer (Carroll and Kellow, 2011: 240). It would also have placed Australia in a strong bargaining position in relation to determining the content of any new work programme for health in the OECD's budget discussions, especially as Secretary-General Don Johnston had informed the OECD Council that 'Members have not shown as much interest in this critical area as I would hope', and that he was concerned about the health agenda and would support the development of further health work at the OECD (Carroll and Kellow, 2011: 241). Australia, clearly, was an exception to the lack of interest he had identified.

As well as efforts to gain support from key OECD officials, longer serving members of the Australian Delegation would have been aware that the OECD's Business and Industry Advisory Committee (BIAC) had supported the expansion of health work at the OECD since at least 1994 and could be counted on for further support. In that year BIAC had not only offered support, but a set of 'principles' for OECD governments to consider when implementing health reforms (BIAC, 1994). The principles asserted that all people should have access to health care services, regardless of their income, with payment being income related. However, it also stressed the need for increased efficiency in the provision of health services and asserted that, while governments should retain control over the redistribution of funds in order to maintain social equity, the role of market forces among insurers and providers of health care services, including hospitals, should be increased. This, it argued, would lead to greater competition in the health care service sector that, in turn, would promote choice and availability of information for patients, while forcing insurers, doctors and hospitals to deliver better care (BIAC, 1994). These were principles that resonated strongly with the staunchly pro-market Howard governments.

As contacts and support were opened and promised, a special meeting of the ELSAC at ministerial level was due on 23–24 June 1998, offering an opportunity to press for further work on health, working with like-minded members such as Japan, the UK, Canada and Denmark. The meeting had its genesis in the May 1995 OECD Ministerial Council meeting which asked the organisation to work on various aspects of reform of social protection systems and services, giving the organisation an explicit mandate to consolidate and analyse the policy implications of ageing populations. This had resulted, in turn, in a high level OECD conference in 1996, 'Beyond 2000: the New Social Policy Agenda', that identified trends that would set the welfare policy agenda in the first decades of the twenty-first century, including the health dimension of ageing.

It was an area of work being strongly led by Japan in the shape of its 'Initiative for a Caring World', first proposed by Prime Minister Hasimoto at the G7 Summit in Lyon, in June 1996. The aim of the June 1998 conference was to follow up on the 'Beyond 2000', conference and to launch a new social policy work programme for ELSAC. Health and ageing issues featured strongly in the draft agenda for the 1998 conference, including 'health care in an era of budgetary stringency', and it was possible that it would raise many of the structural and systemic health issues the Department was then addressing, such as improving the efficiency and quality of service delivery, changes in the public/private health mix, contestability and preventative versus palliative health policies (DHA, 1998a). It was an opportunity the Department firmly grasped, with Secretary Podger attending the conference and the ELSAC meeting.

The growing strength of the support for the Australian position on health led to a formal minute to Minister Wooldridge in July 1998 (DHA, 1998e). It recommended that he note that the Department had taken a much closer and more active interest in the work of the OECD in the previous twelve months, 'in line with the department's corporate vision as a leader in promoting, developing and funding world class health and family services'. As was further noted, the June 1998 attendance by Podger and Rosalky at the meeting of social policy ministers had provided a useful platform to strengthen OECD's health policy agenda:

> [E]xtending it well beyond its well established and well regarded work on health statistics. A number of countries have backed our efforts to achieve a broader health policy agenda and the OECD's Directorate of Employment, Education, Labour and Social Affairs is enthusiastic. (DHA, 1998e)

The Minister noted and agreed that good progress had been made.

AUSTRALIA AND THE DEVELOPMENT OF THE OECD HEALTH PROJECT

The 1998 OECD Ministerial meeting's report stressed the increasing health challenges faced by OECD members and urged the need for further work on health, resulting in a series of meetings of ELSAC's Working Party on Social Policy (WPSP) to consider how it might respond to the recommendations. However, as the Secretariat warned the Working Party, while the ministers might have strongly recommended the new work:

> The resources available for work on social policy remain unclear, even for the short and medium term. The ability of the Secretariat to initiate and complete the items included in this note depends on decisions of the OECD Council (which is the sole body entrusted with determining the work of the organisation) and of Member countries in making resources available for specific projects. (OECD, 1998a)

Despite this sombre warning, by 2001 a proposal for a major new Health Project had been approved, stimulated by repeated Australian suggestions for expanded work on health, together, most importantly, with an offer of voluntary contributions to help fund the work. The Health Project was, initially, a 'one off' project of a temporary nature, with a budget of FF19.5 million, moving health firmly on to the OECD Council's agenda and was strongly supported by Australia (OECD, 2001). The aim of the remainder of this section is to identify the factors that explain this change in priorities and the role of Australian officials and interests in the change process.

As with any change process a variety of factors were involved. The first, as shown by the report from the 1998 Ministerial meeting, was the continuing pressure for further health work emanating from health ministers and their departments, via their OECD representatives, bolstered by the increasing realisation of the extent of rising health costs that would be experienced with the ageing of the member states' populations, as the OECD's work on ageing had clearly demonstrated. Similarly, there had been repeated suggestions as to the need for further work on health contained in OECD publications during the 1990s. Among the most insistent sources of pressure was that which came from Australian officials, including the Australian delegation to the OECD and the senior Australian representatives increasingly in attendance at relevant committee and working party meetings. Officials such as David Kalisch, the Counsellor on the Australian permanent Delegation, Richard Madden, the Director of the AIHW and, following her secondment to DELSA's Health Unit for a year, Dr Vin McLouglin of the DHA. The new Australian Ambassador to the OECD, Tony Hinton (replacing Ralph Hillman) also played an important part, strongly supporting the proposal for an expansion of health work and clearly identifying supporting members, a task vital for a project's success in getting budgetary support (OECD, 2000b). After a meeting of Council's Executive Committee in special session, for example, Hinton was able to report that there was considerable but not unanimous support for the Secretary-General's proposals on health systems and in particular, support for work on indicators of health system performance.

As scheduled, Ambassador Hinton had opened Council discussion on the health topic, supporting the proposal to expand health work and indicating Australia's willingness to make voluntary contributions to support the work. The UK, Denmark, France and Canada were similarly supportive, and Denmark and Canada also offered voluntary contributions. There were, however, major notes of caution from Germany, Japan and Belgium. Also, in later discussions in a following Budget Committee meeting (fortuitously chaired by Ambassador Hinton), the US delegate continued to reserve its position pending seeing the details of the programme, although he supported it in principle. Interestingly, Hinton also reported that 'Some of the sensitivities on the part of the Europeans (and maybe Japan) appear to be linked to bad press associated with recent WHO work in this field', going on to add that 'although, of course, continued US scepticism or otherwise on this project will likely carry the day' (OECD, 2000b).

The second factor was growing pressure from the major OECD members voiced in the G7/8, which had been paying increasing attention to health issues. While G7/8 communiqués made reference to various aspects of health policy from as early as 1980, it became a major agenda item only in 1996–97 under French and American leadership and has remained a major issue (Kirton et al., 2007). In 1996, at the Lyon summit, for example, Japan's Prime Minister Hashimoto proposed the 'Initiative for a Caring World' project aimed at enhancing mutual policy learning on social policies, including health, by OECD countries. As a primary means of achieving the initiative the OECD was asked to prepare a synthesis report, financed largely by the Japanese government, with smaller contributions from the USA and Australian governments, on recent developments in social policy, including health, in member countries (OECD, 1998b: 10).

A third important factor was the positive response by Secretary-General Johnston to this internal and external pressure, expressed in papers he presented to OECD Council in 1999 and 2000 outlining his views as to the future challenges faced by the OECD. He encouraged the development of an integrated, more strategically oriented proposal for a major Health Project by his officials and, working closely with the Australian and a small group of other national delegates, he identified the extent of support for such a proposal and, where appropriate, persuaded members to provide it with support or, at the least, not to oppose it. Given that he had had to lead the major budget cuts demanded by his members on taking up his position as Secretary-General, the push to expand health work must have been a pleasant and positive change, though it did have to take place in a much tighter budgetary context, with commensurately greater competition for resources. Indeed, if it were not for the voluntary contributions provided by Australia and other countries, it is unlikely that work on health would have been expanded in this period.

Johnston made his intentions clear in a note to Council in October 1999, indicating that he would soon be bringing forward to Council some 'concrete proposals' for an increased work programme on health, intended to start the process of gaining a well-defined mandate for the Secretariat from the Council for such work (OECD, 1999a). The proposals emerged shortly afterwards, being placed before the WPSP and inviting discussion and support for a five-year strategy for health policy developed by the Secretariat, shaped in considerable part by suggestions from interested members, including Australia and Japan. The strategy document that resulted from the discussion, soon to be described as the 'Health Project', noted that while much health work had been undertaken by the OECD and was continuing, a number of weaknesses were apparent, including: the limited quality and completeness of the health database; the increasingly out of date work that had been done on members' health systems from the later 1980s and the lack of studies of the five new members that had joined the OECD since 1990; a general lack of analytical work, excluding that undertaken for the EDRC surveys; the one-off, fragmented nature of much of the health work that had been undertaken, often on the basis of voluntary contributions from individual members and the lack of an overall strategic direction. Hence, it concluded that:

> [T]he past contributions of ELSAC could be described as world-class in some respects but also as weighted towards the collection rather than towards the presentation and use of data. Only intermittent attention has been given to studies which have 'completed the circle' by linking policy questions, institutional descriptions, data and analysis. (OECD, 1999b)

A fourth factor was the publication of the WHO's World Health Report 2000. The report met with a critical reaction from several OECD member states, including the USA and Australia, largely because of the surprisingly low rankings the report assigned to the performance of their national health systems, together with concerns as to several methodological weaknesses. In essence, their dissatisfaction, together with their willingness to provide at least part of the additional funding necessary for the additional work on health at the OECD, sharpened their support and those of many other members, for the proposed Health Project and, indeed, a window of opportunity for the Secretariat to propose a further increase in the range of work initially included in the Project. The additional work, unsurprisingly, was to focus on a more detailed examination of health system performance based on OECD, rather than WHO expertise. In a very explicit indication of member sensitivities the Japanese delegate:

> [W]arned against including explicit ranking in the analysis. Mr. Hurst explained that there are no large differences between the OECD and the WHO in terms of their definition and conceptualisation of performance. However, the OECD will concentrate on understanding the causes of variations in performance and will avoid any country ranking. (OECD, 2001)

The Health Project proposal was endorsed by the WPSP and submitted to its parent ELSAC in April 2000, as was an additional paper outlining initial proposals for further work on health in other directorates. A revised version of the latter paper, incorporating the bulk of the proposals from the strategy paper, was submitted to, and discussed by, the OECD Council and Executive Committee in May 2000. The focus of the revised proposal was to be on the measurement, analysis and improvement of health systems performance, in addition to the work already proposed. It was favourably received and the Secretariat was invited to submit a proposal for the implementation of what was now a revised, three-year Health Project in the context of the 2001–2002 Programme of Work and Budget (OECD, 2000d). This was discussed and, in general terms, endorsed at the 2000 Ministerial Council and it was followed, on 8 August 2000, by a letter from the Secretary-General to all of the OECD ambassadors putting forward the proposal for a project for expanded work on health over the next three years. It sought the ambassadors' support at the next budget discussions, asked them to indicate their priorities in the project, requested the additional budget contributions from national capitals (to the total of 19.5 million FF), and also asked them to consider making further, voluntary contributions (OECD, 2000d). In addition, the proposal was discussed on 2–3 November 2000 by the Executive Committee in Special Session, and, on 21 December 2000 Council approved the proposal and allocated FF3 million from the budget for the project (OECD, 2001). The latter funding was also supported by an allocation from the Central Priorities Fund, controlled by the Secretary-General, to a total of EUR520,000 in 2003 and EUR113,000 in 2004.

In summary, the 1990s commenced with OECD work on health somewhat stagnating, dispersed widely across a number of directorates and the NEA, with the exception of the work on health accounts. While there was Australian interest in this work, it was a distinctly minor interest. The decade ended with the onset of the development of a major new Health Project, cross-directorate in nature and supervised by a new steering group of officials. The change, as discussed, was brought about by a combination of internal and external factors, including a continuing, strong push from Australia and, following growing pressure, a sustained and centrally directed leadership role from the Secretariat, led by the Secretary-General, Secretary-General Johnston. The latter, while not unreasonably claiming considerable credit for the Health Project, very much appreciated the leadership and support that Australia had provided (DHA, 2002a).

CONCLUSION

The story of Australian involvement in health at the OECD is one of rapid growth and considerable achievement after a long period of minimal involvement. It demonstrated, again, that a middle power with a clear strategy, experienced officials and a willingness to provide significant funds to support its proposals can achieve an influential position in an international organisation.

While not examined in detail, it also suggests that success in one significant international organisation such as the OECD can spill over into another, adding to Australia's influence. This was most obvious in the case of DHA Secretary Jane Halton, who became one of the two first co-chairs of what became the OECD's Health Committee and whose reputation spread outside of the OECD, as she became an Executive Board Member on the WHO from 2004 to 2007, President of the World Health Assembly for 2007, vice chair of the Executive Board of the WHA 2005–2006, chair of the WHO's Program, Budget and Administration Committee 2005–2007, and chair of the WHO's Executive Board in 2013. As her final term as chair of the Health Committee ended in December 2013 and she moved from the DHA to the Secretary of the Department of Finance in 2014, it will be interesting to see to what extent Australia can continue to maintain its influence in the OECD's health work.

BIBLIOGRAPHY

Australian Parliament 1974. 'Statement No. 3 Estimates Of Outlays, 1974–75, Membership of International Organisations and Other Non-Aid Expenditure', House of Representatives, Procedural Text, 17 September.

AIHW 1995. 'AIHW Annual Report 1994–95', Canberra: AGPS.

AIHW 1997. 'AIHW Annual Report 1996–97', Canberra: AGPS.

AIHW 2003. 'Australian National Health and Welfare Accounts: Concepts and Data Sources', Canberra: AIHW.

AIHW 2010. 'Health Expenditure Australia 2008–09'. Health and welfare expenditure series no. 42. Canberra: AIHW.

Baume, P. 1995. 'Towards a Health Policy', *Australian Journal of Public Administration*, 54(1): 97–101.

BIAC 1994. 'BIAC Discussion Paper for the OECD High Level Conference of National Experts on Health Care Reform, 17–18 November 1994', Paris: BIAC.

Carroll, P. 2013. 'Australia, ECOSOC and the UN Specialised Agencies', in D. Lee and J. Cotton (eds), *Australia and the United Nations*, Haberfield, NSW: Longueville Media, pp. 147–190.

Carroll, P. and Kellow, A. 2011. *The OECD: A Study of Organisational Adaptation*, Cheltenham, UK and Northampton, MA, USA: Edward Elgar Publishing.
DFAT 1995. File No 94/060329 Part 5 Review of Australia's OECD Membership.
DFAT 1998. NAA, File No 94/060329 Part 6 Review of Australia's OECD Membership.
DHA 1992. An undated note in File No 92/25282 'OECD Project on Long Term Care of the Elderly – ACCOFTA'.
DHA 1994. A report from the Australian delegation in Paris on the ELSA meeting of 26–28 September 1994, which was reported as 'overshadowed', by a USA proposal for a major project on the ageing population, including health care issues. File No95/29921 'OECD – Working Party on Social Policy – Long Term Care for the Elderly Project – HSDHFD'.
DHA 1995. 'OECD – Outcomes measures for Health Policy and Health Care', undated file notes regarding various OECD meetings regarding health care for the 1992–95 period, focused on the OECD workshop on Health Outcome Indicators held in Oslo, 18–19 September 1995, funded by Norwegian Government File No 95/30613.
DHA 1997a. 'Co-ordination of Responses to OECD Requests for Information', a memo from Lynelle Briggs, First Assistant Secretary (FAS), Portfolio Strategies Group to the FAS in each division of the Department of Health and Family Services, dated 3 July 1997.
DHA 1997b. Copy of a letter dated 1 July 1997 from Podger to Ann Kern, who had been a Deputy Secretary in Health in Canberra and Queensland and was then a private consultant-academic in Geneva, assisting with the work of the Australian Permanent Mission, Geneva. File No 2002/074662 'International Relations – Meetings – Briefing papers – Relationship between Health and Family Services and OECD – Paris – PSDPI'.
DHA 1997c. A copy of a letter from Secretary Podger to Clive Smee, a senior official in the UK's Department of Health, June, File No 2002/074662 'International Relations – Meetings – Briefing Papers – Relationship between Health and Family Services and OECD – Paris – PSDPI'.
DHA 1997d. 'Minute', to Lynelle Briggs from Lucien Briggs, 14 October 1997, File No 97/23345 'Avenues for Cooperation with the OECD – PSTRIDI'.
DHA 1997e. 'OECD Synthesis paper on Policy Priorities for 1998 Social Policy Ministerial Meeting – PSTRIDI'. File No 97/23340.
DHA 1998a. 'Avenues for Cooperation with the OECD', an undated paper by Susan Ingram, File No 97/23345 'Avenues for Cooperation with the OECD – PSTRIDI'.
DHA 1998b. A copy of an undated, 1998 letter from Secretary Podger to Secretary Dr David Rosalsky of the DSS, File No 98/26756 'International Relations – Meetings – Discussion Papers – OECD working party on Social Policy – October 1998 – PSGIDI'.
DHA 1998c. Copy of a letter from Secretary Podger to Director Alexander of the OECD, File No 2002/074662 'International Relations – Meetings – Briefing Papers – Relationship between Health and Family Services and OECD – Paris – PSDPI'.

DHA 1998d. 'HFS Meeting with Mr John Martin', dated 12 June 98 with a list of issues for discussion. File No 2002/074662 'International Relations – Meetings – Briefing Papers – Relationship between Health and Family Services and OECD – Paris – PSDPI'.

DHA 1998e. 'Expanding the Health Agenda of the Organisation for Economic Co-operation and Development (OECD)', a copy of a minute to Minister Wooldridge from FAS Susan Ingram, File No 98/31075 'International Relations – Policy – Development – OECD Health Outcomes Project Funded by the Department – 1998/1999 PSGIDI'.

DHA 1999a. An undated briefing note. File No 1999/022331 'International Relations – Committees – Discussion papers – OECD – Employment Labour and Social Affairs Committee (ELSA) – Meeting – March 1999 – PSDPI'.

DHA 1999b. 'Minute', August 1999 from Bob Eckhardt to Mary Murnane, regarding WHO's aged care work, File No 1999/048086 'Care and Access – Policy – Aged Care – Aged Care Strategies Development (ACSD) – Briefs and Input for OECD – Other International Meetings and Publications – Pt 10 – ACCPEVA'.

DHA 2000a. 'WHO: Recovery of Balance of AUD250,000 for Research not Undertaken', a fax from the Australian delegation in Geneva to Canberra, File No 2001/020995 'International Relations – Liaison – Organisation – OECD – DELSA – ELSA Cmte – PHDPHP'.

DHA 2000b. Letter from Deputy Secretary Borthwick to Deputy Secretary Jackson of the Department of Family and Children's Services, File No 2000/020350 'International Relations – Meetings – Agenda – OECD ELSAC Meeting April 2000 – PSDPI'.

DHA 2001. A Minute dated 8 February 2001 from Kingdon to Dr Graham, DHA File No 2001/013945 'International Relations – Research – Health Research – OECD Horizontal Health Project and Ad Hoc Group – PSDPI'.

DHA 2002. Briefing notes for Secretary Halton regarding the Ad Hoc Group Meeting 24–25 April 2002, File No 2001/069943 'International Relations – Meetings – Joint Activities – OECD Health Project Ad Hoc Group – Agendas, papers and Briefings – HIIDHCD'.

DHA 2002a. Copy of an Email from Ambassador Forsyth in Paris to Bob Eckhardt in the Department of Health and Ageing in Canberra, dated 3 December 2002, copied to the new Secretary, Jane Halton, noting that he had recently discussed the Health Project with Secretary-General Johnston. File No 02/060461 Trade Policy – International Organisations – OECD Council and Heads of Delegation – OEU 25 Nov 2002 to 19 March 2003.

DHFS 1998. 'Annual Report 1997–98', Canberra: Department of Health and Family Services.

Kirton, J., Roudev, N. and Sunderland, L. 2007. 'Making G8 Leaders Deliver: An Analysis of Compliance and Health Commitments, 1996–2006', *Bulletin of the World Health Organisation*, March, 85(3): 192–199.

Leichter, H. 1979. *A Comparative Approach to Policy Analysis – Health Care Policy in Four Nations*, London: Cambridge University Press.

NAA 1970. File No 69 2095 Part 8 Reconsideration of Possible Australian Membership of OECD, Canberra: NAA.

OECD 1995. 'OECD Economic Surveys Australia 1995', Paris: OECD.

OECD 1998a. 'Work Following the Meeting of ELSAC at Ministerial Level on Social Policy, 23 and 24 June: Implementing the Mandate', DEELSA/ELSA/WP1(98)2, a paper prepared by OECD officials for the Working Party on Social Policy, 25 September.

OECD 1998b. 'Social and Health Policies in OECD Countries: A Survey of Current Programmes and Recent Developments', Vol VI, Labour Market and Social Policy Occasional Papers, No 33, Paris: OECD.

OECD 1999a. 'OECD Challenges and Strategic Objectives 2000/2001', C(2000)166, a Note by the Secretary-General to Council, 19 September.

OECD 1999b. 'Summary Record of the 18th Meeting', DEELSA/ELSA/WP1/M(99)1, held on 21–22 October 1999, Paris: OECD.

OECD 2000a. 'A System of Health Accounts', Paris: OECD.

OECD 2000b. A copy of an email from Paris to Canberra, dated 8 November 2000, summarising a meeting of the OECD ECSS, DFAT File No 00/035784 Trade Policy – Committees – OECD Executive Committee and Executive Committee in Special Session (ECSS)-OEU.

OECD 2000c. 'Current and Future Work on Health at the OECD', C(2000)87, a Note by the Secretary-General to Council, 15 May.

OECD 2000d. 'New Horizontal Project on Health Care', DEELSA/ELSA/WP1(2000)2, a Note by the Secretariat for the 19th meeting of the Working Party on Social Policy to be held at the Château de la Muette, Paris on 16 and 17 October 2000.

OECD 2000e. A Cable from DFAT to Paris, dated 24 May 2000, DFAT File No 00/035354 'Trade Policy – International Organisations – OECD Council and Heads of Delegation – OEU'.

OECD 2001. 'Summary Record of the 1st Meeting', SG/ADHOC/HEA/M(2001)1, Ad Hoc Group on the OECD Health Project held on 26–27 March.

OECD 2011. 'A System of Health Accounts v2', Paris: OECD.

OECD 2013. 'OECD Health Data, 2013', Paris: OECD.

OECD 2014. 'Decision of the Council Concerning the Mutual Acceptance of Data in the Assessment of Chemicals', Paris: OECD, accessed on 30 January 2014 at http://acts.oecd.org/Instruments/ShowInstrumentView.aspx?InstrumentID=263&InstrumentPID=263&Lang=en&Book=False.

Staples, A. 2006. *The Birth of Development – How the World Bank, Food and Agriculture Organization and World Health Organization Changed the World, 1945–1965*, Kent: The Kent State University Press.

WHO 1958. 'The First Ten Years of the World Health Organisation', Geneva: WHO, accessed on 26 January 2017 at http://whqlibdoc.who.int/publications/a38153.pdf.

13. Australia's role in organisational maintenance, reform, and adaptation

The value of the OECD derives primarily from its special character. It has a relatively small membership, with its members being relatively like-minded, liberal democratic countries, with market economies committed to the disciplines of peer review and improving policy through learning and sharing best practice. But it also has a high quality, professional Secretariat that (especially compared with some other international organisations) is very much subject to direction by its 'owners' through the governing Council and its key committees. Australia has played an important part in ensuring that the OECD retains its comparative advantage, as we show in this chapter, through a case study from the early years of Australian membership: the selection of senior Secretariat members that tested the principle of appointment on merit.

We also examine Australia's strategy and tactics in the OECD in seeking to both preserve the special qualities of the OECD, and in attempting to ensure that it adapts to the emergence of dynamic Asian economies in its region, rather than becoming bogged down by the admission of smaller, largely European members that bring little but complexity to the table. As the chapter shows, Australia has played a significant role in the reform of the internal management of the organisation and the enlargement of the membership and the important question of adapting to the global economy of the twenty-first century. But it also reflects critically on the value of the OECD, especially as alternative forums such as the G20 have assumed greater importance.

APPOINTING THE 'BEST AVAILABLE MAN'

The OECD has generally maintained the quality of the Secretariat by appointing its senior staff very much on merit. Even before Australian accession, a keen interest was taken in 1968 in the appointment of a Secretary-General to replace Thorkil Kristensen. Philip Flood wrote to the Secretary of the DEA in December 1968: 'Kristensen's departure will be of particular interest in view of the helpful attitude he has shown towards Australia's relationship with the Organization' (NAA, 1967). Australia was quite happy with the appointment of Emile van Lennep, whose wife had been born in Australia, although she had not lived there since she was two (NAA, 1967a). There had been a move to appointing van Lennep three years earlier, but for reasons unknown this was blocked by France and Kristensen secured an extended term (NAA, 1967b). Australia was quite sanguine about van Lennep's appointment, with Flood noting the OECD's 'more effective work was in the financial field and not in social affairs and manpower, and, unlike Kristensen, van Lennep might be expected to keep the Organization on a narrower path' (NAA, 1967b).

Van Lennep's appointment almost came unstuck when the German Ambassador in The Hague instructed the Dutch government 'on instructions' that German support would be conditional on van Lennep agreeing to there being three Assistant Secretary-Generals (UK, Germany, Italy), in addition to the current two Deputy Secretary-Generals (France and US), as it was apparently unhappy about being placed in a subordinate position to France. In response 'van Lennep properly insisted that he could not be committed in advance on such a question' (NAA, 1967b). Three Assistant Secretary-Generals with those national affiliations (Messrs J.C.R. Dow, R.P. di Caboli and Herbert König) were later appointed in 1971, suggesting that the wishes of larger members of the Organisation were of considerable importance regarding OECD appointments at the most senior levels, though merit was also a consideration (NAA, 1967b). The contests for prestige among members seeking senior appointments continued, and provided Australia with an early opportunity to mark itself out as being more interested in maintaining the integrity of the OECD than pandering to prestige.

Van Lennep was indeed helpful to Australia. When the Chef de Cabinet position opened up in June 1972, he sought an Australian for the position, informing the Ambassador in confidence that he would like to make such an appointment, but the departments could not find a candidate in the short time available. Sweden offered to find a replacement, and provided Mr Hans-Olle Olsson. Understandably, Canada, Japan, and Australia shared concerns over the geographical spread of the senior executive, as all five DSG/ASGs were from the EEC or US, suggesting that, again, competition for positions purely on merit was by no means the sole criterion for appointment, even for smaller powers. This North Atlantic stranglehold proved difficult to break, with Italy adamant in 1973 that they had the right to nominate a person for the ASG position when vacated by an Italian (NAA, 1967c). The Italians were claiming they had a 'fixed long term right' to provide an Assistant

Secretary-General and in particular the 'Aid' Assistant Secretary-General for which the Australian Ambassador considered they had since 1966 'provided two complete dead wood incumbents'. Flood thought the Canadian that had been proposed a very good candidate, and thought Australia should support him, 'unless of course the Italians come up with an excellent candidate (but if they did I would argue he would be better employed helping them start a proper aid administration)' (NAA, 1967d).

Australia made it quite clear to van Lennep that Australia was opposed to ASG positions being considered the preserve of any one country. Italy, with wide European support, was even prepared to support the establishment of a fourth ASG position if geographical balance was sought, and Canada eventually withdrew their candidate in favour of a Japanese candidate (NAA, 1967e).

The Italian Cabinet had apparently given their Ambassador absolutely rigid instructions and threatened to veto the re-appointment of the (French and US) Deputies if they did not get their own way, either as the third or through the establishment of a fourth position, but this would be 'particularly difficult' after strenuous efforts by France, UK, Canada and the US to limit increases in the OECD budget (NAA, 1967f). The Japanese were becoming particularly annoyed that these difficulties were now being encountered, having been asked to find a capable candidate (NAA, 1967g). The view in the DFA was that the holding of 'major OECD positions by the Italians appears to be seen by them as a question of intra-European prestige regardless of the calibre of the Italian candidate concerned or the ill-will created in the process' (NAA, 1967h). Italian occupants of the ASG role were regarded by Canberra as having been 'lack-lustre', and the Japanese candidate was regarded as the 'most promising'. Australia also wished to support the Japanese candidate for 'political reasons' and the Ambassador was asked to advise the Japanese Ambassador of its support before the Council meeting.

Canada blinked first. Their Delegation was told to avoid a situation where Canada alone opposed the Italians, and after van Lennep supported the incumbent Italian (Paulucci) they saw no point in continuing. They regarded the creation of a fourth position as absurd as this, besides being unnecessary, would signal tacit acceptance of the third position being reserved for Italy (NAA, 1967i).

Council decided on 19 December 1973 to reappoint Gerard Eldon (France) and Charles G. Wootton (US) as Deputy Secretary-Generals for two years and to re-appoint Paulucci as Assistant Secretary-General for 15 months, to align the expiry of his term with the terms for Atkinson and Ambramowski, which were due to expire in the first half of 1975

(NAA, 1967j). There was to be a review of the Assistant Secretary-General positions in five months, and the hope was that in filling all three positions in the first half of 1975 a better geographical balance might be achieved and the Italians would not feel they were being singled out.

Canada, Japan and Australia opposed the Secretary-General's proposal to re-appoint Paulucci with 'firm statements, which drew expressions of sympathy with [the] general aim but no support for our position at this date' (NAA, 1967j). After further discussion involving van Lennep (whose term was coming up for renewal), it was clear that further opposition could only take the form of an Australian veto of the whole package, so the Ambassador reluctantly concurred. The Australian interventions helped strengthen the resolve of Canada and Japan and emphasised disquiet about the operation of the 'unanimity rule', with the British, French and Belgian Ambassadors privately communicating that, while they could not support Australia on this occasion, they were committed to a review of the present arrangements, with the French Ambassador stating this to the meeting (NAA, 1967j). Canberra considered that 'the Canadians again appear to have backed down somewhat too easily' (NAA, 1967k). There was surprise at van Lennep's backing of Paulucci, and the Department suggested that the Ambassador (possibly in conjunction with Japan and Canada) might like to make the 'best available man' point once more to van Lennep on an appropriate occasion.

In addition to a desire to ensure better non-European representation at the top of the OECD, Australia also wished to support Japan, and the Japanese Ministry of Foreign Affairs expressed its gratitude for this to the Mission in Tokyo (NAA, 1967l). Seemingly as a compromise, on 10 January van Lennep then announced that he was appointing a Japanese candidate (Professor Oshima) as Director for Science and Technology, along with the appointment of Ron Gass as Director for Education, Manpower and Social Affairs (NAA, 1967m).

The issue continued to affect the OECD through into 1974 and the reappointment of Secretary-General van Lennep, whose term was due to expire in September 1974. Australia supported his reappointment, firstly implicitly by inviting him to visit Australia and then explicitly (NAA, 1967n). Treasury was consulted over support for his reappointment and expressed qualified support, stating that while it had occasionally expressed reservations about his actions 'we do not wish to oppose the recommendation that Australia support his re-appointment' (NAA, 1967o). Trade was fine with the reappointment, and Dr J.W.C Cumes,

First Assistant Secretary, International Organisations Division DFA considered van Lennep had been 'helpful towards Australia and I doubt whether we would support any move to deny him re-appointment' (NAA, 1967p).

Among other Members, Ambassador Cameron wrote, 'support for van Lennep [fell] this side of rapture', with support sometimes 'prefaced by the comment that no-one has come up with an alternative candidate' (NAA, 1967q). Australia and several others urged that the way be prepared for a decision to be taken at the MCM in mid-May, fearing that until a decision was taken, there was a risk that some might attempt to have issues decided in their favour under threat of veto of van Lennep's reappointment. The Italian authorities did not declare themselves, and Cameron thought that 'probably is no more than a typical desire to reserve a possible bargaining position, with no specific purpose in mind' (NAA, 1967r).

A Heads of Delegation Meeting in early May chaired by the French Ambassador discussed the reappointment of the Secretary-General (NAA, 1967s). Support for van Lennep was expressed by Australia, Belgium, the Netherlands, Luxembourg, the US, Finland, France, Norway, the UK, Sweden, and Switzerland. Germany, Canada, Denmark and Turkey expressed support if there was no other candidate, though the Australian Ambassador thought they were well aware there was little prospect of another candidate emerging. Ireland, Iceland, New Zealand and Japan had no final instructions but expected to support reappointment, with Japan stating that he had been instructed to say that his authorities regretted that of the top six Secretariat positions, five were occupied by nationals of the European Community. While they had been outspoken in their criticisms of van Lennep, Portugal had no instructions, as did Austria, Spain and Greece, but they stated that before seeking instructions they would like to know whether there were other candidates and, in any case, felt more time was needed for reflection.

The Italian position was that the appointment of a Secretary-General needed more time for reflection, to take into account the recent increase in membership, the need for balanced representation in senior positions, and the desirability of rotating the position among members. The Italian Ambassador proposed that the issue be discussed informally by ministers at the MCM at the end of May, though not with a view to a decision being taken at that meeting.

Several other Members indicated that they thought more time was necessary to mull over whether they could support van Lennep's reappointment, but the Delegation informed Canberra that this was spurious, as the expiry of his appointment had been known for some time, and they were probably trying to retain for as long as possible a potential means of influence on particular issues (NAA, 1967s). A file note showed that the Australians were wary that the Italians might seek to extract the third ASG position. It was understood that van Lennep was to pay a formal visit to Italy on 16 May 'and he may learn then whether Italians have specific price they wish to exact' (NAA, 1967s).

A few days prior to the Ministerial meeting it was being said that, as a condition of Italian support for his reappointment, van Lennep had agreed that he would not recommend the appointment of *any* Assistant Secretary-General when the terms of the existing occupants expired early the following year, following a clear indication from the Council meeting in December 1973 that the appointment of another Italian Assistant Secretary-General was unlikely. It seemed the Italian government may have decided that no one should succeed them.

At a Head of Delegations meeting on 22 May, no delegation was opposed to the reappointment of van Lennep, although some preferred that it be done at the MCM and others later by Ambassadors. Van Lennep had no objection either way. Valery, the French Ambassador, proposed that at an Ordinary Council Meeting on 6 June he would take the chair and propose reappointment. He asked that any delegation whose authorities had problems with van Lennep's reappointment to make them known then so that they could be resolved at the MCM (NAA, 1967t). It was learned that there was by now a dispute among Italian ministers, and while a decision had now been taken to support van Lennep, it was thought that postponing a formal decision until after the MCM 'would (in some way no one can explain) save face for the Italian government' (NAA, 1967t). And so van Lennep was reappointed by the Council at a meeting on 6 June. The lack of rapture persisted, with Portugal, Greece and Spain expressing both support for van Lennep, but also for their dissatisfaction at the treatment by the Organisation (implicitly by van Lennep) of their countries' interests (NAA, 1967u).

This early baptism in the rather petty European politics surrounding senior appointments was handled well by Australia, and it has generally been an adept player in OECD politics, exercising both skill and caution, and was well regarded by many ambassadors as indicated in interviews with them. As this section shows, Australia has defended its interests vigorously in seeking to maintain what it sees as important principles central to the OECD, but has also demonstrated tact in doing so.

Australia has continued to insist on adherence to 'good governance' and has pushed hard within the OECD on governance issues, holding to the view that the OECD often preached to developing countries on the need for good governance, yet was not following appropriate process itself. One ambassador remarked that the Europeans did not seem to understand the need for procedural fairness and Australia, the US and Canada had numerous battles with them over it, to the extent that the Delegation and Australian staff in the Secretariat who had pushed the reform agenda were marked by the experience: people were afraid to talk to an Australian as they were the only ones pushing hard on the reasoned case for governance reform.

A SOMETIMES TENSE RELATIONSHIP: AUSTRALIA AND THE EUROPEAN COMMISSION

Australia's insistence on adherence to standards of good governance and, as we shall see later in the chapter, in driving reform has been matched by a similar, if measured, insistence on adherence to what it sees as the OECD's core values of trade liberalisation and particularly on its defence against some forces in Europe that have sought to defend the Common Agriculture Policy.

Australia, for example, exercised extreme caution in its continued defence against the introduction of the concept of multifunctionality into the agricultural trade agenda, on the grounds that subsidising European farmers for protecting landscape rather than protecting products was still trade distorting. On 27 February 2001, it noted 'encouraging signs' in a paper to be given by a member of the OECD Secretariat at the ABARE Outlook Conference in Canberra, that OECD work on multifunctionality would reinforce the stance it had taken. However, until this intimation of a favourable policy direction was endorsed by OECD members, posts were asked by cable to be discerning in drawing attention to this paper to minimise the pressure on the OECD Secretariat staff to water down their findings. This proved in vain, as a cable from Paris reported on 23 March that supporters of multifunctionality (the EC, some EU member states, Japan, Norway and Korea) launched a scathing attack on the Secretariat, accusing it of a lack of impartiality because of this paper (DFAT, 2001).

The Australian defence of agricultural trade liberalisation against the efforts of what it referred to as the 'agri-protectionists' to import the concept of multifunctionality was not conducted only in the OECD, however. Australia's case was also prosecuted through bilateral embassies that would press the argument to governments in a coordinated manner, usually at the instigation of the OECD Delegation, and focusing on the US, Canada, New Zealand, Mexico and Cairns Group members such as Brazil, Argentina and Chile. Such a cable on 11 April 2003 read:

> Grateful if posts would make urgent representations to support our efforts in Paris to remove reference to multifunctionality in the Chairman's trade message … We are concerned that this reference would ultimately lead to Ministerial endorsement of this concept, which will be used by the EU, Japan and others to legitimise their interests in this agenda. (DFAT, 2001a)

The cable noted that debate on the role of non-trade concerns in the modalities discussions in Geneva was continuing and Australia would 'not want to be providing added support to the agri-protectionists on this issue'.

Australia had to similarly contain its enthusiasm at the prospect of the appointment of a German agricultural economist, Stefan Tangerman, as the new Director of Food, Agriculture and Fisheries. Tangerman was up against candidates from Finland, Canada, the USA and Japan, and was considered an outstanding candidate and an outspoken critic of the CAP who was well respected internationally, so it was noted that it would be 'interesting to see how the Europeans react'. But it was suggested that 'at this stage it would be prudent not to openly support him as this could be the "kiss of death"'. This stance was undermined somewhat in July 2001 when AFFA got its Minister, Warren Truss, to send a letter to Johnston supporting the Tangerman appointment without clearing it with DFAT, but in the end supporters of Tangerman prevailed (DFAT, 2001).

The issue of agricultural trade has been an important one for Australia, and key to its interaction at the OECD has been its relation with the European Union, both as regards its members and the European Commission. According to one Ambassador, the EU members 'love' the OECD, but the Commission hates it. It provides one of the few occasions where non-EU members get to hear the nuances and views of members, as opposed to the Commission, especially where the Commission has locked in policies (such as trade), as there is often some national *compétence* on many issues. European members frequently let Australian officials know that they agree with Australia but they are happy to let Australia do the talking. Australia often gets 'sicked' onto the European Commission by the EU members. The EC usually attempts to caucus its members in the OECD, but several of them often welcome the opportunity to undermine EU positions, especially those not yet locked in, by breaking with solidarity, even communicating directly with APEC members such as Australia. APEC Ambassadors also caucus, meet monthly and coordinate their activity on a number of issues. By 2006, however, the EC was attempting to exert more control over members. Officials from capitals were apparently receiving phone calls back to their capitals from the Commission over things they said at meetings.

In 2006, Australian relations with the EC became particularly tense. On 21 February the European Commission made representations concerning Australia's opposition to aspects of the EC activities in the OECD, after Australia had challenged both the European Commission's right to chair a management subcommittee and to have the Community's views taken into account in drafting papers (DFAT, 2007b). The legal advice within DFAT was that the onus should be on the EC to explain what 'institutional provisions' in which treaties gave it the legal authority to participate in the OECD and its committees. It was considered that *Supplementary Protocol 1 to the OECD Convention* did not provide a sufficiently clear statement as to the legal authority for the EC to undertake acts such as chairing subcommittees or participating in drafting sessions of the OECD. Instead, the Protocol only noted that representation would be determined by 'institutional provisions' of the treaties of Rome and Paris (1951, which established the European Coal and Steel Community and expired on 23 July 2002).

Australia queried the appropriateness of the EC as a non-member and non-contributor to Part I budget funding belonging to committee bureaux alongside EU members of the OECD – although the EC was making substantial Voluntary Contributions of around €30m at this time. Australia did not question the recording of the Commission's views in OECD papers where appropriate, but resolved to challenge its *compétence* where warranted. For example, at the Council meeting on 15 December 2005, Australia (along with the USA) questioned why the EC had been included as a member and a country in the Medium Term Orientations Survey when it was neither (DFAT, 2007b).

Canberra continued to advocate convening a non-EU OECD members' meeting in Paris to discuss the role of the EU across the OECD. In particular, it was thought such a meeting might canvass the option of granting the EC an enhanced role (including a voting right in Council) in exchange for excluding future EU members, including the EU6 (Slovenia, Lithuania, Latvia, Estonia, Cyprus and Malta), from gaining full access to Council in order to keep decision making in the Council manageable (DFAT, 2007b).

Australia has often found itself in opposition to Europe over questions such as the expansion of membership, but has sometimes been able to counter European ambitions with the support of its often like-minded APEC allies, including the US, although on the question of Russian accession it was left rather isolated by the US. France had made it clear that it wanted Russia as an OECD member, but the crucial move in support of Russian accession came from the USA in 2007. At the ECSS on 19–20 April, at an otherwise low key meeting, the US announced a major policy shift in supporting commencement of accession negotiations with Russia. This decision was apparently made by President Bush, who supported Secretary of State Condoleezza Rice's position over that of Vice-President Dick Cheney. The US acknowledged that Russia did not meet the Noburu criteria for accession at that time, and had ongoing concerns about Russia's democratic values and institutions and its market economy status, but they took a dynamic view which would allow Russian movement towards like-mindedness during the accession process over time, assessed by its meeting a series of specified benchmarks (DFAT, 2007b). This was, perhaps, an attempt by the US to encourage like-minded conduct worthy of an OECD member after the 2004 Russia–Belarus gas dispute and the Russia–Ukraine gas dispute of 2005–2006. Russian like-mindedness was slow to develop, however, with the South Ossetia War between Georgia and Russia in August 2008 and, after its annexation of Crimea in 2014, Russian accession has been postponed.

AUSTRALIA'S ROLE IN OECD REFORM

Australia has been at the forefront of moves to constrain the budgetary expansion of the OECD, seeking to ensure it continued to provide value for money, and has played a prominent role in its reform. It was giving 'active consideration' to its support for all international organisations in 1981/82, and the OECD was no exception. The Delegation was instructed that it would wish to see the 1982 Program of Work and Budget 'determined with strict regard for Member government's policies of domestic expenditure restraint'. This approach was in common with its stance regarding other organisations, stressing that: 'At best we would support a situation of zero real growth for the OECD which is also consistent with our approach on budgetary growth in other international organisations, and in particular those in the UN system' (NAA, 1981). This stance was maintained over the next several years, often to the irritation of smaller EU member states.

Australia, for example, proposed a substantial budget cut in 1996, working closely with the USA, and had it adopted at a meeting of ECSS in October ('Our proposal for a 10 per cent real reduction in the budget over 3 years was accepted' (DEWR, 2008)). While Australia might have taken the lead in this, they were assisted by like-minded members, not least the USA, which was emboldened by an $85m cut imposed on its commitment to international organisations by Congress. The US also pushed hard to change the scale of contributions. The 'solid results' achieved included a mandate to Secretary-General Johnston to cut and prioritise, with a 'large majority' of members agreeing that low priority activities needed to be cut and that the only way to achieve that was through the introduction of majority voting. There was also wide support for a consolidation of outreach activities and the down-sizing of the Centre for Cooperation with Economies in Transition. There was a cool reception for Johnston's later 'vision' for reform unveiled in 2002, and the US marshalled G7 support for down-sizing and reform, with France remaining 'the main laggard'.

On 8 January 2002, the Australian Ambassador sent DFAT in Canberra a cable headed 'OECD Reform Proposals: The "Big Bang", Budget Reform' (DEWR, 2001). Australia had been pressing for reforms to the OECD's budget and planning processes for some years and the Ambassador reported that the Secretary-General suddenly had proposed a major shake-up of the OECD, including terminating committees and working groups by the end of the year and changing the tradition of holding annual ministerial meetings. The proposals were to be discussed at a Heads of Delegation (HOD) meeting on 10 January, and the cable spelled out the views of the Delegation on the issues that arose and the merits of recent reforms.

Australia was not confident the 'Big Bang' proposals would be successful, and considered they probably would have led to an empowerment of the Secretariat relative to the membership. Nevertheless, Australia had supported numerous recent reforms, including the introduction of programme/output oriented budgeting, accrual accounting, and the introduction of a Priority Resource Allocation System (PRAS). Ambassador Forsyth reported that there had been some 'major, embarrassing management problems' identified and addressed relating to the staff pension scheme, the publications programme and accounting procedures, and some of the reforms had not been well implemented. For example, the re-prioritisation of work programmes that should have flowed from the budget cuts in 1996 had to some extent been undone by a dramatic growth in tied voluntary contributions, and those members providing this had generally vetoed any cuts to programmes of interest to them. The PRAS had resulted in only marginal adjustments.

The Secretary-General had prepared a paper in October 2001 setting out his frustrations with the operation of the organisation. Then in late December he produced a paper, 'Committee Reform: A Big Bang Approach', setting out some radical proposals to address those concerns. Johnston was particularly concerned about his inability to direct the directorates, which he saw as 'silos' able to operate effectively as fiefdoms, supported by their corresponding committees and relevant national agencies, limiting the capacity of the Secretary-General, the Council and Budget Committee to prioritise work so that it could adapt the Organisation to changing needs, especially by undertaking cross-sectoral work which was generally given low priority by the directorates (DEWR, 2001).

Johnston's proposal involved identifying key committees and subjecting them to review in 2002, with all other committees and working groups to be terminated before the end of 2002 (unless specifically mandated). He also proposed replacing the annual MCMs with triennial meetings of heads of government and annual meetings of ministers on special multi-sectoral issues, with the composition of the Executive Committee in Special Session (ECSS) to be changed to reflect the composition of these multi-sectoral ministerial meetings.

In addition he had prepared a paper on reform of the budget process, the Hutton Paper, including a proposal to replace the PRAs, and Australia had some concerns over this, particularly its proposal to give the Secretary-General authority to allocate the preliminary budget envelope by work themes such as 'Sustainable Development', which it thought would provide him with excessive discretion over priorities. Nevertheless, Australia put some considerable effort into ensuring budgetary reform was given due attention, especially as Forsyth sensed that the Secretary-General was more committed to his 'Big Bang' approach than to 'measured' reform of processes.

Johnston's proposals received some initial discussion at a HOD's meeting in December 2001, but delegations received the paper only an hour beforehand. Forsyth reported surprisingly strong support for the 'proposed attack' on the committee structure, but the proposal for Heads of Government's (HOG's) meetings was widely debunked, views on cancelling the MCM and multi-sectoral ministerials were mixed, and there was little support for varying the ECSS. Johnston's proposals would have had the effect of strengthening his hand at the expense of the members, who had pushed for reform at the 2001 MCM, and were to take the initiative in developing their own reform agenda, with Australia playing a prominent role.

Australia had not anticipated it would have to discuss the paper at such short notice, but when one delegate suggested that the absence of comment indicated acquiescence, Forsyth intervened to say that this could not be assumed and stated that there were many questions that needed to be thought through, and while he saw some appeal in taking a radical approach to a committee structure where it had proved 'virtually impossible' to terminate activities, this needed to be done in a structured and strategic way. He added that Australia saw the priority as being the measured reform of the 'ailing' budget process, especially as the 2002/2003 budget cycle was about to commence.

Ambassador Forsyth saw the Australian priorities in the reform process as being (DEWR, 2001a):

- To press for reforms that mirror our own approach to budget reform. In this respect we will look to go beyond the Hutton Paper and continue to press for:
  - a corporate plan
  - programme budgets based on a more realistic budget envelope (onus on Directorates to justify rather than on Council to find last minute cuts)
  - inclusion of performance evaluation in budget process
  - a limited shift in resources from silos to the centre
  - voluntary contributions to be covered by the budget process.
- To ensure that work funded by voluntary contributions, which is generally tied and subsidised from the Part I Budget (in some cases heavily so) is either charged at full cost or is appropriately taxed. (We see this as the most appropriate way to shift funds to the Centre of the Organisation. We also note that for the Policy Directorates other than Economics and Trade, voluntary funds are now two-thirds as large as the Part I Budget for those Directorates). To ensure that these funds are subject to new principles and rules.
- To ensure any changes to committee structure reflect, as far as possible, our priorities.
- To ensure a better approach is applied to the review of mandates for committees and working groups which are due to expire and which some members wish to renew.
- To support 'realistic, constructive approaches to MCMs and the ECSS'.
- To ensure that the Enlargement issue is linked to the reform of the Organisation (in part because the Organisation, as presently run, would have difficulty in absorbing new members, and in part as this gives us some leverage in the reform process.

Forsyth noted that the 'Big Bang' proposal was no doubt an opening gambit from a Secretary-General under pressure from the 2001 MCM from many members' delegations, and from the failure of the PRAs to introduce reforms. The USA and the UK were not fully committed to the proposal and the USA suggested at the HODs meeting that perhaps the aim should be to remove a specified percentage of working groups. The consensus process was clearly going to make this difficult, and a major argument could develop over which committees should be 'ring fenced' for review. For this reason, it was expected that the 'thorny issue' of majority voting would be 'resurrected' (DEWR, 2001b).

DFAT cabled the Ambassador on 21 January 2002 stating that it shared his assessment 'that generally speaking the OECD has served Australia well'. The cable added that 'In many policy areas it is a unique forum for analysis, policy development and sharing of best practice between the developed industrialised economies.' It was noted that most Commonwealth agencies 'derive significant value from the work of the OECD' (DEWR, 2001c). This made it important to ensure that this value was advanced and where necessary defended as the OECD entered what might be a period of significant change in terms of internal reform and possible expansion of membership.

Australia agreed that there were too many working groups, and was concerned that it was almost impossible to shut down these bodies, but saw a need for balancing the relative strength of the silos (the line directorates and agencies) and the centre (the Executive Directorate), seeing the strength of the OECD lying primarily in the committee system and the support these garnered from agencies in capitals. While it saw a need for the OECD to be much more flexible and adaptable, and a need to shift some resources to the centre, it did not see that its work programme should be overtaken by cross-sectoral issues. It was also thought to be inappropriate to shift too much authority for establishing priorities to the Secretary-General or the Council, because the 'Secretary-General's priorities are not always the same as ours and most members of the Council do not seem capable of bringing whole-of-government views on priorities.'

The Secretary-General and HODs established three Working Groups at a meeting on 10 January 2002: Working Group 1 on the OECD's priorities, and Programme of Work and Budget (chaired by Ambassador Ian Forsyth); Working Group 2 on the OECD's Committee Structure (chaired by Canada); and Working Group 3 on the Secretariat Structure (Netherlands, chair). After 11 meetings of WG1, and close to consensus, Ambassador Forsyth presented his report to HODs and the Secretary-General in May 2002. His report drew heavily on experience in the Australian public sector, and was greatly assisted by two Australians in the Budget and Strategic Planning area of the Secretariat (Rottier and Bacelj) (DEWR, 2001d).

Forsyth's report recommended a comprehensive, integrated programme of reform that sought to 'lift the OECD from being backward amongst the major international organisations in the area of management reform, to being at the forefront of reform' (DEWR, 2001d). The cable noted that the record of securing even more modest reforms in the OECD was not impressive, but, 'despite less than helpful responses of the OECD's senior executive', there was optimism (ultimately justified) of a good outcome, especially because Australia had been lobbying hard and had secured strong support from most Heads of Mission.

It was recognised that further work was needed on areas such as voluntary contributions, which Australia had successfully pressed as a major concern, because it was conscious that:

> [P]revious attempts to introduce reforms in the OECD have not succeeded and a previous attempt to force reform by across-the-board budget cuts (from 1996) was largely off-set by a rapid and somewhat uncontrolled growth in voluntary contributions. (DEWR, 2001d)

Other areas considered to require further work included: improving staff practices to enhance staff mobility in the Secretariat; the introduction of performance agreements and appraisal in the Secretariat; decision making (with considerable pressure to move from consensus to qualified majority voting on budget issues); and the role of the current salary adjustment system. These were reflective of the kinds of reforms adopted in Australian and other public services from the 1980s, in what became known as 'New Public Management'.

Forsyth secured strong support at the meeting of Executive Committee in Special Session in April and at the MCM in May, but it was noted 'that the Secretary-General and senior executive were showing no enthusiasm, let alone leadership'. Johnston privately challenged ('angrily') the Australian assertion that the OECD was behind other major international organisations in this area, so it provided him with evidence to back this claim (DEWR, 2001d). Australia considered Johnston 'lacked a consistent vision and steadfastness'. It was also reported that he seemed unfamiliar with modern budgeting practice adopted by most members, and thought the need for reform was mostly about the need for Ministers to bring greater whole-of-government approaches to the PWB.

It was reported, however, that Australia had generated 'very good support' for the reform programme among most HODs, including all APEC HODs, and all of the other G7 '(although we are not entirely sure of France)'. The Japanese were continuing to resist attempts to improve oversight of VCs, but had been convinced of the need to have them fully costed and billed. Less progress was made by Working Group 2, in part because the Secretary-General had reportedly asked its Canadian chair to slow down progress (DEWR, 2001d).

Substantial reforms to the OECD's management processes were achieved, with Ambassador Forsyth as chair of the Budget Committee playing a prominent role in the reform of the budget process and evaluation of programmes. Qualified Majority Voting was also introduced for some decisions and, while by no means perfect, the governance of the OECD now resembles more closely best practice among its members (see Carroll and Kellow, 2011).

ENLARGEMENT AND THE ASIA PACIFIC

Australia has pursued with some determination a consistent position on the accession of new members to the OECD, and its interests in pressing for an extension of the OECD to the Asia-Pacific region have coincided with its principled position on preserving the value the qualities of the OECD can provide. The EC has consistently sought to promote the claims to membership of every new member of the EU, even though they might bring little to the table in terms of share of global GDP and thus membership levy contributions. Yet each new member adds complexity to the operation of the OECD and increases the chances of agreement not being reached under the mutual agreement rule. The post-Communist world has seen an expansion in the number of Eastern European countries with the characteristics that would qualify them for membership, but it has also seen the rise of economies in the Asia-Pacific, particularly China, but also other Asian states and those in Latin America, which the USA has also been keen to put forward for membership.

Australia has therefore insisted on adherence to the ('Noburu') criteria for membership that require candidates to expand the relative reach of the OECD in terms of share of global GDP and be in a position to make a meaningful contribution, not least in terms of financial contributions to the organisation. Australia was somewhat sceptical over the case of Russia, which had been given a 'roadmap' for accession, a scepticism justified by subsequent Russian actions that have demonstrated that it lacks 'like-mindedness', to say the least. But, along with the other APEC Members, Australia has also been reluctant to accept every EU candidate, especially the smaller candidates.

Australia also has been supportive of including Indonesia and other Asian nations in 'Enhanced Engagement' activities and was supportive of the credentials of Thailand before the *coup d'état* there in September 2006. While Greece, Spain and Portugal had retained membership under periods of autocratic rule, with Spain and Portugal having acceded to membership while still military dictatorships, and it was felt that they had been influenced positively by OECD membership, democratic government is now considered to be a key criterion for membership.

The Australian objective has been to minimise the number of members around the table, but to encompass as much of the global economy as possible, and it sees it as important to 'ration' places until such time as significant global players (such as Brazil, China, India, Indonesia, and Russia) are ready for accession, limiting overall membership to 45–50 places. Such an extension would expand the 'APEC group' within the OECD, and would advance Australia's interests, and has also generally been supported, unsurprisingly, by the existing APEC members (Australia, Canada, Chile, Korea, Mexico, New Zealand). As Australian Ambassador Chris Barrett put it in a paper to the 2013 Ambassadors' Retreat, 'Our Australian calculus of new membership is that you admit new members to expand your influence in the world ... at the cost of more numbers around the table and more difficult governance' (Barrett, 2013).

The USA expressed a different view, however, when President Obama announced during a visit to Bogota in April 2012 that the US would support accession by Colombia (Obama, 2012). This revealed the hand of the US as regards enlargement and strengthened the 'bloody-mindedness' of the EU, which was able to secure agreement for accession by Colombia and Latvia, followed by Costa Rica and Lithuania a year later – after much 'blood on the carpet'. Turkey and Australia were both disappointed with the result, to say the least, especially as the EU concurs that the influence of the OECD has been weakened as a result of the enlargement decision – although EU dominance has been maintained. Other potential members include Kazakhstan, Morocco, Thailand and Peru. In his presentation to the Ambassadors' Retreat, Ambassador Barrett provided an analysis showing that by adding Colombia and Latvia in 2016 and Costa Rica and Lithuania in 2018, membership would increase by 14 per cent and yet the global economic share would fall by 4 per cent as growth in Asia outstripped that of the OECD membership (including Russia) (Barrett, 2013).

At the same time, the engagement of the OECD with key potential partners has been weakening, with Council postponing Russian accession in March 2014 although engagement with Russia continues at a technical level and engagement with China has intensified, and the focus on small European states has been diverting attention from the large emerging developing countries that have been pursuing their own initiatives, such as the New Development Bank (NDB), formerly referred to as the BRICS Development Bank, established by Brazil, Russia, India, China and South Africa in July 2014. Meanwhile, the OECD is effectively advising European members such as France to undertake reforms that Australia and other APEC and 'Anglosphere' members adopted 30 years ago.

The picture is not quite one of the EU against the APEC group of members on enlargement. The larger European members value the OECD less than the smaller members, such as Austria, Finland and Sweden (which can achieve amplified influence in the OECD), because the larger members have other fora within which they can act, such as the G7 and G20 although, as both lack a secretariat of their own, they have to rely, in particular, on the OECD's resources for analytical capacity and to implement policies, though they also use some of the specialised agencies such as the IMF and World Bank. And the APEC group can fracture, with Japan and Korea Australia's most reliable allies.

Australia has played an important part in establishing an OECD Southeast Asia Regional Programme as a part of providing a pathway to accession for potential members, and managed to divert some Part I funds to this (against some opposition). The US had indicated that it would only support it if there was further reform of OECD governance, including a replacement of mutual agreement by qualified majority voting, but it was not well organised and there was not even any caucusing of the reformist members, while the small members advantaged by the existing system (such as Switzerland, Luxembourg and Finland) were well organised. The introduction of QMV was therefore restricted in scope.

The importance of the South East Asia region had been recognised increasingly by the OECD for several years and the 'Global Reach' Resolution was adopted at the 2013 MCM, calling for the speedy implementation of a comprehensive Southeast Asia Regional Programme. It was proposed that the main objective of the Programme would be 'to strengthen engagement with the region with a view to support the regional integration process and national reform priorities' (OECD, 2014: 2). The scope and nature of the Programme were determined after intensive consultation with OECD Committees, Southeast Asian governments and regional stakeholders. Four clusters were identified:

- Connectivity: boosting infrastructure development, facilitating the flow of goods and services and promoting international investment;
- Enhancing the business climate: regulatory reform, tax policy and SMEs;
- Inclusive growth: skills and education; and
- Cross-cutting work on statistics.

The Programme was to be developed by Regional Policy Networks (RPNs), which would be composed of policy experts from Southeast Asia and OECD countries, operating flexibly and jointly deciding on its work programme, but building on the work programme of substantive OECD and Southeast Asian bodies and dialogue processes. The process was linked to other arenas, such as the ASEAN Business Summit, UNESCAP Trade and Investment Week, APEC Business Forum, a side event to the

Asian Development Bank annual meeting, and a joint OECD–Economic Research Institute for ASEAN and East Asia event, and an OECD Southeast Asia Regional Forum.

Six Regional Policy Networks were established to focus on the following areas: Tax Policies and Administration; Investment Policy and Promotion (chaired by Australia); Education and Skills Development (also chaired by Australia); Small and Medium-Sized Enterprises (SMEs) Policies; Regulatory Reform Policies; Connectivity and the Role of Public–Private Partnerships for Infrastructure Development.

Australia has played a significant and influential role in attempting to ensure that the enlargement of the OECD occurs in a fashion that both maximises its influence in the world by engaging with the most dynamic region in the global economy, yet restricts membership as much as possible to those states that meet the 'Noburu' criteria, designed to bring both gravitas and funding to the table. This effort has not been entirely successful in the face of occasional USA indifference and EU obstinacy, the latter in insisting that each EU accession state, no matter how insignificant, should be admitted to the OECD. Should the OECD lose its influence in the world, with the accession of numerous states that diminish its relative coverage of the global economy while embedding its own internal processes in a 'treacle' of mutual decision (albeit leavened by some provision for qualified majority voting) combined with greater numbers of small members, it will not be for a lack of effort on Australia's part.

A CRITICAL ASSESSMENT

As the earlier parts of this chapter show, Australia has sought throughout its membership to maintain what it sees as the essence of the OECD, especially more recently by trying to limit the past and future Euro-centrism that has recently threatened to stall the extension of influence to the Asia Pacific in what many see as the 'Asian Century', and add as members small states that bring little to the table except additional complexity. There are signs that the esteem in which Australia holds the OECD has been questioned somewhat in the past decade.

The two major issues of concern in 2004 were Outreach and Enlargement. The assessed contribution by Australia to the OECD in 2004 contribution was \$6.8m or 1.75 per cent of the assessed contributions for the main budget – the OECD's 12th largest. By way of comparison, Australia's contribution to the WTO was \$2.1m (or 1.15 per cent), and to UNESCO \$6.6m (or 0.85 per cent) (DFAT, 2004: 1). It is interesting to note that the proportion going to the OECD has grown since Australia joined. When it first did so, the funding was broadly similar to that for most of the UN specialised agencies. Subject to qualification, the relative growth in funding strongly suggests the growing value of the OECD to Australian government as a whole, though, of course, its perceived value to any specific agency rises and falls over time. The value to Treasury, for example, has fallen slowly since the 1980s (with the significant exception of tax work), as can be seen in the reduction of Treasury staff in the Delegation. The value for health, in contrast, has grown substantially.

The Australian view of the value of the OECD, distilled from various sources, can be summarised that it sometimes over-reaches (especially with the ill-fated MAI) and is too keen to assume a 'global' role. But the high quality of its staff and a reputation for objectivity enable it to play a significant role on certain global public good issues such as the promotion of trade liberalisation, the Anti-Bribery Convention, harmonisation of taxation policies, global environmental issues and development assistance policies.

DFAT's priority was the work on trade in the OECD, which was expected to assist progress on the Doha Round over the next year or two, and where the quality and extent of its research and analysis on trade policy compared more than favourably with that undertaken in other international bodies, such as the WTO (which has a different role and lacks sufficient resources for similar analysis), UNCTAD (where much of the work serves the specific interests of developing countries) and the World Bank (the IMF does little work in the same area). DFAT has nevertheless been critical of and disappointed with the Trade Committee, and its Trade Directorate which, under a Swiss chair, and with a French Director, had been more protectionist and less active than Australia would have preferred.

DFAT considered that the then current mission staff establishment was sufficient to advance DFAT's priorities, that there was no need to increase resources (DFAT, 2004: 7). It pointed out that in Canberra the Trade Development Division (TDD), Office of Trade Negotiations (OTN) and International Organisations and Legal Division (ILD) all had officers who provided briefings for OECD meetings. Formal responsibility rested with TDD, which had a dedicated OECD unit with 1.5 FTE plus 5 per cent of the time of the Head of the Market Development and Business Liaison Branch (MDB) and 25 per cent of the time of the Director of Trade Liaison (TLS). The document noted that DFAT Resources devoted to the OECD had been reduced in recent years, as had the involvement of the Senior Executive with the OECD.

It also noted that Australia was closely identified with OECD reforms, but that it could not expect to impose easily additional future changes. It is thought, however, that the OECD already performed at a professional level higher than that of many international agencies. In discussing how Australia might maximise its influence in the OECD, the DFAT has been rather cautious about the benefits of placing staff in the Secretariat, as it is considered that senior Secretariat officials, to be credible and effective, cannot and do not just represent national views and interests. They could give valuable advance notice, and extended contacts, but not much more.

It has been suggested that, when there was a new Secretary-General, Australia could consider running for one of the four DSG positions, with some chance of success, but it was noted that the major contributors (US, Japan, and Germany) look to lock up jobs at that level. Australia's best chance of securing a DSG position was thought to arise should Japan fill the Secretary-General position. As it happened, Australia later put forward its own candidate for Secretary-General, Professor Alan Fels, who had had considerable OECD experience, but lacked the gravitas of having been a minister, unlike the successful candidate, Mexican Angel Gurría.

On enlargement and outreach, Australia has felt that by bringing significant non-member countries to the MCM, the Trade Session proved particularly useful in bringing together both OECD members and non-OECD WTO members and helped in reviving momentum in the DOHA Round after the setback of the Cancun WTO Ministerial. However, the renewed momentum soon stalled in 2008 and was not revived, and then only at a very modest level, until 2013 with the adoption of the Bali Ministerial Declaration in December.

The then Ambassador, Ian Forsyth, considered that the main progress had come not so much from either the OECD trade session or from the mini-Ministerial session, but rather from several informal, restricted meetings that were held in the margins of the MCM (including P5 officials and ministerial meetings and a breakfast hosted by the Minister). In 2002, there had been fewer 'informals' and the mini-ministerial was a more substantive working session. Forsyth was of the view that the various events were complimentary and mutually reinforcing, including in terms of participation. On both occasions the Minister met with interlocutors he valued and was able to discuss directly issues relevant to the Doha Development Agenda (DDA).

Forsyth also noted that Australia covered most OECD work, although not all: for example, DOTARS had pulled back its engagement; it did not engage in all the work on public governance; it did not follow all of the work on environment, or did so 'reluctantly'; it did not follow a lot of the

Outreach work, particularly on Europe – although he did not 'dismiss the global economic and strategic value of that'. Sometimes Australia had to put in a significant defensive effort, such as in work on multifunctionality.

In Forsyth's view, the OECD Trade Committee should have been bringing together high level officials from capitals to discuss a range of DDA and other issues, but in his three years in post, the delegate on Trade Committee had been the FAS OTN twice, Forsyth himself twice, and the AS OTN for the rest. Given the Ambassador's other duties on Council and HODs, it was difficult to guarantee their availability to attend the Committee, and, in any event, he thought it desirable that attendance was from capitals. Prior to mid-2001, the FAS in OTN had attended all meetings and was an active member of the Bureau. Forsyth was 'not sure Canberra always knew what he was up to', but the continuity had clearly slipped since then. Also, the absence of Australia's recognised trade negotiator at the table had meant that it had been excluded from unofficial meetings arranged by the Swiss chair (Luzius Wasecha).

There was a view that the OECD could improve by facilitating wider distribution of its research findings and studies. It was noted that many of these supported Australian policy objectives, but delays in declassifying OECD documents could limit the usefulness of the reports. It was thought that this should be a new objective for the OECD mission, and the TDD could play a greater role in ensuring relevant OECD material reaches a wider audience in Australia.

It was considered that another whole-of-government review of participation was perhaps warranted, and that there was a need to continue to contribute efforts towards improving efficiency of OECD management and work processes.

CONCLUSION

As these examples show, Australia has played a consistent part in seeking to maximise the extent to which the OECD retains its unique character, by appointing its senior staff on merit, though within the constraints of satisfying the major budgetary contributors (such as the US and Japan). It has also played a prominent role in budgetary reform, in reforming the structure and processes of the organisation, and in seeking to maintain its special character as one of a smallish group of like-minded members reasonably capable, within the constraints of the mutual agreement rule, of taking effective action in the face of the determination of the EU to sponsor to membership each and every state that accedes to that institution.

It has not done so alone, but it has done so skilfully, though it has regularly irritated the EC and some of the EU members with its constant criticism of the organisation's Eurocentrism. It has made particular use of close relations with the other APEC members, especially Canada and Japan as well as the US and New Zealand. In so doing, it has assisted the OECD adapt from a largely Eurocentric, 'economic NATO' in the OEEC to administer the Marshall Plan, to a modern organisation increasingly aligned to the rising Asia-Pacific region, not yet as much as it perhaps should be, but more so than it would have been without Australian influence.

There are some indications that Australian enthusiasm for the OECD has waned, at least in DFAT and Treasury, while that of most other agencies has increased or at least been relatively stable, as indicated by the increased voluntary funding provided as well as the work in the tax and health areas. The most recent ambassadorial appointments have been political ones, rather than career officers, and the insights they acquire in the office will not return with them to DFAT or Treasury. There is still an OECD desk in DFAT, but it is now at section, rather than branch level: 'Trade Finance and OECD Section'. Not only the G20 Branch, but the Tobacco Plain Packaging Task Force featured more prominently on the DFAT organisational chart in May 2015.

BIBLIOGRAPHY

Barrett, C. 2013. Unpublished presentation to the 2013 OECD Ambassadors' Retreat.

Carroll, P. and Kellow, A. 2011. *The OECD A Study of Organisational Adaptation*, Cheltenham, UK and Northampton, MA, USA: Edward Elgar Publishing.

DEWR 2001. Cable, Paris OECD to CBR, 8 January 2002, OECD Reform Proposals: The 'Big Bang', Budget Reform, File ET01/11368 Government Relations – Committees 1358 – Organisation for Economic Co-operation and Development (OECD) – Cables and Reports.

DEWR 2001a. Paris OECD to CBR 8 January 2002, File ET01/11368 Government Relations – Committees 1358 – Organisation for Economic Co-operation and Development (OECD) – Cables and Reports.

DEWR 2001b. Cable Paris OECD to Canberra 8 January 2001, File ET01/11368 Government Relations – Committees 1358 – Organisation for Economic Co-operation and Development (OECD) – Cables and Reports.

DEWR 2001c. Cable CBR to Paris OECD. 21 January 2002, File ET01/11368 Government Relations – Committees 1358 – Organisation for Economic Co-operation and Development (OECD) – Cables and Reports.

DEWR 2001d. Cable OECD Paris to CBR. OECD Reform – Report of WG 1 on the OECD's Priorities and Program of Work and Budget. 27 May 2002. File ET01/11368 Government Relations – Committees 1358 – Organisation for Economic Co-operation and Development (OECD) – Cables and Reports.

DEWR 2008. Cable. Paris OECD to CBR/WASH/Well/Tokyo 28 October 1996, File ES08/02225 Legislation and Government Business – Organisation for Economic Co-operation and Development – Briefings Input From Schools Group.

DFAT 2001. File 01/050184 Agriculture Committee 23/01/01 to 22/01/02.

DFAT 2001a. Cable 11 April 2003, CBR to Mexico City/Ottawa/Washington/ Wellington RP: Brasilia/Buenos Aires/Santiago/Geneva WTO/ Paris OECD. File 01/050184 Agriculture Committee 23/01/01 to 22/01/02.

DFAT 2004. Policy Planning Paper. Australia and the OECD: DFAT's Perspectives (n.d., 2004).

DFAT 2004a. Email Ian Forsyth to Anne Pellegrino (Mgr, OECD & UNCTAD Unit (OED)). 18 October 2004 Re: Restricted: Re: Confidential: Review of Australia's Position in the OECD. File 05/060004 International Relations – Conferences – OECD, Review, 2005/06.

DFAT 2005. Minute. 12 October 2004 Mark Pierce, AS, MTB in DFAT File International Relations – Conferences – OECD, Review, 2005/06 05/060004.

DFAT 2007. Cable PO22366H OECD: Secretary-General: Dubious Appointments 3 April 2007 Paris OECD to CBR. CC: Brussels, London, Mexico City, Ottawa, Paris EMB, Washington. DFAT 330/230/160 Political-Economic-International Organisations- OECD – Secretary-General's Programme of Work and Budget (PWB), Budget Committee, Programme Implementation Reports (PIR), OEU. File No. 07/500896-2.

DFAT 2007a. Email Philippe na Champassak to David Spencer 13 October 2006, Role of the European Commission attached to a document 'OECD: Role of the European Community'. DFAT 330/230/160 Political-Economic-International Organisations- OECD – Secretary-General's Programme of Work and Budget (PWB), Budget Committee, Programme Implementation Reports (PIR), OEU, File No. 07/500896-2.

DFAT 2007b. Cable [NZ] Paris to Wellington 26 April 2007 Copied to Denis O'Dea. DFAT 330/230/160 Political-Economic-International Organisations-OECD – Secretary-General's Programme of Work and Budget (PWB), Budget Committee, Programme Implementation Reports (PIR), OEU, File No. 07/500896-2.

NAA 1967. P.J. Flood – First sec to Sec DEA 9 Dec 1968. File A1838 724/4/1/12 Part 1 Organisation for Economic Co-operation and Development – Appointment of Secretary-General and Senior Officials 1967–1975.

NAA 1967a. J.D. McCredie, First Sec The Hague to Sec DFA 21 Feb 1969, File A1838 724/4/1/12 Part 1 Organisation for Economic Co-operation and Development – Appointment of Secretary-General and Senior Officials 1967–1975.

NAA 1967b. P.J. Flood, Permanent Mission to UN Office at Geneva, to Sec DEA 21 February 1969. Memorandum 123/69, File A1838 724/4/1/12 Part 1

Organisation for Economic Co-operation and Development – Appointment of Secretary-General and Senior Officials 1967–1975.
NAA 1967c. Cable 20 November 1973 R.J. Cameron Delegation to Sec DFA, File A1838 724/4/1/12 Part 1 Organisation for Economic Co-operation and Development – Appointment of Secretary-General and Senior Officials 1967–1975.
NAA 1967d. Note from Flood to Dr Cumes: 11 December 1973, File A1838 724/4/1/12 Part 1 Organisation for Economic Co-operation and Development – Appointment of Secretary-General and Senior Officials 1967–1975.
NAA 1967e. Cable 1240 Delegation to Canberra 13 December 1973, File A1838 724/4/1/12 Part 1 Organisation for Economic Co-operation and Development – Appointment of Secretary-General and Senior Officials 1967–1975.
NAA 1967f. Cable 1258 Delegation to Canberra 18/12/73, File A1838 724/4/1/12 Part 1 Organisation for Economic Co-operation and Development – Appointment of Secretary-General and Senior Officials 1967–1975.
NAA 1967g. Cable 1258 Delegation to Canberra 18 December 1973, File A1838 724/4/1/12 Part 1 Organisation for Economic Co-operation and Development – Appointment of Secretary-General and Senior Officials 1967–1975.
NAA 1967h. Cable 1327 Canberra to Delegation 19 December 1973, File A1838 724/4/1/12 Part 1 Organisation for Economic Co-operation and Development – Appointment of Secretary-General and Senior Officials 1967–1975.
NAA 1967i. Cable 1391 OTTAWA- Canberra 20 December 1973, File A1838 724/4/1/12 Part 1 Organisation for Economic Co-operation and Development – Appointment of Secretary-General and Senior Officials 1967–1975.
NAA 1967j. Cable 1265 Paris Delegation to CBR 20 December 1973, File A1838 724/4/1/12 Part 1 Organisation for Economic Co-operation and Development – Appointment of Secretary-General and Senior Officials 1967–1975.
NAA 1967k. Cable 1337 CBR to Delegation 21 December 1973, File A1838 724/4/1/12 Part 1 Organisation for Economic Co-operation and Development – Appointment of Secretary-General and Senior Officials 1967–1975.
NAA 1967l. Cable 3666 Tokyo to CBR, Repeated OECD Paris 28 December 1973, File A1838 724/4/1/12 Part 1 Organisation for Economic Co-operation and Development – Appointment of Secretary-General and Senior Officials 1967–1975.
NAA 1967m. Cable 38 Delegation to CBR 10 January 1974, File A1838 724/4/1/12 Part 1 Organisation for Economic Co-operation and Development – Appointment of Secretary-General and Senior Officials 1967–1975.
NAA 1967n. Memo No 257 27 March 1974 R.J. Cameron (Ambassador) to Secretary DFA, File A1838 724/4/1/12 Part 1 Organisation for Economic Co-operation and Development – Appointment of Secretary-General and Senior Officials 1967–1975.
NAA 1967o. Letter R.J. Whitelaw, First Ass Sec, Overseas Economic Relations Division, Treasury to Secy (Attn Dr J.W.C. Cumes) 3 May 1974, File A1838 724/4/1/12 PART 1 Organisation for Economic Co-operation and Development – Appointment of Secretary-General and Senior Officials 1967–1975.
NAA 1967p. Letter J.W.C. Cumes, First Assistant Secretary, International Organisations Division, to Secretary, DFA, 11 April 1974, File A1838 724/4/

1/12 Part 1 Organisation for Economic Co-operation and Development – Appointment of Secretary-General and Senior Officials 1967–1975.
NAA 1967q. Memo No 257 27 March 1974 R.J. Cameron (Ambassador) to Secretary DFA, File A1838 724/4/1/12 PART 1 Organisation for Economic Co-operation and Development – Appointment of Secretary-General and Senior Officials 1967–1975.
NAA 1967r. Memo No 257 27 March 1974 R.J. Cameron (Ambassador) to Secretary DFA, File A1838 724/4/1/12 Part 1 Organisation for Economic Co-operation and Development – Appointment of Secretary-General and Senior Officials 1967–1975.
NAA 1967s. Cable 507 Paris to CBR 9 May 1974, File A1838 724/4/1/12 Part 1 Organisation for Economic Co-operation and Development – Appointment of Secretary-General and Senior Officials 1967–1975.
NAA 1967t. Cable 580 Paris to CBR 23 May 1974, File A1838 724/4/1/12 Part 1 Organisation for Economic Co-operation and Development – Appointment of Secretary-General and Senior Officials 1967–1975.
NAA 1967u. Memo No 456 6 June 1974 R.J. Cameron Ambassador to Secy DFA, File A1838 724/4/1/12 PART 1 Organisation for Economic Co-operation and Development – Appointment of Secretary-General and Senior Officials 1967–1975.
NAA 1981. Cable CBR to PAR 13/7/81 OECD: Council: 1982 PWB, File A6343 B1981/162 Organisation for Economic Co-operation and Development – Review of Australian Participation – June 1981.
Obama, Barack 2012. Remarks by President Obama and President Santos of Colombia in Joint Press Conference 15 April 2012, accessed 23 March 2015 at www.whitehouse.gov/the-press-office/2012/04/15/remarks-president-obama-and-president-santos-colombia-joint-press-confer.
OECD 2014. *The OECD Southeast Asia Regional Programme*, Paris: OECD Publishing.

14. Conclusions

The aim of this chapter is to summarise and comment on Australia's experience of membership of the OECD. It focuses on: (1) the process of accession and the experience of membership in the early years; (2) the varying experiences of differing departments with the OECD over time; (3) the value of the OECD for policy learning and policy capacity; and (4) Australia and the future of the OECD.

THE PROCESS OF ACCESSION AND THE EARLY YEARS OF MEMBERSHIP

As discussed, the reasons for seeking OECD membership evolved over a period of some ten years and were the subject of considerable debate, marked by a distinct division of views between ministers and their departments. Indeed, in 1960–61 there was little enthusiasm for Australian membership, and it grew relatively slowly in these first few years. This was not a unique experience, for the consideration of membership leading to a final decision to move to an application took nearly thirteen years for the New Zealand government, though, in contrast, it took only four years for the Japanese government (Carroll, 2015). In Australia's case, while the value of membership for Australia as an isolated, middle power was repeatedly stressed, its proponents only slowly gained sufficient strength to overcome opposition.

As with Japan and New Zealand, the Australian government sought access, information and influence in the OECD in order to both protect and advance its economic and political interests by membership of an organisation that seemed likely to grow in status and influence. The time it took to gain full membership was caused mainly by two factors. First, the varying and initially low level of support it perceived for its membership from key, existing members of the OECD, notably the USA, but also the UK. Second was the deep division between senior officials and ministers as to the merits of membership, with persistent and fierce opposition from Deputy Prime Minister McEwen. Indeed, it is possible, in retrospect, that Australia might have gained membership in or about

1963, at much the same time as Japan, had it not been for McEwen's opposition.

The reactions of Australian officials in the early years of membership were similar in that their experiences, at least as recorded, confirmed the expectations of the value of membership put forward in their earlier, pre-accession, domestic discussions and submissions. They found that value, for the most part, in the information, contacts and opportunities for presenting their national interests that the OECD provided. However, not all of their experiences were positive, falling into two broad groups: (1) those negative feelings brought about by the challenges of settling in to membership of a new organisation that, for the most part, were overcome within a year or two of membership; and (2) more persistent disappointment with the value, or lack of it, of the work of specific committees on specific issues, such as agriculture and trade. However, while not examined in this chapter, even these latter, rather negative views varied over time as the work of the committees themselves varied and became more or less valuable. The work of Trade and Agriculture committees, for example, became of far greater interest to both Australia and New Zealand in the years of the Uruguay Round from the later 1980s to the establishment of the WTO.

THE VARYING EXPERIENCES OF DIFFERING DEPARTMENTS WITH MEMBERSHIP OF THE OECD OVER TIME

Australia now has more than 40 years of involvement with the OECD, with extensive, though varying, involvement by numerous agencies, not just those covered in detail here, but others such as successive social security, resources and labour departments, for example. Space constraints and the need to provide depth to the study have precluded exploring every aspect of engagement, and there is much more that could be written about the OECD and related organisations, such as the International Energy Agency (IEA), which Australia did not initially join (a story in itself).

While a wide range of Australian agencies have been involved with the OECD, it is fair to say that their experiences have varied, both from one to the next and over time. AusAID and its predecessors have had a close involvement with the DAC, even before accession to the OECD, as we have seen. Treasury and DFAT have been the agencies with the greatest involvement, especially after the amalgamation of Foreign Affairs and

Trade, and this is only to be expected given the nature of the OECD. But while the focus of the OECD was initially on economics, including trade, it has taken on new areas of concern such as science, education and environment as their inextricable connection to the goal of maximising sustainable economic growth became more apparent.

Education is one such area. Not initially a concern of the OECD, it emerged over time from social affairs, which developed into the Directorate for Education, Employment, Labour and Social Affairs (DEELSA), before gaining its own status as a Directorate in its own right. As we have seen, Australians were prominent in these developments, filling both the Deputy Directorship for Education in DEELSA and the foundation Directorship of what is now Education and Skills. This is the highest level of Australian involvement in any part of the Secretariat, with the most senior Australian in the Secretariat at the time of writing being Anthony Rottier, a member of staff of the OECD since 1993 who was appointed Executive Director of the OECD in November 2012. Rottier was centrally involved in the budgetary reforms in which Australia played a prominent role.

Education is now one of the activities most highly valued by the relevant Australian agency, and others such as Health (in the Directorate for Employment, Labour and Social Affairs) grew in importance, largely because Australia chose to support work in the OECD out of a lack of satisfaction with work being conducted in the WHO. This again highlights how the significance of the OECD for different agencies has changed over time. This extends to the central agencies, Treasury and DFAT, which currently exhibit some signs that they are finding the OECD to be less important than in the past. The appointment of ambassadors that are not senior members of the public service in each agency when their 'turn' fell to each is one such sign, not just in terms of reflecting an inevitable lessening of professional and departmental expertise they bring to the position, but also in terms of what they bring back to their departments.

Ambassadors in the past frequently brought with them the experience of having participated in the work of the OECD's committees, as well as experience in their departments with the OECD's work processes and products, including through interaction with other experienced participants. And upon completion of their posting, they bring back considerable experience of value to their department; this is lost when ambassadors are appointed from outside, and so do not return to their home department.

The OECD, having begun its existence as a kind of 'economic NATO', necessarily had to adapt to the end of the Cold War and the decline in significance of its Eastern Bloc rival, Comecon, and Australia among others, has sought to make it to continue to be of relevance after these and other seismic shifts, such as the rise of the Asia Pacific. These signs of lessening ardour in Australia reflect partly its limited success in reforming the OECD and partly the rise of alternative venues such as APEC and the G20, and the increased pursuit of bilateral or regional trade agreements, such as the Trans Pacific Partnership, where work in the trade programmes in the OECD are of less significance. This decline in importance is by no means shared universally, however, and agencies such as Health and Education continue to find considerable value in the OECD.

As Australia's experience in the OECD indicates, membership of an international organisation does not by any means bring about an automatic increase in influence for a middle power. This will vary over time and, as demonstrated, by the agency involved, some achieving greater influence while others are less fortunate.

MEMBERSHIP, LEARNING AND POLICY CAPACITY

As a small, open economy in an increasingly globalised world the task of gaining and maintaining knowledge of that world and the ability to use it to develop appropriate policy becomes ever more challenging for the Australian government. It is more challenging in at least two senses: (1) in the simple extent of knowledge of an increasing number of countries and markets and their interactions that needs to be absorbed if policy is to be successful; and (2) in the growing need to effectively apply that knowledge in not only national but, increasingly, international contexts, contexts that include an ever-increasing number of international agreements, standards and codes of conduct that have been developed in the attempt to manage the global economy and its ramifications.

Our overall conclusion is that membership of the OECD brought with it a valuable means to the ongoing maintenance and further building of policy capacity in Australia. We use the term capacity building to refer to the process of developing and exercising the ability of an organisation or organisations to meet the challenges, both internal and external, that it faces in relation to the achievement of its goals. The development, maintenance and enhancement of a practical capacity for policy analysis, development and implementation requires relevant knowledge and understanding, combined with the ability to use them in an effective manner to achieve the goals of government. In addition, if that capacity is to be maintained or enhanced then gaining knowledge and understanding must be a more or less continuous process, or its value rapidly declines, especially when faced with a swiftly changing environment.

The OECD is, however, by no means the only international forum that provides, directly or indirectly, such a service to its members, others including, to name just a few examples, the IMF and the WTO (DFAT, 1999). However, it is unique in the extent and variety of policy areas in which it provides learning opportunities, as we have seen, making it attractive, if to varying extents, to nearly all government departments and most agencies, in contrast to the more specialised international organisations with a primarily operational role such as the IMF and the WTO. In addition, for the most part its focus on the richer countries means that there is a greater relevance in its advice for Australia, as a member of that fortunate group of countries facing many broadly similar, but by no means identical issues and policy challenges.

It is important to stress that the value of OECD membership in building policy capacity is not incidental, as one of its primary roles since its inception has been to promote capacity building, although the language of capacity building was not used by those framing its founding Convention. Rather, as indicated in the Convention, its primary aim was, and is, to promote policies designed to achieve the highest sustainable economic growth in a context of expanding world trade, while maintaining financial stability and the development of the world economy, both for itself and for non-members (OECD, 1960). The sense in which the term 'promote policies' is used in the Convention, and has since been interpreted by its members in steering the work of the OECD, makes it quite clear that its efforts are to focus on capacity building in regard to policies that relate to economic growth. This became even more evident with the establishment of a specialised unit with the OECD, the Directorate for Public Governance and Territorial Development (it has had a variety of titles), with its primary focus on the improvement of the capacity of the governments of the member states, albeit largely in relation to the economy. Hence, much, if not all of its work is quite explicitly designed to assist its members maintain and enhance their governing capacity, in relation to whole of government issues, specific policies and, in particular, in relation to transnational issues.

Perceptions of the Value of Policy Learning in Relation to the OECD

There is little doubt that Australia's membership of the OECD is used by public servants to enhance their capacities in regard to the development of policy. All of those interviewed for this study for example, without exception, indicated that the major reason for their continuing, if varying, participation in OECD committees and working groups was that of policy learning, in one form or another. Further, all of those interviewed, bar one, also felt that their aim of policy learning had been achieved, though to varying extents, and that it was a more or less continuous process. Similarly, the bulk of the members of the OECD's Secretariat interviewed felt that the opportunity for policy learning in a cross-national context was the primary service the organisation offered to its members.

When questioned further as to what was meant by policy learning the answers of those interviewed varied, but all indicated that it entailed the acquisition of current knowledge and understanding in relation to particular policy areas, with an emphasis upon the value of the cross-cultural, comparative context provided by the OECD, where they could learn from both their peers and a wide range of experts. Moreover, the bulk stressed that the knowledge and understanding gained for the most part had considerable, practical, policy value, capable of at least informing and, at times, leading to actual modifications to existing national policies, processes and techniques. It was particularly valuable in that it often provided comparative learning about the performance of Australian policy, processes and institutions.

Sources of Policy Learning and the OECD

While the individual experience of policy learning associated with the OECD is as varied as the number of individuals involved, four basic sources of learning seem to predominate, as reported by those interviewed and the records perused, with some overlap between them: statistical data; reports, particularly those in which policy recommendations are provided; peer reviews; and formal and informal meetings and associated discussions.

The OECD publishes comparative data on the economic and social performance of its members, particularly economic statistics but also data related, for example, to education in the shape of the PISA data on educational performance and health data, to name only a few. The data are important for at least three reasons. In the first instance they provide reasonably accurate past and current information on important socio-economic trends at both national and global levels, trends usually examined carefully for their Australian policy implications, both as to existing and future policy (see, for example, the Australian Institute of Health and Welfare's examination of OECD data regarding health trends, AIHW, 2014). While a few of the richer countries can themselves afford to collect data on a global basis, most cannot, particularly where some data, for example, that relating to aspects of economic performance, is often confidential. Second, it provides useful benchmarking data against which to judge national performance, providing important clues as to the efficiency and effectiveness of national policy – for both governments, opposition parties, trade unions, business and interest groups, as in the EDRC reviews and PISA. Third, the OECD's data is important because of its credibility, a characteristic that can add weight to the views of those decision makers who feel that the trends or performance it reveals requires appropriate, remedial action. Those interviewed in DEST, for example, stressed the value of the PISA data and the reputation of OECD statistics for comparisons of Australian educational performance and, as with Porter and Webb noted, its reputation:

> [a]mong scholars is so good that typically the statistics are used without the author feeling any need to justify them as valid measures of the phenomena in question. Similarly, OECD reports are widely used as authoritative statements of knowledge in many policy areas, again often without the author seeing any need beyond the label 'OECD' to justify the authoritative character of the knowledge contained therein. (Porter and Webb, 2004: 7)

As Porter and Webb also point out, the collection and dissemination of data is not a mundane, boring activity, but the definition in quantitative terms of economic and social reality, definitions that can set the framework within which both understanding and future policy developments come to be based. The OECD's definition of 'producer subsidy equivalents', in relation to government subsidies for agriculture is a good example. Government subsidies to agriculture take many different and substantial forms in OECD countries and, to the constant concern of those such as Australia and New Zealand that are relatively highly dependent on trade in agriculture, they result in artificially low prices for many products. Hence, following some decades of pressure from its largely non-EU members and the strongly free market orientation of the bulk of OECD economists, the OECD developed a common measure of government subsidies to agriculture, its 'producer subsidy equivalent', or PSE. The PSE then enabled more objective bargaining among governments in the OECD and, most importantly, within the WTO, about the real extent of subsidies in agricultural policies and their impact. In effect it changed the terms of the debate about agricultural subsidies by making it clear that many previously defined agricultural policies were, in fact, trade-distorting subsidies. It is no accident that a number of Australian academics were influential in elaborating the concept of PSE, and Australian representatives were an important and continuing source of pressure for its development and use.

If Porter and Webb's argument is extended, then in a very real sense the OECD's data, when used to develop ideal-type policy models and standards, is a vital foundation for what it portrays as 'best practice' in policy and governance. Its members are then judged, voluntarily, if not always enthusiastically, against these benchmarks, sometimes blessed with the labels of laggards or leaders, in effect being socialised into the acceptance of the benchmarks as norms by which they should judge their performance, the performance of other OECD members and, importantly, those of their colleagues in Canberra. While policy models and best practice standards do not predetermine the longer term policies developed by governments, they do play an important role in shaping the constraints within which potential, alternative policies are considered, as was found to be the case in the adoption and adaptation of the OECD's 'WALRAS', a world trade model used by the Productivity Commission.

As a glance at its website soon reveals, a great deal of the voluminous output of the OECD takes what can be described as a 'policy template' form, in the shape of a seemingly endless stream of reports and accompanying recommendations, working papers, committee papers and, less commonly, agreements. The bulk of the reports summarise the research work of Secretariat staff (plus, to varying extents, consultants), and members of committees (the latter often supported by staff working with their 'home-based', department or agency), acting on the instructions of, and guided primarily by, the 'bureau', of one or more committees, and which address issues of current or likely concern to the bulk of its members. The members of the committee bureaux vary, but include the chair, vice chairs and a limited number of the members of the committee in question. In recent years, for example, Australian public servants have chaired nine committees (3.9 per cent of the total of which it is a member), and have been vice chairs of sixteen others (6.9 per cent of those of which it is a member).

The extent to which any one of the reports results in policy learning, an increase in policy capacity or, less commonly, an actual impact on national policies, depends upon its perceived relevance and credibility, the extent and type of involvement by the public servants involved and, to varying extents, the ability of the national representatives on the committee to both effectively communicate and persuade key decision makers in their departments and local policy networks as to the merits of the report and its recommendations. Not surprisingly, as a result the influence of OECD reports on policy development varies a great deal from member state to member state, and individual to individual, a view strongly supported by those interviewed.

An example of a report that was particularly influential was a 1982 OECD report authored by the late Peter Wilenski, then a professor at the Australian National University but on secondment to the OECD, that recommended a universal youth allowance as a means of reducing long-term youth unemployment. The following year Wilenski was invited by Prime Minister Hawke to become head of the Department of Education and Youth Affairs in Hawke's first ALP ministry and over the next few years several of the ideas espoused by Wilenski were incorporated into Australian public policy (Vickers, 1995: 59–60). While the circumstances in this case were unusual and, as the head of a major government department Wilenski had both the needed access and opportunity to influence policy, making it more likely that the views he espoused in his OECD report would achieve the Hawke government's agenda and, with modifications, be adopted, there is little doubt that it was the credibility of the OECD that also played an important role in gaining acceptance for his views.

Perhaps a more typical example was a 2001 OECD report reviewing Australia's labour market policies, part of a series assessing national labour market policies in various countries, highlighting the Job Network system (OECD, 2001). While the report was very positive in regard to this novel attempt to introduce market mechanisms into job broking, it also described a number of concerns with the new system that, in part, were recognised by the Commonwealth government, leading to changes to the system (Shergold, 2002). Indeed, most of the Australian public servants interviewed noted that it was very rare for an OECD report and its recommendations to be wholly endorsed and implemented at the national level. Rather, a limited number of specific recommendations might be endorsed, or the general approach suggested by a report might inform future policy developments.

More recent evidence of the influence of the OECD's reports as a source of information in Australian policy debates and the setting of national agendas can be seen clearly, for example, in regard to the recent criticisms of the Commonwealth government's regulatory impact system (RIS) and the quality of regulation made by the Taskforce on Regulation (Taskforce on Regulation, 2006). Its recommendations led to several changes to the RIS, and the Taskforce used the OECD's seven principles of regulatory design as the base from which: (1) to compare the quality of Australian regulation; (2) to help it estimate the cost of regulation for Australian business; (3) as a source of endorsement as to the value of RIS type processes; and (4) to support its case as to the need for regular reviews of regulation (Taskforce on Regulation, 2006: 8, 14, 172). Similarly, in pressing for improved processes for making regulation and the elimination of unnecessary regulation, the Business Council of Australia drew heavily upon OECD data (BCA, 2005: 7, 25). Finally, the Victorian Premier's influential call in 2005 for a third wave of social and economic reform, what came to be called the National Reform Agenda, also drew upon an OECD report to support his case, a report that argued that Australia needed to achieve significant increases in productivity and participation if it was to rise to the never-ending challenge of international competition (Bracks, 2005: 10, drawing upon OECD, 2004).

The information provided in the context of the OECD's peer reviews, such as the EDRC reviews (see Chapter 6), while normally published in report form, deserve particular mention for they are, quiet explicitly, critical assessments of a government's existing policies and, on occasion, of the degree of its compliance with OECD agreements, standards, recommendations or codes of behaviour. Hence, they are directly and immediately relevant in the national policy context, although the objectives of reviews vary somewhat, even within the OECD, with the aims of policy advice, policy coordination and cooperation, information gathering and dissemination being perhaps the most common. As the objectives vary, so can their role in relation to policy learning and the development of policy capacity.

In regard to the peer reviews whose major objective is to provide policy advice the role is clear: to provide comments and proposals in relation to the policy being reviewed so that, if accepted, in whole or modified form, they automatically gain a place on the national agenda and, on occasion, will result in modifications to existing policy, hopefully enhancing the content of policy. The Development Assistance Committee's peer reviews have been, for example, on the basis of a survey of member attitudes, almost unanimously considered to be highly important and:

> On balance, most Members (sixteen) are satisfied with the peer reviews, and the same number declared that the reviews had a high or some impact on their aid policies and practices. (OECD, 2002: 3)

Most OECD peer reviews also have a second objective, that of encouraging policy coordination, cooperation and, sometimes, policy convergence among its members, usually based on a set of policy or administrative guidelines or standards agreed to by members and, less commonly, formal, intergovernmental agreements (see, for example, OECD, 2002: 4). The reviews of members' regulatory reform activities and performance undertaken since the mid-1990s, for example, made seven recommendations for regulatory reform to which all members were encouraged to align themselves and which were used, in part, as criteria for future regulatory reform peer reviews and have been used as bench marks by the Commonwealth government (and the OECD), to assess its regulatory reform (OECD, 1997, 2010).

A third common objective of peer reviews, the narrowly focused information gathering and dissemination necessary for the later analysis and review process, is relevant to national policy capacity from at least three perspectives. The first is that of the government of the country concerned, whose policy is the subject of the review; the second is that of the countries whose representatives are acting as the external assessors for the review, supported by the Secretariat; the third is that of the more general publics and interested non-governmental groups in the country concerned. In all three cases the information gathered has the potential for use in the relevant national contexts, helping to enrich understanding in policy debates by providing a body of policy-relevant information that is already structured around the types of key questions likely to be addressed by participants in those debates. In other words it provides essential material for policy review and development, sometimes enhancing policy capacity.

It should be noted that the information gathered often springs, in large part, from the country under examination, as the core document is often a detailed background report on the situation in the country of a specific member, normally prepared by a group of public servants from the country being examined, although usually based on a standard, OECD prescribed format. This represented a change in OECD policy from the original peer review process conducted by the EDRC, where the background report was prepared by members of the Secretariat, although, even then they were prepared largely on the basis of documents provided by the country concerned (see, for example, Aubert, 2001: 385–386 and Chapter 6 on Economic Policy).

Policy learning is also gained in formal and informal meetings, ranging from a formal OECD committee or working party, to an informal group meeting, one-on-one meetings, or, increasingly, in one of the several large policy forums ('global forums', in OECD parlance), organised each year by the OECD. In essence, the meetings can be regarded as more or less formally organised exchange networks in which the form of policy learning gained is, at least on occasion, an enhanced ability to gain entry to, organise and benefit from interaction with peers working in similar areas in other countries, rather than policy-specific knowledge of the type gained from reports and peer reviews. As indicated by those interviewed, membership of such networks tends to persist over time and to interlink with a range of similar networks in other international organisations notably the IMF, the EU, the World Bank and the WTO, often with the same set of national representatives meeting on a regular basis in differing international organisations, notably Treasury and trade officials.

There is considerable value in membership of such networks, especially for smaller countries such as Australia. It enables public servants to gain advance knowledge of developing international issues, or national issues in the larger states like the USA that are likely to impact on Australian interests, in effect helping to establish which issues should be considered for entry to Australian agendas, with what priority. If, for example, the USA seems to be considering a change in its stance regarding multilateral agreements on investment, it is often within the established exchange networks, including the OECD, that the possible change is first identified by other states and discussed. Similarly, it enables member countries to test out the likely reactions of the other members to possible changes in their national policies and practices before they are fully developed or implemented, in a relatively private fashion. Importantly, it can lead to a withdrawal or modification of planned changes with little embarrassment to any party. At a more modest level, several of those interviewed were able to provide examples of bilateral or multilateral projects conducted outside of the OECD framework that had their origins in discussions in one or more OECD networks.

The OECD is clearly a forum for policy learning that enhances policy capacity. It is, as noted, not the only international organisation that provides, directly or indirectly, such a service to its members. However, the fact that a number of international organisations provide such services in relation to policy capacity is both a blessing and, at least for some departments and their staff, somewhat of a curse. It is a blessing in two senses: (1) in that the international agencies are forced, to varying extents, to compete with each other in the provision and quality of their services, hopefully resulting in at least the maintenance of reasonably high standards for fear of loss of custom; and (2) where the same issues are examined in more than one international organisation member countries thus have the benefit of two sources of advice and assistance. It is a curse in that to gain maximum benefit the departments involved have to participate, if with varying degrees of enthusiasm, in the deliberations of two or more international organisations, a relatively expensive and time-consuming business, often placing considerable pressure on the public servants who have to attend meetings in different international locations and scrutinise a wide range of documents. It caused, for example, difficulties in managing Treasury's then International Economic Division when SES officers at its head were required, increasingly, to be abroad for longer periods of time to attend overseas meetings. The result led first to a merger of two Treasury divisions and their associated branches and later, unusually, the creation of an 'Alternative Executive Director' position to help deal with the increasing workload (Treasury, 1998: 93). The increase in international workload also led, secondly, to two new units in Treasury's Macroeconomic Group (Treasury, 2004: 5).

It is more accurate to conceive of the impact of the OECD in relation to policy learning and capacity by viewing it, not as a consolidated entity, an undifferentiated 'organisational billiard ball', but as a series of loosely linked policy networks, focused around the OECD committees, their subcommittees and associated directorates and departments and agencies at the national level. As with the notion of not one, but a number of national agendas, this differentiated conception of the OECD suggests that one should not generalise about the influence of the OECD as a whole, nor about the influence of any one of its members upon it, but limit such generalisations to the committee network concerned. Hence, from this perspective, the OECD has, at any one time, a varying impact on Australian policy learning and capacity, depending on which network is examined, and vice versa. Further, of course, the impact of any one network will vary over time and from country to country.

One very obvious issue associated with the above notion of multiple agendas and networks is whether or not that fact is taken fully and effectively into consideration at the strategic level by DFAT and, ultimately, Cabinet decision makers, especially when it comes to determining policy directions and coordination across government to achieve the desired directions. The interviews undertaken suggest that:

- Staff within DFAT and Treasury charged with interdepartmental, 'joined up', government, and those within other departments are aware that there is a significant coordination issue posed by international activities, multiple agendas and policy developments.
- In the shape of regular, but infrequent, interdepartmental committee meetings chaired by DFAT or Treasury, there is an attempt to ensure that the implications of the differing issues, agendas and potential policy developments being undertaken in multiple locations within government are identified and appropriately dealt with. However, interviewees also noted that, in practice, far more coordination was achieved by more or less continuous and less formal exchanges between staff in differing departments and agencies.
- There was little systematic knowledge as to how well the formal and informal processes of policy coordination and direction in

relation to multiple agendas and their impact on policy development were performing. Two views predominated among those interviewed who expressed an awareness of the issue: (1) that the sheer complexity of the task made it impossible to achieve effective coordination and direction at a whole of government level; and (2) that it was achieved in relation to a limited number of more important issues, such as trade, where public servants in the trade side of DFAT and Treasury worked very closely with colleagues involved with trade in other departments, for example DAFF, pointing to the close cooperation achieved in recent years in relation to free trade agreements with a number of Asian countries.

AUSTRALIA AND THE FUTURE OF THE OECD

As we have seen in this book, Australia has played a significant part in bringing about change in the OECD, helping in its adaptation to a world that is significantly different from that in which it came into being. Membership has also helped bring about, in turn, change in Australian policies and related activities as it has adapted to changing domestic and international contexts. It has helped Australia maintain and, arguably, increase its status as a middle power.

It has had something of a love–hate relationship with the OECD with respect to its European origins. On the one hand, it has been a useful venue for engaging directly with EU members, gaining insight into, and possibly some occasional influence on, internal European debates, an engagement often not possible in other multilateral arenas, especially where the European Commission has exclusive *compétence*. But the presence of the European Commission in the deliberative processes of the OECD has been a frequent point of contention for Australia, as has the EU ambition that each state that accedes to the EU should become an OECD member.

This has been particularly problematic with the smaller states, which bring with them little by way of extending the influence of the OECD, because they do not represent a significant fraction of global economic output. Nor do they, because of their small size, bring much to the table in terms of contributions to the costs of running the organisation, yet they complicate the deliberative processes by adding yet another seat at an expanding table, decreasing the like-mindedness of members and making agreement less likely, as the OECD becomes more like larger multilateral institutions. Australia and its like-minded APEC partners have succeeded in ensuring that (successively) Korea, Mexico, and Chile accompanied

European accessions, have supported the accession of Israel and the initiation of accession discussions with Colombia and Costa Rica, agreed to by the EU on the condition that discussions were also initiated for Latvia and Lithuania. It also sponsored successfully Indonesia as a 'Key Partner', along with Brazil, China, India and South Africa in 2007.

Australia has thus had some limited success in ensuring that the OECD is of relevance to the fastest growing part of the world economy, but only at the cost of the dilution that has resulted from the acceptance of Estonia, Latvia, Lithuania, and Slovenia. One reason Australia found OECD membership an attractive proposition was that it was not a member of some of the key international groupings, especially the G7. The development of the G20, including Australia, has thus provided an alternative that overcomes this problem, putting it at the table with not only the G7 (indeed, the G8, since it included the Russian Federation), but also the so-called BRICSA nations (see Eccleston et al., 2015). The OECD is still important even if the uncertain emergence of the G20 continues strongly, because it can provide, in part, the analytical capacity that body lacks.

Australia can therefore be seen to be hedging its bets somewhat, continuing to value the OECD (to varying degrees across agencies), but persisting with its long-standing efforts to ensure that the OECD represents value for money and effort. The G20 certainly does not yet, if it ever will, replace the OECD, but the OECD continues to face the challenges of being regarded as the 'club of the rich', engaging with its Key Partners in the rapidly-expanding Asia Pacific, but being poorly represented there among its members.

Australia, since accession, has been an important and influential middle power in the OECD; whether the OECD continues to be as important a venue for Australian participation as it has for the previous 45 years remains to be seen.

BIBLIOGRAPHY

AIHW 2014. 'OECD Health Care Quality Indicators for Australia 2011–12'. Cat. no. PHE 174. Canberra: AIHW.

Aubert, J. 2001. 'On the OECD Experience of Country Reviews', OECD Science and Technology Policy Division, Paris: OECD.

BCA 2005. 'Business Regulation Action Plan for Future Prosperity', Business Council of Australia, accessed at 28 June 2006, at www.bca.com.au/content.asp?newsID=99099.

Bracks, S. 2005. 'A Third Wave of National Reform', based on Allen Consulting Group 2004, Victoria, Melbourne: Department of Premier and Cabinet.

Carroll, P. 2015. 'Access, Influence and Policy Learning in the 1960s and 1970s: Australian, Japanese and New Zealand Membership of the OECD'. A paper presented by invitation at the 'Warden of the West – The OECD and the Global Political Economy, 1948 to Present', Conference, University of Zurich, Rämistrasse 74, 27–29 August 2015.

DFAT 1999. 'Background Note on APEC IAP Reviews', accessed on 23 January 2017 at http://www.dfat.gov.au/apec/meetings/apec1999/1999_reviews.html.

Eccleston, R., Kellow, A. and Carroll, P. 2015. 'G20 Endorsement in Post Crisis Global Governance: More Than a Toothless Talking Shop?', *The British Journal of Politics & International Relations*, 17(2): 298–317.

OECD 1960. 'Convention on the Organisation for Economic Co-operation and Development', Paris: OECD.

OECD 1997. 'The OECD Report on Regulatory Reform – Synthesis', Paris: OECD.

OECD 2001. 'Innovations in Labour Market Policies: the Australian Way', Paris: OECD.

OECD 2002. 'Client Survey Study of DAC Peer Reviews', Paris: OECD.

OECD 2004. 'Getting to Grips with Globalisation: The OECD in a changing World', Paris: OECD.

OECD 2010. 'OECD Reviews of Regulatory Reform Australia Towards a Seamless National Economy', Paris: OECD.

Porter, T. and Webb, M. 2004. 'The Role of the OECD in the Orchestration of Global Knowledge Networks', Paper Presented at the International Studies Association Annual Meeting, Montreal.

Shergold, P. 2002. 'The OECD's Review of Australia's Labour Market Policies', *The Australian Economic Review*, 35(1): 92–6.

Taskforce on Regulation 2006. 'Rethinking Regulation: Report of the Taskforce on Reducing Regulatory Burdens on Business', Report to the Prime Minister and the Treasurer, Canberra, January, accessed at 5 January 2008, at www.regulationtaskforce.gov.au/__data/assets/pdf_file/0007/69721/regulationtaskforce.pdf.

Treasury 1998. 'Annual Report 1997–98', Treasury.

Treasury 2004. 'Annual Report 2003–04', Treasury.

Vickers, M. 1995. 'Cross-national Exchange, the OECD and Australian Education Policy', *Canberra Bulletin of Public Administration*, 78: 52–63.

Index